CHASING SHADOWS

THE UNTOLD AND DEADLY STORY OF TERRORISM IN AUSTRALIA

KRISTY CAMPION

ALLEN&UNWIN
SYDNEY·MELBOURNE·AUCKLAND·LONDON

First published in 2022

Copyright © 2022 Kristy Campion

All rights reserved. No part of this book may be reproduced or transmitted in any form or by any means, electronic or mechanical, including photocopying, recording or by any information storage and retrieval system, without prior permission in writing from the publisher. The Australian *Copyright Act 1968* (the Act) allows a maximum of one chapter or 10 per cent of this book, whichever is the greater, to be photocopied by any educational institution for its educational purposes provided that the educational institution (or body that administers it) has given a remuneration notice to the Copyright Agency (Australia) under the Act.

Allen & Unwin
83 Alexander Street
Crows Nest NSW 2065
Australia
Phone: (61 2) 8425 0100
Email: info@allenandunwin.com
Web: www.allenandunwin.com

 A catalogue record for this book is available from the National Library of Australia

ISBN 978 1 76106 530 9

Set in 12.5/16 pt Adobe Garamond Pro by Midland Typesetters, Australia
Printed and bound in Australia by Griffin Press, part of Ovato

10 9 8 7 6 5 4 3 2 1

 The paper in this book is FSC® certified. FSC® promotes environmentally responsible, socially beneficial and economically viable management of the world's forests.

This work is dedicated to the Australian citizens killed in acts of terrorism, and to the victims of Australian terrorists around the world. It is further dedicated to the individuals who have devoted their lives to countering terrorism and keeping us safe. Finally, it is for those who bear the scars left by terrorism—seen and unseen.

Contents

Introduction   1

Shadows of Empire, 1868–1918
1   The Fenian circle: Irish terrorism   11

The Revolution Generation, 1965–75
2   A socialist utopia: left-wing extremism   37
3   A fascist homeland: the Ustaša   61
4   Quest for state: pro-Palestinian terrorism   87

Southern Cross Terror, 1975–90
5   Spiritual elites: the Ananda Marga   121
6   Promise of vengeance: pro-Armenian terrorism   154
7   Fires in the night: right-wing extremism   181
8   Under sarin skies: Aum Shinrikyo   208

Battle Cries, 1990 onwards
9   White meat: Jemaah Islamiyah   230
10   Caliphate dreaming: the Al-Qaeda franchise   251

11	Civilisation burning: the Islamic State network	278
12	Darkest of hours: the extreme right	311

Epilogue 335
Acknowledgements 339
Notes 340
Bibliography 364
Index 369

Introduction

It was a warm and golden March afternoon. I had the radio playing in my car as I was driving but I wasn't really listening—I was thinking about the weekend, about a visit with family. The normally light-hearted radio channel only caught my notice when there was a sudden switch from celebrity gossip to a serious news bulletin. An Australian citizen—an armed gunman—had fired on the worshippers in two mosques in New Zealand, according to the newsreader. There were reports of multiple casualties, a manifesto, a livestream, and of Christchurch hospitals in lockdown.

'I hope that isn't what I think it is,' I remember muttering.

It was. The months and years that followed were sickening in so many ways. An Australian citizen had committed a terrorist attack against the civilians of our closest neighbour, motivated by extreme right-wing ideology. Fifty-one people had been killed, and another 49 injured. As an expert in right-wing terrorism and a historian who had spent the past few years investigating Australian terrorism, I could not entirely shake the feeling that somehow I should have seen it coming. While I had expected lethal violence to reignite eventually, I never expected it would have happened over the Tasman. At first glance, the history of Australian terrorism seems a short and nasty affair. In earnest, it is far more extensive than even I realised when I started this book.

Chasing Shadows is the first comprehensive history of the Australian experience of terrorism. It explores terrorism against Australians by foreign and domestic organisations—in Bali, the Middle East and elsewhere around the world. It looks at terrorism in Australia—often conducted by Australians in the service of obscure beliefs, such as the Hilton Hotel bombing in 1978. It then considers how Australia has been used by domestic or foreign terrorist organisations, such as Aum Shinrikyo, to achieve their aims. Foremost, however, it addresses the extreme beliefs that give sense and meaning to seemingly senseless and meaningless terrorist violence. This takes us around the world, pursuing dangerous ideologies, distant influences and local inspirations. Its foundations are found in centuries of oppression and wrongdoing, or entitlement and rage, imperialism and conquest—and compelled by all-consuming despair and hope for revolution.

Despite our varied experience of terrorism, our perceptions seem twisted by the dark notoriety created by sensational violence. Terrorism brings with it visions of swathed foreigners exalting under black flags, or white hoods bowed towards tall flames; of zealous bomb-throwers and unstoppable strategists imbued with an otherworldly, destructive genius. Wherever they may be, terrorists seemingly emerge with suddenness from the shadows, bringing terrible violence and dark ideas. Because of the secrecy that shrouds their existence, terrorists can cast long and distorted shadows, becoming an unknown and impossibly unknowable threat. But we *can* know it, and even understand it, if we understand their worldview—their ideology.

At the heart of terrorist violence and its deadly designs is extreme ideology. Simply put, ideology is how we perceive the world around us; it explains the order of things. It is a system of ideas that informs our beliefs and understandings of the world and what we perceive as truth. In an extreme ideology, this truth is anchored in the belief that the world was once harmonious and beautiful. This pure state of being, extremists believe, has been lost—or, in some cases, stolen—from them. They believe that the world around them is rotten to its core, divergent from its authentic nature, or sinking into decadence and decay. They condemn this corrupted order and all the people who exist there comfortably. This rejection and despair, however, are not without hope.

At the core of extreme ideology is a belief in the perfectibility of the world: that it can be returned to a golden age, that lost authenticity can be reclaimed, that the idealised order can be restored. Extremists imagine a utopian order, which is often fantastical or contradictory, and frequently at odds with what the rest of society wants. It is the solution to all their problems, fulfilling their deepest desires, whether personal or political. It comes with a catch, though: in order to achieve this utopia, the old world must be burned to the ground. From the ashes of the old world will come a new world reflecting the harmony and idealised society the extremists seek to achieve.

Barring their way, however, is the rest of society: those who live comfortably in the current order. Their very existence is often seen as a threat to the revolution. At worst, society is blamed for the corrupt order, for the loss of harmony and authenticity. This is where ideology becomes deadly, because it attributes blame for the current state of affairs. And so extremists argue that existing governments are oppressive, that minorities are invaders, that people who hold different political beliefs are traitors, or that those of a particular faith are false. This has fatal significance: it gives terrorists targets for their violence.

This is where the final element of ideology comes into play. Ideology—through its view of the world and by casting blame—also provides solutions. It is like a roadmap leading from a fallen city to a utopian homeland. The signposts along the way tell them how the desired world order can be achieved. In an extreme ideology, these signposts all point to one method for salvation: violence. Extremists deem violence against their enemies to be purifying and cleansing, and the path to reclamation of self or dutiful service to the new world order. This view of violence as purifying and obligatory becomes essential to how terrorists justify their actions. They glorify their willingness to sacrifice everyone and everything to achieve their utopias. They cloak themselves in this sacrifice as though killing innocent people in pursuit of obscure goals somehow ennobles them.

It is in that moment that extremism becomes terrorism. And in this way, too, that extremists reveal themselves for what they are: fringe dwellers who are willing to destroy their own society and everyone in it—including themselves—to satisfy their own desire for change. While terrorism is broadly described as the use or threat of violence in pursuit of political, religious and ideological goals, ideology itself encompasses both politics and religion. Ideology therefore lies at the heart of why people commit acts of terrorism against unsuspecting victims around the world. This is what is behind the events in Christchurch, New Zealand, and what has happened in Australia over the past 150 years.

Drawing on declassified security documents, open-source intelligence, news sources and expert studies, *Chasing Shadows* tells the Australian story of terrorism. Some archival files—especially those related to left-wing and right-wing extremism—were declassified upon my request for this history. Other files, normally restricted from access or lying in forgotten corners of archival collections, I meticulously examined. As a result all archival sources used here are now considered public documents, freely available in the open domain to scholars and the public alike. The history of terrorism threats in Australia covered in this book is therefore underpinned by extensive archival material, in addition to the latest information and detail on contemporary threats. Some few files, however, remain classified and beyond access or use in this history. As time goes on, it is possible that they will be released, and our understanding may well change, and change again. Like all histories, this book is based on what was left behind: those secret documents, cablegrams and communiqués that can shine light on the dark, unfamiliar parts of our story.

In this book, I focus on terrorism attempted or conducted by non-state individuals and groups in Australia, by Australians or against Australians. I have not included official or state-ordered acts. By that reasoning, I have not covered the Battle of Broken Hill in 1915, as the Sultan and Caliph of the Ottoman Empire ordered Muslim populations in Western nations to revolt against Allied Powers in World War I using legitimate religious authority, thereby rendering it fifth-column activity.

Similarly, while governments can also engage in terrorism (often in the form of genocide or frontier exterminations), I have limited this history to the beliefs and actions of individuals and organisations. I have excluded activity perpetrated by labour organisations, such as the Industrial Workers of the World (IWW), because it is an extension of protest and union activity, which is protected under Australian law.[1] The only other group I have omitted is the Black Panther Party of Australia. While the Panthers were considered a threat in the United States, the Australian cell was limited to a few individuals who did not perpetrate any terrorist plot.

To tell the full Australian story, I begin many chapters in foreign nations, with exotic ideas and little-remembered triggers and events that catalysed activity within Australia or against Australians. This fusion of the international and domestic motivations demonstrates that terrorism in Australia is not simply an extension of overseas operations—it is an exchange between the two. As a result, domestic and international terrorism cannot be entirely divorced from one another; they are connected in an adaptive and ever-changing way that effectively makes them a moving target.

By virtue of this, terrorism in Australia has three fundamental characteristics. First, regardless of the terrorist organisation or network, Australian citizens have been, and continue to be, essential to the enactment of terrorist violence and threats in Australia. Domestic groups and networks have international connections, and international groups with interest in Australia tend to have domestic connections. We may perceive ourselves as both isolated and contained, but the tightest border security cannot stop domestic terrorists inspired by international ideas, and nor can it always apprehend international terrorists who, over the course of history, often slipped the very nets designed to catch them.

Second, most international terrorist organisations with interest in Australia actively encouraged their supporters to engage in violence in the service of international goals, against international targets, or to achieve international effects. There have been only two exceptions to this: the Japanese terrorist cult Aum Shinrikyo used its Australian connections only to obtain resources, such as land and chemicals, to further its weapons-testing program; and the Armenian terrorist organisation the Justice Commandos of the Armenian Genocide did not require its Australian supporters to engage in violence. Instead, Australians provided operational intelligence, resources and support functions to the organisation. This is because of the structural nature of these groups, both of which had professional cadres of specialist operatives trained to execute violent acts.

Third, few international terror organisations cared about changing Australia's liberal democratic order. Australia was simply another theatre for action, where international goals could be pursued for strategic effect or leverage elsewhere. In fact, only domestic left-wing and right-wing extremists expressed any genuine desire to revolutionise the liberal democratic order in Australia. Both extremes harboured fantasies of the complete revolution of the very society from which they were born. These threats, more so than others, have both the intent and the power to impact our liberal democratic order.

Knowledge of terrorism in Australia has formerly belonged to only a special few; *Chasing Shadows* is designed to change that. My aim has been to destroy the myths and falsehoods that allow us to blame others for the acts of violence born of our own society. It is written to derive some sort of sense from the chaos created by terrorism, and to do justice to the victims of such calculated barbarism. Only by viewing all of our loss and trauma, bungled plots, thwarted attacks, and victories, can we truly understand terrorism in Australia.

Shadows of Empire, 1868–1918

Long before the Al-Qaeda franchise or Islamic State's caliphate, terrorism transcended national boundaries and populations. There is an obvious strategic logic to crossing borders. It allows terrorist groups to decentralise their resources and diminish their local footprint, reducing the likelihood of detection. It also enables them to expand their influence into multiple populations, enhancing recruitment and financial opportunities. One of the earliest terrorism movements to leverage transnationalism in such a way was Irish anti-colonialism, which demonstrated an early capability to mobilise its diaspora and supporters around the world to action. In such a way, transnationalism magnified the capability of Irish anti-colonialists to conduct lengthy campaigns against superpowers such as the British Empire.

In examining the early days of Australian terror, we can make the following observations. First, Irish terrorism in Australia was executed by people of Irish extraction, including Irish Americans, Irish Australians, and Irish citizens. There were observable links of mutual support between international Irish terrorist organisations and domestic Irish anti-colonial organisations in Australia. Second, while international Irish terrorist groups encouraged Australians to act on their behalf, they had no clear goal for Australia itself: they did not seek to change the Australian democracy or its political order.

Instead, all their goals fixated on liberating Ireland from the colonial shackles of Great Britain. Australia was merely another theatre for action, where international goals could be pursued for strategic effect.

A third observation can be made: despite the actual (and sometimes imagined) scale of Irish anti-colonial terrorism in Australia, it had little impact on the national security establishment. During this period, Australia had no mature or established intelligence and security organisation. Australia's first terrorist assassination attempt left Australian officials reeling with shame and horror.

1

The Fenian circle: Irish terrorism

A prince had never visited Australia before 1868. The antipodean colonies, tucked away on the other side of the world and accessible only by a lengthy sea voyage, were simply not a high priority for the aristocracy of England. When Queen Victoria finally decided to send her second son, Prince Alfred, the Duke of Edinburgh, to lead the first royal tour of Australia, the news was met with jubilation. The prince was 24, and a dashing and decorated naval officer who had recently gained his first command, HMS *Galatea*. Many Australians quickly caught royal fever, enthusiastically planning gauche engagements and social events to impress the prince. It is a pity, then, that he ended his visit with a bullet in his back.

Prince Alfred's voyage began in January 1867, with a schedule that took HMS *Galatea* to the Mediterranean, South America, and the Cape of Good Hope before reaching Adelaide in October that same year. From there, he sailed to Melbourne, and then Sydney. He was accompanied by the esteemed Somerset Richard Lowry-Corry, the Fourth Earl of Belmore, at the peak of his successful parliamentary career. Belmore's presence in the prince's party was significant: from 8 January 1868, he would become the governor of New South Wales. The citizens of Sydney were not only welcoming a prince, but a new governor whose term was doomed to begin with disorder and chaos.

The first few weeks of Prince Alfred's visit were marked with too much enthusiasm and too little caution. A feast for the prince on the banks of the Yarra in Melbourne attracted a crowd of nearly 40,000 people—four times as many as expected—which meant that the prince himself could not attend without risk of being trampled. The crowd turned vengeful at his absence and destroyed the site. In Bendigo, Victoria, a fireworks display upon a model of the *Galatea* designed to impress the prince instead burned to death three young boys who had been playing on it. When Prince Alfred opened a hall bearing his name, it immediately burned to the ground. The festivities in Geelong, Victoria, were overrun by an excessive and enthusiastic mob. Then, during a military display at Flemington Racecourse, again in Melbourne, a sailor lost his hand when a cannon malfunctioned.[1] Such were the early ill omens of Prince Alfred's ill-fated visit.

The outburst of monarchist madness was, however, not the only reaction.

Many members of the Irish-Australian community had migrated to avoid such royal entanglements. They had experienced the bitter fruits of British misrule almost two decades earlier, with the Great Famine of 1846–51. The famine was triggered by a potato blight disease, which struck the Irish staple crop and destroyed up to 75 per cent of the yield. The lower classes of Irish society depended on that crop, but as the potatoes fetched a higher price in England, the British continued exporting what remained of the crop.[2] Over the five-year period, 800,000 people starved to death, and another 900,000 emigrated to the United States and Australia.[3] Although there were pre-existing migration routes between Ireland and Australia, many were now left with little choice but to flee—only a slow death awaited them if they stayed. While the Irish migrants began new lives in Australia, some viewed their emigration as nothing more than exile from their captured homeland.[4]

Suffice to say, some elements of the Irish-Australian diaspora did not welcome the prince with open arms. Instead of celebrating, they protested. One such demonstration took place in front of the grand St George's Hall in Melbourne on 27 November. It was orderly at first, with the crowd singing songs of Irish solidarity. As night fell, the protest turned unruly: stones were thrown, and someone began firing bullets into the crowd from the hall. A fourteen-year-old onlooker, William George Cross, 'screamed, quivered, and fell to the ground': he had been shot in the chest, and was pronounced dead a short time later.[5]

The *Galatea* continued its fateful trip, stopping in Tasmania, Sydney and Brisbane. Although it seemed like the clouds of misfortune were dispersing, it was in fact the lull before the storm. On 12 March 1868, Prince Alfred attended a Sailors' Home Picnic in Clontarf, Sydney. More than 1500 people paid entry and spectated a corroboree performed by 300 Indigenous Australians.[6] While Prince Alfred watched on, a stranger detached himself from the crowd and hurried towards him. When he was within arm's length, he drew a pistol and fired directly into the prince's back.

Prince Alfred fell to the ground and cried: 'Good God! I am shot: my back is broken.'[7]

A bystander, Mr Vial, tackled the assassin and tried to wrestle the gun from him, even while the attacker was again trying to take aim at the fallen prince. In the struggle, the gun discharged once more, hitting another bystander, George Thorne, in the leg. Nearby sailors ran to assist Prince Alfred even as others tried to lynch the shooter. They would have been successful had police not intervened and secured him. Safe in police custody, the assassin refused to give his name. All he said was: 'I have made a mess of it, and all for no good. I don't care for death; I am sorry I missed my aim. I am a Fenian. God save Ireland! I have done my duty and can die for my country.'[8]

This was the first clear example of political terrorism in Australia. The assassin was motivated by anti-colonial ideology, committed to the cause of freeing Ireland of the British. His violence was both instrumental and symbolic: aimed at striking a blow at the heart of the monarchy and the oppressors of the Irish people. Three intentions can be observed from this: first, it was an attempt to force the

British to leave Ireland for fear of other such losses; second, it was a show of force in its own right, that the Irish, after so many centuries of colonial rule, remained defiant; and third, it was an appeal to the Irish diaspora around the world to rise up: their enemy was not all powerful and indestructible. In the pursuit of this goal, the terrorist was willing to countenance his own destruction.

The assassin was Henry James O'Farrell from Dublin, who had resided in Australia for around six months. His family believed that he was studying for the priesthood, but he had a different vocation in mind. He had arrived in Melbourne in 1867, and joined the Fenian Circle, a secret society and a cell of the international Fenian Brotherhood. Other such cells existed in England, Ireland, the United States and New Zealand. O'Farrell claimed his circle was nine men strong. A 'warrant' had come from Fenians in England to the circle's *senex* (chairman), ordering the execution of Prince Alfred. Vowing that they would all abide by the outcome regardless, the circle voted on it. O'Farrell voted against the execution warrant, but for naught: the vote passed. They drew straws to decide who would conduct the grim deed and O'Farrell drew the short straw. O'Farrell had not expected to survive the attack, but his bad luck would bind his life irrevocably to Prince Alfred.

The Irish cause

By the time O'Farrell had migrated to Australia, the Irish cause had coalesced into an undeniably cohesive ideology built on the sturdy foundations of colonial history. It was based on the simple fact that the Irish were once free and now they were not. High-level political manoeuvring back in the twelfth century had led King Henry II of England to secure an 'obscure commission' from Pope Adrian IV to reform the Irish Church, which allowed him to justify the Anglo-Norman invasion of Ireland.[9] The Irish did not submit willingly to British invasion. From 1169, successive British monarchs sought to subjugate the troublesome Irish clans, with Henry VIII finally establishing military control of

Ireland in 1541. This soon expanded to administrative, economic and political control. Ireland became another reluctant colony, another jewel in the British crown. Although Ireland had a parliament, its powers were nominal, and the real power remained with the British administration.

Despite British colonial rule, the Irish retained a profound awareness of their distinctiveness from the English. They held to their identity as Gaels, their separate language, traditions, history and culture. The tighter British administration became, the more this Irish identity was threatened with erasure. English was taught in schools, speaking the Gaelic language was forbidden, and Gaelic sports and cultural pastimes were banned. Gaelic identity and culture were being systematically stamped out, largely through educational restrictions. This threat united the Irish, and 'Ireland for the Irish' became their rallying cry. Nothing less than meaningful self-government and control of Ireland would satisfy them.

Successive leaders arose who sought to throw off the colonial shackles. One was Wolfe Tone, who coordinated with France to lead the disastrous Rebellion of 1798. Clandestine societies followed this failure, such as the Emmet Society, which was established in the United States in 1855 by James Stephens and John O'Mahony. It soon split into two, with O'Mahony leading the new Fenian Brotherhood, while Stephens returned to Ireland and lead the Irish Republican Brotherhood (IRB).[10] The IRB attempted a popular revolt in 1867, the doomed Fenian Rising, which was easily crushed by the British. After this failure, the Fenians committed themselves to violence, believing it was the only way to serve the cause of the Ireland and its people. Fenian assassination circles soon appeared around the world, including Australia.

An Australian circle

Fenian circles followed typical IRB structures to maintain secrecy. Each man was known only to his immediate circle, and strict information hierarchies were in place where only one man from each circle could know the next person in the chain of command. Orders were distributed from the Fenian Central Council to the strata of circles. O'Farrell had relatively intimate knowledge of the circle workings. He also appeared to have inside information on Fenian practices, especially after the recent Clerkenwell prison bombing in London in December 1867. Twelve died and more than a hundred were injured in the blast. O'Farrell claimed Fenians would have tried to rescue the prisoners rather than simply kill people. In the years that followed, it was found that this seemingly indiscriminate bombing was in fact a rescue effort gone wrong.[11]

Despite this, commentators at the time believed that O'Farrell was citing the Irish cause for his own attack in an attempt to accrue more notoriety than shooting a prince could bestow. His own diary, however, indicates his deep political commitment to the Irish cause, even though he was reluctant to execute the attack:

> How if I should fail . . .! I should never forgive myself. Fail! But I cannot; I am alone, and surely I can trust myself. Oh! That the Orangemen would rouse up the apathetic Irish of these parts; one good effect would follow in English capitalists losing heavily by the depreciation of colonial debentures, and the failures consequent on the colonies being in a state of anarchy. If I had had my will, every English ship in these parts should have been destroyed.[12]

The attack shows a clear political motivation: to inspire the Irish masses to rise up and cast off the shackles of colonialism. Through destruction of British property or representatives they hoped to expose the weakness of the colonial powers, and thereby inspire the oppressed to claim their freedom. 'Woe to you, England, when the glorious nine carry out their programme,' O'Farrell wrote exultantly.[13] He held no personal animosity towards Prince Alfred: the prince was targeted because he was a symbol of British power.

Though O'Farrell was fatalistic, his sister Mrs Allan was determined to fight for his life. She arranged an excellent Victorian lawyer, and herself provided testimony in O'Farrell's trial that he was insane and epileptic.[14] The jury were unconvinced and found him guilty in 26 minutes. His activity as a Fenian was not included in the trial. In his sentencing remarks, the presiding judge, in full loyalist fervour, described the crime as a 'cruel and deliberate attempt to take the life of a favourite son of our beloved Queen' and entreated O'Farrell to reflect upon the horror and shame the attack would have caused in Europe.[15] O'Farrell was sentenced to be hanged by the neck until dead.

On 1 May 1868, many gathered at Darlinghurst Gaol to view the spectacle to come. O'Farrell appeared grim and unmoved, quickly mounting the scaffold. He refused to make a final statement. At 9 a.m., the Adelaide *Telegraph* wrote that O'Farrell 'met his richly-merited doom in the most calm, cool, and collected manner'.[16] Afterwards, Dr Carr of the School of Arts shared with a morbidly obsessed press the outcome of a phrenological exam he conducted on O'Farrell. According to Dr Carr, O'Farrell was an intelligent man, but hasty, with little foresight or knowledge of consequences, guided too much by 'false ideas of justice' and 'false ideas of honor', coupled with great concentration and tenacity.[17] He wrote:

> In politics a radical, in spirit a revolutionist, in disposition agreeable, but exacting: proud and self-possessed in manner. It was an organization of power. He would have died alike for those he loved and for those he hated. His intellect, sentiments, and propensities, from the nature of his temperament, required a self-government which he seldom exerted.[18]

Such was the profile of the first terrorist in Australia, based on the pseudoscience of phrenology—examining the shape of the skull. The attempted assassination of Prince Alfred, Duke of Edinburgh, was not the limit of anti-colonial activity in Australia. There were two more incidents of lesser violence that nonetheless indicated the persistence of Irish anti-colonialism, and that contributed spectacularly to the Irish cause.

The rogue whaler

Prince Alfred healed completely from the attempt on his life and returned to England, while Ireland remained under British rule. The event, however, was not soon forgotten, and Irish anti-colonialists from New York to Dublin to London continued to agitate for freedom and to force the British to depart Ireland. One such group was the Clan na Gael (Clan of the Irish), established in the United States in 1867. Led by John Devoy, the Clan's purpose was to encourage Irish anti-colonial sentiment in America, and exploit the protection offered by American citizenship to avoid British retaliation. It was not yet a violent group, but it would be soon. In 1878, Clan na Gael would launch a campaign of terrorism against the British, having capitalised on the success of an operation it conducted in Australia.[19]

Before they could mount any operations, the Clan had to overcome a major problem: it was poor. Because it had little reputation compared to the IRB and the Fenian Brotherhood, it failed to attract the donations it needed to purchase weapons and dynamite to use against the British. Its members decided to raise its public profile through a daring and successful act that would certify their commitment to the cause without challenging the moral convictions of their supporters. Their attention turned to Fremantle Gaol, Western Australia, where about 24 per cent of the convicts were of Irish heritage.[20] The arrival of the convict transport ship the *Hougoumont* in 1868 only added to the Irish population. Six of the ship's Irish prisoners were also military prisoners, convicted of participating in the Fenian Rising of 1867. At the time, military protesters were often sentenced to life in prison for protesting British rule.

The highest-profile prisoner was John Boyle O'Reilly, a poet and activist.[21] In his company was military prisoner Michael Harrington, a decorated soldier from the 61st Regiment, who saw action in the 1857 Indian Mutiny and Sepoy Uprising. Another was the distinguished Colour Sergeant Thomas Darragh, who was waiting to receive his commission, earned through his service in the Chinese War. The third was Private James Wilson, who, like the others, had his death sentence commuted to life with hard labour. The final three were Cranston, Hogan and Hassett, about whom little is known.

A sympathetic Irish priest immediately provided O'Reilly with a means to escape, and soon O'Reilly had absconded to New Bedford, in the United States. There, he met the leader of Clan na Gael, John Devoy—who had also been involved in the Fenian Rising. Together, they conspired to free the prisoners left behind and sought financial assistance from the diaspora. By 1875, the Irish-American community had donated more than $12,000, which the Clan used to purchase a whaling ship called the *Catalpa*. Captained by a Fenian sympathiser, George S. Anthony, the ship departed the United States ostensibly on a whaling expedition, and had caught one whale in the North Atlantic before it docked in Bunbury, Western Australia.

Ahead of the *Catalpa*'s arrival, two Clan agents arrived in Fremantle.[22] They adopted pseudonyms and operated independently of one another. John Breslin, an experienced Clan prison breaker, took on the character of Mr Collins, a rich capitalist studying the country; while Thomas Desmond became Mr Jones, a second-class traveller.[23] They quickly devised a plan of escape, but the plot was immediately thrown into disarray because the *Catalpa* was late and the two agents ran out of money. They had to be rescued from poverty by a generous sum of £500 from a local Irish nationalist organisation.[24]

A second plan was put into motion. It began on the morning of Easter Monday, 17 April 1876. The six Fenians were working unsupervised in some fields.[25] At a signal from the Clan agents, they dropped their tools and fled, making for a prearranged location where horses and traps were waiting for them. The convicts rode 20 miles (30 kilometres) to the wharf, where crewmen in the *Catalpa*'s longboat anxiously awaited their human cargo. The escapees boarded and made for the *Catalpa* as fast as they could. Their absence, however, was quickly discovered. The police sent a steamer, the *Georgette*, in pursuit of the longboat. With the *Georgette* in its wake, the longboat rushed towards the *Catalpa*, disembarking its precious cargo just in time.

The *Georgette* signalled the *Catalpa*, but the Clan ship ignored the police steamer. It wasn't until the *Georgette* fired a warning shot across the *Catalpa*'s stern that it finally hoisted its American colours and identified itself. The shots immediately ceased, and instead a verbal exchange occurred. Police Superintendent Watson demanded the six escaped prisoners be returned to him in the name of the Governor of Western Australia. Captain Anthony claimed to have no prisoners.

'You have, I see three of them, Captain,' Superintendent Watson disagreed. Captain Anthony merely replied that they were seamen, and not prisoners at all. Growing tired of the exchange, the *Georgette* captain threatened to fire upon the *Catalpa*.

'I don't care what you do,' Captain Anthony replied. 'The American flag will protect me.'[26]

And so it did. The *Georgette* abandoned pursuit, and the victorious Captain Anthony sailed back to America, stopping only to hunt whales along the way. The escapees were given a hero's welcome in New Bedford, and the Clan used the success of the Australian prison break to attract substantial donations, which were immediately invested in a terrorist campaign against British interests around the world. The Australian press made much of the story, describing it as one of the 'sensations of the period',[27] and one of the 'most daring projects of the present century', waxing eloquent on the 'intrepid courage' and 'powerful physique' of the rescuers.[28] Needless to say, the act was condemned in London's *Daily Telegraph*, which described the prisoners as an 'expensive nuisance' and proclaimed that 'The United States is welcome to any number of disloyal, turbulent, plotting conspirators, to all their silly machinations.'[29] And welcome they were!

Unsurprisingly, the Western Australian Police Department was not willing to join in the buoyant commentary. The Western Australian Police chief penned a letter to the American police chief in New Bedford, Massachusetts, detailing the escape and requesting information about the escapees.[30] Unfortunately for the Western Australian Police, the police department in New Bedford was controlled by Henry Hathaway, a Fenian sympathiser. Hathaway was a one-time shipmate of the *Gazette*, which had assisted in the initial rescue of John Boyle O'Reilly. Hathaway was not simply aware of the *Catalpa* but had actively assisted O'Reilly and Devoy to carry out the raid.[31] The request for information received no reply.

Wartime tensions

Following the success of the *Catalpa*, the Clan na Gael evolved quickly into a proficient terrorist organisation. It mounted bombing campaigns in England, and with its bolstered reputation successfully continued to raise funds in what became known as the 'dynamite press'. Some of the attacks were spectacular failures, but the concept of violent insurgency was catching on—especially when a rival group, the Skirmishers, was established by Jeremiah 'Dynamite' O'Donovan Rossa. In the midst of this competition, the IRB also began to grow in power, despite its secretive nature. Their primary goal, as demonstrated in its oath, was to achieve an independent Democratic Republic of Ireland, free from British rule.

James Stephens had retained his role as 'head centre' of the IRB over the decades. He had four vice heads, each of whom led a centre, with nine captains, who led nine sergeants, who led nine privates.[32] The regulated information hierarchy ensured that each member of the IRB was known only to their own centre, minimising the risk of infiltration by British agents. It was also itself a keen infiltrator, and saturated other Irish groups, such as the Irish Volunteers, with its agents. Little happened in the Irish resistance movement that the IRB was not across, regardless of whether it occurred in the United States, Ireland or Australia.

Around 1914 and the start of World War I, there was a sudden increase in IRB membership as many Irishmen flocked to the

IRB banner rather than fighting and dying for the British crown. They formed their own militias and drilled in public. On 24 April 1916, the Irish Volunteers and the Irish Citizen Army mounted an insurrection against the British later known as the Easter Rising, seizing control of the General Post Office in Dublin and declaring Ireland a free republic. The British met this rebellion with force, bringing in artillery and a gunboat, and destroyed large areas of the city. The leaders of the Rising were captured and tried in secret military tribunals. Many of them received death sentences, and were executed and buried in quicklime without coffins.[33] The great philosopher Friedrich Engels once observed that all the Irish needed were martyrs: the Easter Rising gave them that. Although the event was tragic, it reignited the flame for Irish freedom in Ireland, and across the Irish diaspora in the United States and Australia.

As the British prospects in the war began to sour, the British commander-in-chief, Lord French, was determined to forcibly conscript Irish men to fight British battles. Seeking to establish control over the movement, he levied charges of conspiracy against the peaceful leaders of the Irish political movement. More than 70 leaders of the newly established Sinn Fein political party were arrested overnight and interned without charge, accused of being party to a vague 'German plot'. There was no German plot: it was a conjured threat to justify the search and seizure of Irish leaders and their offices. It was more convenient for the British to paint the Irish as traitors than to recognise their legitimate claims for self-determination.

On 29 November 1916, a letter was sent from San Francisco to Ireland. It was intercepted by the British, who discovered that the author was John Doran, an Australian. The British demanded that the Australians investigate Doran, stating he was an 'undisguised Sinn Feinner' currently travelling through the United States of America. Doran's letter was accompanied by a postcard depicting Irish volunteers marching at a German relief bazaar, under a German flag.[34] This was seen as evidence of a German plot, and an Australian threat.

An Australian division

Any opposition or perceived disloyalty to the British line became synonymous with treachery and support for the enemy. This atmosphere, in the midst of World War I, made the slightest appearance of disloyalty perilous. The Australian authorities were eager to appease the British: so eager, in fact, that they would make a mockery of themselves and persecute their own citizens without reasonable cause. In the case of the small, relatively inconsequential IRB cell in Australia, the cure was worse than the disease. The group had been small and unlikely to act. From such humble beginnings, it was transformed into a malevolent villain in the imaginations of Australian officials, who interned its members without charge, and then carried out a farcical inquiry to validate the imprisonment. It began with one old man, one young man, and a fondness for invisible ink.

Irish-Australian communities and organisations had long been vocal for supporters of Irish independence. They, like many around the world, were alarmed by the executions of the Easter Rising leaders in April 1916. Instead of suppressing revolt, the executions incited more people to action. In the months that followed, two Irish Australians, Maurice Dalton and John Doran, founded the Australian Division of the Irish Republican Brotherhood (IRB-A) in Melbourne. Maurice Dalton, an old-age pensioner, was a one-time member of a previous circle of the Fenian Brotherhood and had been involved in the Fenian Rising. While Dalton was the old guard, John Doran was part of the new. He was an influential shipwright unionist, and a leading figure of the Gaelic League of Victoria.[35] Doran may not have had his partner's experience, but he did have energy, passion and commitment to the Irish cause.

The newly established IRB-A exploited Irish sentiment in Australia to win recruits, especially from the Irish National Association (INA). The INA was a relatively new community organisation, established in July 1915 in Sydney by Thomas Albert Dryer. The INA's aim was to 'assist Ireland to achieve her national destiny and to foster an Irish spirit among the Irish portion of the community'.[36] Over the intervening year, the INA had gained 1500 members—testament to community support for the Irish cause.

Soon, Doran established a Sydney branch of the IRB-A, with two sub-circles of ten men each. Among the men in one circle were Thomas Albert Dryer and Edmund McSweeney, an insurance officer; in a second sub-circle were William McGuinness, a salesman, and Michael McGing, a hospital gardener. Doran then went on to Brisbane, where he and a Franciscan priest, Thomas A. Fitzgerald, founded yet another branch. The IRB-A garnered more than 50 members in Brisbane, most found and recruited from within the INA.[37] In the space of a few short years, it spread over the eastern seaboard, with offices in Brisbane, Sydney and Melbourne.

The IRB-A's initial goal was to launch a *Catalpa*-like expedition, sailing to America to join John Devoy and the Clan, and then onwards to Ireland to fight the British. This plan swiftly dissolved when Devoy would pay only for Doran's travel costs. Doran left in September 1916 to become the unofficial Australian representative in America, leaving Dryer rather than Dalton in charge of the IRB-A. Doran became close with Devoy and other Irish agitators, and in one letter home he hinted darkly that 'there will be another Easter week before the war ends and it won't be 3,000 men against 20,000 this time'.[38]

To prepare for the fight to come, the IRB-A established an unarmed training camp in the Blue Mountains, New South Wales, and smuggled in Irish propaganda such as the *Gaelic American* and *Sinn Fein* via Irish sailors. Its fundraising efforts were underwhelming, amounting to a mere $194.80, which was sent to America.[39] Dryer was in possession of the Constitution of the Clan Na Gael, which committed its adherents to armed revolution. To all intents and purposes, it appeared that the IRB-A was genuinely committed to the anti-colonial program: members were reading all the right materials, training for combat and fundraising (albeit without great success). But there was no terrorist plot for Australia: their dream was to march with other Irish revolutionaries across the green fields of Ireland and dispel the British using conventional (and outdated) military means.

Given these goals, the IRB-A also took great pains to ensure the secrecy of the group, writing in invisible ink, or in code. Every letter with a torn corner and the code word '*saoirse*' (Gaelic for 'freedom') indicated the presence of invisible ink on the reverse side.[40] The ink was a weak solution of yellow prussiate of potash (potassium ferrocyanide), which, when gently dabbed with a solution of copper sulfate or iron sulfate, would reveal the secret message. One such document was intercepted by government censors: it was seemingly an innocent letter but contained a list of IRB members, detailing their centres and sub-centres in invisible ink. This breached existing prohibitions on secret societies. After a time, the IRB-A became aware of this interception, and thus began avoiding the use of the post office altogether.[41] In response, the Department of Defence began investigating the IRB-A, tracing it back to the INA. The investigation was driven in part by a fear of domestic subversion while on a war footing. They soon uncovered Doran's role in contacting and collaborating with John Devoy, who had also been implicated in the alleged German plot.[42]

The United Kingdom established an Australian branch of the Counter Espionage Bureau (CEB) to track the fifth-column activity—that is, saboteurs and agents provocateurs in league with Germany. Australian authorities assisted the CEB and boosted their own Directorate of Military Intelligence by introducing a series of new regulations that gave such authorities immense domestic reach. Under Section 56(b) of the *War Precautions Regulations 1915*, anyone could be arrested without cause or being given reason to understand their arrest, and their property could be searched. Participation in secret societies was forbidden, and the possession of dynamite was also expressly prohibited (except, bizarrely, for sporting purposes). The *Regulations* moreover suspended normal Australian legal principles and protections, such as trial by jury and habeas corpus, a recourse in law for prisoners detained without charge.

With these new powers, the CEB tracked the IRB-A for months. It soon learned of the IRB-A's first plan: to gather up volunteers who would travel, first to America, and then to Ireland, to aid an armed revolt. The CEB confirmed that the IRB-A was exploiting the unsuspecting INA to recruit, and also that it had connections with John Devoy and the Clan. The CEB became convinced that a German plot was genuinely afoot: that the IRB-A was supplying weapons, people and money to aid the enemy.[43] The link to Berlin was, however, tenuous. One of the internees was found in possession of a leaflet from a non-commissioned officer from the Irish Brigade in Berlin (on which grounds a case for treason was later launched). When investigators discovered that Dryer had German and Irish heritage, his grandfather hailing from Hamburg, he was considered terribly suspicious. A young woman affiliated with Dryer, Miss Kathleen Weber, was also accused of being German, if such a thing can be an accusation. Further investigations revealed she was not a member of the IRB-A, although many other young women were.[44] These women were central to making Sinn Fein badges and flags, which was illegal under the *War Precautions Regulations*.[45]

The government, under pressure from the British, had to be seen to act. Without discovering any serious or damning evidence that Irish Australians were dangerous subversives working in tandem with Germany against the British, investigators concluded that the plot must have been relegated to elite members only. As one secret report found:

> As is not uncommon in the case of treasonable and revolutionary bodies the real aim of the organization was concealed. While sympathy with the Irish Rebels was not disguised, the actual enemy object was apparently known only to an inner circle, and great pains were taken to consider [sic] conceal it from others.[46]

There *were* secret plans among high-ranking Fenians to do more than write covert letters and cultivate favour with prominent Americans, as would be found when key members were uncerimoniously rounded up under the new *Regulations*. On 17 June 1917, on the orders of the acting prime minister, W.A. Watt, a sting was carried out simultaneously in Sydney, Brisbane and Melbourne. The arrests included Maurice Dalton, Thomas Dryer, Edmund McSweeney, Michael McGing, William McGuinness and Thomas Fitzgerald; along with Frank McKeown, a bricklayer. They were imprisoned in Darlinghurst Gaol and told nothing of their charges.

In the midst of arresting Dalton, police actually found a substantiative piece of evidence. Dalton was arrested with a 'Recipe for a severe attack of Cold' in his pocket. It was in his own handwriting, and yet he claimed initially to have picked it up off the ground—and then later changed his story to suggest it was given to him by Jock Wilson of the Industrial Workers of the World (IWW).[47] Investigators believed that the recipe was coded instructions for making 'infernal machines', due to the fact it only had three ingredients, recommended experimentation and was accompanied by a diagram of what appeared to be a clock face. Dalton had experience with gelignite in mining, and investigators began to believe that he had been considering blowing up the magazines at Merri Creek, a mere mile (1600 metres) from his home.[48] That single piece of paper damned the pensioner—whether it was a cold recipe or not!

Seven cells

Desperate to legitimise the pre-emptive arrests, the NSW Supreme Court held an inquiry into the presence of the Irish Republican Brotherhood in Australia in 1918, after the seven men had been interned without charge for a year.[49] A series of high-ranking judges refused to preside over the proceedings, viewing the implementation of the *Regulations* with barely veiled contempt, and public unrest grew. At last, having exhausted the list of eminent judges, the government secured the acceptance of the British-born Justice John Musgrave Harvey. An expert in probate, conveyancing, estate and company law, Harvey did not have the experience in secret societies or political violence required for this task.

Newspapers were censored from criticising the internment. Even politicians were not exempt from this censorship: when Queensland politicians objected to the detentions using parliamentary privilege, the deputy chief censor demanded that their statements be expunged from the proceedings of the Queensland Legislative Assembly. The Queensland premier at the time, Thomas J. Ryan, was apparently not quick enough to reply to this demand. This led to the extraordinary act of Brigadier General G.G.H. Irving taking military possession of the Queensland Government Printing Office in Brisbane.[50] Irving reported that he 'technically and quietly took possession of Government Printing Office this morning owing to printing of Hansard being continued contrary to instructions'.[51] In addition to conventional force, loyalists formed a secret citizens' police, called the Australian Protection League (APL), which compiled information on so-called 'Irish plotters', including Premier Ryan himself.

Justice Harvey heard the inquiry over the space of eleven days, although his powers to make recommendations were limited. A Mr Mack, of Messrs Collins and Mulholland, was the lawyer for the seven IRB-A men. Mack was something of a force of nature. He did a commendable job highlighting the admittedly limited understanding of the prosecution witnesses. In one case, a witness described Wolfe Tone as 'a man who was concerned in an Irish rebellion in England in 1916'.[52] Mack informed the witness, to the laughter of the court, that Tone had been dead for 100 years. Despite Mack's valiant defence, Justice Harvey confirmed the lawfulness of the detentions, though the process itself was described as a farce.[53] The internees were gradually released following a decision by Federal Cabinet, with Dryer the last to be freed.

The dust settles

In the aftermath of the IRB inquiry, security officials took a more proactive stance regarding Irish dissidents in Australia. In May 1918, a secret agent was inserted into yet another community group, the

Irish National Society (INS), in the hope of learning more about its intentions. The official wrote: 'I have instituted secret agent inquiries with a view to getting a list of members and as much information as possible. I have provided the agent with Application Card and instructed party to join Society if necessary.'[54] By September 1918, the agent reported that the INS was avoiding the use of the post office due to the censor. Instead, applications were printed in books of five, and returned to the secretary by hand when they were full. They found the INS had approximately 300 active members, with another 700 memberships expected by Christmas.[55] Surveillance of the Irish groups, however, yielded very little because there was very little to be found. Occasionally, the Fenians would sing revolutionary songs, such as the 'Hymn of Fate' on St Patrick's Day, which cursed England, praised the Irish and encouraged the Germans but that appeared to be the extent of their radicalism.[56]

While anti-colonial activity lapsed in Australia, an Irish terrorist campaign accelerated in Ireland. The IRB was gone, subsumed from within by the Irish Republican Army (IRA), led by the genius strategist Michael Collins. In early 1919, the IRA ramped up its terrorist attacks. British government reports charted 700 'outrages' or attacks from January 1919 to April 1920. From April to May 1920, this number rose to 1700. The outrages included 194 threatening letters to the British Royal Irish Constabulary (RIC); 185 counts of property damage; more than 250 arson attacks especially targeting RIC barracks; some sixteen murders of government officials; a dozen dead policemen; nine dead civilians; and seventeen soldiers robbed of their weapons.[57] Another 300 civilians reported experiencing IRA intimidation, and Dublin Metropolitan Police added 120 kidnappings to the growing tally of IRA depredations.[58]

Between this and the success of Sinn Fein in peaceful politics, a ceasefire was reached between the Irish anti-colonialists and the British in 1921. The Republic of Ireland was established after lengthy negotiations, encompassing all of Ireland save six of the nine Ulster counties in the north. This division would become central to new discord. A civil war erupted in the new republic immediately following the treaty, as Anti-Treatyites wanted control of Northern Ireland as well as the south. This was efficiently quelled by Ireland's new government. In Australia, Irish Australians continued to celebrate their heritage, but the days of agitating for Irish freedom were largely over.

This issue had highlighted an internal need: Australia had to take responsibility for its own security. It was the British, not the Australians, who established the first intelligence organisation in 1916 in the form of the CEB, later called the Special Intelligence Branch (SIB), which was involved in the IRB case. In conjunction with Military Intelligence, it shouldered the burden of World War I security. In the years following the war, the SIB merged with the new Commonwealth Police Force to form the Commonwealth Investigations Branch (CIB). With the outbreak of World War II in 1939, the Military Intelligence directorate again became the primary agency for internal and external security. This was re-configured in mid-1942, when the new Australian Security Service (with ASS as its unfortunate acronym) took over internal security matters.[59] ASS focused on Axis subversion activities in Australia until after the end of the war in 1945, when it was disbanded. Control reverted back to the CIB, now called the Commonwealth Investigation Service (CIS).

Following World War II, internal security remained the domain of the CIS until the Venona incident. In the years following the war, United States and British intelligence services became convinced there was a security leak in Australia involving their own top-secret decrypted Russian intelligence, which they called Venona. It would later transpire that an Australian official in the Australian Department of External Affairs was leaking sensitive US and British intelligence to the Soviet State Security Service. A Soviet diplomat, Semen Ivanovich Makarov, had recruited Walter Seddon Clayton, a senior Australian communist, who in turn recruited a typist in the Department of External Affairs and a member of the wartime Security Service.[60] From there, classified information began to trickle into the hands of enemies—but it would take years to entirely confirm the extent of Venona.

The US used Venona to limit information-sharing with the British, believing (rightfully perhaps) that the UK would continue sharing intelligence with Australia.[61] This led the British prime minister, Clement Attlee, to pressure Prime Minister Ben Chifley into establishing an Australian security service along the lines of MI5.[62] Unsubstantiated claims exist that Chifley directly promised Attlee it would be done. The establishment of a new security and intelligence agency in Australia was therefore not the consequence of Irish agitation, fifth-column activity or subversive Germans: it was because the British, under pressure from the United States, demanded it.

On 16 March 1949, Chifley issued a directive to create and maintain a new security service, with an annual budget of £115,000, called the Australian Security Intelligence Organisation (ASIO). Its primary purpose was to investigate communist activity in Australia and provide security assessments. It was a federal advisory agency, with no executive power or ability to enforce criminal law: its role was purely to collect intelligence on internal and external threats. Within a year, ASIO had taken control of CIS files, hired 141 personnel, and established offices in all major Australian cities. It attempted, at least initially, to cooperate with state police agencies, although this was not always successful: 'political reasons' were blamed for a struggling relationship with Queensland's special branch.[63] The Venona affair hung around like a bad smell and became known within ASIO as 'the Case'. The Case, alongside Soviet and communist espionage and subversion, consumed ASIO's attention for years to come.[64]

The Revolution Generation, 1965–75

In the years following World War II, terrorism became a liberation strategy for colonised peoples around the globe, but little of it came to Australia. Instead, the spectre of terrorism was revitalised in Australia later in the 1960s and 1970s, as much of the Western world was engulfed in the protests and revolutions advanced by feverish dreamers. While protest movements do not fuel terrorism, many extremist movements drew supporters from that energised pool of radicals and revolutionaries anxious for various forms of social change. Amid this activity were schemers, violent extremist organisations and movements that sought to advance their own fringe ideologies. Extremist ideologies, with visions of utopia and fantasies of a radiant destiny, have the power to seize the hearts and minds of wannabe revolutionaries wherever they are in the world, and mobilise them to malevolent ends.

During this period in Australia, there were three main branches of extremism that catalysed directly into politically motivated violence: Ustaša terrorism, pro-Palestinian extremism, and left-wing extremism. All of these threats were supported domestically by Australian citizens, even though all were connected with international networks or inspired by international cult figures.

The fascist Ustaša terrorism network was international and domestic, with numerous Australian cells and organisations involving

Australian citizens. These Australians became the first foreign fighters, uniting with others from around the world to mount incursions into Yugoslavia, with the lurid dream of toppling the communist president, Josip Tito. The Australian Ustaša network was intrinsically connected to international Ustaša counterparts, and their joint goal was altering the political order in Yugoslavia. In this case, Australia was a recruiting ground for Ustaša terrorism and Ustaša terrorists, and the financial powerhouse keeping the international network afloat.

Pro-Palestinian groups such as Al Fatah and the Popular Front for the Liberation of Palestine (PFLP) also recruited Australian citizens and set up domestic cells in Australia. Members supported their cells in numerous ways, from financing to action. Their international connections were strong, and keeping terrorist masterminds out of Australia became a significant focus for border security agencies. These groups, however, had no interest in changing the Australian political order, and focused their efforts instead on the reclamation of historic Palestine through attacking Israeli interests and those of their allies and supporters (including Australia).

Of all three branches, the extreme left was the only threat that sought to change Australia's liberal democratic order. Members of free-floating extreme left-wing cells were Australians, willing to plan and coordinate politically motivated violence in an attempt to coerce the government into backing down on its controversial conscription policy during the Vietnam War. They were inspired by the revolutionary leaders based in far-flung jungles, such as Che Guevara, and imagined themselves to be acting in conjunction with chic middle-class terrorists of the United States and West Germany. This was part of an all-consuming quest for world revolution.

In response to these diverse mobilisations, federal and state law enforcement and intelligence agencies rose to counteract the threat, drawing in unlikely partners such as Australia Post, the Department of Immigration, Customs, and airport security. The national security apparatus would come face to face with pro-Palestinian terrorist masterminds while simultaneously tracking Ustaša terrorists and attempting to penetrate extreme left-wing movements.

2

A socialist utopia: left-wing extremism

The 1960s were pervaded by the twin forces of horror and hope. The Cold War was in full swing, and sudden crises had the terrible power to fundamentally threaten the new and delicate world order. Competition for influence between the United States and the Union of Soviet Socialist Republics (USSR) upset world geopolitics, from Berlin to Cuba, from Korea to Vietnam. Nuclear missiles cast the longest shadows, hidden as they were around the globe, waiting for permission to take their first and only flight. Old men played an elaborate and silent game of chess with counterparts in the Kremlin and shuffled their pawns and bishops around the board. As a consequence of this deadly play, men and missiles moved around the world in soundless response. No matter how many young men caught bullets in the far-flung jungles of the East, checkmate remained a distant fantasy.

The youth of the West began to dread their twentieth birthdays, for around the fringe of the festivities lurked the cold reality of conscription. Once Australian men turned twenty, they were obliged to register their name for the ballot and enter the conscription lottery, consigning their future to the unlucky chance of national service. If their number was drawn, they were obliged to report for two years' continuous service in the Australian Regular Army.

From there, it was a short flight to Vietnam to fight the communist threat, and a longer path back home. Full exemptions from service were difficult to acquire, but temporary exemptions were readily available if the young man in question was a university student. University campuses, then, became the centre of gravity for the anti-conscription and anti-war movement.

When confronted with the expectation of becoming a pawn in someone else's game, these university students shed their secure and rosy Western ideals. The grim realities of 1960s realpolitik revealed the hitherto unrecognised hand of American imperialism. The disillusionment was palpable. Instead of resigning themselves to their situation, many students found their strength in hope. They eagerly embraced the dream of a better world, a world of their own making. And so they marched, they sang, they questioned, and they protested the injustices and hypocrisy of the Western world's Cold War strategies. The insecurity of the future drew many to the far left, where they found identity and community in the culture of rebellion.

This grassroots revolution would leave the various departments concerned with Australian national security scratching their heads. From within the surging and tumultuous student movement protesting the draft and the war emerged a scattering of extreme left-wing groups and organisations that threatened retribution for government action—that threatened terrorism. In the titanic battle between the governments of the West and the forces of communism, there was limited tolerance for left-wing activism and extremism. The threat, in the context of the Cold War, was taken seriously, especially if Soviet sponsorship was suspected. Some counterterrorism authorities believed that domestic groups turning to terrorism was a matter of *when* rather than *if*. From 1969, these groups launched campaigns that seemed to promise that dreadful eventuality. When the dust settled, the record would show that the extreme left was angry enough to burn the existing order to the ground, but not angry enough to kill.

A new order

Revolution was in the air, but not everyone liked the smell of it. Throughout the early 1960s, the far left in Australia was in disarray. The Communist Party of Australia (CPA), the traditional leader of the Australian far left, haemorrhaged student members even as it had an influx of undercover ASIO agents engaged in the war on communism. The CPA tried to distance itself from the Communist International (Comintern) but it was too little and too late.[1] Radical young students turned from them, disgusted by what they perceived as the CPA's ongoing failure to create meaningful political change. Instead, the students galvanised around a fresh source of hope: the New Left.

The New Left became a great unifier of the revolutionary student counterculture around the world. It rejected the so-called 'old' left of communism. Students had no interest in joining the old guard, so marked by failure and division. Although they still held to some of the philosophies of Karl Marx and Mao Zedong, they turned to new philosophers to answer the question of revolution. These included Herbert Marcuse, who theorised that the students, the youth of the world, were the true force for revolutionary change. In consequence, students, frustrated intellectuals, dropouts, misfits and oppressed minorities found meaning in the New Left movement. Political radicalism was a fashionable component of student counterculture, and rebellion was the style of the day.

The New Left pursued an aggressive and idealistic revolution, with plans for Australia and the rest of the world. Its adherents declared themselves committed to participatory democracy, equality, liberty and community. Their goal was the revolutionary reconstruction of society through the creation of decentralised communes, operating on mutually trusting economic and social relationships. Alongside this goal was sexual revolution, including liberation from the constraints of the nuclear family; and civil revolution, with the emancipation of oppressed peoples, including Australia's Indigenous population, and the destruction of the

White Australia policy. This utopia could only be achieved through the complete transformation of society.

The New Left heavily romanticised the undeniably handsome Latin American revolutionaries such as Che Guevara and Carlos Marighella, and elevated them to the status of counterculture celebrities. New Leftists allied with the heroes of the Third World, and consumed book after book on guerrilla warfare. The symbols of war, American imperialism, the police, and the National Service Office became their enemies. The government, which they believed had raised them in deceit and primed them to kill, was imagined as their all-powerful adversary. But beyond all else, the Australian New Left mobilised in opposition to conscription. Seen through their eyes, conscription made them old enough to kill in a society in which they were not even old enough to vote. The New Left offered them an alternative future, a new world order, however unreachable and unrealisable this utopia was.

An international call

Guevara and Marighella didn't care a fig for their legions of student admirers, but from those legions arose a cadre of Western revolutionaries who took on the fight for a New Left world revolution in their name. At the forefront of this activism was the Students for a Democratic Society (SDS), which was established in the 1960s. The SDS became the mouthpiece of student rebellion, and soon recruited nearly 100,000 members worldwide. The SDS was strongest in the United States and the Federal Republic of Germany (West Germany), with smaller elements also present in Australia. They were an activist organisation that largely employed the tactics of peaceful resistance to a supposedly hostile order: peaceful demonstrations, sit-ins, bill-posting and pamphleteering. Like all movements of great promise, the SDS was prone to internal coups as wannabe revolutionaries vied for power.

In West Germany, the SDS spawned an aggressive splinter cell, called the Extra-parliamentary Opposition (APO) movement. This attracted the likes of Andreas Baader and Gudrun Ensslin, who went on to become the leaders of the terrorist group the Red Army Faction (RAF), also known as the Baader–Meinhof Gang. The RAF commenced a bombing and assassination campaign throughout West Germany, targeting businessmen, the US military and the government. In the United States, the SDS was taken over by Bill Ayers and Bernardine Dohrn. They called their cell the Weather Bureau and took their name from a Bob Dylan song lyric: 'you don't need a weatherman to know which way the wind blows'. They soon walked out on the SDS and became better known as the Weather Underground Organization (WUO), an all-American left-wing terrorist group capable of inspiring violence in far-flung regions of the world such as Australia.[2] In 1969, WUO announced that the Days of Rage had come, and promised a revolutionary march of thousands in Chicago. Only a few hundred attended the march and it descended into a riot, incurring substantial property damage.

Embarrassed but hardly humbled, the WUO held the Flint War Council, in Flint, Michigan, and turned to terrorism. The WUO manifesto, released on 18 June 1969, was titled, predictably, *You Don't Need a Weatherman to Know Which Way the Wind Blows*. In this piece, the WUO called for international revolution, hoping to unite the Black rights movement with the socialist cause against US imperialism and the war in Vietnam. From there, it sought to galvanise a student army to become the revolutionary vanguard:

> Young people will be part of the International Liberation Army. The necessity to build this International Liberation Army in America leads to certain priorities in practices for the revolutionary youth movement which we shall begin to apply this summer.[3]

Around the world, students heard this call, and around the world, they answered it.

A domestic reply

One month after this call to arms, a campaign began in Australia. The Australia New Left and SDS had largely evolved in tandem with the SDS expansion in the United States and West Germany from as early as 1966. In its pamphlet 'A Conceptual Revolution of Identity', the SDS listed its priorities as first, to challenge the neo-capitalist system; and second, to provide the impetus for revolutionary change. The group initially claimed that its primary enemies were the universities themselves and the mass media, although there was hardly a consensus behind this. The pamphlet, described as both verbose and boring, failed to galvanise its followers.[4] Glamour and style were all important at a time when radicalism was chic.

Attitude was everything—and invariably led to contested leadership. The Society for Democratic Action (SDA) in Brisbane disbanded as early as 1970 due to such internal upheaval. Other SDS chapters around Australia were factionalised and suffered ongoing conflict, rendering them largely immobile.

Some students believed that the strategy, tactics, and organisation of the Australian New Left were nothing more than 'orgasm politics'—that acts of civil disobedience did nothing to restructure power dynamics because they were not applied sparingly or intelligently. One student, Chris O'Connell, suggested that the movement produce its own ideological manifesto and restructure along Leninist lines in small revolutionary cadres. He noted that:

> The undergraduate radical movement serves a twofold purpose. First, it engages in action designed to undermine the confidence of the people, especially the students, in the goodness of our society, and thus to demonstrate the need of social restructuring along lines of participatory democracy. Secondly, it acts as a recruiting process for the graduate movement, seeking out effective cadres and providing them with training for a strategy that believes in operating within the system to alter the systems [sic].[5]

This strategy of operating within the system to alter the system was a popular one within the left-wing at the time, with a UK Trotskyist group called Militant Tendency using the strategy in the mid-1960s. In the long term, the strategy served only to delegitimise the more mainstream left such as UK Labour Party. Other attempts to produce manifestos, as suggested by O'Connell, also failed. The May Day Manifesto, released in May 1969 by the Revolutionary Socialist Alliance (RSA), stated:

> Violent revolution remains a necessary precondition for socialism. Not simply because rulers cannot be defeated any other way, but because it will only be in the struggle for socialism by revolution that it will be possible to rid ourselves of the collected garbage of our present culture . . .[6]

The RSA was not alone in seeking to create a manifesto encouraging violence. It had serious competition from the WUO on the one hand, and Monash and Australian National University (ANU) students on the other, who wrote their own manifestos, such as that appearing in the student newspaper *Lot's Wife* on 24 July 1969 and 'Manifesto for Change', but these failed to compete with the WUO.[7]

Liberation armies soon emerged: shadowy groups about which little is known and less can be confirmed. They went by the names of the Australian Liberation Army (ALA), the People's Liberation Army (PLA), the People's Liberation Armed Forces (PLAF), the Students Liberation Army Korps (SLAK) and the short-lived RSA.[8] They were a decentralised, autonomous network of cells that engaged in sporadic actions to further the revolution.

Their membership was drawn almost exclusively from university campuses and organisations. Some members were part of multiple groups and organisations simultaneously. Key feeder groups were rumoured to be the Maoist-leaning Monash Labor Club in Victoria, the Trotskyist-influenced SDS in New South Wales (in addition to Tasmanian branches), the anarchist Revolutionary Socialist Student Alliance (RSSA) in Queensland, and the

Leninist-inclined SDA in South Australia. Contra, in the ACT, was also believed to be involved.[9]

The most significant of the groups was, arguably, the PLA. It claimed responsibility for about seventeen major acts of vandalism, fifteen cases of property damage, one theft, eight cases of arson (sometimes Molotov cocktails), two bombings, two attempts to use 'war gas', and one shooting. ASIO believed that the intention of the PLA was to compel law enforcement to brutally suppress demonstrations and protests. This suppression would radicalise the protest movement, which would rise up against the authorities, leading to a revolutionary chaos that the PLA could harness for its own political purposes.[10] The ALA, on the other hand, was possibly a group of students who frequented 116 Greville Street in Prahran. This location was known colloquially as 'the Bakery' in 1969, but it was registered as Alice's Restaurant-Bookshop, where 'you can get anything that's Left' according to an advertisement in the communist newspaper *Tribune*.[11]

Together, these groups were responsible for 25 per cent of all politically motivated incidents that ASIO tracked between 1969 and 1972, spanning nearly 100 incidents of varying severity and linked to New Left motivations. For many students, the revolution was close enough to taste, and promised an immediate release from the lurking danger of conscription. The chic leaders of the New Left in the United States had called for action, and action they would receive.

Phase one: smash

Just over two weeks after the WUO call to arms, the various Australian liberation armies had coalesced and were ready to answer the call. On 4 July 1969, a gang of thirteen young people travelled in three cars to the US Consulate-General in Melbourne and stoned it. They broke eighteen windows, causing $500 worth of damage, and fled. An anonymous call to a radio station claimed it was on behalf of the PLA:

> Thirteen members of the Melbourne People's Liberation Army this afternoon drove up outside the U.S. consulate and stoned it. They successfully demonstrated their opposition to US imperialism and the futility of simple protest and legitimate dissent. We used illegitimate means because we believe in the class struggle through protracted war.[12]

While this kind of claim is not terribly unusual for an aspiring terrorist group or guerrilla organisation, protracted war normally implies outright violent hostilities rather than fatality-free civil disobedience. There is, after all, a chasm of difference between lethal terrorist violence and eighteen broken windows. Nonetheless, the Australian national security apparatus did not take kindly to the targeting of US premises, and concerns regarding the developing militancy of the student movement deepened.

The political and university-based nature of the PLA was evident with the group's next job. On 17 July, the PLA stole a ballot box containing all the electoral votes for the Student Representative Council of the University of Melbourne. A call to the media claimed it was on behalf of the 'Second Division' of the PLA. Again, this act was hardly terrorism, but it shows that some of the PLA, at least, agreed with the SDS that universities were also in bed with the enemy. In Sydney, university students, including Derek Dolstra, stormed a conference between the Student and University Council. In response, three students received disciplinary action—a surprising move given they were entitled to observe the proceedings.[13] The reactions to these minor actions were occasionally hysterical. Patrick Morgan, a Monash University English tutor, wrote:

> Having failed to affect society, the activist students have now turned to their own universities and are trying to terrorize them into setting themselves up as models of the totalitarian nightmare ... The students are permanent revolution [sic], waging guerrilla warfare against modern industrial

institutions... It is pointless to seek for 'intellectual mentors' of the student mind, because there is no student mind.[14]

While this intellectual elitism from an English tutor is not terribly uncommon, it nonetheless articulates the pushback that students were receiving from some university officials because of their radical politics.

The activity soon spread to Queensland. On 8 August 1969, a pamphlet titled 'Struggle' was scattered throughout the University of Queensland. Allegedly written and distributed by SLAK, the pamphlet encouraged its readers to use violent action, including tear gas. ASIO suspected that the pamphlet was written by Richard Francis Shearman under the pseudonym Paul Darcy. They believed that Shearman was a member of SLAK, the Revolutionary Worker Student Alliance (RWSA) and the RSSA, and was henceforth considered by ASIO to be a leader of the PLA in Queensland.[15] Barely a week after this pamphlet was distributed, the PLA smashed two plate-glass windows at Australia House in Brisbane on 14 August, causing $2000 worth of damage. Then, on 23 September, a group of fifteen people worked in concert to extinguish the Flame of Remembrance in Brisbane. Later that night, they also broke more windows at Australia House, with the PLA gleefully claiming responsibility for the activity.

Not to be outdone by their northern counterparts, PLA members generated more propaganda in New South Wales. A Macquarie University student newspaper, *Arena*, circulated in Sydney, published an interview with Derek Dolstra. It frames Dolstra as a key PLA agent at Macquarie University, and Dolstra himself (allegedly) describes the PLA as 'strictly underground, its activities highly subversive, and membership restricted to a revolutionary elite'.[16] This subsequently appeared in ASIO documents on PLA activity in the state.[17] The nature of the revolutionary elite cannot be precisely triangulated, but following the burst of activity in Queensland, it appeared that groups were either working together or competing against each other for prominence.

On 29 September, the South Australian group announced itself in dramatic fashion. In a single night, it launched simultaneous paint attacks on the State War Memorial, the No. 4 Magistrates Court, the Liberal and Country League Headquarters, the Department of Labour and National Service Office, and the Keswick Army Barracks Administration Block. Symbolically, it had declared its opposition to the government, the judiciary, conscription, and the military through these actions. Windows were also broken at the Combined Services Recruiting Office and the Department of Labour and National Service. Caught in the crossfire were a scattering of tollgates, businesses, the racecourse, and railway properties. The PLAF claimed responsibility for this incident in a phone call to the *Adelaide News*, declaring, 'Last night the PLAF was born. It is the Peoples' Liberation Armed Forces,' and warned that '. . . last night's acts of sabotage were only minor. The PLAF will meet increasing political repression with widespread terror activities.'[18] That same night, the PLAF, not satisfied with its first brush with the media, also called the radio station 5AD and described itself as 'A Marxist-Leninist organization which is determined to struggle against the Capitalists and Imperialists until the last Capitalist is hung with the guts of the last Imperialist.'[19]

The PLAF's plan was to supposedly use terrorism to force the changes that its members wished to see. For all their talk of guts and glory, however, their acts of vandalism fell short of the terror they promised. In West Germany, the RAF was blowing up US military bases, while the WUO in the US bombed the Pentagon itself. Daily gun battles occurred between Latin American revolutionaries and government forces. It was simply not on the same scale; it was one thing to claim to engage in terrorism, but it was quite another thing to do it.

The PLAF was not the only group in South Australia. On 8 October, suspected PLA members threw a small bomb—in reality a matchbox of gunpowder—onto the veranda of Andrew Jones, a federal member of parliament, who was known to be fiercely anti-communist. No claim of responsibility was made. Seven days before the 25 October federal election, Jones was again targeted, when the PLAF made telephone threats to petrol-bomb Jones's house. Midnight callers knocked on Jones's door, and he was soon afforded police protection. Nothing further happened, probably because Jones lost his seat to Labor's Chris Hurford in the election.

Not to be outdone by the PLA and the PLAF, the ALA was also competing for prominence, and it aimed higher still. On 1 November, it undertook a 'raid', to use its words, against the Reserve Bank of Australia and the offices of Ansett Transport Industries when it threw bricks through the windows and caused $3400 worth of damage. In a public statement, the ALA aligned itself against conscription and said:

> We intend to do about $10,000 damage for each draft resister jailed—$5000 for the Government and $5000 for big business. The Government is going right off its nut about these windows, but it couldn't give a damn about the lives of Australian kids who have been forced over there.[20]

Opposition to conscription, then, went hand in hand with opposition to the Vietnam War itself. Another $3000 damage was tallied up to the ALA before the end of the year, when windows were broken at the Commonwealth Centre in Melbourne on 19 December; and seven glass windows were broken at Imperial Chemical Industries of Australia and New Zealand on 30 December.

In the midst of this destruction by the ALA and the PLA, the SDS ran a series of conferences to discuss draft-resistance measures. Avoiding the ballot, such as by refusing to register, came with a two-year prison penalty. Several high-profile cases of resistance, such as that of Brian Ross, spurred them on to action. Another resister, P.A. Hornby, had the good sense to flee interstate before his day in court, heading to Victoria to continue to agitate and organise against the draft.[21] The ALA was supportive of these acts of defiance, publicly stating in December 1969 that it stood behind the draft resisters and would do all in its power to avenge them.

According to the ALA, 'We've paid for Gordon REISENLEITER (a person imprisoned in Queensland for two years under the National Service ACT); now we are working for Brian ROSS. We confine our activities to Government and big business which we feel are exploiting the Australian people or the Australian economy.'[22] The ALA also threatened to levy a fine of $50,000 against the government for every ALA member arrested. If the police drew their weapons, fired, or injured an ALA member while arresting them, they promised $1,000,000 in retribution.

Phase two: surge

By early 1970, ASIO reported that the ALA was attempting to escalate its campaign with the acquisition of explosives and weapons. Members boasted of acquiring detonators, fuses and gelignite, while others claimed to possess radio-controlled bombs, plastic explosives, and various firearms.[23] The ALA was also allegedly planning to infiltrate marches, rallies and demonstrations using a series of cadres. The first of these, the Action Cadre, was supposed to protect the leaders from arrest or counter protest. The second, the Battle Cadre, was to act as a guerrilla group within the demonstration and engage in destructive activities under the cover of the protest.[24]

Despite these plans, the year opened in favour of law enforcement when three people from two different states were arrested in relation to ALA activity. Their trials for malicious damage, which were to be heard simultaneously by the County Court in Melbourne, were ultimately pushed back until 1971.[25] They were later suspected of setting fire to a number of schools in Victoria. The PLA was not below national security notice either. ASIO predicted that the PLA would target, first, symbols of capitalism, such as Honeywell Pty Ltd offices around Australia, stock exchanges and oil companies; and, second, symbols of war, including national servicemen and the Lithgow Small Arms Factory in New South Wales.

The South Australian chapter kicked things off early on 18 January, painting anti–National Service slogans on tramway buses in Adelaide. Four days later, two windows were broken at the Labour and National Service Office in Adelaide. No group claimed responsibility for these. The PLA quickly claimed responsibility, however, for graffitiing Adelaide Combined Services Recruiting Office and Commonwealth Offices with anti-conscription slogans on 31 January.

On 2 March, the atmosphere in Melbourne became more serious when an incendiary device was thrown at the US Consulate-General. It resulted in a fire that spread into the Australian American Association premises, causing $7000 worth of damage.[26] Despite the attack's success, it was claimed by neither the ALA nor the PLA, which is odd since it would have boosted the credibility and reputation of either cell as a serious player. Given how many other groups were targeting US diplomatic premises during this time, however, it may well have been the work of an external party.

On 6 March, an ALA member allegedly boasted that they had access to an automatic weapon. The same day, the Monash University Regiment reported that three guns had been stolen from a display case: a .303 rifle, a 9 mm Owen machine carbine, and a 9 mm F1 submachine gun.[27] While the rifle and the carbine had been used in World War II and the Korean War theatres respectively, the F1 had been in service for less than a decade (and remains a popular firearm today). This made it an attractive target for an aspiring terrorist: but would they be able to pull the trigger and take a life for their cause?

Early in April 1970, John Andrew Tully, an SDS activist in Tasmania, demonstrated no such qualms about firing 20–30 rounds into the Hobart branch of the Department of Labour and National Service with a rifle, knowing it was empty on Sunday night.[28] According to ASIO he was convicted of this act, and the event was subsequently incorporated in their list of violent incidents.[29] This was not Tully's first brush with the law: he had previously been charged under the Commonwealth Crimes Act because he wrote a pamphlet encouraging people to disobey the National Service

Act that was distributed around the University of Tasmania.[30] ASIO categorised this shooting as a terrorist incident, although he was not charged as a terrorist, and the magistrate who presided over his court hearing showed little interest in his politics.

ASIO was about to become a target itself. On 3 May 1970, a group of people broke away from the so-called May Day March against the Vietnam War, and broke windows at Honeywell offices and the ASIO headquarters in Melbourne. Three people were arrested in connection with this event, but although it can be confirmed that they were anti-war, it is unknown if they were PLA or ALA. There was a scattering of other events in June, such as the breaking of windows at the South African Trade Commission and the Commonwealth Offices in Wollongong, and shooting at another Honeywell building in Melbourne, but they were not claimed by any group.

Then, on 30 June, the South Australian PLA acted again, and this time it was more serious. A woman threw two stones through the windows of the South Australian Stock Exchange, followed by a bundle of glass vials with a burning fuse. The fuse melted the vials to discharge butyric acid in gas form. This is not dissimilar to capsicum spray and causes coughing and eye irritation. There is no record of injuries, although staff on the floor thought it was a bomb and fled the attack. Two people were arrested and convicted of involvement. This was not the only time that gas was used as a weapon.[31] PLA cells were also suspected of being responsible for pouring butyric acid into air-conditioning units at the US Consulate in Sydney, and throwing it at the building housing the Department of Labour and National Service in Adelaide, although they did not claim responsibility for these attacks.

July 1970 was an especially active period, with the PLA and ALA again targeting capitalist and government symbols. On 2 July, two incendiary devices were thrown into the Australian General Electric's building in Melbourne, causing $10,000 worth of damage when they triggered the sprinklers and destroyed the computer equipment. This was claimed by a new offshoot,[32] whose spokesman said,

'I am speaking for the People's Liberation Front. We have just blown up General Electric in Lonsdale St. Down with all American war-mongering capitalists.'[33] General Electric was targeted for its affiliation with a US corporation that built weapons systems for the US military. On 3 July, a shotgun was fired into the St Kilda offices of ASIO, damaging six windows and narrowly missing an employee. The next day, a Honeywell building in Perth was vandalised. The day after that, bricks and an incendiary device were thrown into the prime minister's electoral office in Melbourne—an event preceded by more than 30 death threats related to opposition to the Vietnam War.

On 6 July, incendiary devices were thrown into Keep Bros and Wood's Melbourne premises, causing $300,000 worth of damage; while an arson attack on McPhersons Ltd that same day left the factory destroyed and almost killed two firemen. The Australian Liberation Front (ALF), a newcomer to the scene, claimed responsibility for all three incendiary attacks.[34] On 15 July, a letter bomb containing white phosphorus arrived at the Department of Labour and National Service in Adelaide. It exploded and nearly injured an employee. A second letter was identified before being opened. On 24 July, a similar letter bomb was received by the Department of Labour and National Service in Sydney—although it failed to ignite. Neither of these letters was claimed by the PLA or ALA, which could indicate that they were the work of a lone actor who shared these organisations' political views.

While it is not known if these attacks were coordinated, the extreme-left cells appeared to be either competing or self-perpetuating. On 1 August, seven bricks were thrown into the home of F.H. Brooks, Director-General of Education in Victoria. The PLA claimed it was in protest at the dismissal of Julie Ingleby from the department. Ingleby, according to the Communist newspaper *Tribune*, had been dismissed because of her husband's role in protesting the Vietnam War.[35] She had been charged with contempt of court during his trial. Mr Brooks was threatened again about the Ingleby dismissal later in August.

Also on 1 August, an incendiary was thrown into the Mobil bulk-fuel store office near Tullamarine airport, but it was not claimed. The store also received a number of threatening calls as the month progressed. On 11 August, Monash University disciplined seven students—and a day later, four windows were broken in the Administration Building. The PLA claimed responsibility. Finally, on 20 November, two windows were broken at Honeywell in Perth. An apparent PLA member called the local newspaper to claim responsibility, further stating that the PLA had a list of firms supplying war materials and that they would be targeted. This proved an empty threat. On 12 August, the PLA claimed responsibility for the destruction of four windows at Monash University, in lieu of those firms.

On 20 August, four incendiary devices were thrown at a container vessel in Sydney, but no group claimed responsibility for it and it could have been connected with environmental movements. On 25 August, windows were broken with bricks at the Combined Services Recruiting Centre in Melbourne. This was claimed by the PLA, but the vandalism of the Australian War Memorial in Canberra with anti-conscription slogans, which occurred on the very same day, was not claimed. On 3 September 1970, propaganda titled 'The Time is Right for Fighting in the Streets' was distributed at the University of Queensland. It gave directions for manufacturing Molotov cocktails and explosives. It was signed under the fictitious name Steve Robins, and ASIO once again suspected this was the work of Shearman.[36]

The most significant event during this period was the Vietnam Moratorium, led by Dr Jim Cairns, and supported by both the mainstream Australian Labor Party and the far-left Communist Party. The Moratorium organisers initially took great care to dissuade marchers from engaging in violence. The non-violent clause was later dropped from the initial Sponsors' Statement for three reasons: first, pressure from the CPA, which actively called for militant activity; second, because the stone-throwing attack on the US Consulate-General building on 4 July 1969 was deemed successful; and third, because it was believed that marchers had to protect themselves from police brutality.[37] This change was opposed by the trade unions, which sought a peaceful demonstration against the war.

In the end, the first Vietnam Moratorium was indeed peaceful, with 200,000 marchers turning out to oppose conscription and the Vietnam War. The second moratorium, on 18 September 1970, was, however, less so, with fewer participants but less peaceful intentions. At this second moratorium a scuffle broke out between radical students and police. Police baton-charged protesters in Melbourne, and nearly 200 were arrested in Sydney. During the chaos, a small bottle containing the chemical chloropicrin was broken, producing a nauseating 'war gas'. Twenty police officers and a large number of civilians were affected.[38]

On 17 October, the words 'fascist pigs' were painted on the steps of the Commonwealth Employment Centre in Adelaide. On 24 October, the Citizens Military Forces (CMF, a forerunner of the Australian Army Reserve) armoury at New England University was damaged by incendiaries, causing $50,000 worth of damage. It was not claimed by the PLA or the ALA. The destruction of windows at Honeywell in Western Australia on 20 November, however, was claimed by the PLA. Around this time, the ALA changed its name to PLA. This was believed to be due to a secret society called the Left Caucus, a covert faction within the SDS that supported street fighting and other militant action.[39] Feasibly, this would have spanned numerous left-wing organisations, including the Monash Labor Club, the SDS, the CPA, the Women's Liberation Group, and other covert groups mentioned earlier. If the Left Caucus did exist, it could have been the centre of gravity of the action groups. Whatever competition had been occurring, the PLA had won. The ALA and PLAF names fell into disuse, and the liberation armies assumed a relatively united front.

By the end of 1970, ASIO had substantial information on the extreme-left groups. In one report they suggest: 'These groups provide an avenue for extremist expression via violent propaganda, and action via "confrontation" operations of a guerrilla-type nature, for numerous extremist-minded individuals both inside and outside the campuses and high schools. They operate to keep discontent simmering with anti-establishment propaganda.'[40]

The events of 1970 had done more than simply keep the movement ticking along: they had also seen intra-organisational competition escalate and then, eventually, dissipate into cooperation. This change would have a significant impact heading into 1971.

Phase three: swarm

Fire was the weapon of choice as the year began, indicating a new attitude to risk: a thrown stone had an admittedly limited ability to cause damage; a fire, however, could wreak great destruction and claim innocent lives indiscriminately. The first incident was a case of arson, targeting the Cadet Training Depot in Ballarat, but while it was commensurate with PLA targeting, they did not claim it. In another unclaimed event, a small explosive device was detonated on the steps of the police headquarters in Adelaide.[41] There was a series of unclaimed arson attacks in February, targeting the 3 Women's Royal Australian Army Corps and 3 Division headquarters in Victoria.

On 22 March, the campaign finally came to Canberra, when the PLA vandalised the Liberal Party headquarters with anti-conscription slogans. There was also growing opposition to apartheid, coinciding with the South African Springbok rugby union team tour planned for June to August in 1971. The popular protest against this tournament meant that the extreme-left groups had a fresh pool of recruits—but it also meant that the national security apparatus had greater numbers of suspects for the numerous incidents of anti-apartheid vandalism. The slogan 'smash apartheid' began appearing frequently as part of a broader student protest movement.

In April, however, the newly coordinated PLA properly emerged. It launched an incendiary attack against the General Electric showroom in Carlton, Melbourne: a small test of its capability. This was the lull before the storm, because on 18 August it launched simultaneous attacks, smashing windows at the Squire Inn Motel in Bondi, where the Springboks had stayed, and the South African Airways Office in Sydney and defacing Sydney Sports Ground, where two matches had been played with anti-apartheid slogans. The PLA called a Sydney newspaper and claimed responsibility. Then, on the night of 1 September, property belonging to the South Africa Consul in Sydney was burnt, along with two nearby boats. Despite this sudden change in targeting, the PLA claimed responsibility. Though primarily motivated by opposition to conscription, the PLA was not insensible to the popular anti-apartheid sentiment ignited by the Springbok tour, which was so widespread in Queensland that it resulted in a state of emergency being declared.

Five days later, on 6 September, the PLA undertook its first real bombing when it placed a gelignite bomb in Torrens River Pump House in Adelaide that blew the door off and painted 'PLA' in great white letters on the wall. The PLA then called the radio station 5KA and claimed responsibility. Despite this new expansion into serious explosives, it was nearly eight months before the PLA launched another attack, and when it did, it showed a new level of coordination and organisation.

Over three days, 9–11 May 1972, a series of attacks took place under the name of the May 10 Action Committee. On 9 May, an incendiary was thrown into Honeywell, Melbourne, causing $100 damage; windows were broken at the Pan Am airline office in Melbourne; and an army vehicle in Queensland was set on fire. On 10 May, protesters marched on DuPont Chemical's Brisbane offices, and a police car was stoned in Brisbane; two more army vehicles were set on fire in Adelaide; and the Department of Labour and National Service and the offices of aluminium company ALCOA in Adelaide were vandalised. On 11 May, windows were broken at the residences of the US Defense air attaché, and of the South Vietnamese Armed Forces attaché in Canberra; and an incendiary device was thrown through the window of General Electric in Melbourne. This was all followed by a violent protest on 12 May in Sydney, Melbourne, and Adelaide, where smokes bombs were heavily used.

This was the PLA's first truly national action, spanning Queensland, Victoria, the ACT, and South Australia. Perhaps the results were less than spectacular, because it was also the group's last major coordinated effort. It claimed a single petrol bomb thrown through the window of the French Consulate on 19 June, but this was its last real attempt. After this sudden swarm in activity, the PLA lapsed.

Phase four: stop

While it was assumed that some elements of the extreme left were later involved with the Campaign for Independent East Timor in 1975, little else really happened. There were the occasional rumours that some members undertook explosives training at Sydney Technical College in 1975 and sought to make letter bombs, but no violence eventuated.[42] The PLA's actions came to an end after 1972. The revolution, like most terrorist revolutions, came to nothing. Its destructive acts were both symbolic and retributive, but lacking in the intent to cause widespread harm or engage in lethal violence. While some members had technical capabilities, it was clear that these were not shared with others. Though there were injuries due to gas attacks, there were no fatalities.

Arguably, the PLA undermined the work of the broader student body, which pursued its opposition to conscription, the Vietnam War and the global realpolitik through largely peaceful and democratic processes. In short, the PLA may have given university students a bad name. More significantly, it also damaged the Australian far left and made the CPA look bad. While the CPA did endorse some PLA activities, it found other actions too extreme, and sought to distance itself from the radicals in an attempt to protect its longstanding quest for political respectability.[43] The PLA and its associated student movements were considered a potential embarrassment or, more optimistically, a recruitment ground for other far-left organisations.[44]

Why, then, did the PLA stop? It was not because of countermeasures. While ASIO had launched Operation Sparrow in the early 1960s and had effectively infiltrated the old guard of the CPA, the New Left was a different beast entirely. ASIO instead launched Operation Whip and sought to infiltrate and monitor the likes of the PLA and the ALA, but it failed to break through the broader university organisations that acted as default gatekeepers of the clandestine groups.[45] Perhaps because of this failure, some in ASIO began to ask themselves whether the groups even existed.

The reason for the dissolution of the PLA could be that they lost their raison d'être, their primary motivation. Conscription finally came to an end. In 1972, following a high-octane campaign by the Australian Labor Party, the reigning Liberal government with its unpopular policies, including conscription, was ousted. Gough Whitlam gained the trust of many left-wing students through his promise to end conscription—and end it he did. Without that key spark for the tinder, the revolution did not blaze but smouldered and then died. The biggest threat to the anti-war, anti-conscription university students had been neutralised. They could go back to their comfortable lives without fear of being sent to fight in the jungles of Vietnam.

Unstructured terror?

Four years after the last PLA-claimed activity, ASIO was still tracking left-wing extremists in Australia, writing that 'almost without exception, the revolutionary socialist groups believe that violence is essential in a revolutionary situation'.[46] Many were still coming to grips with the exact nature of the extreme-left threat during this time. For example, its structure mystified many people because it bore little resemblance to the primary terrorist threats of the time, such as the RAF and the WUO, which were highly structured and hierarchical. The liberation armies did not meet the expectations—in the traditional sense—of what an organised terrorist group looked like.[47] One ASIO report suggested that the leadership fragmentation was to blame for the sporadic and decentralised nature of attacks, driving adherents underground and 'encourag[ing] them to act alone.'[48]

There are several possibilities to consider with respect to their structure. First, it is possible that the PLA and the ALA were simply call signs, noms de guerre, donned by extremists for the purpose of an attack and then discarded, leaving nothing behind. Second, it's possible that they comprised entirely autonomous cells, but given the level of coordination this is unlikely. The third possibility is the most likely: the extreme left-wing cells were all submerged in the broader student movement, and though they initially competed for prominence, they later began to coordinate in order to achieve maximum effect while retaining separate command centres. Instead of a traditional terrorist cell structure, they evolved into free-floating cells, capable of both coordinated and autonomous action.

While ASIO could view their actions as 'unstructured terrorism', the destruction never escalated to the point that it presented a threat to human life. The intent to harm, the use of lethal violence, are integral to how we draw lines between political protest, civil disobedience and terrorism. To that end, the extreme left was not engaging in a level of violence commensurate with terrorism. Fatalities were neither sought deliberately nor achieved by chance. Even the gas attacks and the two minor bombings posed minimal risk to life.

While most of the extreme-left activity could be considered violent activism, the incendiary attacks trod close to terrorism. Arson and firebombing can endanger human life due to their uncontrollable nature, regardless of whether or not the building is empty, as they pose a risk to passers-by and first responders. What is key, then, is the intentions of the act itself. If the intention is to damage vacant property, then it sits within the realm of admittedly violent activism. If the intention is to damage property, knowing it could harm people within, then it sits within the realm of terrorism, in which the murder of innocents is considered an acceptable price to further the cause.

A small number of events crossed the line and ventured into terrorism. This included actions that were attributed to the PLA and ALA but—problematically—not claimed by them directly, such as shooting at the ASIO building, the letter bombs, and the explosive device that detonated in front of an Adelaide police station. Such tactics, regardless of fatality, fit within standard categories for terrorist violence. The difficulty with all these events is that they were not claimed by the PLA or the ALA. Any one of them could have been committed by lone actors supportive of the cause without direct association with the groups. In short, the PLA and the ALA were extreme, but they do not meet the threshold for terrorism.

In a time when protesters are called terrorists for holding signs in the streets of Melbourne or Brisbane, it is important to reinforce terrorism's essentially violent nature in a country that, at the time of writing, has never experienced mass-casualty terrorism. Without any significant loss of life or severe trauma, we risk trivialising terrorism as something mildly inconvenient rather than a coercive use of lethal force and fear. In the case of the New Left, what we can see is a network of extremists coming close to the line in the sand, but ultimately not crossing it.

While the extreme left had been bumbling about, promising to deliver terrorism but ultimately failing to demonstrate the appropriate level of bloodlust required, a serious terrorist threat was ticking away. The Ustaša, a violent Croatian fascist movement, was active in Australia, and to it, bombs and bloodlust were only the beginning.

3

A fascist homeland: the Ustaša

September 16 1972 was a typical busy Saturday in Sydney. Pedestrians hurried about their business, thinking little about shadowy terrorist groups and the dreadful threat of violence that might lurk just metres away. Some unfortunate pedestrians would find their path taking them past the Adriatic and Adria travel agencies that morning. Hidden near the two travel agencies, wristwatches connected to explosive devices methodically ticked towards detonation. Seemingly without warning, one of the bombs initiated. The explosion ripped through the travel agency and burst out onto the street, catching sixteen pedestrians in the blast.

Police responded swiftly and managed to clear the street before the second bomb exploded. Ambulances that screamed to the blast site found that all sixteen victims required hospital treatment: three would be hospitalised for days, and one victim would have their leg amputated. Two days after these Australians bled in the streets, Attorney-General Ivor Greenwood, the minister responsible for ASIO, reaffirmed his belief that there was no Ustaša threat in Australia. This was little comfort to those who had felt first-hand the indiscriminate violence of Ustaša terrorism.

The Ustaša's violence had caught everyday Australians in its crossfire. It had long been a matter of when, not if, such violence would manifest. The Ustaša terrorist network had established a foothold in Australia in the early 1960s and engaged in progressively severe acts of terrorist violence, spanning bombings, murder, intimidation and more. This latest attack had incurred its highest number of casualties in Australia, but was hardly the most fatal assault in its transnational campaign. The Ustaša would become Australia's first real experience of terrorism that was inspired internationally, but largely conducted domestically.

It began with a dictator and dreams of a fascist homeland, and would result in terrorism in Australia nearly 40 years later.

A Croatian führer

The interwar years in Europe saw the birth of fascist movements everywhere. There was the Nazi Party in Germany, of course, led by Adolf Hitler; and the National Fascist Party in Italy, led by Benito Mussolini. A dictator of far less prominence, but no less fascist, was a Croatian called Ante Pavelić, formerly a lawyer and political activist within the Croatian Party of Rights (HSP). The Kingdom of Serbs, Croats and Slovenes had newly become the Kingdom of Yugoslavia under Alexander I in 1929, and Pavelić was one of many who opposed the move. He emerged from the discord and chaos of Yugoslavian politics and formed the Revolutionary Croatian Ustasha Organisation, the Ustaša (which translates as 'insurgent').

It was a fascist organisation first and foremost, galvanised by its hatred of Yugoslavia and its desire for an ethnically and religiously exclusive state for Croatia. In practice, Pavelić sought to deny anyone but ethnic Croatians the right to live in the country, he wanted to conquer all areas he believed formerly belonged to Croatia, and vehemently rejected any compromise with Yugoslav peoples.[1] The nation, Pavelić believed, was defined by its ethnic Croatian and Roman Catholic religious homogeneity: all those who did not conform were seen as unwelcome outsiders (especially Orthodox Serbs). The Ustaša ideology was inherently fascist, seeking to impose conformity and homogeneity upon a select group of people. It was outwardly racist and exclusionary towards other people who had lived on the land for generations.

Pavelić soon fled Yugoslavia and his organisation went underground, receiving finance and training from fascist friends such as Mussolini and the diverse enemies of the newly formed Yugoslavia, such as Bulgaria, Hungary and Austria.[2] Thus aided and abetted, the Ustaša launched terrorist campaigns against Yugoslavia throughout the 1930s. They assassinated King Alexander I and the French foreign minister Louis Barthou in 1934, which forced Mussolini to renounce them. Outrage at the assassination led to the League of Nations passing the Convention for the Prevention and Punishment of Terrorism (1937), which was signed by many countries but never ratified. Ustaša was forced underground until World War II, where it emerged as an ally of the Nazi Party. The Nazis invaded Yugoslavia in 1941 and allowed the Ustaša to administer a Croatian puppet government over parts of occupied Yugoslavia.

Ante Pavelić became dictator, and under his direction the Ustaša enthusiastically pursued Nazi policies and set up concentration camps, such as Jasenovac camp. There, it commenced the systematic extermination of all people who did not fit its narrow ideal of citizenship. It is estimated that 100,000 Jews, Romanis and Serbs were killed in those camps, beaten, stabbed or shot to death one by one.[3] As the Australian ambassador in Belgrade noted many years later:

> It is, I think, impossible for Australians to fully comprehend the bitterness and the savagery during the Second World War in Yugoslavia. It is publicly accepted there that more Yugoslavs were killed by Yugoslavs than by the Germans and Italians combined. Even the Nazis . . . were said at times to have been appalled at the internecine cruelty. Massacres were common and no quarter was given. There was an unsavoury connection between the Catholic Church, the Croatian Ustashi, and the Germans . . .[4]

When the Axis powers eventually conceded defeat, Pavelić ordered the Ustaša to flee to Argentina, Canada or Australia. A large number of Croatians migrated to Australia after 1945, with another wave of economic migrants arriving in the 1960s. Among them, small in number and secretive by nature, were former Ustaša members. By 1981, around 74,000 ethnic Croatians had immigrated to Australia, and enjoyed the political and religious freedoms Australia offered. Only 10 per cent of Australian Croats paid levies to organisations such as the Ustaša. Of that number, moreover, only 100 people were believed to be willing to engage in violence on the Ustaša's behalf.[5]

There were hopes, however futile, that Old World rivalries would be left in Europe, that grievances would be forgotten, and that fascist ideology would be abandoned. Instead, it would manifest in the first sophisticated terrorist campaign in Australia.

Australian Ustaša

After World War II, CIA files indicated that the Ustaša movement internationalised and broadened, reaching out to various Croatian separatist movements and émigré communities around the world.[6] The hub for this international movement was, surprisingly, to be found in Australia, where a number of organisations were linked to the Ustaša and its fresh quest for an independent Croatia. The most prominent of these was the Croatian Liberation Movement (HOP), established by Pavelić from Argentina in 1956. Its Australian branch was founded that same year, and ASIO believed it quickly grew to 25 branches around the country.[7] One high-ranking member appeared to be Fabian Lovokovic, who represented the organisation on *This Day Tonight* among other public appearances. It was later suggested by Senator Lionel Murphy that he had led the organisation since its founding in Australia.[8] As an organisation, it would appear non-violent, and one member was reportedly an Australian public servant called Ivica Kokic, who was also a member of Croatia's 'government in exile', according to the Ustaša Regulations

Handbook published in 1967. He was later billed as the vice-president of the government in exile and described in Ustaša papers as a *satnik* (captain).[9] HOP published a newspaper called *Spremnost* to share their ideology and communicate activities.

The second most prominent organisation was the Croatian National Resistance (HNO), founded by the commander of the Jasenovac camp, General Vjekoslav 'Maks' Luburić, in Spain around 1957. This group was believed to be sponsored by the Soviets, who sought to empower Yugoslavia's enemies. It soon developed a reputation for deadly political violence, engaging in assassinations and aircraft hijackings. In Australia, it was allegedly run by Srecko Rover, who was rumoured to be a former Ustaša officer from the World War II regime, as was his father, Josip.[10] Rover's leadership of HNO was also noted by Senator Murphy in a Senate statement.[11] HNO's publication was *Obrana*.

The third and most extreme of these groups was the Croatian Revolutionary Brotherhood (HRB), established in Sydney in 1961.[12] It was allegedly supported by a Catholic official, Father Rocque Romac, through the Croatian Catholic Welfare Centre, and Srecko Rover from HNO.[13] It was led, for a time at least, by Ante Butković, who was wanted by West German authorities in connection with a mail bombing, while his brother Ivan was connected to Ustaša terrorists who hijacked a Swedish aircraft in 1972.[14] Romac was integral to weapons handling, training, and terrorism in New South Wales, while Rover was the public face.[15] HRB was rumoured to have 100 members, mostly young Croatians who were also members of HOP. The two highest-profile operatives of HRB were Adolf and Ambroz Andrić, who would conduct violent attacks domestically and internationally.[16]

All three organisations were rumoured to be part of the international Ustaša network, despite holding divergent perspectives on the strategies that should be used to reclaim an independent Croatia. They were united, however, in the common cause; according to one sympathiser, 'they want to destroy everything that is Yugoslav and free the state of Croatia from Yugoslavia'.[17] Australia, with the world's third-largest Yugoslav migrant community, became an attractive base for their operations.

Here, the Ustaša network found an unlikely safe haven and a community base of Croatian Australians to support their activities. ASIO, newly established and preoccupied with left-wing threats such as the Soviets, initially paid little attention to this violent movement.[18] Instead, ASIO scrutinised the left-wing Yugoslav Settlers' Association, as its priority was to protect the Commonwealth from subversion generally more so than counterterrorism specifically. The Ustaša were largely targeting the Yugoslav government, not the Commonwealth, so the activity did not fit neatly into ASIO's existing focus. Moreover, right-wing groups were considered by the ASIO director-general, Charles Spry, as 'good anti-communists'.[19]

Training trysts

By 1962, Yugoslavia's leader, Marshal Josip Broz Tito, was 70 years old, and Ustaša likely believed that the time was ripe for a new campaign towards independence. From early 1963, Ustaša elements in Australia began to engage in combat training to ready themselves for the battle to come. In April, photos surfaced of uniformed Ustaša members training with the Citizens Military Force (CMF) in Wodonga.[20] One Ustaša member was holding a submachine gun, and the rest were posing in front of armoured vehicles. The optics of Australian military forces standing alongside uniformed fascists were not good. Scrambling, military officials claimed that the Ustaša were on a picnic and had simply stumbled upon the CMF and seized the opportunity for some photos. There were rumours, however unfounded, that it was actually part of a five-day training exercise. Other training camps were established in New South Wales, run by HOP. These camps were attended by individuals from a number of organisations, including HRB, the Australia-Croatia Society, and a church group alleged to be an Ustaša front.

Some of these individuals were training in earnest. Together with fellow fighters in West Germany and Italy, they swore an oath to engage in acts of terrorism, placing their right hand on a crossed knife and rifle. They trained extensively with dynamite, and refined their techniques to bomb factories, bridges and public buildings in concert with propaganda campaigns. By early July 1963, they were ready. Two HRB operatives from Melbourne, Stanko Zdrilic and Mika Fumic, travelled to Italy, where they joined seven other Ustaša members from other countries. Together, they prepared to launch a sabotage mission into Yugoslavia and incite a mass uprising, followed by a popular revolution. They armed themselves with 14 kilograms of TNT, 100 detonators, five pistols, two daggers, four radios and three maps. Then, sometime between 5 and 7 July, they crossed the border from Italy, near Trieste, into Yugoslavia.[21]

The HRB mission was dead in the water. The Yugoslav Intelligence Service, which routinely tracked Croatian Australians, captured the Croatian Nine upon entry into Yugoslavia. They all received long prison sentences ranging from six to fourteen years.[22] It was later discovered that the Croatian Nine's travel had been paid for by Croatian organisations in Europe and Australia. One of the captured members, Stanko Zdrilic, claimed that they were also assisted by the Croatian Roman Catholic Church in Australia.[23] While this claim was denied by Reverend Josip Kasic, a Roman Catholic priest, who called it communist propaganda, he nonetheless argued that the men were not terrorists but patriots.[24] This was, however, the first instance of terrorists travelling from Australia to foreign lands to fight.

The Trieste mission was not the only sign of an international network mobilising its forces around the globe: there were also indications of domestic unrest. There was a home invasion in far north Queensland in May 1963, when a group of armed and masked men broke into a Yugoslav cane-cutters' barracks and destroyed all symbols of Yugoslavia, including pictures of Tito.[25] There was a violent street brawl in front of the Serbian Orthodox Church in Toowong, Brisbane, and it was rumoured that Ustaša operatives who had trained in northern New South Wales were involved.[26]

Several months later, on 24 November 1963, a group of individuals smashed the windows of the Yugoslav Consulate in Sydney. The Consulate suspected that it was done by the Ustaša, but ASIO believed it was the work of the Yugoslav Intelligence Service, which operated out of the Consulate.[27] Marjan Jurjevic, a prominent Croatian Australian, was beaten on the streets of Melbourne for speaking out against the Ustaša, leaving him with broken ribs. Jurjevic had served as an intelligence officer during World War II, working against the fascists.

Calls for action against the Ustaša network by Labor politicians such as Dr Jim Cairns went largely unheeded. This could have been due to links between Ustaša front organisations and members of the Liberal Party, such as Hubert Opperman, then Minister for Shipping and Transport, and Eric Willis, deputy leader of the Liberal Party, who were photographed at Ustaša functions, standing before photos of fascist dictator Ante Pavelić.[28] The Ustaša network had friends in many high and low places, and the victims of their threats and intimidation were numerous.

Threats manifest

The Ustaša turned to terrorism in Australia in earnest on 7 May 1964. A young Australian Croat, Tomislav Lesic, carried a suitcase bomb towards the Yugoslav Consulate in Sydney, the most obvious symbol of Yugoslavian interests in Australia. The bomb exploded prematurely in Lesic's hands and detonated with such force that it shattered the windows of nearby houses and tore off his legs. Lesic barely survived the blast and was left both blind and crippled. Once conscious, Lesic claimed the suitcase was given to him by communists, although few believed him, given his ties to the anti-Yugoslav movement.[29]

On 12 May 1964, Brisbane schoolteacher Louis Gugenberger received death threats from the Ustaša because he was gathering information on them, which he had given to the Department of External Affairs for translation. The threats, which were both verbal and written, were considered so serious that the South Coast police recommended that Gugenberger receive a firearms permit and taught him how to shoot. A Yugoslav priest, Father Marko Gjokmarkovic, of the Holy Spirit Church in New Farm, Brisbane, received threatening letters from the Ustaša. Father Gjokmarkovic believed it was because of his criticism of HOP and the Ustaša.

A Serbian Australian in Dimbulah, Queensland, Milan Novakovic, was alleged to have stabbed his neighbour, Gojko Radalj, to death with a knife. He claimed that Radalj, a Croatian Australian, was a member of the Ustaša. Queensland Special Branch did not buy his story, and believed that Novakovic 'merely concocted this story to impress upon the jury at his trial that he was a peaceful citizen being hounded by a terrorist organisation, and thus gain sympathy'.[30] Though he was found not guilty on 8 August 1964, Novakovic was later subject to threats. Novakovic's solicitor reported that six cars of armed individuals had cruised past Novakovic's house. When one car was pulled over by police, a search revealed a knife, a shotgun and cartridges. Despite this, Queensland police reported in 1964 that 'no information has come to hand' that would confirm accounts that the Ustaša was operating in the north.[31]

The unrest was not confined to Queensland. A Melbourne police station received bomb threats and was told their officers would be shot if they crossed the Ustaša. In Sydney, three Ustaša operatives broke into a home in Sydney and demanded that the resident tell them the whereabouts of a female communist they intended to murder. The victim allegedly refused to give up the whereabouts of the woman, and was tortured. While this could have been committed by the Ustaša, the waters are muddied by the fact that the Yugoslav Intelligence Service was also operating in Australia—and it had a reputation for extrajudicial activity.

On 19 February 1965, Ambroz Andrić bombed a Yugoslav Settlers' Association dance in Geelong West Town Hall, Victoria. He broke a window hall and threw in a pepper bomb, followed by a bomb containing ammonia concentrate and pyridine. While this was functionally a stink bomb, ammonia concentrate is severely damaging to the lungs if inhaled. This was not intended to be a fatal attack: it was designed to disrupt the event and intimidate the Yugoslav-Australian community. During the trial of Andric for this act, however, witnesses were threatened with death if they testified against him. HNO leader Srecko Rover wore his Ustaša Gestapo badge in the public gallery in support of Andric. Andric was found guilty of the bombing.

Gelignite games

On 17 November 1966, anti-Ustaša campaigner Marjan Jurjevic had another lucky escape. A book packed with gelignite and rigged as a bomb had been posted to him, which was supposed to explode upon being opened. Instead, the bomb detonated prematurely in the General Post Office when it hit the wicker basket at the bottom of the mail chute.[32] This was fortuitous in two ways: firstly, it thwarted the assassination of Jurjevic, and secondly, it prevented the bomb detonating in the mailroom, where six people worked.

About six weeks later, on 1 January 1967, the Ustaša managed to smuggle gelignite into the Yugoslav Consulate in Sydney. Surprisingly, given the Ustaša track record for mishaps, it successfully detonated the explosives, though the building was empty, and no one was injured. Another badly written note claimed: 'we missed you this time you communist bastard but we shall not miss you next time'.[33] Given the advanced and precise nature of the Consulate bombing, the Yugoslav Intelligence Service was suspected of engineering the attack to provoke action from the Australian government against the Ustaša.

Regardless of the mystery surrounding the consulate bombing, from February it seemed like Ustaša violence was escalating. On 19 February, a bomb was thrown into a meeting being held by the Yugoslav Settlers' Association in Fitzroy, Melbourne. On 19 April, a bomb was detonated in a flat in Darlinghurst, Sydney, while a Yugoslavian couple slept inside. On 10 May, ammonia bombs were thrown through the doors of the Geelong Trade Hall during another Yugoslav Settlers' dance.

By September 1967, police authorities went public with their knowledge that Ustaša did, in fact, exist in Australia. It would appear that they were expanding their capabilities, as Queensland Police suspected that small groups of men were quietly drifting up to Queensland to engage in training. Rumours surfaced of an Ustaša training camp in the Atherton Tablelands and another in Dimbulah; and several years later, another such camp was found in Mackay, disguised as a picnic area. State police departments, intelligence agencies and other stakeholders around Australia began to focus on the Ustaša threat. Attorney-General Greenwood of the Liberal Party, however, steadfastly refused to recognise their existence.

On 1 December 1967, a pen bomb exploded at another Yugoslav social function at Richmond Town Hall in Victoria. It is difficult to tell who the target was, between the presence of Marjan Jurjevic, Dr Jim Cairns and the Yugoslav consul-general, Nicholas Zic. The bomb missed all these targets when it prematurely detonated in the hand of a child, leaving him disfigured. A crudely written note from the Ustaša suggested that the attack was 'just letting the Yugoslavs know that they were around'.[34] It was later suspected that the Andric brothers had built the bomb.

For whatever reason, the following year was quiet, with little major Ustaša-associated activity. On 8 November 1968, a bomb was thrown into a south Melbourne home, though no one was reported injured. Another report indicated that the bomb in south Melbourne blew up a car owned by a Yugoslav, but that could also have been a separate incident. On 1 December 1968, Ustaša arsonists gathered at the Yugoslav Consulate in Sydney, smashing windows in an attempt to burn the building down. Unfortunately, 1968 was simply the calm before the storm.

In April 1969, a bomb was detonated in the home of Danica Solunac in Mona Vale, Sydney, injuring her and her 13-year-old daughter.[35] In May, there were numerous threats to businesses, including David Jones, for displaying Yugoslav goods, and Ustaša gangs were racketeering the Yugoslav community. A Yugoslav café owner had his café in Moonee Ponds, Melbourne, destroyed by Ustaša thugs for refusing to pay extortion money. There were repeated rumours of bashings. In June, a large bomb was detonated in front of the Yugoslav Consulate in Sydney, with rumours that it was in association with a Joseph Senic—although his involvement in the violence was not yet established.

The Ustaša also closely monitored ties between Australia and Yugoslavia. When the two governments came close to signing the Yugoslav–Australian migration agreement, the Ustaša bombed the Yugoslav Embassy in Canberra on 28 November 1969. This was followed by an attempt to burn down the Immigration Office in Canberra three days later.[36] On 2 January 1970, a gelignite bomb was detonated outside a Serbian Church in Canberra. Two were convicted of the crime. A couple of months later, in March, a Yugoslav concert featuring Ivo Robić was leaflet-bombed by the Ustaša: each leaflet giving a hit list of prominent Yugoslavs.

On 21 October 1970, a large bomb detonated in front of the Yugoslav Consulate in Melbourne, causing serious damage to the Consulate and twenty homes in the area. Again, Senic was implicated. A Croatian Australian, Senic had tried to travel internationally in 1965, but because his passport was invalid he was denied travel, searched and found in possession of the membership book of the HRB. This intelligence was not shared until 1967, after Senic, undeterred, had travelled to Europe illegally. Once they realised his significance to the HRB, Commonwealth Police (Compol, now the Australian Federal Police) raided Senic's house in March 1967 and seized more than 700 documents. They learned that Senic was the actual leader of the HRB in Australia, and his chapter had kept European chapters afloat with substantial financial support for years. Senic was refused a passport again in 1968. In Europe, however, Senic was implicated in the bombing of a Yugoslav airlines DC-9 over Czechoslovakia on 26 January 1970, which killed 26 people. He was assassinated in West Germany shortly thereafter, allegedly on the orders of the Yugoslav Intelligence Service.[37]

The year 1971 saw four prominent attacks against Yugoslav interests. One attack linked to the Ustaša was the targeting of the Soviet Embassy in Canberra, which was firebombed on 17 January. While the Soviets had at one time sponsored Ustaša affiliates, a shift to support Tito's regime had made Soviet interests a new target. Despite this, old targets were still popular: on 4 July 1971, a bomb exploded near the Serbian Orthodox Church in Melbourne, causing $3000 worth of damage.[38] On 23 November 1971, the Adriatic Trade and Tourism Centre on George Street in Sydney was bombed. This was likely chosen because it was owned by the Yugoslav government through its agencies Yugo-Public, JAT and Central Tourist.[39] On 19 December, a suburban cinema in Newtown, Sydney, was bombed while screening Yugoslav war films.

In the midst of these deadly gelignite games, new players were forming their own teams and joining the field. All supported Ustaša ideology and extremism in one way or another. One was the Union of Croatian United Youth of the World (SHUMS), which published a magazine called *Uzdanica*. At its peak, it had around 100 Australian members. Its emergence coincided with the formation of the Croatian Illegal Revolutionary Organisation (HIRO).[40] A third group, the United Croats of West Germany (UHNj), was also believed to be active in Australia. All three were thought to be primarily youth groups: a sign that the old guard within the Ustaša saw value in expanding its support base.

In 1972 the Ustaša showed no signs of desisting from violence. On 11 January, it bombed a statue of a Serbian war hero, General Draža Mihailović, outside the Free Serbian Orthodox Church in Canberra. On 6 April 1972, there were two coordinated bombings in Melbourne by the Ustaša. One targeted the ANZ Migrant Advisory Centre, and the other the home of Marjan Jurjevic—the second bombing targeting him. A right-wing Liberal senator, George Hannan, insinuated that Jurjevic had planted the bombs himself for attention.[41] This refusal to accept the presence of the Ustaša in Australia was still common, despite all of the bombing and threats and violence. It was about to be put to the test by the Mudrinic affair.

Bombs under beds

On 3 June 1972, Sergeant Robert Turner had a late-night interview with 23-year-old Ivan Mudrinic.[42] Mudrinic did not speak much English, so a police interpreter, Salvatore Romita, translated for Turner. The sergeant had some particularly pertinent questions—most of them relating specifically to why Mudrinic had 231 sticks of gelignite in a bag under his bed. According to Mudrinic, it all began when he was approached by a long-term friend, Ljubo Drevic, aged eighteen.

'Are you really a Croat?' Drevic was said to have asked Mudrinic.

Mudrinic replied that he was, so when Drevic asked him if he would like to do something for the freedom of Croatia, Mudrinic readily agreed. Drevic told him to come to his house a week later.

'We will need you to carry something, but nobody has to know,' Drevic allegedly told him.

A week later, Mudrinic was at Drevic's house. There, in the bedroom, he saw hundreds of rolls of gelignite, half in a wooden box and half in a nylon bag; three rolls of detonating wire; two electric detonators; two tins of gunpowder; a green alarm clock; a walkie-talkie; and some books on politics and guerrilla warfare. In addition, literature associated with SHUMS and HIRO was present in the cache.[43] The two men loaded the cache into Mudrinic's car and—with help from two other young men, 21-year-old Milan Maglicic and seventeen-year-old Mladenko Marvak—the men drove 80–90 kilometres east of Melbourne to Warburton.

On the drive, Drevic told Mudrinic that the explosives had to be hidden until the top man of the Australian Ustaša, Srecko Rover, ordered them to be used. It was, apparently, a test of their allegiance. They unloaded the explosives, wrapped the cache in nylon, concealed it in the bush, and returned to Melbourne. Mudrinic deduced that the explosives were likely meant for the Yugoslav Consulate in Melbourne, although Drevic suggested they were to be sent to Croatia. Two days later, Mudrinic returned to the cache alone and, in secret, removed it and hid it under his bed. Mudrinic then reached out to the one man he could trust, the avowed enemy of the Ustaša in Australia: Marjan Jurjevic. This is what led to his interview with Sergeant Turner.

Despite rumours that this may have been a Yugoslav Intelligence plot to incriminate innocent Croatians, four men went to trial in relation to the Warburton explosive cache. While possession charges were not contested, it appears that the men were acquitted because they may have acted under duress, with some receiving good behaviour bonds.[44] Removing the explosive cache, however, did little to stem the flow of Ustaša violence, especially given that gelignite was used frequently in mining and farming and was not difficult to obtain. What was more worrying was the government's position on the matter: Attorney-General Ivor Greenwood was still publicly denying the existence of the Ustaša. The camps scattered around Australia were still operating in secret, training Ustaša fighters, and readying them for the battle to come.

Fighting in foreign lands

It became harder to ignore the Ustaša camps in Australia, much less the network itself. It was hardly disrupted by an arrest here or a charge and conviction there. The transnational nature of the Ustaša network buffered it from such incidents, and allowed operations to continue elsewhere. These, however, were not necessarily original. Despite the dismal failure of the Trieste sabotage mission, the Ustaša planned yet another incursion into Yugoslav territory. The Ustaša were, by virtue of this, responsible for the first and second manifestations of Australians becoming foreign fighters.

In June 1972, a group of nineteen Ustaša, including the notorious Andric brothers and seven other Australians, travelled to Yugoslavia. These other members included Djuro Horvat, Vejsil Keskic and Mirko Vlasnovic. Their goal was to undertake terrorist missions against the Tito government and inspire the masses to revolution. When they entered the country, the nineteen terrorists expected to find the local citizenry supportive of their efforts to raise a resistance, but this was not the case. The citizenry called the authorities, and the terrorists engaged in a running battle with Yugoslav security forces near Bugojno, killing thirteen Yugoslavs, including Adolf and Ambroz Andrić, before they themselves were mostly killed.

Following the incursion, the Yugoslavs provided an aide-mémoire to the Australian authorities, which resulted in dozens of premises being raided by Compol. Though a great deal of material was seized, no charges were laid immediately. On 30 August 1972, the Australian Embassy in Belgrade, Yugoslavia, sent an urgent message to Compol warning that the Ustaša, angry with its failure at Bugojno, was planning a new round of coordinated attacks. In the 'Fourth of September Plot', the Ustaša intended to bomb international Yugoslav diplomatic missions simultaneously, while another cell would 'deal' with the diplomats.[45] It may be assumed that the Ustaša was deterred from this plot, but not defeated.

It was two weeks later, on 16 September 1972, that the two Yugoslavian travel agencies, Adriatic and Adria Travel, were bombed. As we saw earlier, the attack caused minimal damage to the buildings but injured sixteen civilians. Following this attack and the high number of injuries it produced, interest in the Ustaša and its Australian activities skyrocketed. Ordinary Australians had been caught in the crossfire of a conflict that many had assumed was confined to migrant intracommunity politics. A $40,000 reward was offered for information to assist police inquiries.[46] Within days, ASIO sent agents to Queensland to examine the training camps.[47]

Indeed, much of the lower-level activity was aimed against the Yugoslav and Serb communities. This included harassing phone calls throughout the night; verbal abuse of Yugoslav women about their husbands, and bombarding them with abusive letters and postcards in an attempt to subvert them to the cause; bothering the Consulate with trivial calls; vandalising ships and trains with slogans; and disrupting transport and logistics wherever possible. The purpose of this strategy was to divert Yugoslav Consulate attention from the Ustaša organisations and their activities.[48]

Countering the Ustaša

The Ustaša claimed to practise the three golden rules for guerrilla war: 'constant vigilance, constant distrust, constant agility'.[49] This alone would never be enough to ensure its survival. The raids on dozens of premises in Sydney and Melbourne by law enforcement in August 1972 was the first big counteraction against the Australian Ustaša network. The raids yielded hundreds of documents and other materials, but no charges were laid.[50] At a federal level, Liberal prime minister William McMahon toyed with the idea of a royal commission, despite opposition from Greenwood. Instead, McMahon asked him to prepare a report on terrorism for the Senate. The parameters of the report were expanded when it was realised that no single person or agency was *actually responsible* for countering terrorism in Australia.

The leader of the federal Opposition, Gough Whitlam, continued to challenge Prime Minister William McMahon to take action against the network. Whitlam pointed out that until 1971, the Ustaša had cost the Commonwealth government $29,100 in repairs to the consulates, and the Commonwealth police had expended $29,507 in protecting those consulates. He tabled a motion on 19 September 1972 that the government develop intelligence and police organisations with specialist knowledge and resources to prevent terrorist activities in Australia. A Labor member of the Queensland state parliament, Gerry Jones, also slammed the Liberal and Country parties. He raised the question of the Ustaša camps in Dimbulah and Mareeba, north Queensland, and said: 'The reason the Ustashi fanatics are able to pursue a bombing spree in this country today is the amazing tolerance and immunity extended to them by Coalition governments.'[51] The cause was helped further by the Yugoslavs themselves, who pointed out that Australia was 'the only country which asserted that the Ustasha [Ustaša] organisation did not exist'.[52]

It would later be revealed that Interpol had approached the NSW bomb squad in 1972 with the information that Australia was the international headquarters for Ustaša terrorism. Interpol had demonstrated that Croatian Australians had been involved in a number of overseas terrorist incidents. Damningly, it was also revealed that Compol had petitioned Attorney-General Greenwood to prosecute and deport Ustaša terrorists three years earlier, to no avail. Greenwood was, at best, irresponsible and, at worst, complicit in the endurance of Ustaša terrorism.[53] Despite the efforts of ASIO and Compol, he had refused to act.

As the new year rolled in, McMahon's Coalition government was replaced with Gough Whitlam's Labor government. When Senator Lionel Murphy took over as attorney-general in December 1972, he inherited responsibility for ASIO. This became an unhappy marriage, marred by mutual suspicion and differing perspectives. The situation escalated when a Yugoslav delegation was due to visit Australia. It soon emerged that the UHNj was allegedly plotting to assassinate the Yugoslav prime minister, Džemal Bijedić, during the visit. Despite the swift arrests of four suspects, Murphy began to believe that ASIO was withholding documented information regarding threats to Bijedić from domestic Croatian extremists, as part of an internal conspiracy against the new Labor government. At midnight on 15–16 March, Murphy ordered Compol to enter ASIO headquarters in Canberra and Melbourne with 'sufficient men to secure offices and containers'.[54] The intervention ended peacefully, and Murphy saw the documents he requested, but the Murphy Raid became one of the Whitlam government's 'greatest mistake[s]'.[55]

In February 1973, Attorney-General Murphy discussed the issue of Ustaša terrorism with FBI officials from the United States, and learned that American security agencies had long regarded Australia as a hotbed of Ustaša terrorism. One month later, he was examining the case for prosecution of terrorists in Australia. Attorney-General Murphy's new stance, coupled with the engagement of ASIO and Compol, began to take effect, and vigilance increased. By way of example, on 4 April 1973, the Compol commissioner in Canberra issued an urgent warning to be wary of Ustaša reprisals after three of the Croatian Australians involved in the Bugojno battle were executed by the Yugoslav government, which was shared throughout the relevant agencies.

This was not the only complication that arose from the incident at Bugojno. The immediate question became one of passports. It was not, strictly speaking, illegal for an Australian citizen to travel internationally with the purpose of committing a crime, be it murder or terrorism. Withholding the passports of Croatian extremists was, as a consequence, considered a possible deterrent, but it quickly became bogged down when attention turned to Australians travelling to participate in the supposedly legitimate Croatian 'government-in-exile' (called the Croatian National Council or HNV) conference in Canada in 1975. This was further complicated when ASIO reported that the HNV expressed its commitment 'to the principle of violence in pursuit of its aim for a free Croatia' during the conference.[56]

It was also debated whether passports or identity documents should be issued to Australians overseas who were suspected of terrorist connections. A working group examining the issue found that Foreign Affairs could exercise its discretion in the issuing of identity documents or replacement documents where the applicant was suspected of terrorist involvement. In practice, it meant that such requests from the likes of Josip Kovac, secretary of the Australian HNO arrested in Madrid in connection with terrorism, and Milan Maglicic, who was involved with the Warburton weapons cache, were either deferred or denied. This was designed to prevent their continued travel where it was possible it would result in terrorism.

The question of citizenship also arose when it became clear that some of the suspects were dual nationals. Many Yugoslav-Australian nationals were languishing in Yugoslav prisons, convicted of membership of the HNO, the HRB or the lesser-known Bleiburg Platoon. Some five or six men were convicted of membership, while another thirteen were charged with a variety of other political offences.[57] The question then became what support these dual citizens were entitled to from Australia. Beyond this, the greater question was whether Australians born of Yugoslav parents could be deported back to Yugoslavia. As one document noted: 'deportation power also exists, although it has to be balanced against the doctrine of political asylum'.[58] That same document warned that Australia did not want to garner a reputation or invite criticism for the revocation of nationality, as it would suggest that migrants were treated as second-class citizens. This was a fair conclusion to draw.

Despite no easy solution to the question of citizenship, more practical measures could be, and were, put in place. For example, the NSW police commissioner made the 50-man bomb squad a permanent police unit. Later, a 'terrorist-proof' car was constructed for the sum of $60,000 in Europe, and transported to Australia on an RAAF jet to protect travelling Yugoslav officials. It was equipped with bomb-blast-proof floors, armoured glass windows and bulletproof steel panels, and used engine components from Rolls-Royce, Mercedes and Fiat.[59] Unfortunately, the car was heavy and slow, so it had to be airlifted by a Hercules from city to city whenever Yugoslav officials went on tour, with the unsuspecting Australian taxpayer footing the bill.

Underground or overseas?

As ASIO and Compol closed in on Ustaša training camps in the north, it may have forced parts of the network underground, but it was hardly defeated. On 4 October 1972, the Dimbulah Bridge was bombed. Close to 100 sticks of gelignite, half of those stolen from a nearby mine, were used to bomb the bridge, creating a blast that was heard 5 kilometres away. Only poor explosive placement prevented the bridge from being utterly destroyed. The Ustaša was suspected, due to rumours of its Dimbulah camp.

Shortly thereafter, on 8 December 1972, a car bomb was detonated outside a Serbian Church in Brisbane, killing an American, Thomas Patrick Enright. Investigators considered two competing theories. The first was that the American man was simply the wrong victim, and the bomb had been intended for the thirteen Serbian men inside the church. The second theory was that he detonated the car bomb deliberately, as part of a suicide attack, as he had gone out to his car several times that night. Given what we know of the Ustaša's premature detonations, it is also possible that Enright accidentally triggered the blast and killed himself.

A year passed without any further significant attacks, but understanding of the Ustaša modus operandi had deepened. Messages circulated in the Queensland Police warning of potential Ustaša attacks around significant dates in the Croatian calendar. These included 10 April, the date when an independent Croatia (under the Nazis) was announced in 1941; and 21 April, the date when the Ustaša general Maks Luburić was assassinated in Spain in 1969. In addition, a CIA report states that Srecko Rover and more than 100 of his fellow fighters were disrupted by Australian authorities in the midst of a plan to once again infiltrate Yugoslavia in early 1973.[60] It was a tense time for the Yugoslav community: many Australian Croatians were tracked by police, suspected of Ustaša activity.

Some few were indeed engaged in terrorism. Anton Butković, a leader of the HRB, was believed to have been involved in a mail bombing in West Germany on 4 September 1975. The actual attack, according to a government interdepartmental committee, was undertaken by Ljubomir Dragoja, formerly an Australian resident of six years, who was apprehended while Butković evaded Interpol and reappeared unexpectedly in Australia.[61] Butković's brother, moreover, was a known contact of Croatian terrorists who hijacked a Swedish aeroplane in September 1972.[62] The terrorists used the passengers and crew as bargaining chips and threatened to blow up the aircraft—passengers and all—to force the Swedish government to release seven Ustaša terrorists from prison. It was successful: the incarcerated terrorists were released.

Yugoslavia, too, undertook counterterrorism activities against Yugoslavian Australians. For example, in 1975 28-year-old Marko Nazor was arrested in Yugoslavia. Nazor had migrated to Australia as a young man, worked in Australia, married, built a house, and became an Australian citizen. In 1975, however, he returned to Yugoslavia, allegedly to consider resettling there, depending on how his parents reacted to his wife and children. After his arrest on 13 June, Yugoslav authorities revealed he was a member of the Ustaša, specifically the HRB, having joined in 1968–69. Nazor had sworn an oath in a candlelit ceremony, beside a black-draped table that held a pistol, a cross and books. He was given the code number 208, making him a fully fledged member of the HRB.[63]

The HRB intended for Nazor to join the Yugoslavian Army and prepare for the revolution. It gave him extremist literature and instructional manuals on mining bridges, railway lines and buildings; sabotage; arson; and other activities. It does not seem that Nazor was ideologically committed to the Ustaša cause: in fact, he appeared reluctant to be in involved, refused to recruit anyone else, and had a fear of authority that led him to bury the literature in his garden. When the HRB found out he was returning to Yugoslavia, it demanded he attend training in order to create a *Trojka* (a revolutionary circle) in Yugoslavia. Nazor did nothing of the sort.

The Yugoslav authorities were apparently handed evidence that led to his arrest by the Yugoslav Embassy in Australia. Croatians in Australia had long argued that the embassy was sending 'false' information to Yugoslavia to prepare for their arrest on their return—and in fact one Croatian threatened to burn down the embassy for that very reason. Although there were rumours of a death sentence, Nazor was sentenced to three years for membership of the organisation. What the Nazor incident highlighted, though, was resentment on the part of the Yugoslav government towards Australia for its apparent inability to contain the Ustaša. The District Court judge presiding over the trial, Bozenko Anic, told Australian Embassy officials that he

> found it difficult to understand how a democratic country such as Australia could allow terrorist organisations, which aimed at the overthrow of democracy, to exist within its borders . . . [Anic] felt that even though there were differences between the

legal codes in Australia and Yugoslavia, more could be done to control the activities of terrorist organisations.⁶⁴

As part of the same case, the Yugoslav prosecutor stated that Australia was still the main centre of Ustaša activity, although the change in government meant that many organisations had either fled the country or gone underground.

Some had, in fact, departed Australia. Ante Butković, the incumbent leader of the HRB in Australia, had obviously departed and returned following mission completion (the West German mail bombing in 1975 mentioned earlier). In another case, Josip Kovac of the Canberra branch of the HNO was known to have travelled to West Germany, while others were noted to be in Rome and Canada.⁶⁵ It does confirm Yugoslav suspicions, however, that some Ustaša had gone overseas to build networks, gather resources and potentially launch attacks.

Domestically, there were sporadic violent incidents, but the tempo and momentum sustained in earlier years were gone. On 27 November 1977, the Yugoslav consul-general was assaulted in Sydney; and on 3 December 1977, Ustaša detonated an explosive device inside the offices of the Yugoslav airline, JAT, in Melbourne. On 4 December 1977, a Serbian Orthodox Church in Canberra was attacked, and its bronze statue of Draža Mihailović bombed again.

Following these attacks, the Yugoslav government, convinced that violence was due to escalate, in 1977 provided yet another aide-mémoire to the incumbent Fraser Liberal-National government. The memoir noted the 'absence of adequate and effective measures by the appropriate Australian security authorities aimed at preventing terrorist activities' and warned of the impact this could have on the bilateral relations.⁶⁶ The annexures detailed several Croatian-Australian individuals allegedly raising funds to defend Ustaša hijackers in court, holding meetings, producing propaganda, and staging demonstrations outside the Yugoslav Embassy in Canberra, shouting, swearing and waving flags, making harassing phone calls, and hampering embassy staff. The Australian government, in the face of persistent criticism from Yugoslavia, maintained its stance that these particular activities were within the rule of law and the bounds of legitimate debate and discussion.

Australian Ustaša members overseas nonetheless continued to attack their enemies. On 13 September 1979, for example, former Australian resident Ljubomir Dragoja was arrested in West Germany for conspiring to commit a bomb attack, arson and murder, and training with others to do so. In Australia, the Dragoja arrest was a point of contention in the Croatian community, its organisations unsure how much support to give him.[67] Dragoja had been arrested in Australia nine years earlier, when he was found in possession of gelignite. He had been on his way to blow up a statue at a Serbian church in Canberra.[68]

Aside from disorderly activity, there was a half-hearted attempt to paint-bomb the Yugoslav Embassy in Canberra in 1978; and in 1979 a Croatian extremist group known as the Lithgow Bombers was apprehended in the midst of planning a terrorist campaign in Sydney. They intended to bomb the Elizabethan Theatre with the intention of causing mass casualties, along with travel agencies, Serbian clubs and a water pipeline. At least two members also planned to assassinate two well-known Croatian nationals living in Sydney, including HOP leader Fabian Lovokovic. The Lithgow group were all men, aged between 27 and 32, and seemingly determined to damage Yugoslavian interests (although how killing Lovokovic would achieve that is unclear). Their plans never came to fruition: the six men were instead charged with theft of explosives, conspiring to make bombs, and intending to commit malicious injury.[69] It was the longest trial in Australian legal history to that point, and resulted in convictions and fifteen-year sentences for all six men although doubt around the case persists.

The last event connected with the Ustaša occurred in 1981, when it was rumoured that its affiliates in Australia had posted 40 parcels of live venomous snakes to prominent Slovenians in Yugoslavia. This brought in a Slovenian policy of deep-freezing parcels from Australia for a certain period. But the worst of it was over.

Democracy triumphant

A report produced in late 1980 found that there were 80 incidents of minor violence and eighteen bombing attacks on Yugoslav interests in Australia over a seventeen-year period.[70] The Ustaša's international network had done its damage in Australia, injuring sixteen people indiscriminately, incurring substantial property damage, and intimidating an entire section of the Australian community through threats and violence. With the exception of a select few, much of the migrant community had fled the violence and discord of Yugoslavia, only to be held hostage to Old World rivalries in Australia. The years of fear were, however, finally over.

Why did the Ustaša desist? After all the violence in Australia, and the assassinations and murders overseas, it was the death in 1980 of a single man that halted the perpetual motion of the network: Marshall Tito. Many Croatian Australians celebrated Tito's passing with media engagements and demonstrations. They anticipated immense change following the end of the Tito era, which led many to shift away from the stereotype of bomb-throwing fascists towards respectable and legitimate representation.

A decade later, in 1991, Croatia declared its independence from Yugoslavia. It took four years of conflict to entirely separate from the former Yugoslavia, with sporadic battles leaving lasting scars on the people and landscape. In 1998, the last ethnic Serbian enclave in eastern Slovenia was returned to Croatia under United Nations supervision. Border disputes remain, however, with Bosnia and Herzegovina to the south, and with Slovenia to the north. Croatia is now considered a parliamentary democracy, with a president as head of state, and a prime minister as head of government. Its legislative branch is represented by a unicameral assembly, including eight members who represent Serb, Hungarian, Italian, Czech and Slovak minorities. The Republic of Croatia joined NATO in 2009, and the European Union in 2013. Gone, hopefully for good, is the fascist Ustaša's demand for ethnic and religious homogeneity and the genocidal destruction of fellow citizens.

The Ustaša legacy is one of futile violence and terror, which proves one significant point: terrorism harmed the Croatian cause more than it ever helped. Ustaša's goal was undermined at every point by a dangerous and divisive ideology held to be superior to democratic processes and the democratic will of the people. But the Ustaša was not alone in its dreadful quest that spanned nations, governments and decades. The whole time it had been wreaking havoc in the Australian community, yet another threat was manifesting in political violence and terror. Motivated by the reclamation of Palestine for the Palestinian people, it would leave a mark on nations throughout the Western world, including Australia.

4

Quest for state: pro-Palestinian terrorism

It was Wednesday, 12 September 1973. Sergeant Second Class J.H. Morgan was in an interview room at the Deputy Crown Solicitor's Office in Melbourne. Outside the office, light rain misted the streets of the city known for having four seasons in a single day.

'What is your full name?' police officer Morgan asked the man who sat before him.

'Abdulhamid Abdulla Azzam,' came the reply. Azzam claimed to be a married man with three children. He was Somali, but was born in Palestine on a date no one could remember. He had travelled to Australia on a passport with a false name. It was not this that had brought him to the attention of authorities, but a single piece of his luggage that had a false bottom. It was Morgan's job to find out more.

'Who directed you to come to Australia?' asked Morgan.

'[Yasser] Arafat the Commander General,' replied Azzam, referring to the newest champion of the Palestinian cause and feared leader of the Al Fatah terrorist group.

After several more questions, Morgan got to the crux of the matter. 'One of your suitcases which was overcarried to Sydney has a false bottom in it, it also has markings indicating that a machine-pistol magazine and hand grenades had been affixed to it, what can you tell me about this?'

'I know nothing about this,' came the reply.¹

Azzam, it would transpire, was an Al 'Asifah officer—a high-ranking official in the military arm of Al Fatah and connected to the Black September Organisation (BSO). Just over a year before, in September 1972, eight Black September terrorists had stormed the Olympic Village in Munich, West Germany. It was the Summer Games, styled by the host nation *Die heiteren Spiele*, the Cheerful Games, attracting 900 million television viewers. All cheer was sapped from the event in the second week, when Black September took nine members of the Israeli team hostage, killing two in the process. As the negotiations dragged on, the terrorists demanded a helicopter to evacuate them to the Fürstenfeldbruck Air Base and from there on to Cairo. Unbeknown to the terrorists, police waited in ambush at the airbase, but their rescue attempt quickly went awry, and the ensuing gun battle resulted in the deaths of all of the hostages, a West German police officer and five of the terrorists. This massacre and mayhem occurred in plain view of onlookers and the media. Black September became public enemy number one.

While such a spectacle may be expected to inspire swift and decisive action, the reverse was true. The United Nations became involved, seeking to establish a centralised and transnational counterterrorism response to confront what was so clearly a transnational threat. The problem with that soon became clear, however, according to Australian researcher W. Clifford:

> It was not easy for the United Nations' member states to deal with terrorism. Too many were without clean hands. They had achieved power themselves by using terrorist tactics. Even Israel, most concerned with Arab terrorism, had used terrorism years before the creation of the State of Israel against the British. Kenya had its Mau-Mau, Algeria its action against the French; and some countries were aiding and abetting guerrilla activities in other states.²

As a result, no solution would come from that quarter, nor a truly united response. The Munich attack provoked similar vacillation in Australia, as politicians were unsure whether they should even pass a motion of condolence. They didn't want to risk offending either their Arab or Israeli trading partners.

Instead of being stymied by any swift counteraction, pro-Palestine terrorism was to endure, extending its networks and tendrils around the world, even to Australia. Azzam was just one face of the threat.

Al Nakba: the Catastrophe

Black September was not an insulated or unsupported terrorist group. It was a highly networked and structured terrorist cell, designed to operate on the orders of Al Fatah while maintaining Al Fatah's plausible deniability. Both elements, however, were expressions of the Palestinian cause, aimed at the reclamation of historic Palestine, which organisations such as Al Fatah believed had been stolen from them by imperial powers. Their homeland became a bargaining chip in a geopolitical game, fuelling decades of displacement and grievance.

Before World War I, the land formerly known as Palestine was under the control of the Ottoman Empire. When the Ottomans joined World War I in support of the Central Powers of Germany and Austria–Hungary, Lord Kitchener, the British Secretary of State for War, fomented an internal Arabian rebellion against the Ottomans. To secure the allegiance of prominent warlords, Kitchener promised them a Caliphate, which they believed would include Palestine. At the same time, the 1916 Sykes–Picot Agreement denoted Palestine an international administration zone. A year later, the territory was promised as a national homeland for the Jewish people in the Balfour Declaration. This not only betrayed the Arabs who had supported the British, but it was done without close consultation with Palestinian and Jewish peoples living peaceably in the region.

In 1920, the territory became Mandatory Palestine under British control. In a process referred to as Aliyah (meaning 'ascent'), European Jews began to migrate in large numbers. This migration was seen to be displacing (or overwhelming) the existing Palestinian population. In April 1936, Palestinians began a national six-month strike to protest against Jewish immigration. The British responded to the strike with lethal force, killing 190 Palestinians and injuring 800. Neighbouring Arab leaders advised the Palestinians to end the strike, and encouraged Palestinian leaders to negotiate with the new head of the Palestine Royal Commission, Lord William Peel, a British earl who was investigating the unrest.

After a year, Lord Peel came to a simple conclusion: Palestine must be divided. He formally proposed the Partition of Palestine between Jews and Arabs, a plan met with near-universal condemnation. More revolts followed, leaving nearly 1000 Palestinians dead, as well as nearly 70 Jews and 30 British police officers. In response to the deteriorating security situation, Jewish immigration to the area was restricted in 1937. As a result, millions of European Jews were stranded in Europe when Nazi Germany came into its power and subsequently sent them to extermination camps during World War II. With the end of the war, the newly minted United Nations became involved in the issue.

The United Nations formed an Ad Hoc Committee on Palestine led by the Australian Minister for External Affairs, Dr Herbert Vere Evatt, a lawyer and parliamentarian. A strong champion of human rights, he had been involved in drafting the Universal Declaration of Human Rights. For his part, Evatt was also an advocate of the Partition Plan:

> I think the partition plan was the only solution put forward that had any chance of success. One solution put forward by the Arabians would have given the whole of Palestine to the Arabs and the Jewish people would have been a minority with no real say in the country . . . I think the partition plan was a just solution.[3]

Just or not, on 27 November 1947 the Ad Hoc Committee on Palestine approved the Partition Plan, with 25 votes prevailing against thirteen (with seventeen abstentions). Champions of partition included Australia, the Soviet Union, and the United States, while the vote was opposed by Afghanistan, Egypt, Iraq, Iran, Lebanon, Pakistan, Saudi Arabia, Syria, Turkey, Yemen, and others. Those most affected by the partition condemned it, and despite this the Partition Plan was approved by the General Assembly.[4] The state of Israel was formally established on 14 May 1948.

Sectarian conflict began immediately, and the subsequent years became known as Al Nakba (the Catastrophe). Around 700,000 Palestinians abandoned their homes; some scholars argue that Arab states exhorted people to evacuate via radio broadcast, while others claim the Palestinians were forced to leave due to ethnic cleansing, expulsion orders, and massacres such as the Deir Yassin massacre.[5] Whatever the case, hundreds of Palestinians and Israelis died in the conflict. What followed was a series of military confrontations between the new state of Israel and its neighbours. Among these were the 1948 Arab–Israeli War, the Palestinian insurgency from Egypt throughout the 1950s and 1960s, the Suez Crisis in 1956, and the 1967 Six-Day War. Throughout these conflicts, Israel largely managed to expand its territory. This resulted in ongoing territorial insecurity for Palestinian people, reinforcing convictions that their homeland was lost to them forever.

A large section of the Palestinian population effectively became refugees, seeking safety in neighbouring Jordan and Lebanon. Despite initially welcoming the Palestinians, Lebanon imposed restrictions on their movements, employment, licences and residences. Those in Jordan, however, were offered Jordanian nationality.[6] The Palestinian Arab Refugees Institution was founded in Syria in January 1949 to assist displaced Palestinians by building camps and providing general facilities. Despite that, Palestinian refugees, regardless of whether they were in Syria, Lebanon or Egypt, remained politically disenfranchised.

The Fedayeen rise

While Palestinian anti-colonial sentiment had existed before the disaster and displacement, Palestinian nationalism really began to coalesce into a clear ideology in the 1950s. At its heart, plain and simple, was a return of historic Palestine to the Palestinian people, and the absolute removal of Israel and its Jewish population. The liberation of Palestine, supporters believed, would bring with it the simultaneous liberation of the Palestinian people, who could leave the squalid and hopeless refugee camps, and return home to achieve self-determination.

This ideology developed with the support of regional powers. As early as March 1945, the Arab League was formed by neighbouring Arab states. Its overriding goal was the liberation of Arab states still suffering under colonial domination, but its second goal, perhaps of equal significance, was to prevent a Jewish state in Palestine. It refused to recognise Israel, and instead recognised Palestine as an independent member state. The most significant individual sponsor of the movement was Gamal Abdel Nasser, president of Egypt. From 1953, Egyptian authorities were involved in training and arming Palestinian militants, who became known as Fedayeen (commandos). The Fedayeen launched hit-and-run attacks into Israel from the Egyptian border.

While these incursions provoked a military response from Israel, they failed to further the Palestinian cause in any meaningful way. The Arab League, meanwhile, was struggling under the collective burden of the enormous refugee population the situation had created. It held a series of meetings in Cairo and Jordan, and eventually established the Palestinian Liberation Organisation (PLO) in 1964. The PLO was designed to direct and restrain Fedayeen militarism and pacify Palestinian refugees. It also acted as an umbrella organisation for the Palestinian refugee groups, and a shepherd for the Palestinian hope of return. As a result, it became the figurehead of the nationalist energy.

Within the Palestinian movement there were factions turning towards extreme measures in pursuit of their cause. The tipping point was the Six-Day War in 1967. During this confrontation, Israel soundly defeated the combined might of Syria, Jordan and Egypt, achieving a powerful victory that humiliated the Arab states. But it also worked to galvanise the Palestinian movement towards the single overriding conviction that only violence could achieve the Palestinian goal. From this point on, violence became an essential part of the Palestinian struggle within its militant groups, which launched terrorist campaigns out of Jordan. In 1970 these groups were evicted from Jordan for attempting to assassinate the king, which led them to establish bases in Lebanon.

Palestinian terrorist groups quickly became the most kinetic terrorist threat in the world, responsible for the most significant and international attacks of their time. They became international industry leaders in a deadly profession, launching attacks from Athens to Rome, Bangkok, and the Olympic Games in Munich. Black September, as an operation subject to Al Fatah, was not the sole perpetrator of these attacks. The good intentions of the PLO had not been realised, as other terrorist groups arose and competed with Al Fatah for prominence, such as the Popular Front for the Liberation of Palestine (PFLP). Black September, Al Fatah and the PFLP would have an interest in Australia, and would seek to benefit from Australia's Palestinian population in one way or another.

Compromise and rejection

The divisions within the PLO were numerous but can be divided broadly into two fronts: the Compromise Front and the Rejection Front. This is based purely on their position towards negotiations with Israel. The Compromise Front encompassed the Palestinian groups that were less opposed to a two-state solution with Israel and was open to negotiation on certain points, but still used terrorism against their enemies.[7] Though the term 'compromise' is not widely used, and not really the best word, it is the simplest description of their position. Groups involved in the Compromise Front included the Popular Democratic Front for the Liberation of Palestine (PDFLP), and the Palestinian National Front (PNF). The major groups relevant to Australia, however, were Al Fatah and the BSO.

Al Fatah (a reverse acronym for Harakat al'Tahir al'Filastini) was the most influential group of the Palestinian nationalist movement, more so even than the PLO at one stage. Established in 1959 by Yasser Arafat, Al Fatah enjoyed the sponsorship of Syria, with Syrian political elites using anti-Israeli antagonism and pro-Palestinian sentiment to distract their citizens from problems at home. Al Fatah quickly began to support violent measures against Israel, and it carried out a number of low-grade, low-publicity attacks in 1965 and 1966. After the Six-Day War, Al Fatah changed direction, establishing a secret operations cell, the BSO, under Arafat in August or September 1971.

Its members were drawn from Al Fatah's intelligence cadre known as the RASD.[8] Its founding purpose was to exact revenge on the Jordanian monarchy for expelling Al Fatah in 1970, but it would also be used to execute Al Fatah terrorism around the world. Its first attacks were international assassinations of prominent Jordanians, such as the Jordanian prime minister in 1971, and the attempted assassination of the Jordanian ambassador to the United Kingdom two weeks later. Early success is attributed to the training they received from Egyptian security services. It was the BSO that would propel the Palestinian cause to the world consciousness with the Munich Olympics massacre.

In all, Black September was responsible for 120 attacks, largely targeting the Israeli, Jordanian and Western governments and their diplomatic officials. They mostly used explosives and firearms, undertaking bombings and assassinations, and operated in twelve countries, including Australia. Al Fatah would also accrue considerable statistics of its own. It is believed to have been responsible for 65 attacks, mostly targeting private citizens and governments throughout the Middle East, North Africa, the West Bank and Gaza. It favoured armed assaults and bombings.

Among the competing Palestinian groups, Al Fatah gained unexpected prominence in March 1968 when it engaged in a violent confrontation with Israeli troops at the Al-Karamah refugee camp and, surprisingly, won. This catapulted Al Fatah to prominence among Palestinian groups, and enabled it to gain control of the PLO executive in 1969. It installed its leader, Yasser Arafat, as PLO chairman and began placing its operatives in important administrative positions throughout the network. While the PLO did not engage in terrorism, many of those Al Fatah operatives were connected to attacks. The escalation to terrorist violence was a way for Arafat to lay claim to relevance within the Palestinian movement, so he created a series of cadres to pursue violent objectives. One of these was Al 'Asifah (the Storm), another the Fatah Hawks. Its most deadly offshoot, however, was the BSO.

Although Al Fatah and Black September primarily operated in the Middle East, their international network reached Australia. By 1970, Al Fatah had a branch of eight in Melbourne and another of fourteen members in Sydney, with a national executive of five.[9] ASIO believed these five men were Mahmoud Saadeh, Hana Karker, Mashni, Thabt Dajani and Ibrahim Abou Jaber—all living on the east coast, but none connected to acts of violence.[10] In addition, Al Fatah operative Hamid Meziani allegedly established the Union of Palestinian Workers in Australia, which boasted a further 200 members. Meziani appears to have also operated under the alias of Fouad Abdel Fatah, but his real name was rumoured to be Abdel Kadar el Bileisi. He was believed to be operations officer for all Al Fatah activities abroad, and although he visited Australia to set up the Union, the true base of his operations is unconfirmed.[11]

Conflict with other Palestinian groups was not uncommon, and Al Fatah jostled with Abu Nidal, the most significant of the Rejection Front groups that refused to negotiate or concede an inch of historical Palestine to Israel. Abu Nidal made its name through assassinating prominent members of the PLO in order to stall negotiations. The Rejection Front adamantly opposed any negotiated settlement, which it saw as 'surrender solutions'.[12] Prominent groups included the PFLP, the Popular Front for the Liberation of Palestine—General Command (PFLP-GC), the Arab Liberation Front (ALF), and the Palestine Popular Struggle Front (PPSF). At any one time, some of these groups were backed by Iraq, Libya, Algeria and Yemen. The groups most relevant to Australia were the PFLP and the ALF.

The PFLP was the second most influential group in the Palestinian liberation movement, led by George Habash, a Marxist Christian. Like many of the other groups, the PFLP desired a return to Palestine, but its members imagined Palestine as a modern and secular state. Habash was the mastermind of the group, and the tactician behind its dreadful developments in political violence. It was Habash, of all the terrorist leaders of the time, who championed advancements in the niche trade of aircraft hijacking. The PFLP's first hijacking occurred in July 1968, targeting an Israeli El Al flight from Rome. The attack was a resounding success: the PFLP managed to bring Israel to the negotiating table and secure the release of sixteen fighters in return for the hostages. Habash immediately became a major player in the game. The PFLP was responsible for 167 attacks, where it primarily targeted Middle Eastern and Western governments, diplomatic officials, airports and civilians. Its weapon of choice was explosives, closely followed by firearms. It primarily operated in the Middle East, Sub-Saharan Africa and Western Europe.

It also had an interest in Australia. The PFLP was slightly ahead of Al Fatah in establishing a 'Sydney Group' in 1968, which had a grand total of nine members. These nine, however, connected and sometimes controlled Palestinian Australian community groups, bringing a further 60 people into the fold.[13] The PFLP was initially linked to the Palestinian Arab Club, but it later disengaged from the club. Of the Palestinian Arab Club, ASIO believed Ibrahim Namrawi, Fuad Charida and Yousef Dabit were members of the PFLP. Namrawi was of particular interest, as he was among three people believed to have provided operational assistance to the PFLP, while another, Colin Anderson, allegedly trained with the PFLP in the Middle East.[14]

Soft target, hard visa

Both Al Fatah and the PFLP cultivated support bases in Australia, centred mainly in New South Wales and Victoria. Australia, with a large Palestinian émigré population, seemed a choice location for both groups to rapidly expand their already international networks. They were wrong. ASIO estimated that out of about 150,000 Arab émigrés, only 40 were believed to be supportive of terrorism operations; and of that 40, only ten were thought to be willing to actually participate in or conduct a terrorist operation.[15] There were between 15,000 and 17,000 émigrés in Sydney from Egypt, Iraq, Jordan, Syria and Iran, and another 13,000 were located around Melbourne.[16] This emphasises just how minor support for Palestinian terrorism actually was in Australia.

In fact, there was only slightly more support for mainstream efforts to champion the Palestinian cause. For example, on 25 March 1972 the Australian-Palestinian Solidarity Committee staged a protest in Sydney that was attended by only 40 Australian Arabs and ten European Australians. Given the size of the Australian-Arab community in Sydney, this turnout was extremely low. These groups, much like the activist groups internationally, failed to gain traction in the political mainstream.

Instead, Al Fatah and the PFLP took advantage of support offered by state sponsors, which they had exploited successfully in past operations in Europe. Operatives of Al Fatah, for example, were able to penetrate Italian border security because they were given a solid cover by the Libyan Embassy in Rome. Similar covers were provided by the Iraqi and Syrian governments. Other Arab nations, such as Kuwait, funded Palestinian terrorist groups to the tune of AU$10 million. Iraq, Syria and the United Arab Republic (Egypt) supplied the groups with weapons and training facilities, while training courses were provided by North Vietnam and the People's Republic of China.[17] Instead of recognising the role of state sponsorship, commentators framed this activity as perpetrated by 'refugees driven to despair,' rather than nationalists being promoted or exploited by sovereign states.[18]

The first line of defence, then, was the Australia border. Australian authorities believed that Palestinian terrorist groups developed an ongoing operational interest in Australia from 1970. First, they were concerned about Palestinian terrorists gaining visas and entering Australia; and second, the potential for Palestinian terrorists to be supported by members of the Palestinian-Arab community in Australia.[19] Without the advanced security measures instituted by primary Palestinian targets such as Israel, Australia was considered a soft target. Moreover, Australia's early role in both partition and the recognition of Israel would have justified it as a target for terrorism.

In the wake of the Munich Olympics massacre, there was a heightened awareness of the spectre of Palestinian terrorism. It was this attack, not the poorly attended protests, that concerned the national security community. Nor can it be denied that the attack was not universally condemned by Australian citizens, with individual elements praising the terrorists. The president of the Australian Arab Association, Edmond Melki, said: 'These acts against Israel are necessary ... We are in a state of war and all wars are dirty. This war must be carried to any part of the world and continue until the Arab world and the Palestinians feel that their rights have been returned.'[20]

Melki's sentiments were not terribly radical. The plight of the Palestinians drew sympathy around the world, but sympathy did not generate as much publicity as terrorism. With sympathisers of varying levels of commitment in Australia, the national security apparatus sought to stop the threat in the airport, severing the ties between international terrorists and their domestic support base. There was, however, a way for terrorists to circumvent this hard-border situation.

Return to sender

The first instance of Palestinian terrorism in Australia did not involve anyone from Australia at all. In 1972, there were around 170 cases of letter bombing worldwide (with another 70 the following year). Post office employees had been injured in Geneva, Tel Aviv and Zurich—and all these bombs carried the signature of the BSO.[21] Of that number, ten were intercepted in Australia. Five of the Australian letter bombs had been posted from the Netherlands, two from Malaysia, one from Singapore, and one from Greece.[22] At least two of them were sent to the Israeli Consulate in Sydney. Black September was believed to be responsible. The plot was well planned: it was operationally remote, international, with target locations around the world and sporadic detonation timings. It was, in sum, a plot that provided maximum reach with minimal effort. It also allowed high levels of security for the operative, who would gather the bomb materials in one country and dispatch them from a second country to detonate in a third.

The first wave of letter bombs enjoyed mild success, so a second wave was initiated. A further nine letter bombs were posted to Australia, but were intercepted before reaching our shores: three were detected in the Netherlands, three in Malaysia, and another three in Singapore. All but one had been addressed to prominent members of the Australian Jewish community who had been listed in the *Zionist Year Book*. All were sent inside 6-millimetre-thick ordinary airmail envelopes, containing a mechanical trigger, although the nature of the explosive charge was never revealed. And all were identical to the first wave of Black September letter bombs that wounded people from Tel Aviv to Geneva. None of the second wave reached their targets.

Towards the end of 1972, Black September engaged in another high-profile attack, this time in Bangkok. On 28 December 1972, four Black September operatives seized Israel's embassy in Bangkok, and held six hostages for nineteen hours. Of these six, four were embassy staff and two were the wives of staff members. Throughout the hostage negotiations, Black September demanded the release of 36 Palestinian prisoners being held in Israel. With the help of the Egyptian ambassador, Thai security forces pulled off a successful negotiation in which all hostages were released unharmed, and the terrorists were escorted out of the country.[23]

In response to this attack, the Australian national security apparatus renewed its attempts to stop Palestinian terrorists at the border. It did this by denying visas to anyone suspected of connections with Al Fatah or the PFLP, and tightening restrictions. This was, in part, a successful initiative. On 3 September 1973, it was reported that five to ten Black September operatives would attempt to enter Australia, with an attack planned between 8 a.m. and 10 a.m., at an unknown location on an unknown date. It is possible that the operatives were denied visas, although there were numerous other possibilities for the conspicuous absence of an attack on this date.[24] Nonetheless, security agencies continued to assume that terrorism could be stopped at the airport, an approach that was about to fail in a spectacular fashion.

Undiplomatic immunity

On 24 July 1973, a man who called himself Josef Gurey was issued a passport in Somalia. Around three weeks later, he went to the Australian Embassy in Beirut, Lebanon, and requested a visa to visit Australia for three months. He portrayed himself as a keen businessman, with a plan to investigate import and export opportunities for canned corned beef. His request was approved by Australian officials. A director-general of ASIO would later describe this case as illustrating 'all facets of the modus operandi of Arab terrorists'.[25]

On 29 August 1973, ASIO received intelligence from an overseas source that someone associated with dangerous people would be coming to Australia. The exact details of the information they received remain redacted, but ASIO was clearly aware that a man involved in Palestinian terrorism efforts intended to visit Australia. The timing here was key: other intelligence suggested that

Yasser Arafat was anxious to raise Al Fatah's profile, and was seeking some easy wins on soft targets. To that end, he dispatched eight or nine terrorist teams around the world. Most went to Europe, but one went to the United States and one to South-East Asia, but the final cell was destined for Australia. Within hours, the information had been passed to the departments of Prime Minister and Cabinet, the Attorney-General, Foreign Affairs, and Immigration, and the civil aviation authorities.[26]

On 5 September 1973, a man who happened to look identical to Gurey was issued a passport: only this one was a Somali diplomatic passport in the name of Abdulhamid Abdulla Azzam. He boarded flight AF766 in Bahrain, and arrived in Melbourne on 7 September with one briefcase, one overnight bag, and a suitcase. His suitcase was, however, accidentally overcarried to Sydney, leaving him without some of his luggage. Azzam went on without it, taking a taxi to the Southern Cross Hotel in Bourke Street for two nights.[27]

A day later, Azzam's suitcase arrived in Melbourne. A routine Customs inspection of the suitcase revealed it had a false bottom, and had been fitted with a secret cavity designed to hold a machine pistol, two magazines, and hand grenades. Residue analysis showed that weapons had been transported in it recently. The search also revealed a number of highly concerning documents, one of which was Azzam's green Al Fatah identification card. This listed him as an Al 'Asifah officer—that is, part of the Storm cadre connected with militant activities and BSO. One document was titled 'Main Points concerning Security and Training' with instructions on assassination operations, a list of important people. With it were another two documents of code words. A small radio transmitter and microphone, as used in clandestine operations, were found, along with some pornography magazines.

With the exception of the magazines, this was all quite suspicious.

ASIO placed Azzam under surveillance from 8 September, one day into his Australian adventure. Perhaps not entirely unaware of the scrutiny, Azzam moved from the Southern Cross Hotel to the

Glenborough Private Hotel in East Melbourne, booking the room under the alias Mr Josef. The Glenborough just so happened to be a few doors down from the Melki Milk Bar, owned by Edmond Melki, the president of the Australian Arab Association. Azzam spent his entire Sunday night in the back of Melki's business, and made various visits to the shop over the course of a few days. Sometimes he walked backwards and forwards from his hotel room to the store. ASIO watchers noticed that Azzam went to a certain amount of trouble to act like he did not know Melki, despite the fact he was meeting with a dozen men of Arab appearance in the back of Melki's premises. Azzam later told investigators that this was because he suspected he was being watched.[28]

After only three days in Australia on a three-month visa, Azzam suddenly informed the Glenborough that he would be leaving on Wednesday, 12 September, and gave staff his dry-cleaning. On Tuesday, he requested his dry-cleaning early, stating that he was leaving that very day. He hailed a taxi, arrived at the airport, and bought himself a ticket to Beirut, due to depart in less than two hours. Azzam was detained by Compol just as he was about to board the airplane. He had luggage with him, and the only item missing was the radio transmitter. A day later, he was charged under the Migration Act for three offences: obtaining a visa by false representation, having a false passport, and making false statements on his Incoming Passenger Card. As a security risk, he was refused bail.

Azzam had some serious questions to answer—but few of his responses seemed to be the truth. He had told the Australian Embassy in Beirut that he was looking to do business in canned food. He then told Compol he was looking for a woman called Linda, who was apparently his girlfriend (despite Azzam going on record as being married, with his wife and three children living in a refugee camp). Then, in a later interview he claimed that he was a staff member of the Foreign Relations Commission of Al Fatah, but that his travel had nothing to do with terrorism. He claimed Al Fatah had dispatched him to Australia for three reasons: first, to contact Edmond Melki to assess his potential as a representative of

Al Fatah, as Melki had contacted Al Fatah offering to raise $70,000–$80,000; second, to warn someone called Mahmud Rasheed against speaking in the name of Al Fatah without permission; and third, to explore the possibility of setting up an Al Fatah office in Australia. These explanations were consistent with Al Fatah cover stories elsewhere, although it never actually set up an Australian Al Fatah office.

When he was asked why he was departing so early on in his trip, Azzam said he believed he was under surveillance by Israel. He added that, on several occasions, there had been unexplained knocking on his door in the Glenborough, but if any knocking did actually occur, it was not recorded by the ASIO surveillance team nearby. Azzam further claimed that the Israelis had tried to kill him in the past, and he believed that he was in danger in Australia. During his trial, however, he merely noted that people like him had been assassinated by Israeli operatives in the past.[29]

When asked why he had not travelled on his diplomatic passport, Azzam had two different excuses. He claimed first, that it was more expensive to travel on a diplomatic passport; and second, that the diplomatic passport would make him a target of Israeli assassination.[30] In a blow to Australian immigration officials, it was later suggested that Azzam was awarded his visa in Lebanon while using his actual Al Fatah identity card.[31] Beyond this, Azzam refused to answer any questions relating to his documents, trip timings or suitcase. The suitcase was at the centre of the problem, as investigators later found that a similar one had been used by an Al Fatah agent in Britain.

The questioning of Azzam was not without friction, as ASIO and Compol each vied to protect their own investigations and processes. In a letter, C.W. Harders of the Attorney-General's Department stated that Compol's presence was essentially inhibiting ASIO questioning, while Compol did not want ASIO questioning to interfere with ongoing court proceedings.[32] ASIO wanted to learn what contacts Azzam had, possible targets, and the modus operandi to be used in an Australian attack. To settle the matter, Harding suggested that ASIO be given time alone with Azzam after the court proceedings initiated by Compol. But they were not the only players in the game: both Thai and Israeli authorities also wanted Azzam for questioning, as did the fearsome SAVAK of Iran.

Further investigation into Azzam yielded troubling information. He had travelled to New Delhi, Kuala Lumpur and Singapore in May and October 1972, right before Palestinian terrorists sent letter bombs from those exact cities, addressed to prominent Jewish people in Australia and around the world. Azzam also travelled to Bangkok in November 1972, and again in December 1972. On the second visit, he arrived on the same aircraft as two of the Palestinian terrorists who attacked the Israeli Embassy in Bangkok. He left twenty hours before the attack commenced.

Authorities began to believe that Azzam was the 'point man' of the operation in each city, and had used his Somali passport for diplomatic immunity in order to smuggle in the weapons and explosives for the attacks. Upon arrival, he likely contacted the terrorists and participated in, if not led, the operational planning. The Israeli ambassador to Australia, Moshe Erelle, went further, stating that Azzam was directly responsible for those attacks.[33] The Bahraini security forces later claimed to have confirmed that Azzam was, in fact, one of the five men involved in the Israeli Embassy siege in Bangkok. They knew this because one of the other terrorists was born in Bahrain, and subsequent investigations found all five had been carrying forged Lebanese passports. Tellingly, Bahrain had also been Azzam's transit point en route to Australia in 1973.

This all fitted with the standard Al Fatah modus operandi. It was common practice for the group to have a tactician in headquarters plan an operation, and engage a separate person to lead the operation. The leader then travelled to the target country for reconnaissance and to finalise the plot. Only when the operation was entirely prepared did the leader actually share the instructions with the terrorists who were to execute the attack. The Australian authorities believed that 'Azzam was given this type of brief for the Bangkok operation in December 1972 and a possible operation in Australia in September this year.'[34]

Azzam, it became clear, was an important member of the Black September terrorist wing of Al Fatah, but authorities had no evidence of a plot for which he could be charged. Instead, they charged him with migration offences, of which he was convicted, and arranged his deportation as quickly and politely as possible. He did not serve his six-month sentence, as it appears it was remitted to enable quick deportation. The reason for this diplomatic expulsion was quite simple: the authorities did not wish to provoke Al Fatah and Black September into investing in a significant attack against Australians at home or abroad. The risk of reprisals was high, and the price for any misstep would be paid in blood.

The big issue with speedily deporting Azzam was that few countries in the world wanted him there for any amount of time, even in transit. The governments of Lebanon, Kenya, Tanzania and Mauritius all in turn refused to provide transit facilities for Compol and Azzam en route to Mogadishu, Somalia. The Lebanese were particularly averse to Azzam's transit, stating 'one less commando the better'.[35] At last, the Egyptians agreed to host Azzam in transit, along with the Compol officers. On 25 September 1973, a police escort collected Azzam from Pentridge Prison in Melbourne, and his briefcase and property were returned.

His escort consisted of Compol Inspector Third Class J.B. Burrows and Sergeant Second Class L.N. Elkington. The flight route took the trio from Melbourne to Perth, Kuala Lumpur, Colombo, Bombay, Bahrain, and then finally Cairo, Egypt, without any of them once leaving the plane. Only at Cairo were the trio permitted to disembark. They stayed in a single, dirty bedroom with limited food and water while also 'stricken with chronic diarrhoea'.[36] The following day, they left Cairo and arrived in Aden, where they again remained on the plane. At long last, they arrived in Mogadishu, where Azzam was met by a group of men, including one Azzam claimed to be the Syrian ambassador to Somalia. Azzam gave the Compol officers a letter of thanks and departed.

Some in the intelligence community feared retaliation for the interrogation of Azzam. The day following Azzam's conviction, staff at Australia's Permanent Mission to the United Nations in Geneva noticed that they were being watched by unknown Arabs. In Lebanon, Reuters reported that Azzam had received a nine-month sentence, and had endured harassment from ASIO. In Cairo, another newspaper reported that two members of Australia's intelligence agencies had threatened Azzam, saying that they couldn't protect him from any attack unless he gave them the information they wanted. It also claimed that Azzam had been harassed by Israelis, and that Australia had put sympathisers of the Palestinian cause under surveillance.[37]

In fact, this later report was true. Edmond Melki *was* a sympathiser of Al Fatah, and he *was* placed under surveillance after a search of his home yielded no evidence. That said, reports by intelligence officers found that Melki was allegedly a) considered reliable by the PFLP; and b) considered by Azzam to be the Al Fatah representative in Australia.[38] This was not the limit of Melki's activism: he was also a member of the fascist Syrian Social Nationalist Party. ASIO's surveillance, however, did not unearth any chargeable offence in relation to Melki's activism.

But who was the real man, Josef Gurey or Abdulhamid Azzam? Neither, as it turns out. Azzam's real name was Ibrahim Ismail Abdullah el Khatib Kushia, and he was born near Jerusalem in 1943. ASIO assessed that he had been sent to Australia to support an attack by Black September terrorists, and that he at least had knowledge of the proposed targets for the attack.[39] The terrorists could already have been in Australia. With Azzam intercepted, the terrorists may have become 'frightened and thrown into confusion' and gone to ground, either to await new orders or to leave quietly at a later date.[40]

While intelligence officials refused to accept that there was a Palestinian terrorist footprint in Australia, Azzam had provided information that challenged this belief completely. As one report stated: 'Azzam has told us nothing about his terrorist group except that it exists and he cannot now be held responsible for what his group might do in Australia.'[41] Meanwhile, as authorities were distracted by Azzam, an overseas source reported something quite different. They claimed that on 22 September 1973, four members of the PFLP actually did travel to Australia, and took rooms at the Rome Pension hotel until 7 October before leaving for an unknown destination. Two days later, these four PFLP operatives were rumoured to be in Jakarta.

In fact, an unknown PFLP courier did make it through the airport in February 1974. There are no details about who they were or what they did, save that they were a member of the PFLP and had come via Malaysia. Another two PFLP members were also believed to have arrived in Australia, but their visit was brief and insignificant. That operatives slipped through a hard border raises an interesting possibility: around 24 March 1974, a number of men undertook training in maritime sabotage in Australia. Several months later in June, Al Fatah members conducted a maritime attack on Nahariya, Israel—their first maritime attack, in which they killed a woman and her two children. The terrorists were all killed in their abortive attempt, so it cannot be confirmed if there was any connection with the training in Australia, but it is nonetheless a peculiar coincidence.

Assassination plans

In 1975, a year after Al Fatah disbanded Black September, a different Palestinian terrorist group hatched a plot for Australia. The chief protagonist was a PFLP operative known as Munif Mohammed Abou Rish. Sometime between March and May 1974, Rish visited Australia for three weeks. Travelling under the alias Sami Mosleh, Rish moved between Sydney and Melbourne. He told people he was a journalist for *Al Hadaf*, a weekly magazine used as the political mouthpiece of the PFLP. Rish met with a number of local PFLP supporters, outwardly claiming that he was only in Australia to expand PFLP support in Australian-Arab communities, enhance donations and increase PFLP propaganda.[42]

In fact, Rish *was* a member of the PFLP Foreign Relations Department, but it is suspected that he was far more significant than that. Rish was up to his neck in clandestine activities spanning reconnaissance and strategic planning. After his 1974 trip to Australia, it was learned that he intended to visit again in July or August 1975—but this time with a more specific objective in mind: to plan the assassination of the Israeli ambassador, Esrelle Moshe, as part of a global PFLP offensive.[43] Not one to waste a trip, Rish also regarded three other Australians as suitable assassination targets: Bob Hawke, Isi Leibler and Sam Lipski.

Bob Hawke, at this time, was president of the Australian Council of Trade Unions (ACTU) and federal president of the Labor Party. Neither of these positions made him a PFLP target. It was what he *said*, rather than what he *did*, that ensured Hawke a place on the PFLP hit list. In an interview with the ABC's *This Day Tonight*, he said he supported Israel, claiming that Middle Eastern countries were attempting to 'annihilate' the Israelis. He went on to suggest that Israel should receive more support from Australia, exclaiming: 'By God they have suffered enough, haven't they really?'[44]

The other two targets were representative of typical PFLP targeting. Isi Leibler was a prominent leader within the Jewish community in Australia. He had been a member of the Executive Council of Australian Jewry since 1971, and president of the Victorian Jewish Board of Deputies since 1973. In 1972 he published *The Case for Israel*, which argued strongly that the establishment of Israel in Mandated Palestine was both historically and morally legal. This book, plus Leibler's role and reputation among the Australian Jewry, made him a potential target for the PFLP. Sam Lipski was also a leading light in Jewish circles in Melbourne. The PFLP considered him high profile due to his work in journalism from 1961—for the Nine Network, the Sydney *Daily Telegraph*, the ABC's *This Day Tonight* and *Four Corners*, *The Australian* and the *Jerusalem Post*. In 1973, he was appointed community director of the Victorian Jewish Board of Deputies, where he oversaw a 120-strong network of Jewish community organisations.

PFLP members in Australia were quick to offer Rish assistance, and 'improperly obtained' for him two documents to enter Australia, and devised methods of illegal entry if these failed.[45] Ultimately, the assassinations never went ahead—again, because Rish was prevented from entering Australia to superintend the attacks. This, surprisingly, had nothing to do with Australia and its hard visa policy, and everything to do with France. French counterterrorism forces had recently scattered the French PFLP network. They had been hunting 'Carlos the Jackal' (Ilich Ramírez Sánchez), a Venezuelan terrorist who joined the PFLP and waged five years' worth of terrorism activity before he was involved in the murders of French government and counterintelligence agents in 1975. This prompted a successful counterterrorism crackdown against Carlos and the PFLP network. Having lost the Jackal, the PFLP decided that Rish was too valuable an asset for such an insignificant place as Australia. Instead, he was diverted to France to rebuild PFLP strength. It is suspected that Rish was later killed by Israeli security forces.

It appeared for a time that the leaders of Palestinian terrorism had ceased to care much about Australia. There were still attempts to attract publicity to the cause. Abu Bassam (also known as Lazhari), for example, wrote to Melbourne's *Age* in 1974 claiming to be the Al Fatah representative in Australia. A report to the Interdepartmental Counter Terrorism Committee moreover named an Australian citizen, Joseph Khasho, as a 'leading member of Al FATAH who travels extensively in Europe'.[46] On the other side of things, former ASIO agent Maximilian Wechsler went public in an interview with Channel Nine's *A Current Affair*. He claimed that he had gone undercover among Palestinian groups, and stated categorically that there was a PFLP chapter and an Al Fatah chapter in Australia. Wechsler said that he resigned from ASIO because it refused to take any action against the groups regardless of the evidence gathered against them.[47] Despite Wechsler's claims, an ASIO report from 1976 indicates some level of vigilance, stating: 'There is evidence that Palestinian terrorists have a continuing operational interest in Australia. There is a small number of individuals in the local Palestinian/Arab community who might be prepared to provide auxiliary support for a terrorist attack.'[48]

A successful attack

The world was taking the Palestinian terrorism threat more seriously than the Palestinian refugee crisis. There continued to be tight airport security in Australia, and the Israeli ambassador requested that flights between Australia and Tel Aviv undergo luggage and passenger searches. The threat appeared to slowly creep closer and closer, following a PFLP attack on an oil refinery in Singapore in 1974 in conjunction with the Japanese Red Army terrorist group. Despite the erratic activity, Palestinian terrorism surged again in 1982. This was motivated to a degree by the Israeli invasion of Lebanon as part of Operation Peace for Galilee, aiming to disperse Palestinian terrorists. The operation was condemned internationally after hundreds of Palestinian refugees and civilians were massacred by Lebanese Christians without intervention by the Israeli army. The gloves were off, and Palestinian terrorist groups were about to demonstrate just how hard they could hit. Dozens of Palestinian terrorist attacks, mostly targeting Israel and other nearby locations, followed.

On Thursday, 23 December 1982, an explosive blast shook the Israeli Consulate in Woolloomooloo, Sydney, on the seventh floor of Westfield Towers. The bomb had been placed outside the door leading to the fire stairs and detonated at 2 p.m., blasting a hole in the 20-centimetre-thick solid concrete wall, and a 40-centimetre-wide hole in the floor. All fire doors up to the tenth floor were blown out. A cleaner, Clare Lowry, was injured in the blast and suffered a fractured skull, while a man on the sixth floor was treated for shock.

Five hours later, at 7 p.m., two explosions rocked the Jewish Hakoah Club in Bondi, Sydney. These bombs were placed in the club's underground carpark and damaged a number of cars. Despite the upstairs club being full of athletes, no one was injured. Security around the Israeli Embassy in Canberra, synagogues and Jewish community centres was immediately tightened. In the aftermath, there were two competing claims for responsibility. The consul-general, Dr Moshe Liba, received an anonymous phone call from a woman who claimed the attack in the name of the PLO. Later, an man anonymously called the ABC newsroom in Sydney and claimed the attack in the name of an obscure group, the Organisation for the Liberation of Lebanon from Foreigners. Attacks would continue, according to the caller, for as long as Israel occupied Lebanon.[49]

To investigate the bombings, the NSW Police formed one of the largest ever joint police task forces with the newly established Australian Federal Police (AFP)—a team that was 50 strong. Detective Inspector Ron Stephenson headed the team, which immediately began crime scene analysis, interviews, and examining flights in and out of Sydney. From early on, this was assumed to be an international attack. After three days of investigation, there were no fresh leads in the case. Police appealed to the public to report anyone who had been acting suspiciously near Westfield Towers.

Police believed that the two bombings were the work of the same person or group, organised by one or two foreign operatives who had travelled to Australia. The actual perpetrators, however, had clearly secured the assistance of locals. The clue lay in the wreckage of the Hakoah car bomb—a 1970 Chrysler Valiant. The Valiant had been purchased with the starting intent of blowing it up, as the chassis and engine number had been removed, and an incorrect numberplate, stolen a few days earlier, affixed. The improvised explosive device was set on a timer, with LPG gas cylinders providing the explosive charge, although only one cylinder detonated successfully.

On 9 February 1983, Mohammed Ali Beydoun was charged with maliciously setting off an explosive substance. He was remanded to appear before court on 18 February. Beydoun was a dual Australian and Lebanese national, a postal worker living in Rockdale, married with two children. The case against him was considered to be highly circumstantial, even by the officers involved.⁵⁰ It was alleged that Beydoun was one of two men who purchased the Valiant for $250 from a Michael Cawthorn on 14 December. Cawthorn provided the breakthrough police needed with his identikit image of Beydoun. The Valiant was then picked up by two unknown people on 18 December. Two days later, someone stole Beydoun's sister's car and removed its numberplates, and put them on the Valiant. Beydoun was later released for lack of evidence.

Some authorities suspected that responsibility lay with a new splinter group, the Palestinian 15 May Organisation (15MO). This day, 15 May, had become known as Nakba Day or Palestine Day, when Palestinians typically commemorate displacement in 1948. The terrorist cell was believed to have been formed in 1979 as an offshoot of the PFLP's Special Operations Group. It was suggested that two 15MO operatives flew into Australia to optimise the existing PFLP structures and support base in order to undertake the consulate and club bombings, although this was never entirely proven.⁵¹

In 2012, NSW Police, the AFP, and ASIO formed Operation Forbearance and reopened the case. This was in response to new evidence provided by Mohammed Rashed, who was then languishing in a US prison. Rashed, a Jordanian-born Palestinian, had been caught and convicted for the bombing of a Pan Am flight in 1982 that killed a Japanese teenager. The new operation found that an unknown woman had also been involved in the Sydney attacks. She had attended the caryard on 22 December and paid the balance for the Valiant. They also discovered that the LPG gas cylinders were the property of the State Rail Authority of New South Wales. Despite the revitalised investigation, the people ultimately responsible have escaped justice.

Countering the threat

Investigations conducted after terrorism activities are only one prong of the counterterrorism effort. The threat posed by Al Fatah and the PFLP impacted national security apparatuses and approaches around the world. In Australia, the first real change came not from the consulate bombing or the assassination plot or even the Azzam affair, but from the Palestinian terrorist attack on Israeli athletes at the Summer Games in Munich back in 1972. This international event, rather than the diverse spectrum of local activity, prompted the most decisive action.

Following the attack, Attorney-General Greenwood set up a group for coordinating the various departments against politically motivated violence. The group was later renamed, and then renamed again in 1973 to become the Special Interdepartmental Committee on Domestic Violence (SIDC-DV). The committee received intelligence from both Compol and ASIO, and coordinated with the departments of Prime Minister and Cabinet, Foreign Affairs and Defence. It established a Crisis Policy Centre, an imitation of centres in the Netherlands and the United Kingdom, and designed programs and exercises to ensure counterterrorism readiness. A year later, the SIDC-DV was split into the Special Interdepartmental Committee on Domestic Violence (SIDC-DV) and the Special Interdepartmental Committee on Counter Terrorism (SIDC-CT). This occurred because stakeholders believed the international threat posed by groups like Black September far outweighed the domestic situation.[52]

In its new form, the SIDC-DV was an advisory body focusing on domestic threats to federal authorities and premises, foreign missions and bases, and VIP visitors—in essence, a specialist group for protective arrangements against domestic terrorism. The second committee, the SIDC-CT, was an advisory body that focused on counterterrorism, management strategies and intelligence coordination, with oversight of international terrorist threats such as the Palestinian groups. These committees instituted a number of changes: first, they drew the Department of Immigration into the counterterrorism fold by requesting that it enhance visa checks; second, they tasked the Civil Aviation Authority with reviewing transit passenger rights, tightening aviation security and procedures, and installing closed-circuit surveillance systems; and third, they involved the Postal Commission, which had the unfortunate task of informing the committees that despite magnetometer screening '100% security could not be guaranteed'.[53]

Fortress Australia was slowly taking shape, driven by the national security reasoning that terrorism could be stopped at the border. Background checks of visitors who fit ethnic profiles, especially Arabs and Iranians, became a common strategy to countering Palestinian terror. Profiles were created around the known members of active terrorist groups: for example, the following profile was developed with Black September and the Japanese Red Army in mind:

> Any male or female of Arab or Japanese <u>appearance:</u>
> —aged between 16 and 45 years
> —travelling singly or in a small group (but not a family group)
> —who (in particular) showed signs of tension or of other unusual behaviour[54]

Anyone applying for a visitor's visa to Australia who fit this profile was to have their photographs dispatched immediately to the Department of Immigration for the decision to approve or deny. Customs also became involved, primarily to secure seaports from terrorist incursion. Border security by sea or air became a significant line of defence, as preventing entry was deemed to be 'the answer'.[55] Nubar Hovespian, a PFLP operative who was invited to Australia by supporters in 1975, was successfully denied entry through having his visa refused.[56] As of 1979, however, it was believed that Al Fatah had managed six visits to Australia, although of those six, one had their visa cancelled, and the other, Abdulhamid Azzam, was deported. Beyond these specific incidents, the security forces' fatal misconception was that terrorists were foreign actors who could be stopped at the border. What they underestimated, perhaps, was the power of ideology—which seeps across oceans and borders, and lures citizens into its deadly currents.

Open-air prison

Palestinian terrorism receded as a threat in Australia, and became more centralised in the Middle East. Public opinion on the Palestinian situation, meanwhile, swayed in the breeze, and despite occasional concessions, little change was achieved. While moves were made to combat terrorism internationally, there seemed to be little interest in addressing the issues on which terrorists capitalised. There were small advances here and there with the 1993 and 1995 Oslo Accords between Israel and the PLO, which confirmed mutual recognition between Israel and Palestinians, including the Palestinian right to self-determination. The PLO also enjoyed a small victory when it was granted observer status in the United Nations General Assembly. By that time, 120 countries had recognised the state of Palestine, and had established diplomatic relations with representatives of the PLO. Australia was not one of them. Unfortunately, the accords failed to achieve lasting peace in that contested part of the world.

In 2006, the situation deteriorated again when Israel and Egypt blockaded the Gaza Strip, restricting Gaza exports and degrading the local economy. When rival Palestinian parties Al Fatah and Hamas (formed in 1987) put aside their conflict in 2011, some believed that reconciliation with Israel would soon be possible. Unfortunately, tensions flared again in 2014, when Hamas, then ruling Gaza, kidnapped and murdered three Israeli teenagers, leading to Israel's Operation Protective Edge. Seven weeks of conflict claimed the lives of thousands of people. The year 2018 marked 70 years since Nakba, meaning that the Palestinian problem has now become the longest and largest refugee crisis in modern history. There are 7.54 million Palestinian refugees around the world, and 720,000 internally displaced persons. Of the total number, 5.3 million receive aid from the United Nations and charity agencies.

Around 2 million Palestinians remain on the Gaza Strip, which is so densely populated that it had been described as 'the world's largest open-air prison'.⁵⁷ In March 2018, Palestinian refugees and political parties launched the Great March of Return, where 70 per cent of Gaza's Palestinians marched on the Israeli border and demanded their Right of Return to the lands allocated to them in 1948. Israel responded with force, killing fifteen and injuring 1400. In subsequent rallies, Palestinians have continued to protest the blockade, and fire-kites have been used to destroy Israeli agricultural land. Since then, import restrictions have extended to fuel and gas, leaving many homes with only an hour or two of electricity every day. Many Palestinians depend on humanitarian assistance to survive, unemployment is high and the economy is in tatters. Ceasefires between armed groups and Israel do not last, as evidenced by the May 2021 conflict, which left over 250 people dead, with a quarter of the casualties children.

The refugee camps remain, the Palestinians' hope for return fades, and the conflict continues.

Southern Cross Terror, 1975–90

From the mid-1970s, the terror threat changed again. The social agitation from the revolution generations largely subsided and, with it, left-wing extremism. The Ustaša and pro-Palestinian terror networks of the 1960s and 1970s evolved and moved on. That is not to say that extremism subsided; rather, new movements came into prominence. The 'moving target' of terror continued to shift and adapt. New ideologies rose and fell, threats developed, fresh tactics were devised, even as key figures were neutralised. During this new period of terror, there were four major threats relevant to Australia: the religious sect Ananda Marga; pro-Armenian terrorism; right-wing extremism; and the Aum Shinrikyo doomsday cult.

These groups had similar characteristics to those that had come before: they were internationally linked and domestically engaged. All movements during this period had strong international connections and inspirations. New extremist ideologies from India, Armenian diasporas and Japanese extremists were successful in establishing a presence in Australia, while the Australian extreme right continued to propagate its domestically embedded (and often internationally inspired) ideologies against its fellow citizens.

All of these threats were also able to recruit Australians and establish domestic support bases. In the case of Ananda Marga, domestic sects provided the people and support that ultimately resulted in

Australia's first fatal terrorist bombing. For pro-Armenian terrorists, Australians provided the local knowledge and resourcing required for international operatives to conduct targeted assassinations. Right-wing extremism was predominantly championed by Australian citizens. With Aum Shinrikyo, domestic support was potentially limited to one woman, who provided the local legitimacy required for the cult to experiment with weapons of mass destruction in the Australian outback.

Of these threats, most groups advanced international strategic goals, attempting to coerce governments and their representatives. These goals included freeing political prisoners, forcing a target to change a policy or admit wrongdoing, or advancing a chemical weapons program for use elsewhere. In one instance, it was even believed that the Japanese Red Army arrived in Australia to conduct such an attack but then inexplicably departed without doing anything. Only the extreme right sought to target Australian citizens specifically, and to change Australia's liberal democratic order. To them, democracy was a thing to be spurned, and they sought to bend their fellow Australians to their will, conducting an internally directed campaign of violence.

The national security apparatus rapidly maturing in response to these threats would be faced with the worst attacks yet seen in Australia, with people dead in Australian streets. Again, border security and visa bans became essential to the fight against terrorism. The national security apparatus itself would change in response, undergoing its own reviews to better serve the Australian people and protect the constitutional order.

5

Spiritual elites: the Ananda Marga

It was lunchtime on 13 February 1978. A three-man crew of council workers was operating a garbage truck, doing their normal rounds. Forty-nine-year-old Bill Ebb was driving the truck, as he always did, while his two colleagues dismounted to manoeuvre the bins. One was William Favell, a 36-year-old from Dulwich Hill, and the other was Alec Carter, 37 years old from Bronte. Both men were married and had young children at home. Ebb pulled up the truck alongside the George Street entrance of the Hilton Hotel: they were running early that day and were keen to get the job done. Little did they know that earlier that day an anonymous caller had phoned the *Sydney Morning Herald*.

'You'll be interested in what the police are going to be doing at the Hilton soon,' the caller said cryptically, and made a vague reference to a bomb.

The next call went to the Sydney Criminal Investigation Branch of NSW Police.

'Listen carefully,' instructed the anonymous caller with a foreign accent. 'There is a bomb in a rubbish bin outside the Hilton Hotel in George Street.'[1]

Unaware, Ebb, Favell and Carter diligently went about their work. Favell and Carter dismounted the truck and positioned the bins for Ebb. It was 12.40 p.m. The bins emptied into the back of the truck, and the compactor began.

'There was a sheet of flame, an enormous blast and glass flying everywhere,' Ebb recalled.[2] A bomb concealed in the bin had detonated, ripping apart the back of the garbage truck, sending deadly shrapnel through the air. The force of the blast and weaponised fragments of steel from the truck hit Favell and Carter, killing them instantly.

'I think they were dead before they hit the ground,' Ebb said.

A journalist on the tenth floor of a motel a few blocks away from the Hilton felt the shock hit her room. The windows of nearby shops were shattered, and broken glass and shrapnel littered the road. Bodies were strewn in the street, caught in the blast or lacerated by the sheets of glass. One man was thrown more than 15 metres. Pieces of the truck, twisted into dangerous metal projectiles, were found 30–40 metres away.

Also caught in the blast was NSW police constable Paul Burmistriw, aged 31. He never made it home, having received severe head injuries in the blast that took his life more than a week later. Many other police officers were wounded: Constable Terry Griffiths was struck in the legs with shrapnel, leaving him in a serious condition in hospital; Sergeant John Hawtin received wounds that required surgery; and Constable Rodney Wither was also injured. A hotel waiter, Colin Nicholls, received serious shrapnel wounds but he survived the attack, while his colleague Christine Bidarp and many other bystanders suffered minor lacerations and were treated at the scene. Three men were dead and eleven were injured. The attack on the Hilton Hotel was the first fatal terrorist bombing in Australia's history.

Soon, rumours abounded that the culprits were linked to Ananda Marga, a newly established religious sect governed by an obscure Indian guru.

In service of humanity

The Ánanda Márga Pracáraka Saṁgha (the Organisation to Propagate the Path of Bliss), also known as Ananda Marga (AM), was established on 7 November 1955 in India under the leadership of Prabhat Ranjan Sarkar. Also called Shri Anandamurti or more affectionately 'Baba' by his followers, Sarkar was a railway clerk and revolutionary who vociferously opposed the caste system in India. In so doing, Sarkar was essentially opposing the entire Hindu conceptualisation of how the world should be structured, which made him a threat to Hindu orthodoxy in India.

Sarkar was the chief ideologue of AM—at this stage, its one and only guru. He believed that current religions, such as Hinduism, offered only the worship of false gods. Instead, he posited that there was a single Supreme Consciousness: an omnipresent divine entity. It was only through returning to the worship of this entity that humanity could be reborn and achieve true bliss, living in harmony in a single holistic system in which all religious, social and economic concerns were governed. His ideology was universalist (not nationalist as is commonly suggested) because he was not concerned with a single nation or people, but with the entirety of humanity.[3] His origins may have been in India, but his dreams were truly global.

Sarkar was highly critical of the concept of non-violence; he believed that within every person raged a great and constant battle between the forces of good and evil. He required his worshippers to engage in eternal struggle, guarding constantly against the innate immorality of human nature. As one scholar noted:

> In Ananda Marga, non-violence is considered impossible *per se* because violence is the basis of the world's evolution, both at the microcosmic and macrocosmic level. Violence directed at oneself is legitimate when it is used to accelerate individual evolution towards liberation; violence against persons in society is legitimate to perpetuate the socio-cosmic order. Therefore, individualized spiritual practices bring the initiate toward accepting violence as a necessary component of human incarnation.[4]

Violence, then, was essential to the group's understanding of themselves and the world around them. It was through such violence that bliss—freedom from earthly temptations—could be achieved.

Sarkar taught that liberation could only be achieved through revolution. The entire restructuring of humanity in accordance with his own teachings was required, led by a revolutionary vanguard known as the Sadvipras: the spiritual elite chosen by Sarkar. They alone were sufficiently beholden to the Supreme Consciousness, and would hold all-powerful political positions to interpret its will. They alone were engaged in a cosmic battle to defend the world from impurity and immorality. The masses, according to this belief system, could only worship them. Under their enlightened rulership, all current forms of government and religion would become obsolete. In order for this to occur, revolution was not simply desirable, it was the key pathway to wrest power from the ruling classes.[5] Sarkar, though opposed to terrorism, claimed that 'Like materialism, spirituality based on non-violence will be of no benefit to humanity. The words of non-violence may sound noble, and quite appealing, but on the solid ground of reality have no value whatsoever.'[6] The reality, then, was revolution: both within oneself, and against the status quo.

Sarkar's sect quickly gathered followers among the lower classes of Indian society, becoming a quasi-religious charity organisation. Its slogan was 'In the service of humanity'. Its members adopted strict dietary practices, and engaged primarily in meditation, yoga and study. They attempted to live sustainable lifestyles, such as by growing their own food, often in communal living arrangements. These were called Master Units (or sometimes Land Projects) and were designed to showcase the harmony and achievability of Sarkar's vision. Master Units were essentially self-sufficient agrarian communities. The public face of AM, by virtue of this, was one of peace and harmony, with all members striving together to achieve bliss.

Despite this communal striving, organisational ranks developed, and AM swiftly became both structured and hierarchical. The vast majority of members were Margis, general members who followed the soft-core practices such as taking a vow of secrecy, following certain moral rules and restrictions, and studying. Other Margis were 'local full timers' (LFT), highly regimented organisational workers living in non-cloistered monasteries, having renounced all kinship ties and entered absolutely into the world of AM.[7] A small number of elite members, perhaps under 1600, became *acaryas*. The *acaryas* underwent extensive training, and performed administrative and spiritual functions for the sect. A subset of *acaryas* were *brahmacaris*, who followed 111 rules and restrictions, including celibacy, and were subject to relatively soft punishment; while *abadhutas* were stricter still, and subject to greater ritual violence, such as naked beatings, to absolve their sins and bring them closer to bliss. The most elite, however, were *purodhas*, who, having reached the pinnacle of discipleship, engaged in secret rituals and practices.[8]

Not content simply with the religious organisation, Sarkar launched AM's political wing, PROUTist Universal (PROUT), to achieve his vision by other means. PROUT, or Progressive Utilisation Theory, devised by economist Ravi Batra, adopts a mix of capitalist and communist economic ideas, while simultaneously opposing both and accusing them of materialism. PROUTists believed that a violent revolution between Eastern and Western economic systems was not only inevitable but desirable, and would pave the way for spiritual revolution. PROUT claimed to be a socialist entity, promising the basic provisions of life to all people to enable them to achieve bliss. In their political campaigns, PROUTists levelled many accusations against the Indian government, which in turn monitored PROUT and AM closely.

AM soon expanded out of India and began to set up Master Units around the world. It was relatively successful in this venture, and within a few years had millions of followers in India and 35 branches worldwide.[9] By 1971, Sarkar claimed to have 8 million followers in India, Britain, the United States, Canada, the Philippines and Australia.[10] These branches were managed by an orderly network. First, there were two world headquarters, in Calcutta and Denver, that managed seven sectors that neatly divided the world. The US Sector controlled North America and Mexico; the Nairobi Sector had a foothold in Egypt; the Georgetown Sector in Guyana covered parts of South America and the West Indies; the West Berlin Sector coordinated Europe; the Hong Kong Sector covered Taiwan and Japan; the Manila Sector covered South-East Asia; and the Australasian Sector covered Australia, New Zealand and the South Pacific.

AM in Australia

The two major chapters for AM were based in Wollongong and Armidale, although there were others. All Australian chapters reported to the Australasian Sector, which reported to both World Headquarters.[11] There was an Australian presence at least by 1970, with a sister chapter in New Zealand. There was considerable exchange between the Australian chapters and the chapters in New Zealand (such as Wellington) and the United States. Trans-Tasman links were assisted by travel arrangements between both countries, which allowed travellers from New Zealand to come and go in Australia without a visa.

In the Australian AM constitution, high importance was placed upon the realisation of Sarkar's objectives, committing its members to social welfare first and foremost, and instructing them to engage in social work, relief work, schooling and childcare, aged care, medical care, and literary and artistic endeavours, as well as spiritual, moral and cultural upliftment through all spheres of life.[12] Group mottos encouraged followers to self-realisation, service and self-discipline. Tantra, meditation and yoga became popular; followers also adopted dietary restrictions (prohibiting garlic, onions, meat and eggs) and recited mantras. The Master Units in Australia ran primary schools and children's homes, officiated weddings, and attempted to run for electoral office, the last of these with limited success.

There was also a PROUTist faction within AM in Australia. With their small numbers, the PROUTists believed they would be unable to speed up the looming revolution, and instead sought to build up a support base. One Australian member suggested that PROUT could influence government decisions by inserting agents into influential government positions and getting sympathisers elected to federal parliament. Australian authorities remained convinced that Sarkar was the head of both AM and PROUT, despite the organisation's claims that the two were separate.[13] He was likely the nominal leader, but left the day-to-day functioning of his religious network to his elite *acaryas*.

In Australia, one of the key *acaryas* was Abhiik Kumar, the spiritual director of the Ananda Marga for Australasia, and described as a 'violent man by nature'.[14] Kumar, whose real name was Jason Holman Alexander, travelled extensively using a variety of aliases, including Jon or John Hoffman, Mark Randall, David Hart, James Manly and, most commonly, Michael Brandon.[15] Kumar alone could recognise new members as Margis after an indoctrination and screening process; he alone was responsible for appointing the regional AM committees; and he alone could veto all committee decisions.[16] There is little that Kumar could not know and actively manage in his organisation.

Other leaders included *acarya* Brahmacarinii Mahashveta, Brahmacarinii Tilottama, and Brahmacarinii Bodhiishvara (spiritual names were assumed in AM's elite ranks), who were involved only in the peaceful administration of AM.[17] This included teaching at schools, marrying couples, running yoga and meditation sessions, recruiting, and engaging in humanitarian and public service acts. They even established a communal orchard in Queensland, likely as part of a Master Unit.[18] The expansion of the order through recruitment of new members continued.

Training to become a Margi involved a month of rigid discipline, fasting—or minimal food intake—and long hours of study, cold showers, and sleeping on bare wooden boards. This austerity was not unusually sinister. It was only when new Margis were required to surrender all their worldly goods to the organisation and sever all contact with family and friends outside the order that it manifested cult-like characteristics. This enforced a financial dependency on the sect, reduced freedom of movement, and imposed social isolation. The LFT members were treated differently, and it was rumoured that a military-type obedience was enforced by certain *acaryas*. Domestic authorities assessed the obedience to be so absolute that the 'AM leadership has the capacity to direct individual members to undertake a terrorist role' without the knowledge of the broader AM community.[19]

Throughout the 1970s, AM had anywhere between 300 and 500 adherents in Australia. They were typically middle class, educated and aged between twenty and 35. Disillusioned with conventional values and modern life, followers often relied on social security payments and chose to live in AM Master Units, adopting an austere lifestyle of meditation and worship. Many were apolitical, with the exception of the 50 or so adherents suspected of PROUTist politics—of which twenty were also feminists committed to the revolutionary objectives.[20]

Turn to violence

Sarkar was soon to pay a high price for his swift rise in popularity. In December 1971, he and his most trusted lieutenants were arrested by the Indian government using emergency powers, and charged with the murder of six fellow Margis. The Indian government alleged that six Margis who had attempted to leave the organisation were murdered by AM and buried in the jungles near Jamshedpur in 1970. Sarkar and his co-defendants claimed they were being framed by the government, but all four were convicted and received life sentences. While Sarkar's legal teams launched appeal after appeal, he himself undertook a hunger strike.

Fearing for Baba's life, seven of his followers went so far as to burn themselves alive in protest at his imprisonment. Two of the immolators were German women who burned themselves to death on the steps of a Berlin church. The agitation for Sarkar's release was becoming both global and violent. In the context of this gory self-sacrifice, the Universal PROUTist Revolutionary Federation (UPRF) splintered off from the PROUTist political movement. It was the UPRF, concealed within the various arms of PROUT and AM, that would launch a transnational terrorist campaign, aided and abetted by sympathisers around the world. The first sign that UPRF was capable of serious violence occurred in 1975, when the Indian railway minister, Lalit Narayan Mishra, was assassinated in a bombing attack in Samastipur, India. The blast also killed three other people. While many suspected AM, the sect did not claim responsibility.

Following Sarkar's imprisonment, the general attitude of AM in the Pacific changed. A New Zealand Margi, Hari Deva, claimed that AM became increasingly militant and had 'people handpicked for the purpose of overthrowing governments by violent means'.[21] This cadre formed an elite guard and trained to become master saboteurs, capable of stealing weapons from military installations and managing explosives. Within the space of a few months, there was violence associated with the cult in the Australasian Sector. In October 1975, three New Zealand Margis were interrupted by police while stealing explosives. The extremists took an officer hostage and escaped in a police car, only to be apprehended shortly thereafter. Their aim was to blow up the Indian High Commission in Wellington. All three were convicted and jailed. An Australian, Timothy Jones, was allegedly involved in this plot. While he was not arrested, Jones was believed by Compol to have 'been involved in the conspiracy to commit the bombing'.[22] The New Zealand police disagreed, while ASIO had not yet commenced investigations into AM.

The UPRF, meanwhile, was gaining traction as a security threat. Towards the end of 1977, ASIO assessed that: 'UPRF is probably a clandestine group of senior AM members which operates without the knowledge of the AM movement as a whole, and that the campaign of violence may be internationally coordinated.'[23] Before this assessment, however, it is unlikely that the small spate of incidents in Australia in 1975 was part of a greater and centrally organised plot. The Indian High Commission in Canberra, for example, only received threatening phone calls from people they presumed to be AM members—not quite reaching the severity of the Wellington plot.[24] Meanwhile, in July 1976, two people in Bunbury, Western Australia, were arrested and convicted for trying to blow up a woodchip gantry. One of the would-be bombers was allegedly a Margi, but this turned out to be a false alarm: the attack was motivated by environmental concerns rather than the freeing of Sarkar.

Knives in the dark

Towards the end of 1977, threats against Indian representatives in Australia ceased to be empty. On 24 August, the Air India offices in Sydney were splattered with blood by Paul Maurice O'Callaghan, president of an AM chapter in Sydney. Two days later, a pig's head was placed in the office of the consul-general for India in Sydney. On 27 August, a bomb hoax targeting Air India Flight 1415 was claimed by the UPRF. Two days after that, the Indian High Commission in Red Hill, Canberra, was damaged by a suspicious fire, which the UPRF claimed as a firebombing. The damage was valued at $130,000. On 2 September and again on 11 September, the Indian consul-general's house in Sydney was stoned at night. As the harassment of Indian officials continued, the risk of genuine violence increased.

The first proper terrorist attack associated with the UPRF occurred in Australia on 15 September 1977. 'The first thing I can recollect after going to sleep is a pain in my chest,' recounted Colonel Iqbal Singh. 'My hands moved subconsciously to the area of the pain . . . and I realised I had a dagger in my hand. It was straight and erect in my chest . . . I can't recall if I pulled it out.'[25] Colonel Iqbal Singh was a military attaché of the Indian High Commission in Canberra, and the newest target in the campaign to coerce the Indian government to free Sarkar. Around 1.45 a.m., a Margi called John William Duff had broken in to Singh's Red Hill house via the bathroom window, and crept into the bedroom where Iqbal and his wife Darshan lay sleeping. Duff stabbed Singh, leaving the knife in his chest, and watched him wake. The first thing Iqbal saw was Duff, a stranger to him, wearing a white scarf and aiming a gun at him and his wife. As Duff made them get out of bed, Iqbal hid the knife in the sheets. Duff noticed, and beat Iqbal with the barrel of his gun before retrieving the knife.

Duff marched Singh and Darshan out of the bedroom and into their own car, holding Darshan at knifepoint while keeping the gun trained on Iqbal. He ordered Iqbal to drive. The car left Red Hill and turned on to Mugga Lane—a relatively deserted area at that time of night. Iqbal accelerated the car rapidly around a corner, and turned to wrestle Duff for the gun. Iqbal pulled the trigger multiple times, but the firing pin landed on an empty chamber. In the scuffle, Duff stabbed Iqbal in the chest again. Iqbal managed to gain control of the firearm, and broke its stock before throwing it out of the car, as he did with the knife. The car, uncontrolled, left the road and crashed into a ditch. Finally, Iqbal and Darshan managed to subdue their assailant.

'I have got nothing against you. It is against your Government,' Duff told them.[26]

When the Singhs saw headlights approach in the night, they feared that Duff had an accomplice and fled into a field, leaving him to make good his own escape. The Singhs were later rescued by a truck driver, Jeff Schubert, and rushed to hospital. Iqbal Singh required intensive care, and did not leave the hospital for eight days. The day after the attack, the leader of the local AM chapter issued a statement claiming they did not support Duff and nor did they have any connection to the attack. The police quickly identified Duff, and the Singhs readily confirmed he was their attacker. The footprints at the scene were matched to Duff, as was the gun.

When he was arrested, Duff allegedly confessed to an Inspector Brown, detailing how he was a member of AM and that the attack was intended as ransom 'in exchange for Baba [Sarkar]'.[27] Duff explained that he chose the Singhs because he couldn't go to India, so a domestic attack was his only option. He was charged with two counts of kidnapping, attempted murder and grievous bodily harm. He was convicted by jury and sentenced to nine years in jail. He later appealed the conviction, but was unsuccessful.

Shortly after the attack by Duff, the UPRF posted its claim of responsibility to the Indian High Commission, signed by its Central Command:

> The Universal PROUTist Revolutionary Federation claims full responsibility of the attempt on the life of Indian Military Attaché Iqbal Singh last night. A continuous programme of assassination will proceed until political prisoner P.R. Sarkar is unconditionally released. As we are established throughout the world the next attack may take place anywhere any time. Officials and lackeys of the Indian High Commission, Consuls, trade offices, and Air India are all considered suitable targets. The Indian Government should realise the sincerity of our claim that the failure of immediate release will bring blood on their hands. Do not fail to heed this warning. The next attempt will not fail.[28]

With these chilling words, it appeared that UPRF was gathering momentum. Additionally, the *Dharma* magazine published by AM in Australia shortly after the attack conceded it was possible after all that the perpetrator was an AM member.

On 22 September, someone threatened to rape and murder Indian diplomats if they were not paid $100,000 immediately. This anonymous threat was issued to the Indian vice-consul in Sydney, R. Alagh. The activity was not confined to Australia: on 29 September, a threat was made to the Indian Embassy in Kabul: 'You and three members of your Embassy are marked for assassination; one suicide squad is now leaving Nepal and will be there when you receive this; remember Chanberra! [sic] We will not stop until Anandamurti [Sarkar] is released by your Government.'[29] 'Chanberra' is likely to be a misspelling of Canberra, referring directly to the Singh attack. Nothing came of this threat, nor of the message sent to an Indian tourist office in London on 9 October that promised an assassination campaign. All threats are believed to have been engineered by the UPRF.

Safeguarding Indian establishments was further complicated by the suspicions of insider involvement. In the wake of some stone-throwing targeting diplomatic premises, investigators found that some of the windows had been broken from the inside. The stones used were then found hidden in a toilet used by an employee, Ramish Chand. Excluding this complication, the authorities soon suspected that there were tangible connections between the violence domestically and internationally.

When a bomb threat was made against the train of Indian prime minister Morarji Desai on 11 October 1977, it was believed possible that this was connected to incidents in Australia. One report indicated: 'An overall view of the evidence suggests a connection between incidents in Australia, Afghanistan, and London which, together with previous acts of violence in New Zealand lead to a reasonable conclusion that at least some of the Ananda Margis are following a central theme in the furtherance of their criminal acts to secure the release of their leader, P.R. Sarkar.'[30] These Margis committed to violence action were possibly UPRF, a secret network concealed within an otherwise peaceful and well-meaning organisation. The denouncements of violence by many Margis were genuine: they did not know that there were wolves in the midst of their flock.

Not everyone took this threat seriously: an ASIO minute dated 17 October 1977 alleges that most AM activities focused on childish vandalism, empty threats and mysterious attacks. The writer believed there was no evidence of weapons training at any of the AM retreats around Australia, or even in sects around the world. Combined, this did not 'create a sufficient threat for any already overworked Police force to devote a great number of extra man hours into probing Ananda Marga in depth'.[31] Two days later, they would be proven wrong.

The UPRF rises

On 19 October 1977, the threats ceased to be empty, as Michael Meneghini found out the hard way. Meneghini was an airline clerk at Air India in Melbourne, and an Australian national. He was working at the front counter of the Air India offices that afternoon when a man entered and spoke with a female employee. He claimed he had a letter for the manager, Mr Zellner, who overheard the conversation and immediately became suspicious. He went to his office, closed the door and began to ring the police. That's when the screaming began.[32]

The attacker had waited until Michael Meneghini turned around, and then stabbed him in the back with a 200-millimetre knife, puncturing his lung and narrowly missing his heart. Two female workers witnessing the attack screamed, and watched as the attacker fled. An ambulance raced Meneghini to hospital and fortunately he survived the ordeal. According to Indian High Commissioner Jagdish Ajmani, a letter was left by the attacker addressed to Air India and Prime Minister Desai.[33] The note was signed by the UPRF, and called for the release of Sarkar:

> The Universal Proutist Revolutionary Federation has pointedly engineered the attack on Melbourne Air India Staff to demonstrate that all Indian Government employees are considered suitable targets for our program.
>
> We repeat that continual program [sic] of assassination will proceed, with employees of Indian High Commissions, Consul, Trade Offices, and Air India targets, until Shrii P.R. Sarkar is unconditionally released.
>
> As you should realize from the warning in London this week. The world wide programme has now begun, from the first few steps in Australia, we are now ready to begin our program similtaneously [sic] in several countries around the world . . .[34]

This was no longer a campaign of empty threats, but the early steps in a transnational assassination program to free an Indian guru.

After the attack, Victorian police visited AM chapters in Melbourne and reported that they 'had obviously been expected'.[35] Despite this focus on Melbourne, some began to suspect that the attacker had fled to Western Australia. The AM presence had the benefit of legal advice from a noteworthy authority. Police noted that after an AM incident in their jurisdiction, this legal specialist was fast on the scene. In any event, Western Australian police made a swift arrest following a tip-off from ASIO. They wrote:

> The West Australian Police are satisfied that a man arrested in Perth a few days ago in connection with the Air India stabbing in Melbourne, was in fact responsible. However, Ananda Marga, Perth, has produced a number of members who claim to have been with the suspect in the sect premises at the time of the incident. Their stories cannot be shaken but are not believed. The suspect has been released and is now being sheltered in the Ananda Marga premises in Perth.[36]

The suspect in question was George Jekic. Meneghini had only glimpsed his assailant before the attack, so was unable to identify Jekic in the line-up. He did, however, assert that he was 80 per cent sure it was Jekic, because Jekic's voice was 'exactly the same as that of his attacker'.[37] Two other witnesses also claimed the perpetrator was Jekic, while a third witness disagreed.

Western Australian police conducted a search of Jekic's Perth address, and although he was initially helpful, he soon became difficult and refused to go to the station for questioning. When cannabis was allegedly found in his pocket, he was arrested and taken to Police Headquarters. While police believed Jekic was responsible for the stabbing of Meneghini, 'they did not have enough evidence to arrest him'.[38] Jekic was charged for possession of cannabis. During his trial for cannabis possession, Victoria Police had another reliable witness in the court room who sighted Jekic, and adamantly maintained Jekic was not the Air India attacker. Ultimately, no conviction for the Air India stabbing was ever made.

Threats, warrants and visas

Two days after the stabbing of Meneghini, there was a series of claims and threats. Apparently, on the same day AM claimed responsibility for the theft of Australian Army munitions, bomb threats were made to Red Hill Primary School in Canberra, where the children of Indian diplomats were students. Another threat was made to Air India, with callers claiming they would hijack a flight out of Sydney. Both of these threats were unrealised. Despite that, the Air India stabbing had re-energised awareness of the threat, and Australian agencies began collaborating with international counterparts regarding the UPRF and AM. Attorney-General Peter Durack permitted a telephone intercept warrant on 19 December 1977 on an AM member, even though only two months earlier ASIO deputy-director Harvey Barnett had objected to that same measure. The perception of the Ananda Marga threat was changing.

Three previous Cabinet decisions had attempted to handle the growing AM problem. The first, around 4 October 1977, was a suspension of consideration of AM's requests for official recognition or financial assistance; the second continued that suspension. AM members, or people actively involved with the organisation, were banned from entering Australia from around 20 December 1977.[39] AM members were also denied citizenship applications. It was soon realised that three AM schools in Australia were in receipt of Commonwealth assistance to the value of $46,000, while eight individuals were registered AM celebrants. All financial support and recognition to the schools was cut off immediately, and the celebrants deregistered.[40]

While these were perhaps easy fixes, there was a real problem regarding visa applications. In a memo to ASIO, the Australian Embassy in Washington DC pointed out that 'in practice there is very little that can be done to establish whether a visa applicant is a member of A.M.'[41] The senior liaison officer in Washington reinforced this, noting that migration officers had no indicators to assess if applicants were Margis; some migration officers were not

Henry O'Farrell was a member of an Australian Fenian Circle, an Irish terrorist network that executed targeted attacks against British interests around the world. He would become Australia's first terrorist when he attempted to assassinate Prince Alfred in 1868. SLNSW

Prince Alfred was attending a Sailors' Home Picnic at Clontarf wharf when he was shot in the back by Henry O'Farrell. The crowd nearly lynched the would-be assassin, who only survived due to the actions of police. SLNSW

Two university students burn their national service registration cards at a rally in 1966 in protest of forced conscription to fight in the Vietnam War. The unpopularity of the war and conscription policies created the impetus for left-wing extremism centred around university campuses. *The Age*

The widespread opposition to the Vietnam War and subsequent conscription policies was evident at the Vietnam Moratorium in Melbourne in May 1970. Extreme left-wing cells were rumoured to be present at these marches, forming Battle Cadres to protect leaders and counter police. Bruce Postle/ *The Age*

Police inspect the damage left by the bombing of a Yugoslav travel centre in Melbourne in 1975, which was undertaken by Ustaša terrorism. The Ustaša targeted Yugoslav interests around the world as part of their campaign for an independent Croatia. *The Age*

A large bomb detonated in front of the Yugoslav Consulate in Melbourne in 1970, severely damaging the building and many of the surrounding premises. Prominent Ustaša extremists were believed to be responsible.
Peter Mayoh/ *The Age*

A 1970s Chrysler Valiant contained a timed IED. It detonated under the Jewish Hakoah Club in 1982, in coordination with another bomb outside the Israeli Consulate in Sydney. Representatives of Israel had long been a target of pro-Palestinian terrorism. NSW Police Force

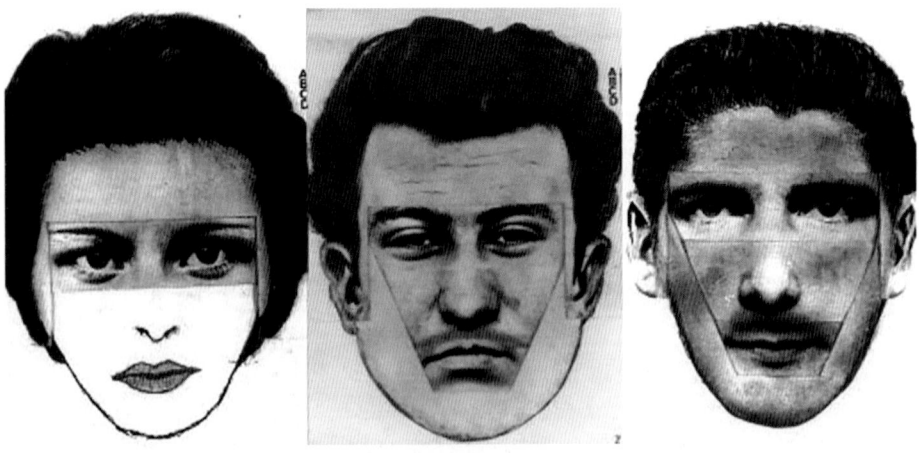

Police released an identikit image of the suspects involved in the bombing of the Hakoah Club and the Israeli Consulate in 1982. It was believed that pro-Palestinian terrorists were behind the attack. NSW Police Force

A Margi protests peacefully in 1978. Ananda Marga was a religious sect that primarily engaged in peaceful protest seeking to secure the freedom of their imprisoned guru, Prabhat Sarkar. W. Gibson/*SMH*

On 13 February 1978 the Hilton Hotel was bombed by suspected Margis, killing three people and injuring eleven. It was believed that a violent sect had emerged within the ranks of Ananda Marga and had perpetrated the attack. Rick Stevens/*SMH*

Sarik Ariyak, the Turkish consul-general to Australia in 1980, is pictured here with his wife. She and their daughter were both witnesses to his assassination outside their Sydney home. This was part of a worldwide assassination campaign by the Justice Commandos of the Armenian Genocide. *SMH*

Police officers stand near the car of Engin Sever. Sever was the bodyguard of Turkish consul-general Sarik Ariyak, and shared his fate in the 1980 slayings. His car, much like Ariyak's, was left riddled with bullets. The perpetrators have never been convicted. *SMH*

Australian members of the German Nazi Party stand in front of the Nazi Party flag in Tanunda, South Australia around 1935. Australia was home to many Nazis at a time when fascism was surging in popularity. NAA

The German Club in Perth celebrates Adolf Hitler's 50th birthday on 20 April 1939. German clubs around Australia were co-opted by many organisations serving the Third Reich. Hitler's birthday is still celebrated today by neo-Nazis. NAA

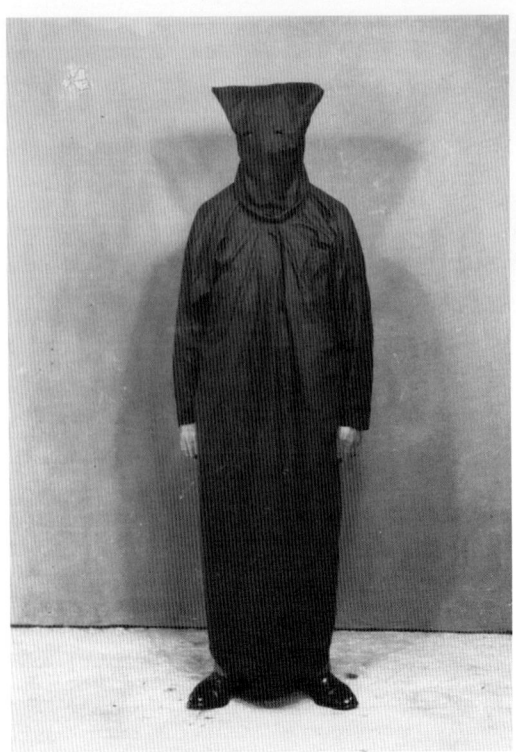

The New Guard—and the more secretive internal sect The Association—was one of the early iterations of white supremacy in Australia. This costume was worn by members in the 1930s, shortly before they disbanded. NAA

Detectives inspect the damage left by a firebombing at the Man Lin restaurant in 1988. It was executed by the Australian Nationalist Movement as part of a greater plan to drive people of Asian descent out of Perth—an essential element of their quest for an all-white Australia. Bell Publishing

trained to question applicants about AM; there were no provisions in existing visa questions about AM associations; and 70 per cent of visas were issued by mail, with the individuals never actually sighted by migration officers.

Beyond this, travellers between Australia and New Zealand did not require a passport, and didn't have to complete an incoming passenger card. This was raised as a national security issue by the Department of Labour and Immigration as early as 29 July 1974.[42] The department claimed quite rightfully that this created a problem for intelligence insofar as it was a gap in the stones of Fortress Australia. Strangely, the Department of Immigration opposed attempts to institute visa requirements for direct-transit passengers, arguing that it would add considerably to their workloads. This weakness in the system would not be fixed until jihadists flew airplanes into the World Trade Center in 2001. It is likely that the loophole was exploited by the leadership of AM, who could effectively use New Zealand as a backdoor into Australia from anywhere else in the world.

The visa ban was not only difficult to apply, it was also easy to avoid, as it was well established that AM members travelled under aliases. This would lead to the next event. On 1 January 1978, Air India Flight 855 took off from Bombay, carrying 213 passengers. Four minutes after take-off, the airplane crashed into the sea 3 kilometres from the airstrip, killing all 190 passengers and 23 crew. The official story was that wing failure had caused the crash. A document sent to ASIO's 'Scorpion Melbourne' telegraphic address, however, told a different story: 'That Air India officials in Perth are satisfied that the Bombay crash was the result of sabotage—the story of wing failure has been advanced for purely commercial reasons by Air India in an effort to minimise potential passenger fears.'[43] Air India also retrieved the black box, which confirmed that the Boeing 747 was functioning normally when the crash was triggered by an explosion in the centre fuselage. It was surmised to be the work of the transnational network aiming for the freedom of Sarkar.

Western Australian police suspected that Australians may have had something to do with the attack. The wife of a noteworthy AM leader had taken a flight from New Delhi to Bombay around the same time as Flight 855. She was in Bombay airport at the time of the crash, and caught the next available flight back to Perth, Australia,[44] although no connections to the doomed Flight 855 were ever proven. She was nonetheless denied normal entry to Perth airport, but eventually allowed temporary entry only because her children were waiting for her.[45] During this time, Abhiik Kumar was also in India. It is not known when he had departed Australia, but it was believed that he would not return.

In the midst of this, three new militant factions with affiliations with the AM sect were emerging. One was the Voluntary Social Service (VSS), which specialised in training young men in paramilitary and guerrilla activities under the guise of relief work. It was thought to have been established in Australia in 1978, and was coordinated through the VSS Global Headquarters in Manila. The VSS was a uniformed organisation, with military discipline and rank structures. Members undertook training with crossbows, and in unarmed combat and first aid. All senior AM members were required to undertake VSS training, and some even theorised that VSS provided security services for senior AM leaders.[46] One analyst working on the VSS argued that the AM shouldn't be underestimated as a 'bunch of hippies'; while AM was cultivating a harmless public image, the VSS was developing its paramilitary and terrorist capabilities.[47]

The VSS had a female equivalent in the Girls Seva Dal (GSD), sometimes referred to as the Girls Volunteers. The GSD, another AM front, was considered a feminist training camp, where members were preparing to assist armed forces in times of emergency. The camp was located on the western outskirts of Sydney, and the women were photographed dressed in combat fatigues and army boots, and engaging in paramilitary exercises. It was suspected that the training included the use of firearms. When the camp was raided well after the heyday of AM in 1985, it was assessed as a low-level threat.⁴⁸ The UPRF and the VSS were deemed far more likely to engage in violence.

To that end, ASIO provided an assessment to Cabinet on AM at the start of 1978, stating

> while Sarkar, the founder and leader of Ananda Marga, remains alive and in prison in India, isolated but dangerous acts of violence will continue to be directed against Indian establishments and officials in Australia by individual Ananda Marga members, perhaps describing themselves as belonging to the UPRF. Further violence ought to be anticipated should Sarkar die in prison.⁴⁹

This assessment was reinforced in early January 1978, when factions of the UPRF/AM released a pamphlet called 'The Way of Peace: A Recipe for Revolution', which outlined a strategy for violence.

In response, authorities recommended 'a blanket rejection for visas for all foreign AM members entering Australia in view of the forthcoming international AM conference in Australia and the visit of Mr Desai in February 1978'.⁵⁰ Already, there were concerns for the Indian prime minister and his upcoming visit to Australia. Desai was visiting NSW to attend the Commonwealth Heads of Government Regional Meeting (CHOGRM). The visa ban became inextricable from CHOGRM, documents noting that 'the reason for the imposition of the ban is to ensure the security of the heads of Commonwealth countries (including the Indian PM Desai) attending a meeting in Sydney in early February, 1978'.⁵¹

The ban was a good idea, but once again was based on the same flawed assumption that domestic terrorism in Australia came from elsewhere rather than from within, that it wasn't perpetrated by Australian citizens. This time, like so many others, the terrorists were already here waiting, and in February 1978 they claimed three innocent lives.

The Hilton tragedy

CHOGRM was a biennial offshoot of the greater Commonwealth Heads of Government Meeting (CHOGM). Although CHOGRM no longer exists, its original aim was to enable cooperation between governments on matters of regional interest, and reinforce connections between India and Australia, and with smaller Pacific nations. The meeting was attended by twelve Asian and South Pacific Commonwealth nations. Prime Minister Desai attended, as did leaders and dignitaries from, among others, New Zealand, Fiji, Tonga, Sri Lanka, Malaysia, Singapore, Bangladesh, Nauru, Samoa and Papua New Guinea. Each brought their own agenda, spanning security issues such as the drug trade and international terrorism, industry protectionism, trade, and renewable resources. At this CHOGRM, a Singaporean-led working group wanted to explore ways international cooperation could better counter the international terrorist threat.

With so many potential targets, it was a matter of national significance to keep dignitaries safe. Security was divided between Australia's relevant agencies: Compol undertook close personal protection of dignitaries; NSW Police was responsible for the hotel's external security and most of its internal security; and ASIO completed audio counter-measures before the meeting, although they had no personnel on the ground. Despite this united front, some believed the Hilton Hotel security was 'still far from stringent'.[52] Police checked ID cards at the door, but visitors were not searched or subjected to X-ray or explosive checks, despite the facility having been installed in the foyer. One journalist claimed he managed to bluff his way past police right up to the eighth floor, while another man simply ignored police orders to halt and walked through to the hotel's shopping arcade.

CHOGRM was scheduled to begin on Monday, 13 February 1978. The dignitaries arrived on schedule, and everything appeared to be going (relatively) to plan. That lasted for all of three hours: at 12.40 p.m. the explosives detonated in the city council garbage truck. The confined spaces of the rubbish compactor magnified the blast force, which in turn magnified its destructive power. In this case, the explosive force was directed outwards, tearing the thick metal asunder, expanding the blast radius, claiming the lives of three innocent men, and injuring eleven bystanders.

First responders immediately, and correctly, assumed that the real targets were the attendees of CHOGRM. Prime Minister Malcolm Fraser made the swift decision to relocate the dignitaries to a rural retreat in Bowral, New South Wales, bringing the schedule forward by several days. The military was called in to escort the dignitaries. This required an Executive Council minute, duly signed by Governor-General Sir Zelman Cowan, which overturned decades of previous practice in Australia, by which police and civilian agencies—not the military—maintained domestic order.[53] Some found the legality of military intervention questionable. In several earlier cases, however, Commonwealth support had been requested by states to curb domestic violence.

In these cases, neither the Constitution nor the Defence Act were invoked: in practice, it was based on the request of the minister responsible. Under Section 119 of the Constitution, the military can be deployed domestically, but only when a state requests assistance from the Commonwealth to restrain domestic violence and is supported by the governor-general under Section 51 of the Defence Act; or when the Commonwealth government needs to protect Commonwealth interests (in sum, to protect itself, rather than to protect the state in question). While the agreement of the state was not mandatory, it was considered unlikely to occur without state cooperation.[54] Despite the support of New South Wales, Fraser took the latter avenue to deploy the military domestically.

Decorated Vietnam veterans Brigadier David Butler and Lieutenant-Colonel Murray Blake were given the command of 2000 troops, drawn from Holsworthy base west of Sydney. Before the Executive Council minute was even signed, four army helicopters had reconnoitred Bowral. By 6.30 a.m. the following morning, 800 troops were securing the town, searching drains, bins and hedges, while others secured the Hume Highway and the Sydney–Melbourne railway. A VIP train left Sydney as a decoy, while some dignitaries were conveyed in Chinook helicopters. Others were moved by car, including Desai, escorted by fifteen police motorcycles and five escort cars each. Two Iroquois helicopters carrying snipers escorted each vehicle group. Journalists were put on a bus and told they would be taken to the train: it was another ruse, as the bus travelled the 130 kilometres to Bowral nonstop. In rural areas, soldiers were stationed along the road every 500 metres; in urban areas, soldiers were stationed every 30–40 metres.[55] Up to 45 armoured personnel carriers were positioned along the route.

This activity was taken at the significant personal risk of military personnel. At the time, no one knew what the legal repercussions would be if they were compelled to use lethal force. It was only a month later that the Attorney-General's Department released clarification on the judicial rights and duties of Australian Defence Force (ADF) personnel when aiding a civil power. Because martial law was not declared, all activity by the ADF was subject to common law. While the ADF had legal authority to 'take whatever steps were necessary, including the use of reasonable force', ADF members were personally responsible, under common law, for any excessive force used.[56] In the event, such force was not required; the CHOGRM diplomats made it to the retreat without incident, and the meeting continued.

Back in Sydney, rubble lined the streets. Bodies lay in morgues. Blood dried on the pavement. Investigators were faced with a crime scene for which there was no precedent in Australia. There were numerous potential targets for attacks, from Singapore to Malaysia to India. NSW Police and Compol joined forces for a shared investigation. They sought witnesses and offered a $100,000 reward for information. In particular, they sought information about a young woman who was seen carrying a cardboard box near the hotel twelve hours before the explosion. One witness said he met the girl, who called herself Penny. She was a New Zealander there to protest abortion (which was odd given it was not a high-priority CHOGRM agenda item), and requested that the witness show her the Hilton.[57] Although Penny was ultimately cleared, it must be remembered that New Zealand too had an Ananda Marga sect that was prone to violence.

Two days after the Hilton Hotel bombing, three AM members were arrested in Bangkok in possession of explosives, thwarted in the process of planning a bombing. Two of the members were Australian. All three were believed to have recently spent time with Abhiik Kumar, who was attending an AM Conference in Kathmandu to the north. His links to the Bangkok bombers were considered highly suspicious.[58] When Compol officers travelled to Bangkok to question the Australians, they quickly realised that the Margis believed Compol was complicit with Indian intelligence, supposedly engineering a conspiracy to destroy AM.

Ten days after the Hilton Hotel bombing, on 23 February, ASIO provided another minute to Cabinet in which it reaffirmed earlier statements that AM violence was likely part of an internationally coordinated effort rather than coincidental or imitative violence. It had, however, been unable to prove its hypothesis that a secret group of leaders within the broader AM movement was responsible for the violence. ASIO reported that it had 'no information which would link AM to the Hilton bombing incident on February 13th. However, the possibility cannot be ignored and ASIO continues to monitor the Movement as closely as possible.'[59] No one, it seemed, had the answer so dearly sought.

As time went on, the conviction that AM/UPRF were involved grew and newspapers reported that the sect was under suspicion. AM itself was also complicating the investigation. A Compol officer had a conversation with AM spokesperson Tim Anderson and Abhiik Kumar in Sydney on 31 March 1978. Instead of supporting the investigation to bring the killers to justice, Anderson and Kumar appear to have baited the police. They told the Compol officer that they had an AM agent in the Department of Defence in Sydney (a fact already known by both ASIO and NSW Police), and suggested that not only did they know the name of ASIO agents who had infiltrated AM but also that they had successfully converted them. Moreover, they claimed to be funded by ASIO itself. They blamed the Indian Embassy for the violence in Australia, and accused Compol of heavy-handedness against Australian Margis held after the Bangkok arrests.[60]

The investigators concluded that they needed someone on the inside of AM. Richard Seary—a former member of the Hare Krishna movement and soon to accrue historical infamy—became that someone. While Seary infiltrated the AM in the months following the Hilton attack on behalf of police, ASIO also penetrated the organisation with an agent of its own. This was in addition to phone taps, which indicated that AM members were becoming rather 'security conscious'.[61] A police telex sent in April 1978 suggested that AM in New South Wales was on the alert for 'agent penetration by police and security services'. The leaders of AM, moreover, made contingency plans should an agent be discovered: the 'case should be blown up in the media'.[62]

In fact, AM was successfully penetrated by both Seary and the ASIO agent. Seary soon made connections with three prominent AM leaders: Tim Anderson; Paul Shawn Alister, who once led AM in New Zealand; and Ross Anthony Dunn, believed to be the leader of PROUT in Australia. All three had undergone VSS training.[63] Seary ingratiated himself with this leadership team with surprising swiftness. Four months later, he was in a car with Alister and Dunn driving to the home of Robert Cameron, the Sydney leader of the National Front of Australia and former leader of the NSW Nazi Party. The plan was to bomb the residence, unaware they were under the observation of police.

The three men were quickly arrested in possession of a functional explosive device, comprising ten sticks of gelignite, a timing device and a detonator. It is odd, however, that such a well-made bomb was part of such a poor plan, given that Cameron had not lived at that residence for fifteen months. Seary told the arresting officers that Dunn and Alister had confessed to the Hilton bombing en route to Cameron's house. Anderson was also later arrested. All three suspects allegedly spoke freely of their crime in front of the detectives—and warned of further violence to come. This could never be proven, as none of the detectives had switched on the tape recorder.[64]

The ensuing investigation was plagued by claims that the attack was Seary's idea. Alister, Dunn and Anderson were charged with conspiring to murder Robert Cameron, and the attempted murder and attempted grievous bodily harm of the arresting officers: Detectives Burke, Gilligan, Godden and Summerfield. Immediately following the men's arrest on 20 June 1978, AM released a statement to the press. Among other claims of harassment and AM victimisation, it stated that the arrests were 'clearly a further step in the increasing harassment of Ananda Marga by Commonwealth and State police and a part of their on-going campaign to discredit and destroy Ananda Marga in Australia'. It continued: 'According to Mr Anderson, the State Police are carrying out a personal vendetta against him at the same time as endeavouring to further discredit Ananda Marga. He states that since his arrest a number of death threats have been made against him by police officers and that he has been bashed while in custody of CIB detectives.'[65] The statement further suggested that any trial of the members would likely be biased. While in prison, the defendants claimed that they were denied contact with their spiritual adviser, Acarya Abhiik Kumar.

Although they were convicted in conjunction with the testimony of Seary, this was later considered unverifiable. Their conviction was overturned in 1985, and they were released. Seary later published an ebook called *Smoke 'n' Mirrors*, detailing his undercover experiences.

The commissioner's garden

The Indian High Commission in Canberra had been a focal point for AM attacks before the Hilton bombing, and was the scene of another incident a little over a month after the bombing. The head of Protective Services, A.P. Fleming, reported to Compol that back on 20 March 1978, two vehicles containing eight AM members had pulled into the driveway of the High Commission and parked near the front door. The contingent was led by Tim Anderson and Julian van Towsey, the mastermind behind a new secret code AM used to communicate. Police responded to the incident, although it took them a significant amount of time to convince Anderson and his crew to leave.

This episode cannot be divorced from what followed: one week later, an attempted bombing took place. On 27 March 1978, an ACT police constable was patrolling the back fence of the Indian High Commissioner's residence when he detected a bomb made of gelignite and hidden in a canvas bag, complete with an alarm clock attached to the detonator. The clock had been set for just after 3 p.m. A second bomb was discovered nearby in the Commissioner's garden. The Indian High Commissioner, Jagdish Ajmani, noted that he received two phone calls that afternoon, at about 3.10 p.m., and on both occasions the caller hung up after hearing Ajmani's name. He believed the calls were from AM.

AM members in Australia suggested that the Indian High Commissioner planted the bomb in his own garden to frame the AM. This claim was ridiculed by Ajmani, given it could have harmed his own family. Further investigations revealed that the bomb was planted by a man and woman who had been cycling past. The man was described as 180 centimetres tall with black hair. The woman was slight with shoulder-length brown hair. Despite this lead, the investigation failed to progress, plagued by rumours of rivalry between ACT Police and Compol, with one ACT Police official claiming that Compol was not 'adequately trained or equipped' to handle such situations. Moreover, its officers had apparently 'shown ineptitude' on 28 March 1978, when a young man hanged himself in the residence of the first secretary of the Indian High Commission. These comments may stem from bitterness that Compol did not notify ACT Police of the High Commission bomb until four hours after it was discovered. No charges were ever laid for this attempt.

Code for peach?

Four to five months after the Hilton bombing, Compol obtained a copy of the AM codebook, and a letter between Julian van Towsey and Paul Alister explaining how it worked. The code had three parts: a numbered list of letters and words; a list of codes that related to each letter; and an alphabetical list of codes and numbers. The development and exploitation of this code could indicate two possibilities: that the AM in Australia had developed a siege mentality; or that it was engaging in clandestine activity it didn't want intercepted. Towsey instructed Alister to eat the instructions with his breakfast muesli. So much for AM's dietary restrictions!

'In this way,' explained Towsey, 'if it is intercepted by the enemy, they would never get the whole code, only part of it.'[66]

While there was a list of AM devotional words, other codes suggested the increased securitisation of the group. TAB meant 'Commonwealth Police', while TCF meant 'Commonwealth Police are here'. TEZ meant 'ASIO are here', and TJK 'do not come here'. The code listed a surprising collection of words, some of which beg the question as to how much they were used: while AJG for 'self-defence', BNJ for 'destroy' and BGY for 'counter-revolutionary' were likely used often, one can only wonder at BII for 'crocodile', FUW for 'peach', or DIC for 'lick'. Breaking the code, however, did not appear to break the Hilton case.

Between 1978 and 1979, an ASIO agent in AM reported that leftover explosives from the Hilton attack were hidden in a storage locker at Macquarie University. This intelligence was shared with NSW Police, who searched the lockers but turned up nothing of interest. Two years later, a storage locker at the University of New South Wales was opened due to unpaid fees. There, an unsuspecting staffer called Patricia Elson found a black duffel bag packed with gelignite, detonators, breaker switches, gloves and batteries.[67] The locker was leased in the name of a student-turned-midshipman then aboard HMAS *Melbourne*. Historian Rachel Landers' investigation suggested that the student was a drug addict who traded his student card for collateral. It is possible that the card ended up in the hands of AM; shortly thereafter, forensic experts were able to link the locker cache to several other AM bombs.[68]

In 1989, eleven years after the Hilton attack, AM member Evan Dunstan Pederick confessed to the crime. Pederick had once told a fellow Margi: 'Do not worry about killing people—you kill flies and ants and cockroaches so don't worry about people and should people be on the run from police for killing others then they should be sheltered from the police and the police should be given false leads.'[69] With this grim perspective in mind, Pederick described his bomb as containing twenty sticks of gelignite and capable of being detonated by a radio-control signal. He was targeting Prime Minister Desai, but he attempted detonation when Fraser was greeting the Sri Lankan prime minister—apparently unaware of what his target even looked like. The device failed to function, and Pederick left town. Eleven hours later, the bomb detonated when disturbed by the garbage truck. All of this, he alleged, was in conjunction with Tim Anderson. Pederick was convicted and sentenced to twenty years, while Anderson was later found not guilty on appeal. Pederick was released after eight years because of Anderson's acquittal.

Several books have since been published, seeking either to indict or exonerate the people thought to be involved in the Hilton attack. In 1986, Tom Molomby mounted a vigorous defence of Anderson, Alister and Dunn in *Spies, Bombs and the Path of Bliss*. Paul Alister himself published *Bombs, Bliss and Baba* in 1997, in which he said he 'felt God to be by his side' throughout the trial. Tim Anderson also wrote in his own defence in *Free Alister, Dunn and Anderson*. The most noteworthy account of the Hilton attack, however, was presented by historian Rachel Landers. In their official history of ASIO during this period, *The Secret Cold War*, John Blaxland and Rhys Crawley, who enjoyed extensive access to ASIO records, described her account as 'contentious and fascinating', but stopped short of taking a position on whether her history was accurate: 'While Landers' account does not necessarily accord with the ASIO records, it nevertheless presents another important angle on the case.'[70] Lander's investigation pointed the finger at the leader of AM in Australia, Abhiik Kumar, although ASIO records were not entirely clear on this front. He denied the allegation.[71]

The Hilton Hotel terrorist attack remains a riddle to the general public. Conspiracies abound regarding the role of the police, the military and ASIO in the attack—with regard to either their actions or inaction. Some have even gone so far as to imply that ASIO orchestrated the attack in order to enhance its powers, but similarly contentious claims have been made about the military in light of their domestic deployment.

Path to freedom

The AM presented a caring mask to the community, professing its innocence and pointing emphatically to its good deeds. Many, no doubt, were law-abiding people who were deeply committed to Sarkar's peaceful objectives. Most of the members grew fruit in orchards, studied, meditated and sought to achieve internal mastery in pursuit of bliss. Their work in the community, and their reputations, were sabotaged repeatedly by high-ranking members of the AM/UPRF nexus, who gloried in destruction. They too wore caring masks, but behind them they hid twisted goals, and used threats, intimidation, disruption and death to achieve their ends.

These extreme elements did not seem to care who was caught in the crossfire of their ambitions. On 12 June 1978, for example, AM made a death threat against a Senior Constable Fyfe due to his involvement in arresting senior AM members at a demonstration in 1976, and subsequent AM claims that he committed perjury in their court cases. Then on 4 July 1978, the navy's Lieutenant Andrew Michael Stackpool received a threatening phone call from the UPRF telling him he was on the AM 'kill list'. Stackpool, at the time, was working with the Department of Defence at Russell Offices, in Canberra, and was aware of the AM movement and the PROUTist threat.[72]

So what brought an end to the skirmish that Ananda Marga devotees had initiated in Australia? Sarkar, the man they worshipped, was finally released from prison. He and his co-defendants had long stated publicly that they would achieve freedom through legal measures rather than violence or terrorism. Their case made it to the Patna High Court in July 1978, and their appeals were upheld. It was learned that the prosecution had rested its case on a single, unreliable witness, Madhwanand Awadhoot. Then there was the issue of the bodies. Of the six victims, only three were positively identified, two were unidentifiable, and the sixth was never found. Sarkar and his co-defendants were set free.

The violence was over—or so it seemed. The religious sect remained, but in Australia its appeal began to wane. Intelligence agents attributed this to four things: first, the imprisonment and deportation of senior AM members; second, Abhiik Kumar, aka Jason Alexander, had weakened the organisation as a whole; third, older and steadier AM members had left the group; and fourth, the organisation was in the hands of younger, less experienced members who were unable to provide the leadership that senior members had demonstrated.[73]

AM also did little to help itself or its public image. On 16 August 1978, Roger Lindsay Thompson, a member of AM, threw pamphlets into the Press Gallery of Parliament House. A few days later, on 23 August 1978, an AM member stashed a fake bomb inside Kings Hall, Parliament House, where it was discovered by an ACT police officer. Alongside the bomb was an inactive alarm clock, 200 pamphlets identical to those thrown by Thompson, and a strip of saffron cloth. AM members claimed responsibility. It was known that Abhiik Kumar and other AM were in Canberra that day, driving in a Queensland-registered vehicle.

Abhiik Kumar was demoted from his rank of spiritual director of the Australasian sector towards the end of 1979, and was transferred to administer a sports club in Europe. Peter Athos became the new spiritual director, and his leadership was seen as moderate. He guided the group back towards Sarkar's more peaceful tenets, and the group began supporting a range of causes such as feminism, environmentalism and Aboriginal land rights.[74]

Upon his release, Sarkar undertook a worldwide tour of AM communities in 1979. Despite months of lobbying by adherents in Australia, his visa was categorically denied. Twenty-five AM members threatened to starve themselves to death in protest of this decision, but no fatalities are recorded. Following this, Compol received threats from someone with an Indian accent claiming that there would 'be problems at the airport and that AM were planning something crazy on Air India'.⁷⁵ Again, no attack eventuated. Instead, there was a slew of bomb hoaxes in protest of Sarkar's visa situation. ASIO in Melbourne informed Compol of three bomb hoaxes around March 1979. On 26 March 1979, at 4.11 p.m., a man rang police headquarters in Sydney and claimed that AM had hidden a bomb on Town Hall Station Platform 2. At 4.16 p.m., a man rang Bankstown Station saying there was a bomb hidden on the 4.48 p.m. Lithgow train, to detonate between Blacktown and Penrith. At 4.23 p.m., a man rang Bankstown Station again and said the same thing, except that the bomb would explode between St Marys and Blacktown. No explosions occurred, and police searches yielded no devices.⁷⁶

Aside from these hoaxes, things appeared to quiet down in Australia until the return of Kerry Susan Ping (also known as Kerry Lawrence).⁷⁷ Described in ASIO documents as a radical feminist, Ping was an AM member who returned to Australia from India sometime in 1980. She established a clandestine group known as the New Humanist Society, or NHS. Its aims were to accelerate society towards revolution through violent agitation: this, it was suggested, would lead to global worship of the Sadvipras—the enlightened AM elite.⁷⁸ Sarkar was the nominal head of the NHS, and it was believed that his bodyguard, Pajnath Pandey, was involved in its early formation. Organisationally, NHS fell under the remit of Sovan Sinha, the global secretary of the VSS. Sinha attended NHS meetings, and was involved in the conduct of its activities—at the very least, to ensure they were in accordance with both AM and Sarkar.

According to now-public ASIO documents, Ping successfully recruited about fifteen AM adherents to NHS, and together they engaged in paramilitary training. This included the use of firearms, explosives, knife fighting, unarmed combat and other security techniques. Some members were believed to have purchased high-powered rifles. There were also rumours that Sinha requested that Australian NHS members acquire poisons, although there is no evidence of this forming part of an attack. Ping's phone was tapped and her mail monitored.

In September 1981, as Australia was due to host CHOGM, ASIO had reason to believe that violence was a real possibility. As a result, thirteen Ananda Marga houses were raided by law enforcement, which yielded a couple of handguns, literature and a floor plan of the Melbourne Wentworth Hotel, the scheduled venue of CHOGM.[79] NHS members were also found in possession of the *Anarchist Cookbook*, a bankbook with a balance of $100,000, and a large quantity of AM literature. Finally, there were numerous newspaper cuttings regarding the Hilton Hotel bombing in 1978, and security arrangements for the imminent CHOGM.[80] The raids served as a deterrent, and no attack by NHS eventuated. Following the raids and resultant publicity, along with censure by Peter Athos and condemnation of violence by Sarkar himself, the NHS disbanded in May 1982.

A troubled legacy

The AM had spread to Australia wearing a respectable face and, for the most part, its adherents sought to improve themselves and their communities. But a group of extremists within the organisation had turned to violence, hiding their actions from their fellows, and engaging in a terrorism campaign against Indian institutions in Australia. The organisation as a whole, instead of uniting with Australian society and authorities to uncover killers in their midst, closed around them and harboured terrorists who considered the death of innocents an acceptable price for the freedom of their guru.

For all that, the UPRF terrorism did not achieve the release of Sarkar. All it did was harm the innocent and turn people away from the broader AM movement. The conspiracies that then developed around the Hilton attack served to expose the fault lines within the counterterrorism community and damaged the trust Australians placed in their national security institutions. The violence at the heart of AM ideology was partly responsible for the actions and behaviours of its constituents, and allowed them to feel justified in terrorising, injuring and murdering their fellow citizens.

The activities associated with AM did, however, have a marked impact on Australia's national security apparatus. Demand for a review of Compol was strong in 1977, driven in part by the Hilton Hotel bombing. In the aftermath, the Fraser government ordered a review into Australia's security services, including Compol and ACT Police, and invited Sir Robert Mark of the United Kingdom to undertake that review. Mark was a highly decorated and distinguished policeman known for rooting out corruption in the police force, and had vowed to 'arrest more criminals than we employ'.[81] This earned him the nickname the 'Lone Ranger of Leicester'.

The results of the Mark report were tabled in federal parliament on 14 April 1978. It was Mark's view that ACT Police and Compol should be replaced with a new, single organisation, which he called the Australian Federal Police This new force would have six primary responsibilities: policing the ACT, investigating infringements of Commonwealth law, training and coordination for counterterrorism activities, Special Branch duties and coordination with state special branches, escorting VIPs, and the security of airports. He also mandated that the AFP be equipped with explosives experts and bomb dogs, forensics and analysts.

This legislation to amalgamate Compol and ACT Police and create the AFP, however unpopular, was tabled on 10 May 1979 and passed in June. Mark was offered command of the AFP but refused, stating that 'no consultant should benefit from his own recommendations'.[82] Instead, Sir Colin Woods, who had overseen the amalgamation, became the first commissioner of the AFP. Woods was another British career policeman who had spent time in every single division of Scotland Yard during his 30 years on the force. His résumé and qualifications were impressive, but this did not excuse his crime of being an Englishman. Ted Innes of the ALP went so far as to declare that the appointment 'reeks of colonialism'.[83] The early days of Woods's command largely involved calming hysteria about jurisdictions, at which he was largely successful. The new force became active in October 1979 and remains to the current day.

6

Promise of vengeance: pro-Armenian terrorism

It was 17 December 1980. A 500cc Honda motorcycle, recently spray-painted black, waited with engine humming on a quiet street of an affluent coastal Sydney suburb. It carried two riders wearing dark helmets and one held a pistol close. As darkly clad as the motorbike and its passengers were, their plan was darker still.

At 9.45 a.m., the Turkish consul-general, Sarik Ariyak, walked out the front door of his home in Dover Heights in Sydney's eastern suburbs. His bodyguard, Engin Sever, was parked opposite his house—as always. Sever had been hired a year earlier following threats on Ariyak's life. He had a successful career in security behind him, and was familiar with the neighbourhood and the consul-general's routine. Sever waited in his car and watched as Ariyak climbed into his own vehicle. The consul-general liked to drive himself, and Sever would follow in his own car. It was what they always did.

Unknown to Sever, the black motorcycle and its riders kicked into action. It roared up the street and pulled to a halt beside Sever's vehicle. The pillion passenger dismounted and raised their pistol, firing several times at close range. Sever did not see it coming: within seconds he was slumped in his seat, dead. The assassin then calmly walked over to the consul-general's car. They raised their pistol again and opened fire, riddling Ariyak's body with bullets. The Turkish consul-general in Australia was dead.

The assassin turned and remounted the motorcycle behind their partner and the motorcycle roared off down the streets of Dover Heights. Behind them, they left two dead bodies, twelve 9-millimetre bullet casings, and numerous witnesses including two shocked schoolboys who had watched the killings from their bus stop. The motorcycle was found 2 kilometres away, padlocked to a pole, leaving no indication of where the assassins had gone.

In the hours after the slayings, as the international media was slowly waking up, an anonymous male caller made a claim of responsibility to the press:

> I have a very important message. Please don't interrupt. I am speaking on behalf of the Justice Commandos of the Armenian Genocide. We have just shot the Turkish Consul in Sydney. The operation falls within the bounds of our revolutionary movement which started in 1975 with acts by our commandos in Vienna, Rome, Madrid, Paris and the Vatican. The attack was in retaliation for the injustices done to the Armenians by the Turks in 1915. Our attacks are aimed at Turkish diplomats and Turkish institutions. We will strike again. I repeat, we are the Justice Commandos of the Armenian Genocide.[1]

The consul-general was the eighteenth Turkish diplomat to be assassinated in a worldwide campaign. Pro-Armenian terrorism, which had left bodies scattered around the world since 1973, had finally made it to Australia.

The Armenian cause

The various terrorist groups advancing the Armenian cause did not speak in riddles: they made their grievances and intentions very obvious. In 1915, the Armenian people in the Ottoman Empire (later Turkey) were the victims of a coordinated extermination campaign: the first genocide of the twentieth century. It occurred in three waves. The first, engineered by police chief Ismail Canbolat, involved the mass arrest, deportation and murder of prominent Armenian intellectuals around 24 April 1915. The second was permitted by the Three Pashas of the Ottoman Empire, Grand Vizier Talaat Pasha, Enver Pasha and Jemal Pasha, within the context of World War I, where all able-bodied Armenian males were rounded up and forced to the front lines as labourers, soldiers and cannon fodder. Simultaneously, the third phase involved gathering the women, children and elderly, and forcing them on so-called Death Marches into the Syrian Desert, where they were raped, abused and left for dead on the roadside. More than a million Armenian men, women and children died.

The genocide of the Armenian people is a contentious topic: after World War I, the new Turkish government refused to acknowledge it. There was a series of half-hearted war crimes trials in Turkey, but a disappointingly small number of people were actually condemned, much less convicted. Many architects of the genocide fled Turkey, and began new and successful lives abroad. Their new host countries, more often than not, refused to extradite them to stand trial, allowing them to escape prosecution and continue their lives around the world. Justice for the Armenian people seemed distant. In frustration, the socialist Armenian Revolutionary Federation (ARF), known as the Dashnaksutyun or Dashnak Party, launched Operation Nemesis in the early 1920s. This has been described by terrorism historians as one of 'the very rare instances of a terrorist undertaking to avenge the annihilation of a people and to right a wrong'.[2]

Under Operation Nemesis, the architects of the genocide were hunted down wherever they were hiding and eliminated. It began on 15 March 1921, when Talaat Pasha, the Grand Vizier of the Ottomans and the engineer of the genocide, was shot in the head on Hardenbergstrasse, Berlin. The assassin, a young Armenian who had lost his entire family in the war, was acquitted unanimously by a German jury. On 5 December 1921, Sayid Halim Pasha, the Grand Vizier who preceded Talaat Pasha and had signed papers ordering the mass deportation of Armenians, was shot in the head in Rome. His assassin was a 22-year-old who successfully evaded arrest. On 17 April 1922, Behaeddin Shakir, an organiser of the genocide, and Jemal Azmi, the 'Butcher of Trebizond', were shot dead in Berlin. On 21 July 1922, Jemal Pasha was shot dead in front of the Secret Police headquarters in Georgia. One by one, Operation Nemesis was working its way down a list.

For all its methodical nature, Operation Nemesis missed three targets. Ismail Canbolat, the former police chief of Constantinople who had arranged the extermination of Armenian intellectuals, escaped the wrath of Operation Nemesis through the good fortune of being hanged by President Kemal Atatürk in 1926 on conspiracy charges. Dr Nazim Bey, who arranged many deportations, was also hanged in 1926 for conspiring against Atatürk. The only one of the Three Pashas who escaped vengeance was Enver Pasha, who was killed on 4 August 1922 fighting the Bolsheviks in Bukhara. By and large, Operation Nemesis was a tactical success, but it was also a strategic failure. While the architects had been removed, the Armenian desire for recognition remained unfulfilled. The Armenian cause was at risk of being forgotten by a world eager to move past such horrors.

While justifying the genocide of European Jews twenty years later, Adolf Hitler himself said, 'Who, after all, speaks today about the annihilation of the Armenians?'[3] Who indeed? Following World War II, the mighty powers of the world were forced, a second time, to face the reality of genocide, this time engineered by Nazi Germany and its fascist allies around the world. For a moment, it seemed that recognition for the Armenian genocide was within reach, but this proved to be a false hope, and the decades passed with little change.

Many Armenians, by this point, had found homes in different nations around the world. They lived in Australia; in the former Armenian Republic of the USSR; in Beirut, Lebanon; and Los Angeles in the United States. While the world seemingly forgot, the Armenians, wherever they were in the world, remembered the magnitude of their loss. In the 1960s, mass demonstrations occurred, eventually leading to the installation of a genocide memorial in Yerevan, Armenia. Every year on 24 April, crowds gathered and laid wreaths in memory of the genocide. While this was a small win, it did not bring justice to the victims. Recognition had been actively denied them—and the United Nations proved itself incapable of tackling the issue. In 1973, for example, a United Nations Sub-Commission on the Promotion and Protection of Human Rights included a single paragraph on the Armenian genocide. Turkey opposed the paragraph, and it was subsequently removed from the report. Many were appalled by the United Nations' stance, construing it as supporting the powerful and privileged over the victims of injustice.

The Armenian situation simply needed a spark, and came through the actions of Gourgen Yanikian. Born in 1895 in Erzurum, once part of Armenia but now in Turkey, Yanikian had been studying at the University of Moscow when World War I broke out. He volunteered for the Russian Army in order to travel back to his family and homeland, then under Ottoman rule. Upon arrival at his family farm, he found that Turkish soldiers had killed two of his brothers and 24 members of his extended family. Yanikian survived the war and returned to his studies, eventually migrating to Iran, then to the United States. By 1972, he was living in California and writing letters urging the Armenian people to wage war on Turkey—to no avail.

On 27 January 1973, Yanikian, posing as an Iranian in possession of a stolen Ottoman painting, lured two Turkish diplomats to a hotel room. There, he shot them dead. He reported himself to the police and calmly confessed to the crime. The public prosecutor, David Minier, claimed that Yanikian's purpose was to create an Armenian Nuremberg and finally bring the world's attention to the genocide.[4] This did not happen. Instead, the attack spawned two separate yet interlinked terrorist organisations: the Armenian Secret Army for the Liberation of Armenia (ASALA) and the Justice Commandos of the Armenian Genocide (JCAG). These two organisations would carry out dozens of terrorist attacks around the world for the next decade. The targets were primarily Turkish diplomats, and few countries were immune.

Revolution and terror

The central trigger for the terrorism campaigns was recognition, but it brought with it a number of other essential expectations. The first was the restoration of the Armenian homeland, and the hope that the Armenian diaspora could lay sole claim to historic Armenian territory. The second was reparation to assist the survivors. The third was revenge, and the emotional solace and satisfaction that such an act would bring.

In these groups, much like other terrorism movements discussed in this book, extremism occurred within the shelter of a broader, peaceful community and movement. In all such groups, hidden insiders bound together with a deadly purpose and, strategically concealed—as Mao would say—as a fish in the shoal, were able to secure freedom of operations. This allowed them to pursue their goals without attracting obvious scrutiny. In the case of Australia, the broader Australian Armenian community was, by and large, peaceful and well integrated into wider society. Within this population was the ARF, which became the primary mouthpiece for Armenian will both domestically and internationally.

Founded in 1890 and determined to fight for the national self-determination of the Armenian people, the international ARF had been attempting to achieve recognition of the genocide for years without success. It had branches all around the world, including Los Angeles and Sydney. The Youth Federation (ARF-YF) was an offshoot of the main body. Neither of these two organisations were terrorist groups; they were activist organisations using peaceful tactics to achieve the desired change. Rogue members of the ARF-YF, however, despairing of peaceful processes, are thought likely to have also been members of terrorist organisations.

The ARF-YF was designed to represent the passionate Armenian youth, who were impatient for real change. In 1975, the first expression of this emotion manifested under the leadership of Hagop Hagopian and Hagop Darakjian, who established ASALA. This group soon became one of the most extreme factions championing the Armenian cause, and from 1975 onwards engaged in an increasingly violent and lethal terrorism campaign. Beyond its avowed goals, ASALA was a Marxist group and formed alliances with other like-minded terrorist groups at the time, such as the Kurdistan Workers' Party (PKK), with which it launched joint attacks. ASALA also claimed to work with Palestinian groups and radical left groups, such as the Italian Red Brigades and the Japanese Red Army.[5] It developed a disdain for other Armenian groups, despite having a common cause. ASALA claimed that the ARF was in bed with the CIA in an attempt to delegitimise the organisation.

Terrorist expert Laura Dugan has suggested that 'Rather than lose its young people to ASALA, ARF founded its own terrorist group', JCAG.[6] It is widely established that JCAG was an offshoot managed by the international ARF parent organisation, and indeed such links were also suspected in Australia, where organisations could not afford to lose the support of the youth.[7] The ARF-YF was haemorrhaging members, so JCAG was created as a lure to keep the young people where their elders could control their impulses.

Because of this internecine competition between the two new groups, JCAG hated ASALA just as much as ASALA hated JCAG. Much like ASALA, however, JCAG had established its headquarters in Beirut, where they called the nerve centre of the operation Piro (central bureau). Piro controlled, or at least connected, JCAG support cells and operatives around the world. Records of JCAG leadership are sketchy. Abraham Ago Ashjian was the leader of JCAG until he was assassinated by his fellow members for considering cooperation with ASALA in 1982. His successor, ironically, was then assassinated by ASALA.

The rivalry between ASALA and JCAG was bitter. They were driven half by a desire to kill Turks, and half by the desire to win the battle for the hearts and minds of young Armenians around the world. Both groups were eager to claim the other's successful attacks in an attempt to boost their own public profile. ASALA had strength in numbers, but JCAG was wealthier. It received financial assistance from the ARF, and attracted further recruits through the ARF-YF. An ASIO report suggests that it had 'identified a JCAG support group in Sydney within the ranks of the Armenian Revolutionary Federation (ARF) Youth Federation ...'[8]

The two organisations became locked in a deadly spiral of international terrorism. It began in 1975, when ASALA and a group protesting the imprisonment of Yanikian both claimed responsibility for the bombing of a Turkish Airlines office in Beirut. By October that year, ASALA had turned to assassination, killing Turkish diplomats from Vienna to Paris to Beirut. Throughout their decade of international activity, ASALA was suspected of being involved in 186 attacks, including 145 bombings and 26 assassinations. It targeted airlines in 69 instances and government officials in 49. Six times, it directly targeted other terrorist groups such as JCAG. Ironically, the early assassinations in Vienna and Paris in 1975 were also claimed by JCAG, which, in sum, was linked to 23 assassinations and 22 bombings. In the wake of this combined violence, dozens were dead, and hundreds injured around the world.

Wherever there was support for the assassins of JCAG and ASALA, death and destruction seemed inevitably to follow.

The killing years

International terrorism against Turkish interests, rooted in the Armenian cause, began sporadically in late 1972. By 1975, the killings began to indicate the growing professionalism of the two organisations. On 22 October, a Turkish ambassador was killed in Vienna. Two days later, the Turkish ambassador in Paris was killed. Two years later, on 9 June 1977, the Turkish ambassador to the Vatican was assassinated. These were merely the first in a long line of assassinations and bombings around the world by Armenian terrorists. Some of the attacks were simple assassinations, while others were more sophisticated, such as the bombing of the Turkish Representative Office in Paris on 8 July 1979; the Turkish Bureau for the UN in New York on 12 October 1980; and, that same day, the bombing of the Turkish Representative Office in Los Angeles.

By early December 1980, Armenian terrorist campaigns had developed momentum. Their assassinations largely occurred in major cities of Western countries—wherever ASALA or JCAG found they had sufficient support and connections. They left a line of bodies in their wake from Los Angeles to Boston and New York; and in major European cities, such as Copenhagen, Madrid, Paris and Vienna. While bombings were a rarer occurrence in the early days of Armenian terrorism, they tended to manifest in locations where a successful assassination had recently occurred. This could indicate the reliability, or perhaps cooperativeness, of local JCAG or ASALA support elements in the target locations. By 1979, all of their activities escalated dramatically. The handful of bombings per year suddenly increased to 31, and the one or two yearly assassinations rose to six in 1980 alone.

Attempts to counter this terrorism with force were met with retribution. When Swiss authorities detained two Armenian terrorists, for example, they faced an onslaught of seventeen bombings and 30 other attacks.[9] Investigators learned to tread lightly or face retaliation. Australia was not ignorant to the threat posed by Armenian terrorism to Turkish targets domestically. In 1980, the Department of Foreign Affairs requested a 100 per cent increase in its budget to protect Australian diplomats.[10] Given the frequency of attacks against Turkish targets, it is likely that the Turkish diplomatic service had similar concerns. After death threats towards the end of 1979, the Turkish consul-general in Australia, Sarik Ariyak, had hired Engin Sever as a bodyguard sometime in December 1979. In the following months, an allied intelligence service advised ASIO that a threat against Turkish interests in Australia was possible, and Ariyak's security was tightened further.[11]

It was to no avail. Ariyak and Sever were gunned down in cold blood a year later. Their routine had become predictable, and their movements had likely been studied by the assassins and their domestic supporters for some time. The two schoolboys were not the only witnesses: Ariyak's wife and eight-year-old daughter, who had been waving goodbye from the front door as they did every morning, saw the man they loved as husband and father murdered. That morning, they saw two members of a terrorist organisation kill a man because he was a symbol, a representative of a distant government.

There were two claims for responsibility. As we saw at the beginning of this chapter, one claimant was male. His words were cool and composed, and said the attack was the work of JCAG. The other call was from a woman, who called the AAP office in Sydney at 10.20 a.m.: 'The attacks are in retaliation for the injustice done to the Armenians by Turkey in 1915. We are the authors of the above-mentioned act. We have no connection at all with the so-called Armenian Secret Army [word] and Turkish institutions are our targets, the Armenian genocide [sic].'[12] This message was garbled and rushed, in a way strikingly dissimilar to the composed and confident nature of the attack. While the male caller proved impossible to identify, the female caller gave police a new lead. Investigators concluded that she was aged in her teens to mid-twenties. Her accent suggested that while she was not a native English speaker, she had learned English in Australia and could have been a resident for a few years. Given the division between JCAG and ASALA was not known among the general public, her reference to a Secret Army made her a person of interest.

But the lines of inquiry regarding the female caller quickly led nowhere. Instead, police began to focus their attention on the motorcycle. It was reported in the press that the motorcycle had been stolen from a Steven Singh in Drummoyne. Regardless of where it was procured, it was not driven until the day of the assassination and abandoned shortly thereafter. Inquiries regarding the padlock securing the bike to the telegraph pole also went nowhere. Witnesses could offer little beyond noting that the motorcyclist and pillion passenger were near the site an hour beforehand. They had sat and waited for their targets to emerge.

Police were also under pressure from the Turkish ambassador to catch the assassins—and quickly. A $100,000 reward was offered for information leading to their capture. On 3 February 1982, this reward was increased to $250,000, in a joint move between Attorney-General Durack and NSW Police.[13] Still no one came forward. The reward was renewed in 1987, again in 1990, and again in 2020.

Investigators advanced two different theories: first, that Australian citizens had committed the murders; second, that international commandos had executed the attack with domestic support.[14] It was a typical strategy for Armenian terrorists to utilise local sympathisers for plot preparation and reconnaissance. A well-planned attack, informed by local knowledge of the terrain and professionally executed by trained operatives, was a deadly combination. ASIO, moreover, believed that the terrorists received operational support from members of a JCAG cell concealed within the peaceful Armenian community in Australia.

This cell was believed to have no more than six members, and to operate without the knowledge or support of the broader Armenian community.[15] As a result, the ARF, with its suspected links to JCAG, was raided by ASIO. Documents were seized but for a long time were useless, given they needed to be translated and Armenian translators were scarce. It was suspected that there was a group of radicals in an inner circle of the ARF, which ASIO described as 'a dozen hard-core anti-Turkish fanatics' who attended the ARF Congress in Beirut in August 1980 and therefore had international links.[16] Beirut was, after all, where the Piro was located. It proved impossible, however, to establish if this inner circle had any prior knowledge of JCAG operations, or had supported the assassination.

ARF offshoots and feeder groups were also suspected of militancy, and there were some minor indications of preparatory behaviour. The motto of the Armenian Scouts run by the ARF was, for example, 'Be Prepared. Today we are scouts but tomorrow we will be soldiers.'¹⁷ But this was hardly proof of an assassination. Also under suspicion was the Sardarabat Youth Branch of the ARF in Sydney, named after an Armenian victory over Turkish forces in 1918. The Sardarabat Youth Branch was essentially a feeder group for the greater ARF, and most of its 90-odd members were engaged only in sporting and social activities. Again, there was little to tie any of these cultural organisations to the slayings.

Muddy waters

The whodunit soon had more bad answers than good information. Members of the public, of the Turkish community, of the Armenian community and, of course, of the intelligence community all had differing opinions as to who might have been responsible. Some were more outlandish than others: one theory, dismissed by Turkish authorities, was that extreme left- or right-wing Turkish groups were engaged in false-flag operations, killing targets under the cover of Armenian terrorism to discredit the Armenian cause.[18] It is unlikely, however, that pro-Turkish groups would assassinate Turkish diplomats and draw attention to a cause they hoped the world would forget.

This left police laboriously following up on leads that often went nowhere. In one instance, police found that anti-Turkish handwritten pamphlets had been scattered through a park near Railway Square in Sydney's CBD. They contained messages such as 'Sarik Ariyak consul general NSW was assassinated by the Turkish terrorist group of NSW—the "Kurtulus" all murderers and cowards', and accusing Mehmet Ali Ağca of responsibility.[19] Ağca, a nationalist Turk and member of the Bozkurt (Grey Wolves) fascist organisation, which was associated with the Turkish National Action Party, had attempted to assassinate Pope John Paul II on 13 May 1981.

In another instance, now-public ASIO documents noted that a woman called Dzovig Balian, who had ties to ASALA, claimed she knew the killers. She had been living in Australia for five years, and was married to Nerses Keshishian. Balian claimed that her husband's cousin, Hagob Keshishian, could be one of the assassins. Balian herself had worked with Esther Basmadjian in Beirut, whose brother was Aram Basmadjian, a convicted ASALA terrorist. Interestingly, Aram Basmadjian once used the pseudonym Raffi Balian. One of the investigators thought Nerses and Hagob might have been 'real herrings'.[20]

The waters were further muddied by politics. A Syrian Embassy staffer in New Delhi, for example, was identified by British intelligence as a colonel in the Syrian security service, which was known to act in a support capacity of ASALA, suggesting potential state involvement. Another Turkish consul-general believed the assassination could have been undertaken by Kurdish separatists, given the well-established links between ASALA and the PKK.[21] There were also rumours within the Turkish Australian community the pro-Turkish Bozkurt was involved. No evidence was found to confirm any of these claims.

Other rumours suggested that if the Turkish community didn't believe the assassination had been carried out by a Turk, it would have retaliated against the Armenian community.[22] There were also anonymous allegations that there were a large number of undocumented Turks who could be extremists. Some were alleged to have overstayed their tourist visas in Australia, or were seamen who deserted their ship when it docked in Australia. While a document from NSW Police considered this a possibility, ASIO pointed out that given the unsettled political climate in Turkey, the deserters may simply have been in opposition to the government.[23] The claim was followed up by police, who tracked down fourteen deserters, to no avail.

In early August 1982, investigators pursued a new lead, as detailed in ASIO documents. Soon after the assassination, two Armenian taxi drivers were heard over the radio saying that 'Mardik' had 'succeeded'. The man they were talking about, Mardik Boghossian, was an Armenian Australian and supposedly the leader of a small group within the ARF. Coincidentally, Boghossian flew out of Australia, destined for Beirut, at 1 p.m., just over three hours after the attack.²⁴ Other sources disagree, and claimed he was technically in Hong Kong at the time of the shooting. Despite having been exploited by Ananda Marga, New Zealand remained a popular backdoor into Australia, as noted in ASIO records with respect to the matter.²⁵ It was therefore possible that he transited back from Hong Kong to Australia via New Zealand in secret without any record being kept of his entry or exit (this travel loophole was closed in July 1981). This lead went nowhere, as police did not uncover any evidence implicating Mardik in the killing.

It was soon established that a number of Armenian Australians had attended a secret meeting in Beirut, where political assassinations were discussed. It was alleged that members of the Sardarabat Youth Branch, among others, had been present. While this indicates a developing political extremism among a very select group of Armenian Australians, it still didn't establish the terrorists' names. What it did do, however, was allow for ASIO to obtain a number of telephone intercept warrants.

One of these was against Silva Donelian, a member of Sydney's Armenian community with links to the Sydney ARF-YF. If sympathetic to the assassins, her position was hardly unique; subsequent ASIO investigations found that 'almost every Armenian felt sympathy for the assassins', just not for the assassination.²⁶ Finally, on 13 September 1982, the intercept of a telephone conversation between Nina Alexanian and Silva (possibly Donelian) gave them a slight lead.

At the start of the conversation, Silva congratulated Nina. When Nina queried the greeting, Silva replied that 'another one bit the dust today'. This could have been in reference to the assassination of Bora Suelkan, an attaché to the Turkish Consulate in Bulgaria, four days earlier on 9 September 1982. Silva indicated that the perpetrators were 'ours'—by which she could have meant JCAG. The discussion continued, with Silva criticising ASALA. Nina then said, 'Let them do it. As long as they do not get caught . . . If they go free like you.'²⁷ The intelligence officer wrote in the now-public ASIO document that the conversation suggested that 'both women especially Silva appear to be privy to the existence of JCAG. Nina's last comment certainly implies that Silva has "escaped" capture, most probably for her part in some terrorist act'.

But this too ultimately led nowhere.[28] The conversation, regardless of context, would hardly persuade a jury. The investigation, which had spent so long chasing leads, had reached a stalemate.

Game of whispers

The assassinations also provoked an inquiry into the Australian Federal Police, as some people suggested that it occurred not because a professional terrorist cadre had domestic support but because the AFP had failed to provide Ariyak with adequate protection. As a result, the AFP set up Turkish VIP Protection Units. ASIO's role in the affair was also subject to debate, given the media reported that ASIO was tipped off about the plot months earlier by an allied intelligence service. ASIO documents tell a different story, indicating there was no warning of a planned JCAG attack.

Security was also tightened around diplomatic premises. The Turkish Embassy and residence in Canberra received 24-hour protection, with static guards at the front and rear of the buildings. Mobile patrols passed every twenty minutes, and a bomb search was carried out daily. In Melbourne, the consul-general, vice-consul and attaché also had 24-hour static guards, as well as mobile patrols visiting frequently. The consular office received an extra guard too. In Sydney, however, the consul-general was given only one 24-hour guard, and the consular office one static guard during business hours.[29] All of this was merely defensive: JCAG and ASALA remained operational and in the wind.

In 1983, ASIO began to suspect that JCAG Sydney was building towards a violent action. On 9 March 1983, for example, the Turkish ambassador to Yugoslavia, Galip Balkar, was assassinated in Belgrade. Another two people died, and four were injured. More attacks were anticipated, and airport security was tightened for Armenians leaving and entering Australia. Sometime in May 1983,

ASIO intercepted a phone call between Silva Donelian and Krikor Keverian, who was on holiday in Los Angeles, the centre of JCAG activity in the United States. Before Keverian was due to depart for Australia, he received communications from Silva, who reminded him to bring back 'important things' from the United States.[30] ASIO took this comment seriously.

A game of whispers ensued. Another alleged JCAG Sydney member, Levon Demirian, had been living in Beirut since June 1981. This was also unlikely to be a tourist trip, given that Beirut's frequent military conflict made it a relatively undesirable holiday destination. Demirian's return to Australia was scheduled for 13 July 1983. Before he left, he called Nina Alexanian and said he was returning early because something 'had been brought forward'.[31] As Alexanian was an associate of Donelian, some officials began to suspect that these whispers between Alexanian and Demirian were connected with Keverian's return and his 'important things'.

A picture began to develop that the four were possibly coordinating something. Australian authorities were poised, ready to act. On 12 July 1983, when Keverian returned from Los Angeles, his bags were selected by Customs for searching. He was found to be in possession of four handguns, ammunition, speed loaders, special grips, cases and holsters. Keverian was arrested immediately and charged under the Customs Act for making an untrue statement to a Customs officer. He pleaded guilty (these circumstances led to Krikor being subjected to 24-hour surveillance for a time).[32] Upon hearing the news of Keverian's arrest, Demirian immediately cancelled his flight back to Australia. There is a likelihood that, without guns or operatives, a terrorist attack similar to the 1980 assassinations was prevented by this arrest.

ASIO had detected sympathisers among the ARF-YF in Sydney, where the cell still numbered around six.[33] A now-public memorandum to the National and International Security Committee of Cabinet stated that all in all, ten Armenian Australians were under close scrutiny, among them Silva Donelian, Nina Alexanian and another suspected member of the Sydney cell, Krikor Keverian (who was subject to 24-hour surveillance).[34] Maintaining surveillance on these individuals was justified due to the continued campaign against Turkish diplomats throughout the world.

Smuggling made easy

It was not just Keverian and Demirian who were involved in attempts to smuggle weapons into the country. Another was Armenian Australian Agop Magarditch. He lived in Sydney at a premises also associated with Jano Assadourian.[35] Both men were known to ASIO, but Assadourian was of particular interest to authorities. ASIO had considered turning him into an informant as a way to penetrate JCAG Sydney, but abandoned this idea when it discovered how hostile he was to the authorities. Assadourian was one of the organisers of the yearly ARF-YF camps in Kanangra, New South Wales, known as 'army camps', which brought him to the notice of ASIO.[36] He was an avid shooter, and frequently practised pistol shooting with Keverian at a range in Malabar, south-eastern Sydney. In short, he was too radical and potentially dangerous for ASIO's purposes.

Agop Magarditch was a different story altogether. He had recently returned to Australia after spending around four years in Los Angeles, the other JCAG hub. His belongings were being slowly shipped from LA while he arrived earlier via airplane and stayed with Assadourian. It was believed that the JCAG LA had hidden weapons and operational equipment in that shipping container, for use in a terrorist attack in Australia. The closer the container got to Australian shores, however, the more nervous Magarditch became. He had heard about the arrest of Keverian on 12 July, and his paranoia was not entirely unfounded.

An ASIO briefing note said: 'It is our suspicion that MAGARDITCH, on hearing of KEVERIAN's arrest, panicked and reported the weapons.'[37] Although he did so under a fake name, it was well known that it was him (Magarditch's fake surname was merely his wife's maiden name—an unimaginative choice, to say the least). When the incoming shipment was searched, it was found to contain a submachine gun, five handguns, a lock-picking set, smuggling books, disguises, ammunition, handcuffs and more.[38] There was also a large amount of literature, including books such as *Death Dealer's Manual*, *The Perfect Crime and How to Commit It*, *Smuggling Made Easy* and *Assassination Theory and Practice*.

As the links between the Sydney and Los Angeles cells became more apparent, they came under closer scrutiny by authorities. At the same time, links between the two were becoming more obvious. For example, an Armenian Australian, Kegham Sarkissian, was believed to have been involved in an attempted bombing against the honorary Turkish consul in Philadelphia.[39] This was one of fifteen incidents of Armenian terrorism in the United States between 1975 and 1982.[40] In May 1982, three American ASALA members were thwarted as they attempted to bomb an Air Canada airplane en route to Los Angeles. The trio were arrested and convicted, and the subsequent crackdown on JCAG LA significantly reduced its freedom of operations. These arrests could be why it was instead assisting with attacks in Australia and elsewhere.

The range of equipment supplied by JCAG LA gave operatives the capability to conduct a complex hostage-taking attack instead of a simple assassination. This was not beyond the realm of possibility, as on 27 July 1983, five members of JCAG took three hostages in the Turkish Embassy in Lisbon, Portugal. In the ensuing conflict with Portuguese security forces, the terrorists' explosives detonated, killing all five terrorists and two others. Some of the more experienced terrorists had come from Beirut, which remained a hotbed for Armenian terrorism.[41] It is possible that the Australian attack was meant to coincide with the one in Lisbon, as JCAG had previously demonstrated the capacity for internationally coordinated events.[42]

Despite the significance of the weapons cache and instructional manuals, Magarditch was not charged with any criminal offences. There were at this time no laws that encompassed preparing for or supporting terrorism offences. Moreover, Magarditch's actions exposed a loophole in the law: it was not an offence to have prohibited goods in unaccompanied baggage if they were *declared*, moreover, a delay was permitted in declaring unaccompanied baggage until it was opened. Magarditch, having declared his arsenal, went free. The cache, predictably, was confiscated.[43]

It is unknown how Assadourian responded to Magarditch's betrayal. Within a matter of weeks, he moved on from Magarditch and had been appointed as Keverian's bodyguard.[44] Two things can be inferred from this: first, Keverian was a significant member of JCAG Sydney and therefore worthy of protection; and second, JCAG was worried that Keverian would be targeted by either Turkish or Australian authorities. Keverian and Assadourian continued practising at pistol ranges, and sought to evade ASIO's 24-hour surveillance.

Levon Demirian, meanwhile, finally left Beirut and returned to Australia sometime in September 1983. As there was no record of him passing through Australian Immigration, it was suspected that he used an alias to travel. One report concluded 'Such an entry would suggest an operational motive.'[45] With JCAG LA scattered and JCAG Sydney lacking in expertise, it was believed that Demirian, fresh from Beirut, was an operational commander. ASIO only discovered his return, in fact, when Keverian visited him at his family home. This confirmed suspicions that an attack had been planned, and that it involved Demirian, Keverian and Assadourian. Their identification by ASIO likely compromised any potential operation from the outset.

That did not prevent the suspects from attending Armenian camps. Before a long weekend early in October, Keverian shopped for clothing at an army disposal store. It soon became evident that this was for a camp the ARF-YF was holding in the Megalong Valley in the Blue Mountains west of Sydney. Despite the presence of children at the camp, it appears that covert training took place, with a roving piquet, a duty watch and two-way radios observed. Six suspected members of JCAG Sydney were there, including

Keverian, Donelian and Assadourian.⁴⁶ This was not the limit of the training, either. Sometime between August and September, two female members of the ARF-YF (one of whom was Silva's sister, Seta) were believed to have attended JCAG camps in Athens, Greece; Seta posted a parcel of books and other items back to Australia.⁴⁷

Surveillance of the ten primary JCAG suspects in Australia continued. Others had been subject to telephone interceptions since 1981, including Krikor Keverian, Nina Alexanian, Silva Donelian and another individual. As a result of suspicious conversations, the interception operations on these four suspects continued well into 1983. An extensive interview program was also launched within Armenian communities, aiming to gather intelligence and deter potential threats. Unfortunately, while it was one thing to talk to members of the community, it was another thing entirely to infiltrate them. ASIO noted that 'agent operations against the Armenian community are very difficult due to its clannish and close-knit nature. That arises from its strong sense of nationalism and its widespread and uniting hatred of Turks.'⁴⁸

On 2 December 1983, ASIO intercepted a phone call between Assadourian and an unknown man called Eddy. The conversation indicated that the two men were attempting to use a third party to purchase items for $150 each. ASIO believed they were trying to obtain firearms for use in an attack, an assessment reinforced by Eddy and Assadourian's attempts to talk in code. Assadourian in particular complained that 'things have gone cold because the pressure is so great'.⁴⁹ Despite this, on August 1983, the counter-terrorism alert was raised at 'special counter terrorist risk' level and remained there for some time. The timing coincided with the looming anniversary of the assassination of the consul-general. The Australian Embassy in Ankara, Turkey's capital, had also received reliable intelligence that an attack was likely.

The Department of Foreign Affairs disagreed with the alert, conceding that while it still believed JCAG was planning an operation in Australia, in the absence of any indication on its timing, the alert level should be lowered. When the ominous date passed without any attack, Foreign Affairs again requested that the alert level be lowered due to costs. A document from December 1983 stressed that protecting Turkish VIPs was very expensive. In addition to 98 AFP officers engaged in protection duty, the team also required three explosives sniffer dogs. Operational costs were $750,000 per month (more than double the outlay before the 1980 assassination). NSW and Victoria police had also been assisting in patrol and escort duties, although this cost was not counted.[50]

The easiest solution, of course, was to bolster Fortress Australia and harden the border to international terrorists—overlooking the fact that domestic activity could not be affected by this measure. Travel restrictions were put in place for all people of Armenian descent. One cablegram noted that although it was difficult to identify travelling Armenians, their surnames generally ended in 'ian', 'yan', and 'oun', while another document specified an age range between eighteen and 25.[51] ASIO's 1982–83 annual report firmly stated that 'the major threat currently is from the activities and intentions of supporters of Armenian terrorism in Australia'.[52] It would carry this perception into the next year.

Revolutionary armies

By 6 October 1983, there were hints of a new player joining the game. When the leader of JCAG in Beirut, Abraham Ashjian, was assassinated, JCAG underwent internal reorganisation.[53] The new, remodelled JCAG now claimed its attacks under the moniker the Armenian Revolutionary Army (ARA). It announced itself in typical fashion, with an attack on the Turkish Embassy in Lisbon on 27 July 1983. Despite the new name, it was believed to essentially be the same organisation, with links to the ARF-YF.[54]

Under warrant, ASIO continued to monitor the conversations of JCAG suspects, and installed microphones and transmitters in their homes. In 1984, ASIO justified its intrusion into private domains by publicly stating that Armenian terrorism remained a major threat in Australia.[55] The ARA continued to conduct international operations, such as the assassination of Turkish diplomat Evner Ergun in Vienna in 1984. Following the operation, the ARA issued a communiqué (abridged here) stating:

> The Armenian Revolutionary Army [is] claiming today's attack against Mr Evner, a Turkish diplomat posted to Vienna, Austria, [and] continues to battle according to its plans . . . Our combat which emanates from the National Liberation Struggle of the Armenian people is undertaken against the reactionary Turkish government. It will conclude when, taking note of the legality of the Armenian Cause, the Turkish government begins negotiations with the representatives of the Armenian people. Until then, we will continue our struggle with the same resolve expressed by our suicide commandos in Lisbon and we warn the Government of Turkey as well as its representatives in the four corners of the world . . .[56]

It was not purely successes claimed by the ARA either. In September 1984, two ARA terrorists were killed in Topkapi Palace, Istanbul, when their explosives detonated prematurely. A month later, the ARA issued a communiqué stating:

> This is the price which our fighters are willing to pay, according to their militant commitment . . . Our target is the Turkish reactionary government, through all of its official representatives. As long as it will continue to falsify history and deny the legitimate rights of the Armenian people, we will not give it any respite. We will strike them in Turkey proper, where we have the benefit of assistance and active support of the Turkish clandestine revolutionaries . . . the A.R.A. states it will attack the Turkish government in the four corners of the world until the Armenian people regain their legitimate rights, on its historic lands absusively [sic] occupied by Turkey.[57]

On 13 March 1985, three ARA terrorists stormed the Turkish Embassy in Ottawa, Canada. They held a dozen hostages captive for more than four hours, before finally surrendering to police. A civilian security guard died in the process. The terrorists included the chairman of the ARF-YF in Canada. As it was the sixth attack since 1983, it was seen as confirmation that the ARA was the new operational name for old JCAG elements.

Energised by the embassy siege in Canada, ASIO began to suspect that JCAG supporters were planning local violence in early 1985. This was driven partly by its assumption that JCAG Sydney was under the 'operational authority' of a northern American cell, presumably JCAG LA, which was also suspected of involvement in the Ottawa siege. With the 70th anniversary of the Armenian genocide looming, authorities were worried about an outbreak of Armenian violence. One assessment suggests, however, that ASIO had JCAG Sydney well covered:

> The JCAG cell inn [sic] Sydney is aware that it has been subjected to intense ASIO (and police) interest since 1983. That interest has been reinforced only recently by a co-ordinated programme of ASIO interviews of people close to cell members. ASIO's success in 1983 in preventing the entry of JCAG-linked Arms into Australia, and its subsequent operational activity against cell members, could be expected to create a fear in the local cell that we have been successful in securing penetration of it.[58]

Although this was a sound assessment, ASIO may not have had the cell as well covered as it thought, because it unfortunately had no warning for the bombing a year later.[59]

False dormancy

On April 1985, JCAG Sydney proved that it was not idle; it was simply planning. When the Turkish foreign minister visited Australia on Anzac Day 1985, an unknown vehicle attempted to join his motorcade. It was stopped, and an investigator found that the young occupants were part of the ARF-YF and in possession of photos of the foreign minister. This was dismissed as an obscure prank. In a threat assessment on 24 April 1986, authorities stated that they were not aware of any planned violence, and that 'The JCAG/ARA and ASALA, the two most prominent Armenian terrorist groups, have been dormant for about 18 months.'[60]

While serious terrorist activity appeared to be subsiding, the political wing was highly active, as the ARF had ramped up its attempts to gain political recognition through the United Nations. The supposed dormancy was attributed to infighting within ASALA itself, which had splintered into two or three factions. One faction wanted to retain the strategy of attacking Turkish representatives, while the second, more radical splinter group wanted to target associates of Turkish interests. One of these may have been responsible for the spate of murders of senior ARF members in Beirut, or, conversely, it may have been the third ASALA splinter group, which called itself the ARF-Revolutionary Movement (ARF-RM). The traditional enmity between ASALA and ARF had flared up, and now ASALA sought to liquidate traditional ARF leaders. Six months later, those assessments would be redundant.

Sometime in mid-November, Hagob Levonian visited Melbourne for a 'discreet weekend of fun',[61] which to him meant two things: women and sex. To ensure his wife didn't discover his infidelity, Levonian's close friend, Levon Demirian, rented a car for him. According to Demirian, this was quite a common occurrence for the two men. Demirian also put the accommodation charges on his Diners Club card, which was 'not a known or approved practice of the JCAG'.[62] To the innocent onlooker, it could simply have been two friends covering for one another, until something unexpectedly went bump—or rather boom—in the night.

At 2.30 a.m. on 23 November 1986, a bomb exploded in the boot of a Holden Torana parked directly under the Turkish Consulate in Melbourne. Four kilograms of explosives were used in the bomb, which was inadvertently triggered by Levonian. All that was left of him were 50 kilograms of human remains scattered around the burning vehicle. An area of nearly 1 square kilometre was cordoned off. The blast triggered a gas leak, which was quickly brought under control, while 70 firemen worked to control fires that had broken out. Nineteen shops on Toorak Road were damaged, one of these destroyed completely. It also prompted the evacuation of fifteen war widows who had been living in a set of flats owned by the Department of Veterans' Affairs.

A police task force comprising AFP, state police and army explosives experts was set up to investigate the bombing. Demirian, meanwhile, booked a direct flight to Beirut, but investigators uncovered his involvement in the bombing and detained him before he was able to flee. Demirian was charged with conspiring to commit an illegal act that would have endangered lives, intentionally and maliciously causing damage to a building, and endangering lives with an explosive device.

By skill alone, Levonian's remains were finally identified when a police fingerprint expert, Sergeant Peter Pangrazio, found a 2-centimetre slice of human palm two full days after the bombing. It was matched to prints on a raffle ticket belonging to Levonian. As a result, Demirian's charges were upgraded to include the murder of Hagob Levonian. Investigators also found 174 sticks of gelignite in the restaurant where Demirian worked as a cook; a receipt showing that he had rented the Torana; and a notebook containing the address of the Turkish Consulate, details of consulate staff movements, and elaborate diagrams of the consulate and its circuitry and wiring. ASIO ascertained that Demirian had been closely involved in the bomb-making preparations, and may have been assisted by his brother, John Demirian.[63]

Levon Demirian was found guilty of all charges and sentenced to 25 years in prison. He appealed the murder charge, which was successfully overturned. In total, he served ten years. This was the last JCAG attack in Australia.

A bomb too far

The cessation of JCAG/ARA and ASALA terrorism has been the subject of a great deal of study. It is hard to switch off multiple cadres of professional, experienced terrorists—many of whom faked their deaths and operated under false identities to achieve their international ambitions—especially when those ambitions had not yet been realised: there was no greater recognition of the Armenian genocide; there had been no restoration of Armenian lands; and no reparations had been paid. All they had achieved was revenge. So why did both groups desist by 1988?

The beginning of the end was the ASALA attack on Orly Airport in Paris on 15 July 1983. At 2.15 p.m., a suitcase bomb detonated prematurely on the luggage conveyor belt, killing five people immediately and wounding another 56. Three more later died of their wounds. Forty of those injured were Turkish, mainly because that particular flight was destined for Istanbul. Police believed the bomb was intended to go off mid-flight. Despite the great unpopularity of the attack, ASALA claimed responsibility. The group was already plagued with instability because of Israel's invasion of Lebanon, which compromised the security of the Beirut Piro. This is likely why so many abortive plots and attacks featured in Australia and the United States. In addition, ASALA was suffering leadership problems. The Orly attack led to an internal revolt, power struggles, waning recruitment and a loss of popular support for the ASALA mission.[64]

As long as ASALA had maintained a fiction of the moral high ground, it had not been universally condemned. The Orly attack violated an unspoken moral code: it was, in sum, one bomb too far. JCAG went down with ASALA's ship—their spiral of competitive violence had held them together in a deathly grip. While JCAG did not suffer the same insecurity as ASALA, and remained highly organised and professional with a selective targeting program, it too disbanded. Experts have suggested that with the disbandment of ASALA, the JCAG/ARA's raison d'être was simply gone. Moreover, the ARF was well aware that associations with terrorism could harm the Armenian cause more than they could help. In light of its renewed push for recognition through legitimate measures, it is possible that it, too, sought to curb the violence.

Terrorism, again, failed to achieve the strategic objectives of those who wielded it. They accomplished neither recognition, reparations nor restoration. All they achieved was a hollow, empty revenge that branded the Armenian diaspora as suspect communities, creating internal suspicion and discord. Armenia ultimately achieved independence in 1991, following the dissolution of the USSR. At the time of writing, Australia does not formally recognise the Armenian genocide. Other countries, however, have made greater advancements. In 2016, Germany's parliament voted to recognise the Armenian genocide, joining 29 other countries in recognising the loss and suffering of the Armenian people. In response, the Turkish president, Recep Tayyip Erdoğan, said: 'I am addressing the whole world. You may like it, you may not. Our attitude on the Armenian issue is clear from the beginning. We will never accept the accusations of genocide.'[65]

7

Fires in the night: right-wing extremism

The Ustaša was not the only right-wing threat in Australia. While extremists were running a campaign against Yugoslavian Australians, another element of the extreme right was emerging. This element was domestic, composed of a motley crew of white supremacists, garden-variety fascists, anti-government agitators, neo-Nazis, and a few Odinists and Christian Identity adherents for good measure. Since the 1920s, this diverse assembly of right-wing extremists had developed undisturbed in the dark corners of Australian society, where knowledge of them—and indeed concern about them—was largely relegated to small teams in intelligence or law enforcement tasked with disrupting their nefarious activities.

These groups and movements arose organically in the Australian context, or were cultivated from afar by foreign states such as Nazi Germany. Some were isolationist and protectionist in nature, while others were overtly connected to fascist and National Socialist systems around the world. Ultimately, in the dark heart of the extreme right lie the entwined serpents of privilege and entitlement. Supporters champion their own unique privilege to rule and control the lives of others, to compel submission and obedience to their will, and to enforce gendered norms and relationships. This is the deadly power they believe they hold, and yet are too privileged to be subject to themselves. Their world is populated with manufactured truths that they believe implicitly—truths that uphold their privilege and separateness, imbue them with a sense of greatness, and promise them the recovery of great power and status.

Ultimately, in the 1980s, local right-wing violence and beliefs coalesced in the Australian Nationalist Movement (ANM) and its campaign of terror against Perth's Asian community. ANM, following a long tradition of disruption and coercion, set Perth aflame, wreaking millions of dollars of damage, and seeking to foment a revolution that would destroy Australian society, burn it down to the bedrock, and build it anew as a white ethnostate practising racial segregation to maintain the racial purity of white Australians.

Explaining the extreme right

Before turning to the ANM campaign, we must first understand the extreme right. Because of the term 'right wing', many mistakenly believe that right-wing extremism is simply an extension of mainstream ideas. But important distinctions must be drawn to understand the shape of the threat. Given it is a matter of national security, the term must not be used as a slur to delegitimise those we oppose, but to give meaning and shape to the way an individual or movement perceives the world. To do this, we must ask ourselves two primary questions.

First, why is it right? The term 'right' in contemporary politics has long been equated with support for existing hierarchy and authority, observance of duty and tradition, and order. A mainstream individual in the right often seeks to maintain that sense of order and stasis, but will also support incremental changes based on tried and true measures. They are not, in short, revolutionary, but seek to maintain the status quo where possible and reasonable. In the moderate sphere, the right is very popular—as testified by the success of numerous mainstream democratic parties.

Second, why is it extreme? The extreme right takes that support for hierarchy and authority far beyond the pale, seeking a political nexus of authoritarianism, anti-democratic beliefs and exclusionary nationalism. In practice, the extreme right is authoritarian because its adherents seek to compel people to live a certain way, whether they choose to or not, and to sacrifice their personal freedoms to the regime (such as forcing a homosexual to conform to heterosexual 'norms'). They hold the regime to be righteous and pure, and all other political parties such as the left to be false or corrupt. Authoritarians therefore reject political pluralism, and seek to establish unchallenged political authority. Authoritarianism is often supplemented by an obsession with the traditional, whereby authoritarians glorify in a traditional and 'natural' order or way of living, thereby restricting individual choice. They reject the modern world as decadent and degenerate, and seek a retrograde world order, often based on the heterosexual nuclear family. While they promise freedom, the extreme right actually seeks to enforce submission to an idealised order without popular support.

At the heart of the extreme-right worldview is a seething mistrust for democracy, its processes and its principles. Representative democracy is a process that confers power to the people, and as such is a mechanism for the will of the majority that also ensures the protection of minorities. Contradictorily, the extreme right believes democracy allows the weak to reign over the strong. They do not accept the equality of peoples, and resist all expansions towards equality, believing it to be unnatural. In fact, many in the extreme right believe that to expand the rights of others is to minimise or reduce their own, despite all evidence to the contrary. To that end, the extreme right believes that democracy is rotten to the core: it cannot be salvaged, it must be destroyed. A revolution, triggered by acts of violence and terrorism, is required to cleanse the world and make way for the authoritarian utopia.

Above all else, the extreme right exhibits exclusionary nationalism. Nationalism as defined famously by Benedict Anderson describes the 'imagined communities' in society that are both limited and sovereign: binding together peoples within certain geographical boundaries who are believed to share common language, beliefs, history or origins—sometimes contrary to historical fact. As one scholar noted, 'nationalism is not the awakening of a nation to self-conscious: it *invents* nations where they do not exist'.[1] With regard to the extreme right, the nation (and the nationalism it produces) is frequently imagined in terms of racial exclusivity. Nationalists imagine that their nation comprises a single 'race', a select community of people who conform to their ideal racial integrity or purity—often ignoring the multiculturalism inherent in their own histories. The people who do not conform to their imagined nation, such as religious, sexual or ethnic minorities, 'promiscuous' women and left-wing opponents, are seen to be unnatural and a threat to their nation's survival. Non-conformers are rejected from membership to this exclusive club, despite holding the same human and citizenship rights. Those who do conform find their identity exalted and sacred, and united in a collective grandeur that extends beyond the individual. Such ethnonationalism has immense power because it can promise people a radiant destiny, and mobilise them to sacrifice everything in pursuit of it. It was such nationalism that demanded and received the 'colossal sacrifices' of World War II.[2] It is only fitting, then, that the clearest examples of extreme-right ideology can be found in that war-torn period of history.

Roots of the extreme right

The extreme right in Australia historically comes from the same species but represents two different genera: international fascism and grassroots ethnonationalism. After the chaos of World War I and the economic uncertainty that followed, extreme-right ideologies such as fascism and National Socialism (hereafter Nazism) began to gain traction among European and also Australian communities. Charismatic fascist leaders arose, such as Italian dictator Benito Mussolini and Adolf Hitler, who reimagined German fascism as National Socialism.

In Australia, international fascism was largely considered to be the consequence of German immigration, which began anew in the late 1920s following a previous ban. Migrants moved to areas such as Tanunda in the Barossa Valley, South Australia, and were considered (however erroneously) to have brought their political allegiances with them from their homelands. This is why historians believe that the first Nazi stronghold was formed in Adelaide as early as 1932, and strongholds in the other states soon followed. The Australian chapter of the National Socialist German Workers Party (NSDAP; i.e. the Nazi Party) formed in 1934, and the Australian Security Service believed it had nearly 100 local members by 1938, which increased substantially in 1939.[3] The main priority of the NSDAP in Australia was to revive concepts of German identity and establish links between German-Australian community groups. Although its members were initially community oriented, they became increasingly anti-Semitic, racist and fascist.

There is a reason these parties were exclusively German-Australian émigrés: it was a membership requirement. Members came from Berlin, Hamburg, Eggenberg (in Austria), Schesslitz, Bremen and Leipzig, to name a few. Among them were tradesmen, merchants, artists, a ship's captain, engineers, managers, a doctor and a lawyer.[4] While the NSDAP was monitored by Australian security services, their knowledge of the movement was also informed by foreign intelligence partners. In 1939, a secret memorandum from the Netherlands alleged that citizens of German origin were pressured to join the Nazi Party wherever they lived, and forced to contribute 25 per cent of their income. Failure to do so could lead to the imprisonment of their relatives in Germany. In some cases, donations were coerced, while in other cases financing, sabotage, and espionage may have been viewed as acts of loyalty in the service of the radiant destiny of the Third Reich.

Central to this effort in Australia was the Auslandsorganisation (overseas organisation), an extension of the Third Reich that sought the 'complete domination of Germans living outside of the Reich'.[5] It did this through exploiting its Aussenhandelsamt (Foreign Trade Office) and the German Chambers of Commerce in foreign jurisdictions. Its core objective was the creation of a *Schicksalsgemeinschaft*—a 'community of "fate" between Germans inside and outside Germany, which can overcome all troubles'.[6] Between 1938 and 1939, the Auslandsorganisation took control of all Nazi activities in Australia. Around the same time, the Union of Germans in Australia and New Zealand (Bund des Deutschtums in Australien und Neuseeland) was formed. It too was soon subject to overseas control. This was a concern to Australian authorities, which were monitoring the subversion of citizens by fascist regimes. The Department of External Affairs noted that 'the danger therefore lies in the fact that overseas NAZIS [sic] in a time of war may be called upon to serve the fatherland, not by rushing to Germany and joining fighting forces, but by remaining where they are and conducting acts of sabotage and espionage'.[7] Despite these ill omens, very little serious violence was conducted by Nazis in Australia during World War II, although fascism lived on.

The other side of the extreme right in Australia emerged from grassroots ethnonationalism. It too arose during the interwar period, and, like fascism, was stoked by economic uncertainty and Depression-era paranoia. This homegrown extreme right imagined a glorious Australian past, saw a society in decay, and sought to achieve a grand future. While numerous movements arose around Australia, the most eminent example was The Country in New South Wales. Led by rural elites, it soon attracted 30,000 members.[8] They were fiercely opposed to all left-wing politics, which they perceived as communism, and believed Premier Jack Lang was a Bolshevik in disguise. The movement stockpiled arms and ammunition, gathered information about left-wing enemies, and engaged in vigilante street fights with unionists. Soon, The Country fractured into the Old and New Guard.[9] The New Guard was formed in 1931 by Eric Campbell, a Sydney solicitor. Its membership largely comprised former military officers, but it also attracted some working-class men to its ranks. Its mission was to prepare for intervention in the event of communist-engineered social breakdown. It was fiercely opposed to left-wing politics and trade unions, applauded fascist politics, and believed it stood for 'country' values. In time, its numbers expanded to 36,000, with members drawn from all classes of society. They frequently engaged in street fights with trade unionists, wharfies and opposing labour groups—the most notorious of which was the infamous Battle of Bankstown in 1931. The New Guard also fought with the Australian Labour Army, while the 800-strong Constitutional Guard appears to have formed specifically to defend against New Guard attacks.[10]

On the other side of this grassroots mobilisation were the Odinists, a cult established and led in Australia by Melbourne solicitor Alexander Rud Mills. They believed that modern Christianity was debased 'Jew-worship', and the only way to restore Australia to greatness was through Odinism, a form of racist paganism that honours and seeks to revive Norse heritage, practices and beliefs (in which Odin was the principal god). These Norse beliefs are venerated by the extreme right as a warrior religion, and the time of the Vikings reimagined as one of racial integrity, purity and strength. Without Odinism, Mills believed the white race would become 'a race of mongrels'.[11] Highly connected in international fascist circles, Mills met Adolf Hitler in Munich in 1930. He was interned during the war due to his direct connection to Hitler, although he himself believed it was because of his involvement with the Australia First Movement.

The Australia First Movement (AFM) was established in October 1941 by William J. Miles and Percy R. Stephensen, who ran a right-wing gazette, *The Publicist*. The movement had a strong hostility to the 'Jewish race', and its adherents were 'keen advocates of Australian nationalism'.[12] It was divided as to its hostility to Britain and America, and friendliness towards Japan. A number of members interned under the National Security (General) Regulations during World War II were accused of attempting to prejudice the war effort and spread ill will.[13] They were rumoured to have a hit list of Australian politicians that they would assassinate when the Japanese invaded, and were connected to Mussolini through a member's wife. The AFM diminished rapidly after World War II, although its members also developed ties with the Australian League of Rights that would persist for decades to come.

A dormant network

Following World War II, Nazism was discredited but not entirely discarded. The Holocaust had claimed the lives of 6 million Jews, and millions more died because of Nazi persecution, including 7 million Soviet civilians, 3 million Soviet war prisoners, 1.8 million non-Jewish Poles, 250,000 disabled people, and hundreds of thousands of homosexuals.[14] Despite the staggering loss and overwhelming scars that the Nazi Party left on the world, the extreme right endured. The grassroots movements continued to develop domestically, and international influences continued to arrive in Australia. Numerous Nazi war criminals immigrated to Australia after the war and gained citizenship. In fact, during this time, 'no information relating to wartime activities or to political background is required of applications for the grant of Australian citizenship'.[15] These war criminals rarely attempted to attract attention, and leadership of the extreme right was assumed by Australians.

The most prominent post-war movement was the Australian League of Rights (ALR). It was an international organisation, with an Australian chapter established in 1946 by Eric Butler. It was libertarian in substance, opposing big banking, big business and big bureaucracy. Its members were also Anglophiles, who thought that the only guarantee of individual liberty would come from Britain, and they were staunch loyalists to the British crown. They believed that the Jews had tricked Britain into entering World War II, and were responsible for bringing the British to their knees.[16] Anti-Semitism was a central belief. During a time when anti-Semites around the world routinely penned forgeries claiming to be Jewish-authored works articulating plots for Jewish world domination, Butler himself penned one version of *The Protocols of the Elders of Zion: The International Jew*.

Butler also encouraged covert tactics to achieve political significance, and accordingly the ALR sought to erode the democratic system in four ways: infiltration of the National and Liberal parties, where it sought to undermine and replace core party values with its own; elite penetration, whereby it hoped to capture leadership positions in these parties; policy penetration, where it bloc-voted and stacked in target parties; and finally, cultivating agents of influence, whereby it formed grassroots groups to pressure targeted politicians.[17] This strategy of infiltration would be used decades later by the right-wing group the Lads Society. In any event, the ALR sought to game the democratic system and increase its own power without actually having popular support among the community.

The ALR had connections in New Zealand, South Africa, Canada and Britain, and became a sprawling network of chapters, in addition to forming domestic front groups to lobby on its behalf. These included the Women Who Want To Be Women group and the Christian Alternative Movement. In 1964, the ALR established what it called 'Voters' Policy Associations' or VPAs, whose members believed they were engaged in a life and death struggle raging throughout the world. The VPAs believed themselves responsible for engaging in recruitment drives, propaganda and pressure activities to alter government or party policy. This activity, too, soon faded. ASIO kept the group under surveillance until 1984, when the threat was assessed to be low enough to reduce coverage by one-third.[18] Despite this, individuals with links to the ALR went on to establish organisations of their own and engage in violence.

Beyond the ALR, one of the most prominent right-wing leaders was a journalist called Frank Browne. He dreamed of Australia becoming a 'muscular white nation' lording it over the Pacific, with a small government and a large military.[19] Browne briefly led the ill-fated Australian Party between 1955 and 1957, which managed to garner only a few hundred members. What Browne did achieve was a Nazi identity in Australia that provided the bedrock for subsequent neo-Nazi culture and led to the establishment of other neo-Nazi groups, such as the National Australian Workers Party, established in 1959 by some of Browne's acolytes.

Following Browne were other failures to form an extreme right-wing party in Australia. In the mid-1950s, Arthur Smith tried to establish the Australian National Socialist Party, which followed Nazi doctrine.[20] Personality clashes between the leaders of the movement were a persistent weakness. Smith tried to revamp the party between 1966 and 1968, recognising that it had failed to gain resonance with the Australian people. He tried to rebrand from the jackbooted stereotype of Nazis, and replaced swastikas with Akubras—a move that would be mimicked by the extreme-right group Antipodean Resistance decades later. In 1968, with the resignation of Arthur Smith, the National Socialist Party of Australia (NSPA) was formed under the leadership of Edward Cawthorn, Ferenc Molnar (a Holocaust denier), Leslie Ritchie and John Stewart.[21]

The NSPA contested the Senate elections in 1970s, its candidates in Queensland scoring as many as 12,000 votes, and netting another 8000 in New South Wales and 1800 in Victoria. At the time, ASIO believed that support for the NSPA was derived more from its anti-communist stance than any great devotion to its policies.[22] The NSPA opposed the Vietnam Moratorium, and staged counterprotests against Jewish and student groups. It was rumoured that the party had a secret 'kill list' of 100 prominent Australian politicians and businessmen, and an elite EAGLE guard of fifteen. There were also claims of a training camp in Emerald, east of Melbourne, which ASIO thought to be false. ASIO also believed that some members were responsible for incendiary bombs that damaged left-wing businesses in Melbourne.[23] The NSPA was weakened internally as a result of its leadership, infighting and relatively small membership. Its members' beliefs made them the enemy of radical student groups, communists, Jews and Australian society at large. '[They are] a lunatic-fringe extremist political organisation promoting a Nazi-type "ideology" abhorrent to the population at large, and maintaining its very identity through acts of provocation directed at its main ideological targets—jews [sic], communists and radical left-wing bodies generally,' an ASIO report found in 1971.[24]

Such fringe dwellers were likely responsible for the importation of Nazi paraphernalia from abroad in 1963. Two Brisbane residents imported stickers stating 'Hitler was Right' and 'Unite and Fight';

leaflets and stormtrooper magazines; literature catalogues; a Nazi armband; and neo-Nazi music from Hatenanny records. Other packages were sent to a man in Geelong who was deemed mentally unstable by police. As there was no provision against the importation of such materials, the parcels were released to their addressees. Three months later, the same stickers were used against a Sydney synagogue, supposedly by a nascent group called the Australian National Socialist Movement (ANSM).

The ANSM also called itself the Australian National Workers Party, and NSW police documents note that three prominent members were allegedly Brian Raven, Donald Alexander Lindsay and Graeme Royce, although Arthur Smith was also once a member.[25] Police investigations tied the ANSM to the American neo-Nazi George Rockwell, and two prominent British fascists, Oswald Mosley and Colin Jordan. More than 500 stickers were thought to have been imported and disseminated.[26] This dissemination was among the first signs that such a network was reawakening in modern Australia. The transnational fascist network created in World War II had not died, it had merely gone dormant.

Two politically motivated events could be attributed to the extreme right during this time. The first occurred on 8 July 1970 in Canberra, when a piece of masonry was thrown through the window of the residence of Kevin Townley Dobson, a stipendiary magistrate (and later acting chief magistrate). Dobson had recently dismissed a charge against prominent anti–Vietnam War campaigner M.J. Kahan. Kahan, as a left-wing activist, was loathed by the NSPA, whose members were considered the most likely suspects. Targeting the judge was an act of retribution for his ruling. A year later, on 8 March 1971, another left-wing opponent was targeted. A gelignite bomb detonated inside the residence of Senator-elect Arthur Gietzelt of the Australian Labor Party in Caringbah, Sydney. The attack caused extensive damage, although it is not clear who was actually responsible. Because of Gietzelt's anti–Vietnam War campaigning and his left-wing politics, it is possible that this attack was conducted by the extreme right.[27]

Two main leaders emerged from the NSPA movement towards the end of the decade: Robert John Cameron and Rosemary Sisson. Cameron became publicly involved with the NSPA in 1974, when he unsuccessfully stood for Senate election. He quickly rose through the ranks to become national secretary and deputy leader. He often courted media attention by making outrageous statements, such as that the NSPA had stormtrooper training camps and death lists, and suggesting that 187 of its enemies could be killed by joint NSPA and Palestinian commandos. He was considered responsible for damage to left-wing bookshops, and engaged in threatening behaviour towards left-wing political opponents. In 1976, he dubbed himself 'Führer'—which drove the Melbourne NSPA to distance itself from his brand of politics.[28]

Rosemary Sisson, meanwhile, was a Victorian arts–law graduate who worked for a time in the Australian Public Service. She had a keen interest in South Africa, Rhodesia (now Zimbabwe), and the United Kingdom—hotspots for white power movements—and visited all three. She also served in the Army Reserve as a radio operator. Sisson became involved in the movement in 1975 due to her 'overriding awareness of the differences between white people and other races',[29] although her travel history would suggest that this was a long-term fascination. She began attending Melbourne NSPA meetings in 1977 after she returned to Australia, and also became involved with the Eureka Students League, a student-based neo-Nazi group (not to be confused with the communist Eureka Youth League). Intelligence reports note that she was 'less adversely qualified' for leadership than her comrades.[30]

The Melbourne Nazis seemed to have increasingly divorced themselves from the stereotypical Nazi image, and no longer supported the more provocative Sydney NSPA led by Cameron.[31] Now-public ASIO documents suggest that towards 1977 a member of the Sydney NSPA told the Melbourne NSPA that Jeremy May intended to establish a National Front group in Melbourne. ASIO documents suggested that May was the 'Overseas Organiser of the British National Front'—and he was believed to have been active in both South Africa and New Zealand previously.³² When May met with the Melbourne NSPA he told them that John Tyndall, then deputy chairman of the British National Front and co-founder of the New Zealand White Commonwealth Association, had instructed him to create a National Front in Australia.³³ The transnational network was beginning to take shape.

Melbourne members of the NSPA, largely driven by Rosemary Sisson and Jeremy May, created a steering committee to coordinate negotiations with Tyndall and British counterparts. While they agreed to many elements of Tyndall and May's proposal, they disagreed with pledges of loyalty to the British crown, as these would be not be well received among some of their supporters; and they disagreed with the expulsion of Aboriginal peoples, who the NSPA believed were entitled to live in Australia. This was no inclusive gesture on behalf of the NSPA: in their ideal state, Aboriginal peoples would be excluded from citizenship, 'confined to their native reserves at all times and . . . strictly controlled in population'.³⁴

The Melbourne group was in direct competition with the Sydney Nazis, as they had heard rumours that political aspirant and neo-Nazi Arthur Christian Tane³⁵ had also contacted Tyndall in order to create a National Front in New South Wales, which was subsequently reported in a now-public Department of Foreign Affairs document.³⁶ The Melbourne group was worried about missing out on the prestige that would come from a clear connection with Tyndall, and seeing its already scarce membership flock to the Sydney groups. In any event, Sisson's Melbourne group beat the Sydney group to the punch, and the National Front of Australia (NFA) was established early in 1978. It planned an inaugural conference for June 1978 and invited National Front officials from the United Kingdom, New Zealand and South Africa, demonstrating the value it placed on international contacts to convey legitimacy and authority.³⁷

The event was a failure. Only nine people attended the conference in the Southern Cross Hotel in Melbourne. In its charter, the group declared commitments to:

- developing economic and political ties with other Anglo-Celtic populations
- coordinating trade and defence ties within the Commonwealth
- closer ties with the United Kingdom and the Commonwealth
- strengthening the White Australia policy and the repatriation of non-white migrants
- a 'better deal' for Aboriginal peoples, by which they meant corralling them in reserves, controlling their population numbers, and excluding them from citizenship
- economic ideals similar to Social Credit (i.e. a living wage, nationalised industries, farming incentives)
- enforcing law and order, and criminalising drugs and homosexuality
- expanding the defence forces.[38]

It was recorded that Sisson became national coordinating convenor, Lawrence Ronald Morton national vice chairman, Walter Heinrich Edward Wilhelm Krull treasurer, while Robert Valentin Furlan and David Greason (who was only sixteen) assumed no positions.[39] Greason later wrote *I Was a Teenage Fascist*, while Furlan currently runs a charity that aims to 'promote co-operation among English-speaking peoples through cultural and educational programs'.[40] Of the remaining attendees, one was a journalist for *The Age*, two are unknown, and the final attendee was probably an ASIO officer. The details of the meeting were reported in newspapers the very next day.

Shortly thereafter, Robert Cameron began to claim he had also established an NFA branch, as did Antonius Heintjes in Brisbane, despite Sisson rejecting association with the two. While Heintjes soon retracted his statements, Cameron did not. It appears he may have gone on to establish his own NFA regardless. Cameron was disowned by Sisson's NFA because of his violent rhetoric, which undermined her attempts to develop a respectable reputation that promoted Nazi ideals but no longer looked explicitly Nazi.[41]

Cameron and Sisson's manoeuvring was for naught. As is common among these groups, the NFA failed to achieve any meaningful political significance due to infighting between its leaders, and by 1984 it had disbanded. This demonstrates, however, two key facts: first, there was domestic support for extreme-right organisations in Australia, however small; and second, political organisation had to this point failed to trigger the authoritarian utopia.

Race hate emerges

The NFA had focused on strengthening the White Australia policy, deporting non-white migrants, criminalising homosexuality, and deepening ties with white countries. These same motivations were to endure, and become part of the impetus for the new surge in activity that was to occur in the late 1970s and 1980s. National Action (NA) emerged, and with it the Australian Nationalist Movement, and together they would incite a significant surge of extreme-right violence in Australia. They shared similar ideas to the fascist movements of the past, both domestic and international.

The leader of NA was James 'Jim' Saleam, who was based in Sydney and founded the National Resistance Group in 1977, which evolved into the National Alliance in 1978.[42] The National Alliance merged with the Immigration Control Association in 1981 to form the Progressive Nationalist Party. These groups collapsed, and eventually Saleam formed NA in April 1982.[43] NA focused initially on opposing the attendance of students from non-European backgrounds at Sydney universities. Over time, its worldview came to adopt many positions popular within the extreme right. NA claimed Australia for the white man and opposed immigration. NA members explicitly dismissed democracy as a myth, and articulated conspiracies that a Zionist lobby was enforcing immigration and multiculturalism.[44] NA also engaged in homophobic activity, targeting the Pitt Street Uniting Church because of its acceptance of homosexuals (and migrants). It particularly targeted Asian Australians and left-wing opponents, both on and off university campuses, with street violence. Beyond this, the NA engaged in intimidation campaigns in Sydney; storming the Uniting Church; burning female effigies on a female minister's front yard; firebombing a union member's car; and harassing members of the gay, lesbian, and migrant communities.[45]

NA member Jack van Tongeren, a former member of the Australian Army, is rumoured to have challenged Saleam for leadership. When this failed, he returned to Perth and established a splinter group, the Australian Nationalist Movement (ANM) in 1985. He greatly admired Adolf Hitler and the operations of Nazi Germany.[46] He, too, had travelled extensively, meeting with neo-Nazi figures in the United States, United Kingdom and Europe—even visiting Holocaust sites with his international allies. He styled himself the 'supreme leader' of ANM.[47] The group itself was an anti-Semitic white-supremacist organisation, opposing ethnic minorities and left-wing political opponents in Australia. ANM rejected the presence of all ethnic migrants (especially Asian Australians) and multiethnic relationships, and believed that the 'Zionist Occupation Government' was secretly controlling the nations of the world to enforce multiculturalism. Multiculturalism, according to the ANM, was designed to weaken the Aryan 'race', suppress its natural genius and render it a slave. Beyond all this, ANM believed the white 'race' in Australia was being replaced, and that this replacement was being engineered by vast and malevolent powers.

Of course, not all members entirely understood van Tongeren's ideological beliefs: some were merely so-called 'street rats' seeking an outlet for violent impulses. ANM's aims were based on the US book *The Turner Diaries*, by a prominent leader of the Ku Klux Klan. According to a senior ANM member:

> Our ethos was to terrorise the Asian community through any means possible from arson to anything such as murder ... The basic aim was to discourage other Asians immigrating to Australia and it was also intended to terrorise occupants here to such an extent that they would leave the state.[48]

With such an objective, ANM soon spread across Australia, setting up chapters in South Australia, Queensland, New South Wales, Victoria and Tasmania.[49] Beyond van Tongeren, the leadership included John van Blitterswyk as second-in-command; Russell Willey as third-in-command and treasurer; Christopher Bartle; Wayne van Blitterswyk, who owned land they needed, and Judith Lyons, who acted as an accessory.

ANM tried to divide itself into two wings: a militant wing and a political wing. The Australian Nationalist Movement was the political wing, and the Australian Aryan Army (AAA) the military wing. John van Blitterswyk was the commander of the AAA, which appeared never to move beyond the conceptual stage.[50] In order to advance the AAA, the ANM set up a training facility on a farm in Bindoon, east of Perth. The Bindoon bunker was technically a farm, but it also contained a shelter, a lookout and a rifle range (ANM called it, optimistically, Radical Ranch). ANM planned to use it as a training ground for soldiers in the revolution, while van Tongeren's home in Gosnells became the ANM headquarters. In an attempt to make the ANM respectable, Jack van Tongeren filed an application to register the ANM as a legitimate political party in February 1986. In February 1989, van Tongeren contested the seat of Helena as an ANM candidate. His election platform was based on resistance to the 'Asianisation of Australia and to Zionist control of Australia'.[51] During the election, he had the house of one of his own members firebombed and shot at so that they could claim the insurance money (with which the member subsequently absconded). Van Tongeren attracted 300–400 votes but did not win the seat.

Shortly before his political failure, van Tongeren did what some fringe radicals do when they begin to realise the community doesn't support them: he turned to coercion and threat. The propaganda campaign began in 1987, and had escalated to destructive acts by the end of 1988. The ANM plastered 400 posters all around Perth on buses, walls and depots. Perth citizens were shocked to wake up on 7 December, an otherwise typical Monday morning, to see posters emblazoned with the words 'Asians out or race war', and 'Don't lose your job to an Asian. Join the ANM. Stop the Invasion'.[52] Although the initial propaganda targeted ethnic minorities, ANM leaders were open about the fact that their 'real enemy behind the scenes' was Jews. This campaign was not merely the work of the ANM; it claimed to have received the support of local skinhead gangs. Afterwards, the ANM attracted substantial publicity and media attention.

'They are steadily outbreeding and dispossessing Australians,' van Tongeren told the newspapers, referring to Asians. 'It's a basic racial instinct—a healthy mechanism to safeguard our race and culture.'[53] These statements, though shocking, were legal. At the time, Western Australia had no anti-discrimination legislation; only New South Wales had outlawed racial vilification. Without legal recourse, a number of anti-racist groups formed in Perth to counteract and combat the ANM's threatening campaigns. The ANM, undeterred, continued spreading misinformation about minorities, especially Blacks and Jews, and threatening them. One poster, which John van Blitterswyk and van Tongeren posted themselves, claimed 'Media Cover-up. Holocaust a lie. Seek the Truth'. The Minister for Ethnic Affairs, Gordon Hill, caught them in the act of postering. He pulled a poster down and reported it to police, which eventually led to van Tongeren and van Blitterswyk being fined for property damage. In response, van Tongeren said, 'I've done nothing wrong. I was standing morally correct before my nation for which I am fighting by the eternal law.'[54]

His belief in his righteousness was about to spawn a nine-month crime spree and campaign of violence, primarily targeting Perth's Asian population.

Fires in the night

Synchronous to propaganda and electoral efforts, the ANM made a long-planned strategic shift from propaganda to politically motivated violence against the Asian-Australian community in late 1988. Its tactic of choice was firebombing. The ANM sourced a sprayer, which it used to spray petrol under the eaves and onto the roofs of their target locations, smashing windows with bricks to disperse more petrol inside the buildings. Once the target was soaked with petrol, they threw a Molotov cocktail and fled to the next target. On 1 September, Jack van Tongeren, John van Blitterswyk and Chris Bartle firebombed the China City Restaurant in Como, causing $7000 in damage. It never reopened. That same night, the three men also firebombed the Man Lin restaurant in Karawara, causing $100,000 worth of damage. On 22 November, the ANM firebombed the Golden House restaurant in Bellevue. The fire damage alone was $45,000, which, as the building was not insured, destroyed the business completely. It never reopened. The ANM had moved beyond threats, and now sought to drive out Perth's multicultural community through coercive violence.

A new group formed in an attempt to combat the ANM called Aussies Against Racism (AAR). Unfortunately, it was infiltrated by John Bain of the ANM, under the alias Dennis. On 13 January, the AAR planned to meet up and paint over the racist ANM posters. Instead, AAR member Nicholas Smurthwaite was lured into a parking lot in Kardinya shopping centre by Bain. Once there, Bain disappeared, and Smurthwaite was confronted by eight people wearing balaclavas, green overalls and military boots. One held a knife to Smurthwaite's throat and the other ANM members beat and choked him, and clubbed him to the ground. They fled when a car approached, leaving Smurthwaite so badly injured that he was hospitalised. It later transpired that van Tongeren, John van Blitterswyk, Bartle and Willey were involved in the attack, while other ANM leaders, including Judith Lyons, Wayne van Blitterswyk, and Mark Ferguson were implicated.

On 16 January, the ANM firebombed another Chinese restaurant, the Ko Sing in Ferndale, causing $17,500 worth of damage. Two days later, on 18 January, the ANM firebombed the Ling Nan restaurant in Mirrabooka, and caused $39,500 worth of damage. On 28 January, another member of AAR was targeted. Helen Carroll was away from home for a week, and when she returned she found that her car had been set alight and destroyed, apparently by van Tongeren and John van Blitterswyk.⁵⁵

After these attacks, the ANM turned its attention away from firebombing Asian restaurants and towards stockpiling for the imagined race war. It began to break into businesses to steal the resources it needed to reinforce its bunker and finance the group's activities. The thefts started on New Year's Day 1989, when Russell Willey broke into General Bulldozing in Guildford, stealing computer equipment and cheques. During the January rush, the ANM broke into businesses in Welshpool and stole six chainsaws and 1000 sandbags. These were secreted at the Bindoon bunker.

But the ANM was not the only extreme-right threat: on the other side of Australia, NA endured under the leadership of Saleam. In January 1989, there was a drive-by shooting at the house of Eddie Funde, an African National Congress leader who campaigned against apartheid. On 27 January, police charged Saleam with being an accessory before the fact, and alleged that he supplied Jason Frost and Michael White, the two shooters, with the firearm, in addition to balaclavas, gloves, ammunition and Funde's address. After the shooting, White and Frost had hidden the gun under the floorboards of White's house, and it was collected by Saleam the following day. Police very quickly finalised their investigation, leading to the NA cadre being charged.

Back on the west coast, the ANM was in full swing. On 2 February, it broke into Tandy in Cannington, stealing two-way radio equipment and electronic scanners in about 30 seconds. Willey and Bain were the key culprits. Around 9 February, the van Blitterswyk brothers and Willey broke into a Vox Adeon store in Myaree, stealing $20,000 of video recorders and cameras. On 19 February, Willey led a team and broke into building supplies company Alco in Cannington, stealing 25 sheets of fibro. Around 24 February, the ANM struck again, this time targeting the Vox Adeon store in Willetton. They smashed their way in, stole fifteen TVs, twenty video recorders and ten compact disc players to the value of $30,000. Four days later, they smashed their way into Hilti

Ltd in Victoria Park and stole construction tools and drills for the Bindoon bunker.⁵⁶ On 10 March, the ANM stole computer equipment from Belmont Management Corporation in Cannington. On 16 March, the ANM raided the A&M Bookshop in Willetton, stealing a cassette player, a fax machine and a typewriter. Between March and April, they broke into National Mutual Life, Direct Digital, and General Bulldozing, stealing cheques and computer equipment, and Vox Adeon, where they stole household goods. The group also stole cement mixers, wheelbarrows and ladders to further the construction of the Bindoon bunker. On one occasion, they stole a getaway car from a man married to an Asian-Australian woman.

All of this theft was, in essence, resource acquisition to prepare for violent confrontation, with the sandbags, cameras, scanners and cladding designed to reinforce the bunker. But it appears that the ANM continued stealing far beyond what they actually needed, as the resale of stolen items could be a source of revenue. The break-ins continued with such regularity that the ANM could no longer store all of its ill-gotten goods. The group had to rent a house in Thornlie to store dozens of TVs and other household merchandise.

The worst ANM bombing came on 25 May, when members returned to the Ko Sing restaurant, perhaps dissatisfied with the damage they caused in their previous attack. In a technological leap, they made an explosive device with power gel (commonly used in mining) wrapped in wire. When it exploded, the wire became shrapnel, and was embedded in the ceiling, tables and walls of the Ko Sing. No one was injured, but the explosion caused a further $50,000 in damage. Reports stated that the blast was so strong it 'lifted the roof off the building'.⁵⁷ In May and July, Western Australian police charged Jack van Tongeren with possessing explosives and unlicensed ammunition, but more was needed to put an end to their spree of theft and arson.⁵⁸

Operation Jackhammer

By August 1989, the ANM had caused more than $1 million in damage in Western Australia. In response, a 36-strong law-enforcement team was put together in an operation codenamed Jackhammer. The operation order read: 'The task force was created to investigate the movements of the ANM, the primary role and objective was to apprehend these offenders who had been blatantly committing a series of offences and terrorising the ethnic community.'[59]

And that they did. Operation Jackhammer investigated the ANM for six weeks. Soon, the Jackhammer team received a tip-off about the house in Thornlie, which was full to the brim with stolen electrical goods. Detectives staked out the house, and when John van Blitterswyk and Russell Willey arrived at the property four nights later, Jackhammer ambushed the two men. On 4 July 1989, the second-in-command and third-in-command of the ANM were caught red-handed.

A breakthrough came when Willey, who was also conveniently the treasurer of the ANM, turned informant. In exchange for immunity, he told police all that they needed to know. They, in turn, protected his life. Willey led them to weapons caches, including one in Huntingdon, New South Wales, that held a rifle and silencer, and another in Kensington, Western Australia, with a rifle and twelve detonators. On 8 August, Willey wore a wire and went for a drive with van Tongeren, prompting his leader to talk about the firebombing and theft. This was the last item of evidence that Operation Jackhammer needed. On 14 August, Jackhammer officers executed simultaneous arrest warrants across Sydney and Perth.

The Bindoon bunker was the highest-risk target, as detectives didn't know if the site was rigged for ambush, or if the ANM would engage in a shootout. Fortunately, this did not occur, and van Tongeren, John van Blitterswyk, and Judith Lyons were arrested at Bindoon without violence. Wayne van Blitterswyk was arrested while prospecting on the Eastern Goldfields, and Chris Bartle at his home in Perth, while Mark Ferguson and John Bain were arrested in Sydney. Within hours, the leadership of the ANM was facing a total of 159 charges. Their assets had been frozen, and the extradition of Ferguson and Bain to Western Australia was looming.

The ANM threatened to get even, issuing threats against the police, their families and witnesses only two days after their arrest. Bizarrely, two days later, Jack van Tongeren changed his tune: he gave Operation Jackhammer's Arson Squad the ANM party flag, complete with a Nazi swastika. He wrote: 'From a general to the soldiers, I concede the battle of round one to the arson squad but not the war.'[60] It was a small concession, but he was not yet ready to give up the fight. The ANM members refused to record pleas during the trial, claiming to be 'political soldiers'.[61] They also attempted to represent themselves, which ultimately led the judge to enter not-guilty pleas on their behalf.

It was thirteen months before the trial was concluded, in part because of a Nazi murder then being tried in the Supreme Court that cast a shadow over the possibility of a fair trial for ANM members. During the ANM trial, van Tongeren used the courtroom as his grandstand:

> I convinced my comrades of the justice of our cause and I led the attack. I threw the first Molotov cocktail. I fought the enemy by talking and by posters and I fought the enemy on the streets . . . If I die in jail as the people who run the country intend, then I will defy the corrupt legal code until the end. Australia is worth it.
>
> Yes, I am unrepentant and I will stay that way. The time has come to fight. Damn your rotten laws. Australia forever.[62]

The trial also revealed the ANM had discussed murdering senior police officers and government ministers, blowing up ships, and breaking prisoners out of jail and arming them. Despite a futile hunger strike by van Tongeren, on 15 September 1990 a District Court jury in Perth handed down a guilty sentence. Jack van Tongeren was convicted of 53 crimes, and sentenced to eighteen years. John van Blitterswyk, the second-in-command, was sentenced to fourteen years' gaol, while his brother Wayne van Blitterswyk, the explosives expert, was sentenced to ten years' gaol. Mark Ferguson and Judith Lyons were each sentenced to three years' gaol and three years' probation.

Back on the east coast, Jim Saleam was again in front of a judge: this time for conspiring with a fellow, John Rex Anderson, to firebomb the car of Peter Coleman. He appealed this conviction, claiming he was entrapped by his wife, among others.

Self-cannibalism

In the midst of this organised activity by extreme right-wing groups, there were also instances of sporadic violence. There were firebombing attacks on Jewish premises in Sydney in March 1989, for example, targeting a girls' school and a youth club, and a bomb threat was made against the Jewish Hakoah Club in Bondi. In another case, Dane Sweetman, a neo-Nazi, and an accomplice assaulted a man they believed to be gay in Thornbury, Melbourne, while Sweetman was on bail for armed robbery offences.[63] There were a series of firebombs thrown against a Jewish residential college in Sydney in January, and against synagogues in Melbourne in March and April 1990. There was also violence of a more lethal and personal nature from fringe elements connected to the ANM or NA movements.

In August 1989, while the ANM leadership was being arrested, a young ANM member called David Locke was living in Jack van Tongeren's Gosnells home. On 2 September, his body was discovered by an eleven-year-old boy in a creek in Gosnells: Locke had been bashed to death and his throat had been slit. The night before, he had been at a pub when fellow ANM members William Patrick Monaghan and Wayne Robert Napier happened across his path. The conversation turned to the ANM court case, and Locke apparently expressed an intention to aid the prosecution as a witness.

'Willy [Monaghan] was pretty pissed off about it, putting other people in for no reason, there is no benefit of it,' Napier said in a videotaped statement. Napier himself was annoyed because 'you want to go to the pub after work and relax—you don't need some guy filling your head with crap'.[64] After Locke left the pub, Monaghan and Napier followed him, and murdered him. They were charged two days later with wilful murder, and both received life in prison.

Similar intergroup tension was evident on the east coast in connection with NA. On 23 April 1990, Perry John Whitehouse, a member of NA, shot and killed fellow member Wayne David Smith. In a bizarre happenstance, ASIO recorded the entire murder, having previously planted listening devices in the NA headquarters in Sydney's inner west, where Whitehouse was planning the murder. It is suggested that Whitehouse decided to kill Smith because they had had a disagreement about Saleam and the shooting of Eddie Funde's house. Whitehouse pleaded guilty.

In the midst of the ANM and NA practising self-cannibalism, another small neo-Nazi group was active in Melbourne. Its members had attacked Jewish families in the street, vandalised a Jewish library, and desecrated twenty Jewish gravestones. On 23 April 1990, a dog walker stumbled across the dismembered body of a 29-year-old man in the Yarra River in Kew, Melbourne. Victorian Police identified the body, which had been tied with rope and wrapped in foam, as that of David Noble of Adelaide. On the weekend before his death, Noble attended a neo-Nazi party celebrating Hitler's birthday on 20 April. Other attendees included Dane Sweetman, Martin Bayston and Sean Shilling. Sweetman was a 'proud member of teenage skinhead gangs, had a fixation with Nazi doctrines and an antipathy towards homosexuals'.[65] He was a petty and violent crook. He was close friends with Martin Bayston, a 27-year-old neo-Nazi. Shilling, however, was a 'street kid' under the influence of the other two.

Sweetman and Bayston decided to kill Noble because he had become 'an annoyance'.[66] They told Shilling they intended to assault Noble, encouraging Shilling to join them. During the assault, Sweetman hit Noble on the head with a pickaxe, while Bayston stabbed him twenty times with a boning knife. Shilling kicked Noble several times in the head. They then cut off his legs to fit his body in the boot of their car, and dumped the body in the Yarra River. When they were arrested, Shilling alone pleaded guilty to the murder. As a result, while Shilling receiving a seven-year sentence, Sweetman and Bayston were sentenced to twenty and eighteen years respectively. During the trial, Sweetman yelled at reporters, 'You Zionist maggots are going to get it—Sieg Heil.'[67]

Returning to the dark

With the arrest of the leaders of the ANM and NA, these groups effectively collapsed. Prominent and open extreme-right organisations ceased to parade before the media. Instead, they returned to the dark places within fringe subcultures wherein extreme-right worldviews endured: in some cases, they developed in isolation, but primarily they evolved with contact with like-minded extremists around the world. With little regard for the origin of many extreme-right conspiracies, their willing domestic supporters nurtured their beliefs, their sense of alienation from a broader society that, too soon, forgot them and their desire for a white revolution in Australia. But fascism tends to linger, even where it is not accepted.

The groups that enabled this endurance are diverse, but significant proponents include the Women for Aryan Unity, the Southern Cross Hammerskins, Blood and Honour, and associated skinhead gangs. There were also remnants of the fascist Ustaša, which retained a minor presence in Australia. There were also elements that drew on American traditions, such as the Confederate Action Party, plus anti-government militias in Queensland, stirred up by the 1996 gun-control legislation. Aryan Nations had a minimal, although marked, presence in Australia, as did the Ku Klux Klan. The Loyal Regiment of Australian Guardians, the AUSI Freedom Scouts, and the Abolish Self Government Coalition were rumoured to be in the mix. Inconveniently, given the number of right-wing extremists serving time in prison, the extreme-right groups also formed in correctional facilities. In 1995, ASIO warned of an 'upsurge in the activities of religious extremists, doomsday cults, neo-Nazis, and right-wing militia groups', according to the *Canberra Times*.[68] That same year, the grave of Eddie Mabo, the campaigner for Aboriginal rights and the revolutionary who saw Australia's doctrine of 'terra nullius' overturned, was desecrated by suspected neo-Nazis in Townsville.

The disjointed campaigns of the Australian extreme right did not come to an end with the close of the century. Despite changing in some ways, they were still a distinct threat, and still adhered to very much the same belief systems and strategies as the right-wing extremists before them. What is significant, however, is right-wing extremism in Australia has been both international and domestic from its very genesis. Extremists developed and maintained connections with the extreme right internationally, while Australian citizens, whether born here or elsewhere, were intrinsic to the movement.

Unlike other terrorism threats, however, their goal was to rip the very fabric of Australian society apart. They did not pursue a change in some distant land, but in Australia, driven by deep-rooted and twisted fantasies disconnected from actuality, in pursuit of an imagined utopia. They, much like the extreme left, sought to fundamentally alter the political and democratic order in Australia. Unlike the left, however, their goal was to transform it into an authoritarian state that enforced societal conformity at the expense of personal freedoms, that sought to alienate and terrify ethnic Australians and religious minorities, and to ultimately crush the democratic system whose freedoms they enjoyed. This threat, given time, would soon rise again.

8

Under sarin skies: Aum Shinrikyo

Up to this point in Australian history, terrorism had manifested in three main ways. First, terrorists of extreme-left or extreme-right persuasions were domestically driven and internationally connected, but concerned primarily with altering Australia's liberal democratic order. Second, international terrorist organisations recruited Australian supporters, who offered both financial and operational assistance for international campaigns aimed at foreign political orders. Third, Australia generally made for an attractive target for terrorism because of its independent media guaranteeing international publicity, and because its national security apparatus was not yet as developed as that of other Western nations.

This would change in the 1990s with the rise of religious fundamentalism in the form of Japanese doomsday cult Aum Shinrikyo. This cult would leverage its domestic supporters to take unique advantage of Australia's vast and lonely wilderness. Its work in the Australian outback provided a freedom of operations that contributed directly to its development of biological and chemical weapons programs designed to accelerate the apocalypse and bring about the end of days. Aum Shinrikyo's chemical dreams would take it all around the globe, and ultimately saw it become one of the most unique terrorist threats of the twentieth century, paving the way for religious terrorism to come.

An apocalyptic vision

Aum Shinrikyo was founded by charismatic cultist Chizuo Matsumoto. Born to a poor family, Matsumoto was partially blinded by glaucoma as a child. He sought admittance to university early in his adult life but was unsuccessful. To support his burgeoning young family, Matsumoto founded an acupuncture business that sold fake medicines in addition to more traditional compounds—all without the appropriate licensing. He also began practising yoga around 1981, and became interested in some of the new religions arising in Japan that challenged the established order.

Since the 1950s, Japan had become rife with new religions. Some of these religions were influenced by Shinto beliefs, others by science, Buddhism and Christianity. Some were hugely popular and gained nearly a million followers, while others catered to cliques of only 5000 or 6000. These new religions offered young Japanese professionals something different: a belief structure that freed them from the confines of post-war Japanese society. The new religions were often a combination of major religions, from which they drew their social acceptability and legitimacy, and offered spiritual liberation, freedom, leadership and self-discovery.

The key social demographic attracted to the new religions in the 1980s were the educated, intelligent youth of Japan's elite classes. The new religions symbolised a dramatic departure from the strict conventions of Japanese life—and, significantly, offered these people the opportunity to realise their dreams. The youth were frustrated by their slow social progress in Japanese society, and, like all frustrated idealists, they began searching for meaning, community and social progression elsewhere. The new religions offered them creative freedom, a broader and daring scientific licence and, more importantly, an escape from Japan's 'conformist social environment'.[1]

In this context, Matsumoto founded his own yoga studio called Aum Shinsen no Kai (meaning 'Aum Immortal Wizard Association'—Aum itself being an acronym inspired by the Hindu gods of creation, continuation and destruction) with only fifteen members.

Matsumoto changed his name to Shoko Asahara, and the yoga studio quickly became a cult centred on his personality and his narcotics-induced prophecies. Soon, Asahara renamed his organisation Aum Shinrikyo (meaning 'Supreme Truth') and began building a belief system that included elements of other religions, offering his followers a higher level of spirituality and emancipation from earthly concerns. This was, in sum, a new religion in its own right.

Asahara's teachings drew from Hinduism, exploiting yoga practices and preaching austerity, in addition to Buddhism, championing the idea of rebirth and transmigration. He also drew on Christianity, and its interpretation of Armageddon, and was inspired by the writings of Nostradamus. Born in 1503, Nostradamus also worked with medicines and failed in his academic career (much like Asahara). Asahara drew on biblical stories to make various predictions regarding the end of the world. Most significantly, perhaps, Asahara was also influenced by science fiction, notably the *Foundation* series of Isaac Asimov, in which a visionary psychic historian predicts the future and foresees the unstoppable decline of intergalactic empires. Amid great adversity, the protagonist creates the Foundation to preserve the accumulated knowledge of mankind, with the hope of forming a new and enlightened society once the period of decline and barbarism is over. In time, Asahara began to perceive himself as a similar protagonist, predicting the end of the world and offering humanity its last hope for salvation.

Asahara believed that he could foresee the Third World War occurring in 1997: a nuclear war triggered by the United States of America that would bring an end to all life on earth. Asahara charged his members with spreading the word of doom in return for their salvation and a place in the post-apocalyptic world order: a utopia that could only exist under him and his teachings. Gaining membership to Aum and securing a place in this utopia, however, came at a price: it required followers to donate all of their material belongings and resources to the cult, and sever contact with their friends and family. They lived in isolation from the rest of society, most of their engagement with outsiders being limited to recruitment attempts. Aum soon boasted nearly 50,000 members, primarily drawn from society's young, educated elite.

As word of Aum spread, so too did media coverage of its leader. Asahara attracted attention by saying wild things, claiming he could both fly and levitate, and designating himself both as Christ and the Enlightened One from Buddhism. Asahara also played upon the common quest for meaning and self that pervaded alternative spirituality at the time. In 1986 he said,

> For the first time I stopped and thought, 'What am I living for? What must I do to overcome this sense of emptiness? . . .' The desire to seek after the ultimate, the unchanging, awoke within me, and I began groping for an answer. That meant that I had to discard everything. Yes, everything that I had. It took great courage and faith, and great resolution.'[2]

Such statements resonated with those on quests of their own. Aum promised its followers deeper meaning and metaphysical gratification on the one hand, and seemed to promise professional advancement and the realisation of ambitions, after great sacrifice, on the other. Ten per cent of Aum members became *shukkesha*, severing all ties with their families, and committing themselves (and all their worldly resources) entirely to the Aum mission.

Early on in his preaching, Asahara had plans to change Japanese society for the better and create a utopia. This phase lasted four years until, in 1988, Asahara began to believe he was the messiah of the coming global apocalypse. He believed the disintegration of the Soviet Union, the unification of Europe, and Halley's Comet were all signs pointing towards the end. He began to teach his followers that the end was nigh and inevitable. Instead of a utopia, Asahara began planning a nuclear shelter. His preaching also became more extreme, and disavowed society as corrupt, decadent and doomed.[3] This deep conviction in Armageddon became the focus of Asahara's teachings. The forces of evil, he promised, would destroy each other, and only the revolutionary elite of Aum would survive. World-engulfing violence lay on the path to securing the salvation of their souls.[4] Once the ash had settled, they believed that the new world order would begin under Aum's spiritual and political leadership.

Shoko Asahara ruled his cult with an iron fist. Any disagreement or opposition from his followers was met with threats and violence.[5] A culture of submission was fostered and maintained through groupthink, heavy drug use, sleep deprivation and violence. There was also no leaving Aum: followers who sought to escape the cult found themselves trapped and helpless. Part of this was financial: new recruits were required to donate their assets and income to Aum, which helped the cult financially control its followers while also strengthening its economic position. Other income was derived from Aum's high-pressure fundraising activities, insurance fraud and a suite of other criminal activities. Because Aum was technically a religious organisation, it was exempt from various forms of taxation, which only contributed to its wealth—and its power.

The Aum Shinrikyo Victims Society was established in 1989 by the families of captive Aum members. They sought to assist followers in escaping the cult, believing that some members were being held against their will. Aum responded with violence: a lawyer who was representing the families associated with the Victims Society was kidnapped, along with his wife and their one-year-old son. All three were murdered by Aum members, who confessed to the crime only years later.[6]

Aum's weapons program

In time, Asahara began to preach to a small inner circle that violence was required, not just to survive the apocalypse, but to trigger it. It was not simply the 1989 killings that indicated their turn to violence: in 1988, for example, Aum attempted to purchase 250 tons of sarin from a US weapons supplier, which turned out to be a US Customs front.[7] Beyond these sporadic attempts, Aum's weapons program began systematically in February 1990, after Asahara engineered his own personal embarrassment. In that month, Asahara and 25 of his members stood for election to the

Lower House of Parliament in Japan but did not gain a single seat. This failure damaged Asahara's delicate sense of self-importance, and he turned on the society he believed himself destined to lead. Immediately after the election, Aum began plotting Armageddon. The cult's new goal was to overthrow the Japanese government by force, seize control and catalyse the apocalypse. To achieve this, it needed weapons.

Young, brilliant Aum scientists were sent to meet with Soviet specialists, although it took a few years for the relationship to bear fruit. Aum purchased the blueprints for AK47s and began domestic production in 1994. In June that year, Aum also purchased and smuggled an MI-17 cargo helicopter from Russia into Japan. Aum didn't rely solely on the Russians: in 1994 adherents broke into the Tokyo Metropolitan Police Department to steal data, and into the Hiroshima factory of Mitsubishi Heavy Industries to steal technical information on tanks and artillery systems.[8] Conventional military confrontation, however, was not Asahara's favoured option: his preference was biological warfare.

To that end, he charged one of his virologists, Seiichi Endo, to head a program to create biological warfare agents.[9] As Health and Welfare Minister of Aum, Endo held a high rank, and his ministry worked closely with Aum's Ministry of Science and Technology. As part of this role, Endo became integral to Aum's biological weapons programs, despite having little skill or training in biological agents. He persisted, and in April 1990 he and his team attempted to manufacture botulinum toxin. They developed the agent as a spray, which they dispersed around Tokyo while Asahara lectured to his followers from the safety of Ishigaki Island. The team targeted a US Naval Base, Narita International Airport, the Japanese National Assembly (Kokkai) and the Imperial Palace.[10] The idea behind targeting the US was to prompt World War III between the US and Japan. Fortunately, the attack failed, and no one succumbed to the toxic spray.

Endo also tried to weaponise a non-toxic strain of anthrax, believing he could genetically engineer it to be lethal. Without the requisite knowledge of bacteriology, he again failed. His experiments produced noxious fumes from an Aum laboratory in Koto, Tokyo, in June 1993, which led to around 100 people making complaints about the smell. Later, it would be discovered that the fumes were another test attack, dispersing anthrax bacilli.[11] In 1992, Aum sent a member to Zaire to procure the Ebola virus—which also failed. There were numerous other attacks using biological agents, including an unsuccessful botulinum attack against the Japanese royal family during the wedding of Prince Naruhito in June 1993.[12] The biological weapons program under Endo was paused due to these ongoing failures. Instead, Asahara ordered his personal physician Dr Tomomasa Nakagawa and his Minister of Science and Technology, 30-year-old Masami Tsuchiya, to pursue a chemical warfare program in 1993.[13] This ministry comprised some 300 young members, many of whom were scientists, and as part of this program they would be brought to Australia.

Outback toxins

The vast emptiness of Western Australia attracts thousands of tourists each year, but also people with malevolent intentions and, in this case, people with something to hide. On 22 April 1993, the Aum Minister of Construction, Kiyohide Hayakawa, landed in Perth. His ministry was responsible for acquiring Aum's land and facilities, and military hardware, and carrying out the occasional assassination (e.g. the killing of the lawyer and his family in 1989). In his party was Yoshihiro Inoue, the Intelligence Minister of Aum, whose primary role was to gather scientific and technical materials, often through burglaries such as the one at Mitsubishi Heavy Industries, infiltrate the Japanese defence force, and gather intelligence on the Japanese government's plans to counter the cult.

Hayakawa and Inoue's goal was to hire a real estate agent who could procure them a large, isolated property with confirmed deposits of uranium. They spent nearly a week inspecting properties in Western Australia, South Australia and Tasmania.[14] Ultimately, they purchased a lease for Banjawarn, a property of some 190,000 hectares in the middle of nowhere: 300 kilometres from Kalgoorlie, 80 kilometres from Jindalee Base, and 600 kilometres from Perth. It cost the kingly sum of $570,000—a small price for so wealthy an organisation.[15] Following the purchase, Aum created a shell company called Mahaposya Australia Proprietary Limited, jointly directed by Asahara and Japanese-Australian woman Yasuko Shimada, who was a member of Aum. Following the lease purchase, Aum learned that the property terms allowed people to enter the land while prospecting for minerals. They attempted to prevent that by obtaining eight mining licences for another $37,600. Aum then created Clarity Investments Proprietary Limited, a subsidiary of Mahaposya, which permitted them to prospect on the property, ostensibly for gold.

This was all a smokescreen. Banjawarn station gave Aum the privacy it needed to test its chemical weapons on living creatures, and the chance to procure high-quality uranium for its nascent nuclear weapons program. Hayakawa, who had originally developed Aum's relationship with Soviet scientists, praised the quality of Australian uranium and considered purchasing Russian nuclear warheads.[16] Soon, Aum was consulting geologists about the intricacies of exporting uranium.

In September, 25 Aum members including Shoko Asahara, his virologist Seiichi Endo, and his physician Tomomasa Nakagawa, flew from Japan to Perth. This was a significant event, as a number of other ministers also attended, including Hayakawa, Inoue, and Niimi Tomomitsu, Aum Minster for Home Affairs, who maintained cult discipline through coercion and violence. They took technical equipment, gas masks and digging tools as excess baggage, which cost them another $20,000. This was searched by Australian Customs, which charged them a $15,000 importation fee. When Customs officers found that two glass bottles labelled as hand soap actually contained hydrochloric acid, they seized two crates of chemicals and equipment. Endo and Nakagawa were charged, and they pleaded guilty to the offence.[17] This brought Aum onto the Australian Federal Police radar.

Despite these items being confiscated, the remaining Aum party continued on from Perth to Banjawarn, where they set up a chemical laboratory. Denied its chemicals by Customs, Aum did two things. First, it used its subsidiary companies in Australia to purchase more chemicals from wholesalers, and second, it financed a member to fly to Melbourne and back in a single day to procure those chemicals that were harder to replace. Once equipped at Banjawarn, they built a laboratory called Toyoda, and began to produce sarin gas and different types of mustard gas. They tested the sarin on 29 sheep, which resulted in the animals' deaths. The experiment was considered a success. The leaders returned to Japan, leaving behind cultists to continue searching for uranium, while others left the station one by one.

By now, however, the AFP had officers watching Aum comings and goings in Australia. Asahara attempted to return to Australia on a tourist visa, with two aides and seventeen bodyguards: this visa was denied through cooperation between the AFP and Immigration. In all, some twelve separate visa applications were rejected by the Australian government, which effectively rendered Aum's Australian operation over. Despite many repeated applications, only two low-ranking members were allowed back to Australia, and they travelled once again to Banjawarn to act as caretakers of the property. They failed to manage the vast station, and soon the Western Australian Pastoral Board ordered them to cull 2000 sheep that were showing signs of neglect.[18] Instead, Aum cultists destroyed the lab, burned most of the remaining equipment and sold the property. All that was left were about 32 litres of hydrochloric acid, more than 12 litres of ammonia, 5 litres of perchloric acid, 7.5 litres of nitric acid, more than 7 litres of chloroform, and a small amount of potassium dichromate.[19]

Unwittingly, Australia had hosted a terrorist group experimenting with weapons of mass destruction. Aum Shinrikyo's experimentation in the Australian outback would set in motion an attack that, Aum hoped, would lead to the apocalypse.

The production of sarin was not the limit of Aum's experimental weapons program. Masami Tsuchiya also produced 200 kilograms of mustard gas; 20 grams of soman, a nerve agent used by Germany in World War II; 20 grams of tabun, the world's first nerve agent; 20 grams of cyclosarin, classified as a weapon of mass destruction; phosgene, a chlorine gas; and 3 litres of hydrogen cyanide.[20] This activity, however, was bound to leave a trace. US toxicology professor Anthony Tu, an expert on sarin gas, devised a way to detect degraded sarin (methylphosphonic acid) in the soil, and assisted Japanese police with their detection processes in 1994. His subsequent article was published that year, and was read by Nakagawa, Asahara's physician.

Nakagawa went to Asahara with concerns that Tu's paper would assist the Japanese Police to discover their sarin production. By this time, Aum Shinrikyo's experimentation in Australia had borne fruit, and they had several laboratories in Japan manufacturing high-quality refined sarin gas. Aum Shinrikyo was so alarmed by Tu's research that it commenced the destruction of 70 tonnes of refined, high-quality sarin gas. Nakagawa later told Professor Tu that they 'decided to destroy the sarin so that the Japanese Police would not know we made sarin when they came to our facility to inspect'.[21] Ultimately, there was too much sarin to destroy, so Nakagawa and Tsuchiya, the Minister for Science and Technology, attempted to hide what remained.

It was in that same research article by Tu that Nakagawa and Tsuchiya got the idea to manufacture the VX nerve agent, an agent so dangerous that it is classified as a weapon of mass destruction. Tsuchiya made the VX a month after reading Professor Tu's article. VX was subsequently used to murder Tadahito Hamaguchi in 1994, after he helped ex-Aum members escape the group.[22] The VX was transported to Osaka in a syringe, and kept cold in an icebox. While some Aum cultists acted as lookouts, others grabbed Hamaguchi and injected the VX into his neck. He died ten days later.²³ Hamaguchi was not the only victim of Aum's experiments: in January 1995, Aum gassed the head of the Aum Shinrikyo Victims Society, a man named Hiroyuki Nagaoka, who survived but was left in a coma.²⁴ In February, Aum kidnapped and murdered a local administrator by lethal injection, and incinerated his body in one of its underground bunkers.

The violence of Aum was not only directed at external threats. Under the orders of Home Affairs Minister Niimi Tomomitsu, six former members of Aum were held captive in one of the group's facilities. Another member, pharmacist Otaro Ochida, was hanged in an Aum facility and his body incinerated. The remains of another eight people were later found in the incinerator. It was only through death that members could escape Aum. Membership of the cult was a life sentence.²⁵

The Tokyo attacks

Japanese police were not idle throughout this activity, and frequently inspected the many properties held by Aum. The cult became, rightfully perhaps, paranoid of being discovered in its many nefarious activities, while still conducting sporadic acts of violence against internal and external enemies. Police pressure contributed to Aum destroying much of its refined sarin, which would later have a significant impact on how many people died due to their violence. The two major attacks that followed made use of impure and lower-grade sarin gas, which resulted, fortunately, in few fatalities.

The first major plot was executed on 27 June 1994, when members of Aum Shinrikyo drove around a neighbourhood in Matsumoto, unleashing sarin nerve gas as they went. They were targeting three judges who were deliberating on a fraud case against them. Although all three judges became ill, they did not succumb to the sarin. Collateral deaths did occur; the gas killed seven people and injured about 500 others. The legal decision was delayed. Aum did not claim responsibility, and Japanese police initially treated it as an industrial chemical accident. An American chemical warfare expert,

Kyle Olson, however, knew better. He believed the 'accident' had all of the major indicators of a dry run for a major terrorist attack. Olson was largely ignored by Japanese authorities, even though he had travelled to Matsumoto to analyse the case.[26] In January 1995, Olson wrote again, warning of the vulnerability of the subway system to such violence. This warning, too, achieved nothing.

Two months later, it was too late. On 20 March 1995, five Aum terrorists boarded the Tokyo subway on three major lines that would arrive at Central Station within four minutes of each other. They had eleven canisters filled with sarin, which they punctured to unleash the nerve agent. Panic ensued at Central Station as the three trains arrived successively, with terrified passengers flooding out the doors, many choking and having coughing fits. Thirteen people died as a consequence of the gas, and more than 5000 panicked commuters were injured from both the gas and the panicked crowds. The low number of fatalities can be attributed to the low-quality sarin and a flaw in the gas delivery mechanism that caused the canister to leak slowly instead of spray.[27]

Following the sarin subway attack, Japanese police raided Aum buildings and arrested many of the leaders. The raids also brought the Australian link to light. Within a week of Tokyo, AFP and Western Australia Police had converged on Banjawarn station. The *Canberra Times* reported that station managers at Banjawarn found whisky bottles full of acid. Investigators confirmed that sarin gas had been manufactured at Banjawarn and used to kill the 29 sheep.[28] During the investigation, Japanese businesses in Australia received letters from abroad threatening to target them with gas attacks—most likely an attempt to threaten Japanese authorities via their overseas representatives. These threats were not treated as serious, despite the wealth and reach of Aum around the world.

Subduing the cult

In the aftermath of the Tokyo sarin attack, Japanese authorities came down hard on Aum Shinrikyo. Aum was initially undeterred and continued to enact violence. It was allegedly responsible, for example, for the attempted assassination of the commissioner-general of the National Police Agency only ten days after the Tokyo incident. Then, on 5 May 1995, Aum is alleged to have conducted another gas attack at Shinjuku station, this time using sodium cyanide. The device failed to function, which prevented a possible death toll of 20,000. A letter bomb detonated in the office of the governor of Metropolitan Tokyo on 16 May, injuring one. On 4 July, another hydrogen cyanide attack failed in the Tokyo subway system when cannisters were found in rest rooms, having failed to function. Ultimately, the violence was staunched by the arrest of Asahara and most of the leadership of Aum. Over the ensuing months, police conducted over 500 raids on more than 300 Aum properties, and gathered over 66,000 pieces of evidence. About 240 cases were prosecuted against 398 members of the cult.[29]

Shoko Asahara and his senior leadership were charged with seventeen crimes, including the production of sarin, LSD, truth serum and assault rifles; the sarin gas attacks in Matsumoto and Tokyo; three acts of murder; one act of assault and murder using VX; and one act of assault and murder using sarin.[30] Asahara was found guilty and sentenced to death by hanging. He and his disciples continued to appeal their convictions for the next 21 years. In 2016, the last appeal was dismissed, paving the way for Asahara and six others to be executed on 6 July 2018.

As is often the case in such cults, thousands of members of Aum Shinrikyo had little knowledge of the violence. The religion, as a result, lives on in contemporary Japan, although it has since been renamed Aleph.

Aum was hardly the first religious organisation to turn to terror: Ananda Marga was also a global network with rogue internal elements committed to violent action. It, too, had supporters around the world. Aum was, however, distinct in two ways: first, its membership came from the educated elite, whose knowledge and skills were exploited in direct support of the organisation; and second, its economic aggression, in conjunction with its tax exemption status, allowed it to become wealthy. This wealth was funnelled directly into Aum's projects with a single-mindedness originating with Shoko Asahara himself. In short, Aum was an early demonstration of what a terrorist organisation could achieve with the right staffing and resources.

While its violence focused on Japan, Aum had a truly global vision of destruction and apocalypse, which meant it was willing and able to use nations around the globe. Aum's engagement with Russia, and trips to Zaire and Australia, finally proved the old Australian dictum that terrorism could be stopped at the border. In essence, for the first time in Australia's history, terrorists had conformed to national security logic and expectations. There was little in the way of structured domestic support of Aum in Australia, making it an exception to the rule that terrorist organisations in Australia had numerous supporters who facilitated or directly contributed to their campaigns.

Despite its exceptional nature, Aum would be surpassed by religious terrorist organisations to come. While it had been pursuing its toxic ambitions in Japan, Australia and elsewhere in the world, a new terrorism threat had been forming in the Middle East. This threat would also be deeply religious in nature, its authors twisting and misinterpreting structured religious systems to suit their own ends. It had its own apocalypse—and its own paradise—and would wreak any violence to achieve it.

Battle Cries, 1990 onwards

At the start of the 21st century, the major global threat looming on national security horizons appeared to be separatist terrorism. This was shared between the Provisional Irish Republican Army (PIRA) and its splinters in the United Kingdom; the Liberation Tigers of Tamil Eelam (LTTE) in Sri Lanka; the Kurdistan Workers' Party (PKK) around Turkey and Iraq; and a scattering of terrorist networks in South America that relied more and more on the global drug trade to finance their depredations. All these organisations and networks had evolved since their origins, departing from their left-wing (Marxist–Leninist) roots and focusing on separating from the state powers they deemed illegitimate. Some of this separatist terrorism overflowed into Australia in a haphazard fashion—perhaps distracting from the dreadful terror to come.

Before 2000, some Australians had sympathised with terror, supported it, funded it, and a few had engaged in it, but the targeting of Australians by foreign terrorist organisations was hardly standard practice. A case in point is PIRA, which—it was rumoured—received funding from the Green Cross of Australia, while the Official Irish Republican Army received support from the Sean South and Fergal O'Hanlon Society, the Connolly Association, and the Northern Ireland Civil Rights Association.[1] These supporters engaged in fundraising activities and demonstrations, and also offered safe haven for terrorists; in 1974 it was reported that five suspected IRA members migrated to Australia and sought assisted passage for their families. That Australians were killed by PIRA in 1990 was quite by accident.

In a case of mistaken identity, two Australian lawyers, Stephan Melrose and Nicholas Spanos, were stalked by an Active Hit Unit of the PIRA for several days while they were on holiday in the Netherlands. The unit believed they were British secret service officers attached to a nearby base. While the two Australians were sitting in a parked car in Roermond town square, the hit unit ambushed them and shot them to death. The alleged killers were Gerald Harte, a known PIRA terrorist, three other men and a woman (wanted in West Germany). They were aided by an unsuspecting local nurse, who later turned witness against them. Harte was convicted of the crime and sentenced to eighteen years, although this was successfully appealed, which in turn led to enraged British MPs denouncing the Netherlands and demanding their expulsion from the Anti-Terrorist Trial Group of European Community Nations.[2] In a surprise move, the PIRA claimed the attack and issued a formal apology for the killings. This event shone light on PIRA fundraising in Australia, especially their use of the construction industry to hide financing activities through ghost employees. It would later transpire that Australia became one of the retirement locations for PIRA terrorists, two of whom were wanted in connection with unsolved killings during the Troubles.

In another case, Australians were alleged to have engaged in fundraising to support the LTTE. Three men, Aruran Vinayagamoorthy, Sivarajah Yathavan and Arumugam Rajeevan, raised more than a million dollars for the LTTE between 2002 and 2005, and sent electrical equipment to the group. They were arrested, despite the fact that at the time the LTTE was not proscribed by Australia and, more to the point, there was a ceasefire between Sri Lanka and the LTTE. The LTTE was acting as a de facto government, and the resources were intended to assist in the humanitarian effort. Following judicial criticisms of the arrest process, and the allegation that the arrests had been at the request of the Sri Lankan government, the terrorism charges were withdrawn. The three men instead pleaded guilty to charges of funding terrorism on 24 December 2009, shortly after the Sri Lankan military killed some 20,000 people in its offensive against the LTTE.

In another case in August 2010, some seventeen properties in three states were raided by counterterrorism officials in relation to fundraising for the PKK—one group that routinely fell in and out of ceasefires with its target state. All of this activity, however, was rather beside the point, because the prime threat at the start of the new millennium would not come from such separatist organisations: beyond all else, it would come from international religious extremists motivated by twisted Salafist interpretations of Islam.

Salafi extremism did not start on 11 September 2001, the day that became the watershed for such extremists. The skies were clear and blue when the first hijacked aircraft struck the north tower of the World Trade Center shortly before 9 a.m. As smoke billowed, a second aircraft struck the south tower. About half an hour later, a third hijacked aircraft dove into the Pentagon, even as a fourth—destined for the White House—went into a death roll over an empty field in Pennsylvania. The passengers of United Airlines Flight 93 had called their families and said goodbye; then they had revolted against the hijackers and stormed the cockpit. None survived the crash, but this was not the end of the dying. Just before ten in the morning, the South Tower appeared to sink into the earth, consumed by a cloud of ash, dust and debris, causing an immense loss of human life, both within the building and outside it. Twenty-nine minutes later, the North Tower joined its fellow, the dreadful fall of a doomed behemoth making its first—and last—descent. Nearly 3000 lives were lost. In stark contrast to the clear blue skies of dawn, a great grey cloud bloomed over the island of Manhattan. In a sense, the cloud remains there even to this day.

While the northern hemisphere struggled to comprehend the enormity of what it had witnessed, the southern hemisphere slept. Australia slept. And we would awaken to a new day in which the world as we knew it—the trajectories of lives, of geopolitics, of coercion and terror, threat and death—had changed irrevocably. In the wake of the dreadful loss, the shock and the seemingly senseless act, men in high places talked resolutely of vengeance. In other halls, in other cities, other leaders made promises that would exact a considerable price. Australia's Prime Minister John Howard committed his forces and the fate of his people to the United States cause:

> if those who died last Tuesday are not, in the judgment of history, to have died in vain, there is an obligation on all of us to persevere, to travel the distance, to persist and to root out the evil that brought about those terrible deeds. But, in the process of responding, we must do so with care as well as with lethal force. We should understand that barbarism has no ethnicity and evil has no religion. Both around the world and within our own society, we should take pause lest we engage in the evil of scapegoating individual groups within our society . . . wouldn't it be a terrible, tragic, obscene irony if in responding, however we do it as individuals or as nations, to these terrible terrorist attacks we forsook the very things that we believed had been assaulted last Tuesday in New York?[3]

It was in this spirit that Australians would become involved in the long War on Terror. This commitment, moreover, would see Australians targeted in acts of terrorism both at home and abroad, by the likes of Jemaah Islamiyah, Al-Qaeda, Al-Shabaab and Islamic State. This would turn previous historical trends on their head: now Australians were fair game for international terrorist attacks, as symbolic and evocative targets to convey the terrorists' ideological and strategic objectives.

Nor was this legitimisation of targeting Australians confined to such international terror networks. The Australian domestic extreme right—which had suffered setbacks in the late 1980s—resurged. This time, Australians were willing to kill, motivated by a dark ideology pervaded by a false sense of privilege, imagined perils and the quest for racially pure ethnostates. This willingness would see Australian right-wing terrorists target their fellow citizens—their own societies—exploiting where possible the freedoms of their own state in their quest to destroy it. Because this quest was restricted by Australia's pre-existing securitisation (especially gun control), they would instead aim their barbarism at our closest allies. This manifested in 2019, with the deadly attack by an Australian against civilians in New Zealand.

Both terrorist movements deemed targeting Australians as valid and legitimate in their quest for utopia.

9
White meat: Jemaah Islamiyah

Whenever a breeze comes from the south-east, kites fly tranquilly over the island of Bali, Indonesia. The brightly coloured kites, some up to 10 metres long, are launched by Balinese villagers from July to October: a poignant message of thanks to the Hindu gods for abundant crops and a healthy harvest. The capital city of Denpasar and its seaside towns present a vibrant contrast to the serene kites in the sky above: their streets are alive with good-willed chaos, as street vendors cook fragrant meals, music booms, tourists laugh, and the Balinese people share their lives and culture. Few who caroused in Bali thought seriously about the threat of terror: much less terrorism directed at them.

Paddy's Pub was a prominent tourist watering hole in Legian, Kuta, that often attracted crowds of Australian, British and American visitors. Situated as it was on a central nightlife strip, it was popular with young tourists interested in drinking and dancing in the tropical Bali nights. On 12 October 2002 it was like any other night, except, unbeknown to the jubilant crowds, a bomb had detonated at 6.45 that evening in front of the Philippines Consulate in Manado City, nearly 3000 kilometres away in northern Indonesia. News tends to travel slowly wherever the music is loud and the people are carefree. The crowd at Paddy's Pub would not have known of this terrorist attack, and yet their lives were to become inextricably bound with it.

A little over three hours later, a young man called Jimi walked into Paddy's Pub. He wore a heavy tartan-lined black vest: an unusual garment to wear on a humid Bali evening. The vest was packed with explosives concealed within five lengths of PVC piping. Jimi was there for a single purpose: to fulfil a single commitment. At 11.08 p.m., while the tourists drank cocktails and the Balinese staff moved about the venue, Jimi took his last breath and detonated his suicide vest. The bomb exploded outwards, tearing through Paddy's Pub: the blast churned through the venue and turned everything it touched into deadly shrapnel, including Jimi himself. All that remained of him was his decapitated head and lower legs.

Horrified holiday-makers surged out of Paddy's, believing they would be safe from the bloodshed and violence in the open air of the streets, even as a fiery inferno began taking hold of the pub. Not far away from Paddy's Pub and the neighbouring Sari Club lingered a white Mitsubishi van. It had been stripped: its back seats had been removed and replaced with more than 1 tonne of improvised explosive compounds, made using potassium chlorate, sulfur, aluminium and TNT, then packed into twelve four-drawer plastic filing cabinets. These cabinets had been connected with military-grade detonating cord made of pentaerythritol tetranitrate. The man inside the van, Arnasan, too, was there with a single purpose.

Seven minutes later, more than 350 people jostled in the streets outside Paddy's Pub. Some were injured, having escaped the carnage in Paddy's, others were first responders, bravely fighting the crowds and the chaos to deliver first aid to the severely wounded. Bodies still lay in Paddy's Pub—silent now, where music had once sounded. The violence, however, was not yet over. The white van was motionless—and people stood nearby, not reckoning on its menace. At 11.15 p.m., Arnasan detonated his vehicle bomb. Little would remain of the van, which detonated with a force equivalent to 150 kilograms of TNT. The blast force was so strong that it registered on the seismographs of neighbouring countries. It blew a crater in the street, smashing through a water main, and set fire to nearby buildings. Those present described the blast as a fireball that 'seemed to be consuming people'.[1]

Ten minutes later, at 11.25 p.m., while Legian was engulfed in fire and blood, another bomb detonated. This one had been placed outside the US Consulate in Denpasar, only 10 kilometres away. No one was injured; the losses that dreadful night were all in Kuta, in streets that were once vibrant with life, now a scene of horror. As the ash settled, 88 Australians would be identified among the dead, alongside 38 Balinese and a scattering of tourists from all over the world. In all, the fatalities rapidly climbed to 204, with another 209 people injured.

This was the greatest loss of Australian life since World War II, and it was at the hands of Al-Qaeda's first and most faithful friends: Jemaah Islamiyah.

Indonesian extremism

To understand the fatal events in Bali in 2002, we must first understand the nature of extremism in Indonesia and the connections the extremists forged with Al-Qaeda. Without Al-Qaeda's involvement, it is entirely possible that the attack would have manifested very differently. The people of Bali, a largely peaceful Hindu community, were as much victims of the terrorist attack as the Australians, although they were considered acceptable collateral damage by violent Salafists, motivated by an extremist interpretation of Islam. Outside of Bali, Indonesia is primarily a Muslim country, where more than 225 million people identify as Muslim.

There is a long history of extremism by violent Salafist elements of Indonesian society. As far back at the seventeenth century, Indonesians resisted Dutch colonial rule. During World War II, similar extremist elements of Indonesian society joined Axis powers to root out their colonial rulers. After 1945, a traditionalist Islamic political party called Masyumi emerged, and it took on the quest for West Javanese liberation from colonisation. Masyumi soon became connected with two violent guerrilla units: Hizbullah and Sabilillah.[2] They were trained by Sekarmadji Maridjan Kartosuwiryo, an Indonesian Islamist mystic who merged these units into a single organisation called the Darul Islam Heroes. When the Dutch eventually departed Indonesia in 1949, Kartosuwiryo began a campaign to overthrow the secular government.[3] On 7 August 1949, he declared an Islamic State of Indonesia (Negara Islam Indonesia).

Darul Islam was a violent Salafist organisation, but what is Salafism, and how does it relate to Islam? Salafism—meaning 'followers of Mohammed and his companions'—is an interpretation of Islam that follows a strict, and at times twisted or literal, interpretation of the Quran. Its adherents teach that the end of days—the apocalypse—is nigh. This is because they perceive society as decadent and degenerate, existing in a state of pre-Mohammedan barbarism and ignorance, referred to as *jahiliyyah*. To overcome this state of discord, violent Salafists embraced jihad, violent struggle. To most Muslims, jihad refers to the internal struggle to stay true to their faith. In a few contexts, however, it can also refer to Holy War as declared by a caliph to defend the lands of Islam. To Salafists, jihad is interpreted as a neglected duty, a forgotten pillar of Islam mandating violence in order to return Islam to the purity and glory it enjoyed under the Abbasid caliphs. Salafi jihadists argue that violent jihad is the duty of all Muslims to re-establish the Caliphate and institute Sharia law, make church and state inseparable, and purify the lands of Islam to make way for a new utopian golden age.

In time, the Indonesian government managed to contain Darul Islam, and in September 1962, executed Kartosuwiryo by firing squad. Darul Islam, and Kartosuwiryo's ideology, persisted beyond his death, influenced, perhaps, by a rising tide of Islamist fundamentalism in certain parts of the world. With the Iranian Revolution in 1979, and the successful overthrow of the Shah and his replacement with Grand Ayatollah Ruhollah Khomeini, a new

Islamic theocracy was born in the Middle East that was an inspiration to all Islamists around the world, both Sunni and Shia.

While Australian authorities became concerned that such a revolution could occur in Indonesia, an Indonesian scholar, Abdurrahman Wahid, disagreed. He argued that Islam in Indonesia was not highly politicised and claimed that while Islam was experiencing a revival in certain elements of the Sunni community, the Iranian Revolution would have no direct effect. The indirect effect was more powerful, however, empowering Muslims to voice dissatisfaction with the government, and raising their hopes for a similar change in circumstances.[4]

The Iranian Revolution was connected, indirectly, to the revival of Islam in Indonesia. The vice president of the World Islamic Organisation, Mohammad Natsir, said: 'For centuries Muslims were colonized by foreigners. After becoming free in this mid-century they have been groping in their attempts to carry out their ideals . . . Now there is an opportunity to apply them.'[5] The Australian Department of Defence suspected that Natsir himself sought to exploit religious divisions between Muslims and Christians. Rapid economic growth and mobilisation over the preceding twelve years had led to increased social inequity, and 'created the conditions for excessive corruption, ostentation, and decadent living to flourish'.[6]

An Australian career diplomat in Indonesia, Paul O'Sullivan, also suggested that the revival was linked to a desire to return to a purer way of living, to simpler times: 'The result is a strong desire to conjure up in the imagination a past that was great, and a desire to re-enact that past. The past was thought great because it was pure— no alcohol, no liberal attitude to sex, no abuse of political power, and little economic exploitation of the weak by the rich.'[7] A strict observance of Islam was seen as the best panacea for these societal woes. Indonesia already had a well-established political Muslim identity in the United Development Party (DPP), which received, generally, 29 per cent of the vote at elections during the 1970s. A small surge in support led to the ruling Golkar (Group of Workers) Party curtailing the DPP's power.[8]

One way Golkar tried to achieve this was by threatening to recognise the Kebatinan movement as a new religion. (The Kebatinans were Javanese mystics whose belief system was a syncretism of Buddhist, Hindu and Sufi Islamic practises—a sect opposed by the Muslim Party.) Golkar also gave the Ministry of Religious Affairs portfolio to a high-ranking military officer, Lieutenant General Alamsyah Prawiranegara, who instituted measures to address Muslim discontent, such as regulating proselytism by Christian missionaries.

The origins of Jemaah Islamiyah

As the 1970s progressed, four branches of extremism emerged in Indonesia. The first was the separatist Free Aceh Movement (GAM) seeking independence for Aceh province. Two were student movements, Younger Generation of Indonesian Islam and Islamic Youth Movement, both supporting Islamic revival. The last was Komando Jihad, an organisation with close ties to the Darul Islam movement.[9] Some believe that Komando Jihad and Darul Islam were one and the same.[10] Unlike the former three branches, Komando Jihad was a strict Salafist organisation and willing to use violence to achieve its ambitions.

Komando Jihad executed a series of robberies to fund their operations. Their first series of attacks occurred in 1976–77, targeting Christian facilities in Sumatra: the Immanuel Hospital in Bukittinggi, and a Methodist church and Christian school, Budi Murni College, in Medan. They then switched to targeting Padang, where they bombed the Nurul Imam Mosque, the Riang Cinema and the Apollo Bar. After the Padang attacks, they scattered leaflets claiming responsibility in the name of the Indonesian Christian Youth Movement. This was a false-flag campaign, which they hoped would ignite sectarian tensions between the Christian and Muslim communities.

When this failed to catalyse into widespread violence, Komando Jihad planned another campaign targeting electrical and communication infrastructure. There were also rumours of a plot to conduct a Jakarta bombing campaign targeting the Senen commercial centre, the Monas National Monument and the Pertamina Building. In response, the Indonesian authorities arrested a large number of Komando Jihad members. Following the crackdown, many Darul Islam members went underground or fled to Malaysia.

Two significant leaders soon emerged from the shadows of Darul Islam, both Indonesians of Yemeni descent: Abu Bakar Ba'asyir and Abdullah Sungkar. Both were highly active in Islamic organisations, and began preaching on a conservative radio station. In 1970, together they set up an Islamic school in Java called Pondok Ngruki, where they began to spread their more extreme beliefs. They soon connected with the Darul Islam movement and expanded their networks and deepened their commitment to Salafism, which drew the attention of authorities to them. This was warranted in part because of the organisation's plans to assassinate President Suharto, and a bombing campaign in the eighties. Both fled to Malaysia after their arrests were ordered in the eighties, and from there they helped establish the Moro Islamic Liberation Front (MILF) and, later, Jemaah Islamiyah (JI).

Ba'asyir and Sungkar sought to train Darul Islam cadres for battle against the Indonesian regime, and reached out to an Arabian millionaire who was rumoured to look favourably on Salafist causes. His name was Osama bin Laden. Within a matter of years, Ba'asyir, Sungkar and some of their followers had travelled to Afghanistan and trained in the camps on the Pakistan–Afghan border. There, they received religious instruction from Abdullah Azzam and Osama bin Laden, and helped his army of mujahideen to fight against the Soviet invasion. This experience forged close ties between the Indonesian extremists and the mujahideen of the Middle Eastern battlefields. When Al-Qaeda emerged from the rubble of Soviet withdrawal in 1989, members of JI and MILF continued training with Al-Qaeda.

By 1992, Ba'asyir and Sungkar had broken with Darul Islam entirely and formed JI. While still closely linked with the MILF terrorist group, JI soon expanded to have cells in Malaysia, Indonesia, Singapore and Australia. These cells, called *mantiqis* (territories), were headed by different teams. Mantiqi I, based in Singapore and Malaysia, was focused on intelligence collection and fundraising. Mantiqi II, based in Indonesia, focused on fighting jihad. Mantiqi III, in Mindanao, the Philippines, provided a great deal of training at MILF camps. All *mantiqis* were ultimately expected to obtain military capabilities.

Friends of Al-Qaeda

The friendship between Al-Qaeda and JI soon bore fruit. As part of the relationship, the JI operations chief, Riduan Isamuddin, alias Hambali, would collaborate directly with Al-Qaeda. Hambali grew up in West Java and, after graduating from Allanah Islamic School in Cianjur, moved to Malaysia in 1985 looking for work. While there, he married a local woman and attended the local mosque—where Abdullah Sungkar was known to preach. After six months, Hambali was sent to Afghanistan to train for jihad. He remained there for a year and a half before returning in 1988.[11]

Hambali became a significant operative in Indonesian jihad, and travelled throughout Malaysia and the Philippines promoting jihad and forging alliances with other jihadist groups such as MILF. When JI established the Mantiqis to raise funds, gather resources and conduct attacks, Hambali had first pick of their capabilities. He could overrule any of the Mantiqis and use their resources at will. He was, in effect, the most powerful operative of JI, abetted by Al-Qaeda. In 1999, he made contact with Al-Qaeda's strategic mastermind, Khalid Sheikh Mohammed.

Khalid Sheikh Mohammed was the uncle of Ramzi Yousef, who undertook the World Trade Center bombing in 1993, which killed six and injured 1000. A Pakistani, Mohammed was raised in Kuwait and, like many, joined the jihad against the Soviets. He went to a training camp run by Abdullah Azzam, and forged links with the mujahideen who would become Al-Qaeda. After his nephew

Ramzi's bombing in 1993, he went on the run and ended up joining Al-Qaeda, becoming a recruiter, financier and operational planner. Khalid Sheikh Mohammed and Hambali were tasked with coordinating attacks in South-East Asia against American interests and, later, Australians as well. They were supported in their efforts by Mohammed Atef, the military chief of Al-Qaeda, and Ba'asyir of JI. Together, Khalid and Hambali planned an attack using the Australian chapter of Jemaah Islamiyah, known as Mantiqi IV.

Omar al-Faruq was another Al-Qaeda operative in the arena: a Kuwaiti who had fought in Afghanistan with bin Laden and the other mujahideen, he was dispatched to Indonesia in 1998. Al-Qaeda directed him to take over local jihadist cells and channel them towards Al-Qaeda objectives. To keep his cover, he married a local Indonesian woman, Mira Augustina, who had no idea he was a terrorist.[12] From that point on, he formed many plans to wage jihad in Indonesia, including violence against Christian churches.

An Australian *mantiqi*

While its goal may have been an Islamic state in Indonesia, JI was prepared to transcend international boundaries to achieve it. In Australia, a chief factor in the establishment of Mantiqi IV was Rabiyah Hutchinson. Born in Mudgee in 1953 as Robyn Mary Hutchinson, Rabiyah moved to Bali in 1970 and married a Buddhist. They had one child together before the relationship broke down and she moved to Jakarta. In Jakarta, she married an Indonesian named Bambang Wisudo, and had two daughters with him. In the 1980s, she left Wisudo, converted to Islam, changed her name to Rabiyah and moved to Malaysia.[13] There, she worked at Pondok Ngruki and became close with Ba'asyir and Sungkar. She became an ardent follower of their ideology, and married a fellow adherent, Abdul Rahim Ayub.

The newlyweds moved to Australia, where, under the direction of Ba'asyir and Sungkar, Ayub set up a new JI cell called Mantiqi IV. By the time Ayub was given this task, he and Rabiyah had separated.

She would go on to remarry several times, including to a senior Al-Qaeda leader, Mustafa Hamid. Abdul Rahim Ayub continued to establish Mantiqi IV in Australia, a task he shared with his twin brother, Abdul Rahman Ayub. They recruited from the Indonesian-Australian population, and arranged for Ba'asyir and Sungkar to engage in speaking tours in Australia (at least until Sungkar's death in 1999). According to scholars Shandon Harris-Hogan and Andrew Zammit, not all converts were Indonesian: of the fifteen to 30 members, at least three who wanted to fight were Australian Caucasian men: Jack Roche, Andrew Wenham and John Bennett.[14]

Al-Qaeda, which wielded substantial influence over JI, decided that Australia was an attractive target for terrorist activity. The upcoming Sydney Olympics was suggested as an opportune theatre for attracting publicity. A plan was concocted in Al-Qaeda headquarters to have Mantiqi IV launch an attack against Israeli interests in Australia during the Olympics. Targets included the Israeli Embassy, the Israeli Consulate, and a prominent Jewish Australian mining magnate, Joe Gutnick.[15] Mantiqi IV, however, was not operational, and had little in the way of a military capability. It was also in strife financially, and funds were occasionally misappropriated for personal use. As a result, in 1998, Mantiqi I sent one of its seasoned fighters, Asman Hashim, to train Mantiqi IV fighters at Victoria Falls in the NSW Blue Mountains.[16]

From then, Hambali took command of the operation from Al-Qaeda, and forged ahead with the plot.[17] Because Al-Qaeda believed a Caucasian would have more operational effectiveness, Hambali arranged for Andrew Wenham to travel to Afghanistan for training. Wenham refused to go, so Hambali asked Rahim Ayub for another fighter. Rahim sent Jack Roche instead. 'I was drawn in bit by bit, given information in dribs and drabs. It wasn't until I got to Afghanistan I realised they had this whole thing organised way before I came into the picture,' Jack Roche would later tell the media.[18]

While training in Afghanistan, Roche met Khalid Sheikh Mohammed and Hambali. They apprised him of their plan, and he was taught to build explosives and monitor targets. He was ordered to recruit two more Caucasians for the attack, but this was met, more often than not, with outright rejection. In his own words, Roche felt 'out of his league' and had little desire to harm innocent people. In over his head, Roche turned to ASIO on 14 July 2000 and was put on to an officer called Don. 'I said to them, "Look, I've just returned from Afghanistan, I've just met with Osama bin Laden, I'm extremely or very concerned about developments within, amongst certain elements of the Islamic community here in Australia",' Roche said.[19]

He requested an interview with ASIO, and offered to work with them. No one called him back. Roche claimed he called ASIO two more times, making the third call in August merely a month before the Sydney Olympics. He had Hambali's home phone number, email address and home address, and the contact details of Khalid Sheikh Mohammed, and was willing to share them. September 11 had not yet happened: few were interested in a ragtag gang of religious extremists. Eventually, Ba'asyir or possibly Rahim Ayub cancelled the attack on the Sydney Olympic Games. Roche would later be charged with conspiracy to commit an offence for the plot to bomb the Israeli Consulate, to which he pleaded guilty.

Early attacks

JI did not embrace mass-casualty terrorism from the outset. Its first attack was actually a highly targeted assassination that nonetheless killed bystanders and missed the target entirely. On 8 January 2000, JI detonated a car bomb in central Jakarta as the Philippines ambassador, Leonidas Caday, was in his limousine en route to the embassy. An embassy guard and a female street trader were killed, and another twenty were injured. Caday survived. This early failure in January may have prompted the wave of support that JI was to receive from Al-Qaeda. In June 2000, Ayman al-Zawahiri, Al-Qaeda's number two, in the company of Al-Qaeda's secret operative Omar al-Faruq, travelled to Indonesia to create a new terrorist group. But al-Zawahiri

Shoko Asahara, born Chizuo Matsumoto, was the charismatic cult leader of Aum Shinrikyo. He believed that initiating the third world war would pave the way to a future utopia. He, along with other Aum leaders, was executed in 2018. Alamy

Banjawarn station, as seen by air, was purchased by Aum Shinrikyo in 1993 with the help of an Australian member. There they experimented with poison gases and tested their lethality on sheep. Nic Ellis/ *The West Australian*

Wanted posters of prominent members of Aum Shinrikyo in the Tokyo subway. This site was to be the target of their sarin gas attack in 1995. The attack killed 13 people and injured over 5000 more. **Alamy**

First responders attend the Tokyo sarin gas attack, which targeted three subway lines simultaneously in rush hour. Although the sarin was less refined than that tested in Banjawarn, it nonetheless affected the breathing and vision of the thousands of people exposed. **AAP**

On 12 October 2002, three bombs were detonated in Bali. The two biggest bombs—one a suicide vest and the other a vehicle IED—were triggered in Kuta. Much of the area was destroyed by the blast and the inferno it caused. AAP

During the 2002 Bali bombing 88 Australians were killed—the largest element of the 204 fatalities. The terrorists of Jemaah Islamiyah had been deliberately targeting white foreigners on the advice of Al-Qaeda. Alamy

The Bali Bombing Memorial commemorates the Australians who lost their lives in the attack. It is positioned at the original site of Paddy's Pub—and across the road from where the vehicle bomb was detonated. Wikimedia Commons

Around 2770 people died on 11 September 2001 when Al-Qaeda operatives flew two hijacked aeroplanes into the World Trade Center in New York, and a further 21,000 people were injured. The terrorist attacks had followed a series of actions the then little-known terrorist group Al-Qaeda had enacted against the United States. Wikimedia Commons

Another 190 people died and 106 people were injured on the same day when a hijacked aeroplane was flown into the Pentagon by Al-Qaeda operatives. Their objective was to provoke the United States into a protracted and damaging conflict. Alamy

Hostages flee the Lindt Café siege in 2014. They had been held at gunpoint by Islamic State supporter Man Haron Monis for a number of hours. The siege ended when Monis killed a hostage and the café was breached by police. AAP

Over 150 Australians travelled to Syria and Iraq between 2014 and 2018 intent on joining the Islamic State group. Many died in suicide attacks, and later in the broader conflict when the Caliphate fell. Alamy

Khaled Sharrouf was involved with the Al-Qaeda–inspired cell in Sydney, investigated under Operation Pendennis in 2005. He subsequently travelled to Syria and fought on behalf of Islamic State. He is presumed dead.

Neil Prakash travelled to join Islamic State in 2013, and became a prominent propagandist and controller. He was the first Australian to have his citizenship revoked due to his terrorism activities.

Abu Bakr al-Baghdadi was one in a long line of leaders of Islamic State, but the first to crown himself caliph in 2014. He died in 2019, a year after the so-called Caliphate fell. AAP

Osama bin Laden (left) was the first leader of Al-Qaeda and was behind the September 11 attacks. When he was killed in 2011, leadership was assumed by his right-hand man, Ayman Al-Zawahiri (right), a career terrorist from Egypt. Al-Zawahiri remains in charge of Al-Qaeda.
Wikimedia Commons

The office tower of Norwegian prime minister Jens Stoltenberg was bombed in 2011 by right-wing terrorist Anders Behring Breivik, killing eight and injuring 209. He then travelled to Utøya Island and murdered 69 teenagers. Breivik was a noted inspiration to Australian right-wing terrorist Brenton Tarrant. Alamy

Far-right crowds including Reclaim Australia protest Muslim immigration in Melton in 2015. Anti-Islam sentiment is a common feature of Australian right-wing extremist ideology, as they claim white Australians are being overwhelmed by people of other ethnicities. Shutterstock

Extreme right-wing ideology was a feature of the 2019 attack on the Al Noor Mosque in Christchurch, New Zealand. Australian citizen Brenton Tarrant killed 51 people and injured 49 in his attacks. Alamy

Right-wing extremism persists in Australia in various forms, including neo-Nazis. This Antipodean Resistance sticker, with the slogan '21st century Hitler Youth', photographed in Bathurst in 2018, reflects their commitment to Nazi ideology. Alamy

instead bound JI even closer with the Al-Qaeda cause and developed a secret league of mujahideen in South-East Asia.[20]

The mujahideen league met for a second time in November 2000, and decided that Christian churches and US interests in South-East Asia were to be the primary targets for joint Al-Qaeda and JI violence. Hambali attended the meeting, as did al-Faruq and Khalid Sheikh Mohammed. Scarcely a month later, on Christmas Eve, the bloodshed began. The churches were full of worshippers. In a display of synchronicity and organisation, more than 37 Christian churches in Indonesia were bombed, killing nineteen and injuring 118. The explosives were made by JI master bomber Fathur Roman al-Ghozi, whose alias was 'Mike the Bomber'. Even though JI did not claim responsibility, it was widely known that it and Hambali were behind the blasts.

Less than a week after the Christmas Eve bombings, Hambali directed his resources against more soft targets. Once again, Mike the Bomber constructed the IEDs. MILF also assisted, backed by Al-Qaeda. On 30 December 2000, the Philippines celebrates Rizal Day, a public holiday to commemorate Jose Rizal, a national hero. People commemorate Rizal in parks while flags are flown at half-mast. In 2000, holiday-makers flooded the public transport system. Within the space of 60 minutes, JI bombed five strategic points around Manila, including a petrol station near Dusit Hotel, a park near the US Embassy, a fuel depot at Ninoy Aquino International Airport, a Quezon bus station, and a train arriving at Blumentritt Station. They killed 22 people and injured another 100.

Falling towers

Al-Qaeda was not only pursuing operations in South-East Asia. Under the direction of Osama bin Laden, Al-Qaeda launched an assault directly on the United States. In a plot that came from the dark imagination of Khalid Sheikh Mohammed, and was facilitated by Mohammed Atef, four separate airliners were hijacked in the United States on 11 September 2001 (9/11). Two of those planes were flown into the north and south World Trade Center towers. The third was crashed into the US Pentagon. The fourth was destined for the White House, but when its passengers realised this, they rose up against the hijackers and downed the plane in a field in Pennsylvania. None survived. Soon after, the World Trade Center towers collapsed, and the ash that settled over Manhattan was a pall of mourning.

On this single dreadful day, this meticulously planned attack claimed nearly 3000 lives, ten of whom were Australians, but Al-Qaeda's pace did not falter with this successful US mission. Even as armies gathered around the world, and a new generation of military leaders committed themselves to an Afghan campaign, Khalid Sheikh Mohammed had a new plot ready. In conjunction with Hambali, he planned for JI and Al-Qaeda to launch a joint operation in December 2001. Hambali, once again the operations chief, secured the help of Mike the Bomber and the Singaporean cell of JI, Mantiqi I. Mohammed Atef of Al-Qaeda gave them the green light.

The plan was to pack 21 tonnes of ammonium nitrate into seven trucks. Once armed with the industrial explosive ANFO, these trucks became vehicle-borne improvised explosive devices. They would be detonated by suicide terrorists at key locations around Singapore, including the US Embassy, Israeli Embassy, Australian High Commission, British High Commission, a US naval base, and other American targets. In such a small and densely populated nation as Singapore, the effects of the blast would be devastating. The plotters used a number of codewords to remain off the grid. They called Westerners 'white meat', while Singapore was referred to as 'soup', and Malaysia as 'market'. It is no accident that Australians were targeted in Singapore and, later, Bali: Al-Qaeda and JI had considered Australia in their scope since 2000.

The plan was near execution: Mike the Bomber had been flown into Singapore, and Hambali had met him at the airport with operatives of Mantiqi I. Four tonnes of explosives had been sourced, but another 17 tonnes were needed. Then, seemingly by chance, an Al-Qaeda suspect who was under surveillance unknowingly led authorities to the Singaporean cell, exposing them and thwarting the chemical purchase. Singaporean police quickly unravelled the entire plot and thwarted it. While Singapore, the Philippines and Malaysia began arresting suspected JI members, Indonesia, unfortunately, did not crack down on the group because its Internal Security Act had no provision to arrest people unless they were suspected of committing a crime. As a result, 200 JI members moved to Indonesia and Thailand.

Deterred, but undefeated, JI turned to fresh plots.

Terror in Bali

By now, Australian security agencies had a fair idea that Australia was in the terrorist firing line. The security assessments had been passed on to the Department of Foreign Affairs and Trade (DFAT), and travel warnings sought to deter Australians from holidaying in Indonesia. Perhaps some Australians took the travel warning seriously, but many did not. Jack Roche's information was now outdated and the opportunity to crack down on Khalid Sheikh Mohammed and Hambali had been missed. Mohammed, who was still at large in South-East Asia, began to plot a new attack, one as spectacular as before, in conjunction with Hambali. Because of the Singapore failure, they didn't go for hard targets like naval installations. Instead, they aimed at soft targets, such as Western holiday-makers enjoying the wonders of Bali.

A team was assembled combining JI, Al-Qaeda and MILF operatives. Hambali and Mohammed became the directors, while Mohammed also contributed AU$30,000 to the plot. They had many operatives on the ground. Noordin Top, a Malaysian-born accountant, was appointed head of logistics. Dr Azahari Husin of the University of Technology Malaysia, a man whose actions would ultimately claim more than 250 lives, built the bombs. Imam Samudra, a long-time JI member, was the field commander. Huda bin Abdul Haq, known as Mukhlas, was put in charge of the attack itself.

Mukhlas was, at this time, believed to be a leader of Mantiqi I. His two brothers were also involved: Amrozi bin Haji Nurhasyim purchased the chemicals and rented a white Mitsubishi van with Balinese plates, while Ali Imron was the driver. They also recruited a few Indonesians to be the suicide bombers, including Jimi and Arnasan.

'We sat in the car in front of Sari Club. I saw lots of whiteys dancing, and lots of whiteys drinking there, that place—Kuta and especially Paddy's bar and the Sari Club—was a meeting place for US terrorists and their allies, who the whole world knows to be monsters,' Imam Samudra claimed.[21] 'Australians, Americans, whatever—they're all white people,' Amrozi laughed.[22]

At the time of the attack, there were 22,000 Australians on holiday in Bali. While Samudra was reconnoitring the Balinese beach strips, Australian tourists enjoyed the sun and sand. While Amrozi was sourcing chemicals, Australian tourists relaxed with evening cocktails. While Azahari Husin was building the vehicle bomb and a suicide vest, Australian tourists danced into the night. While Jimi and Arnasan prepared to die, Australian tourists were living life. For 88 of them, their lives would end that night, stolen by terrorists pursuing an obscure cause that had little to do with their actual targets.

At 11.05 p.m., Jimi entered Paddy's Pub on Legian Street. Three minutes later he detonated his vest.[23] Arnasan waited in the van outside the club. In case he lost his nerve, the van was rigged with four different detonation systems: one trigger controlled by Arnasan, a mobile phone trigger, a timer, and a booby trap. Nothing was going to stop the bomb from detonating. Nothing did.

On 12 November 2002, Al-Qaeda claimed responsibility, and Osama bin Laden proclaimed:

What happened since the attacks on New York and Washington and up until today, such as . . . the killing of the British and the Australians in the explosions in Bali . . . as well as some other operations here and there, is but a reaction and a retaliation (an eye for an eye), undertaken by the children of the Muslims who are devoted to defending their religion and the teachings of their Messenger . . .

So why are your governments entering into one alliance after another alliance with America, by attacking us in Afghanistan? And I specifically mention Britain, France, Italy, Canada, Germany, and Australia.

We have warned Australia before against taking part in a war in Afghanistan, in addition to her despicable attempt at separating East Timor; she disregarded the warnings until she awoke to the sounds of explosions in Bali. Then she falsely claimed her people are not targeted . . .

So as you kill, you shall be killed, and as you bomb you shall be bombed, and wait for what brings calamity.[24]

Operation Alliance

While some ran away from the terror in the Balinese streets, many ran towards it. Locals and tourists alike began searching through the wreckage, offering assistance, even ferrying the wounded to hospitals on the back of mopeds. The Indonesian National Police reached out to the Australian Federal Police, and Operation Alliance was born. Australian federal agent Gary Brook was a team leader in the Joint Counter Terrorism team. He received the call about the Bali bombings at 5.00 a.m. on 13 October 2002, less than six hours after the attack. By 7.30 a.m., he was organising a team, even while aware that some of his own had been caught up in the attack. 'We knew some were injured but we didn't know how many or how badly,' he later said.[25]

At its height, 500 AFP members would be engaged in Operation Alliance, 100 of them working at the bombsite. Other AFP experts in investigations, forensics, IT, media, intelligence, disaster victim identification, communications and administration were involved in the enormous task. Two AFP agents who had been en route to Jakarta to teach a routine forensic investigation management course to an Indonesian laboratory were abruptly rerouted to Bali. Federal agents Julian Slater and Cliff Frost soon arrived and were integral to crime scene integrity, encouraging security at the site to prevent contamination. Families, locals and survivors had been worried about the bodies in the streets, which were being packed with ice to prevent them from rotting. Slater and Frost sourced four or five refrigerated shipping containers from Java, and removed the deceased from the humid Bali streets.[26]

AFP agents worked to assist the Indonesian authorities, to identify not only the victims, but also the perpetrators. The breakthrough came when investigators found the chassis number of the van stamped on the chassis rail. This led them to Amrozi, whom the Australian media would dub the 'smiling assassin'. Amrozi was arrested first. He confessed to the Bali bombings proudly, and named Samudra and Imron among his co-conspirators. After their arrests, Amrozi and Samudra taunted the survivors and their victims' families, displaying no remorse. Only Imron showed remorse and cooperated with police. Because of this, he alone was spared the death penalty.

Amrozi, along with Samudra, was executed by firing squad at midnight on 9 November 2008, six years after the attacks. For the high-level terrorist strategists, a different fate was in store. Hambali was captured by joint US–Thai forces in Thailand in August 2003, and sent to Guantanamo Bay, the US prison on Cuba. Khalid Sheikh Mohammed was captured by the Pakistani Inter-Services Intelligence Directorate in March 2003, and immediately turned over to US forces, which took him to Guantanamo Bay too. Mohammed Atef had been killed in a US bombing raid around 19 November 2001 as part of the War on Terror. For a time, Noordin Top and Azahari Husin escaped authorities.

Ten years after the 2002 Bali bombings, the pain and grief had not faded. *The Australian* ran a story for which the reporter interviewed victims' families. Dave Byron, who lost his daughter Chloe in the bombing, told the media: 'I learned some terrible things. I learned what terrorism meant. I saw people terrorised that night. I saw people curled up on the street screaming in terror.' His daughter, the 'light of his life', was gone.[27]

The Coogee Dolphins rugby league team lost six of their players in the Sari Club. Jane Elkin, the sister of one of these players, Dave Mavroudis, said, 'To be honest, this 10-year anniversary doesn't change how you feel, it's as hard as every other anniversary. I'm not interested in going to Bali and I doubt I ever will.' This feeling was echoed by Ross McKeon, who lost his wife Lynette and one of his daughters, Marissa. 'They say that time cures all but all it really does is deaden the pain.'[28]

JI endures

Terrorism in Indonesia was not the sole domain of JI—the Free Aceh Movement (GAM) was also operational, and engaging in terrorist attacks designed to secure Aceh independence from Indonesia. JI remained, however, a major player in the region: a position influenced by its friendship with Al-Qaeda. In 2003 JI struck again, detonating a car bomb outside the Marriott Hotel in Jakarta. The hotel was another Western hotspot, a favourite of embassy staff and American businesses. Twelve people died and another 150 were injured. The hunt for Western fatalities remained a key priority for violent Salafist terror groups, which took their directions from Al-Qaeda.

Two years after the Bali bombings, Salafist terrorists again targeted Australians, one of the most present and enduring symbols of the West in Indonesia. On 9 September 2004, a car parked in front of the Australian Embassy gates in Jakarta. It was 10.30 a.m., when the streets were busy and the blocking of the embassy gates was not noticeable. The car suddenly exploded, detonated by the suicide terrorist in the driver's seat. The blast carved a crater in the road nearly 3 metres wide. Nine people died—all Indonesians—and another 150 people were injured in the streets and nearby office buildings, where windows turned into shrapnel. The

Australian Embassy was largely unharmed, except for some damage to the gates. The Indonesian police chief, General Da'i Bachtiar, identified the attack as the work of JI, and believed the bombmaker was Azahari Husin.

Husin was a gifted mathematician who had studied in the University of Adelaide during the 1970s. He subsequently gained his PhD at a British university, and moved to Malaysia to lecture at the University of Technology Malaysia. He, like many before him, fell under the teachings of Ba'asyir, and became a born-again Muslim. He was one of many sent by Ba'asyir to Afghanistan and the Philippines for jihadi training, part of which was in explosives and bomb-making. As a result, he became the top technical expert of JI, even writing a 50-page terrorist manual. He attracted the name 'Demolition Man'—and it stuck.

His bombs would claim the lives of Indonesians and Westerners indiscriminately. A case study for this is the JI attack in Tentena, a town in central Sulawesi, off the beaten track but attractive to tourists for its natural wonders. In May 2005, Husin provided JI with two bombs set to detonate fifteen minutes apart. The first was placed in a crowded marketplace, the second outside a police station. The first bomb exploded, and as first responders rushed out of the police station, they were caught in the second blast. Twenty-two civilians died and a further 60 were injured.

Five months later, in October 2005, JI struck again. It was school holidays in Australia, and many Australians had flocked to Bali. A popular attraction is Jimbaran beach, a location famous for its hotels, sunny sands and austere limestone cliffs. Tourists can dine directly on the beach at one of the open-air *warungs* (cafés and eateries), toes tucked in the sand and the stars shining above, surrounded by the sound of soft waves hitting the shore.

At 7.00 p.m. on 1 October 2005, the *warungs* were busy, with people eating dinner and enjoying the ambiance. Two suicide terrorists walked into one *warung*, each carrying a backpack estimated to contain nearly 10 kilograms of explosives. They detonated within seconds of each other, killing thirteen people and injuring

50 more. A few minutes after that, and miles away, a third suicide bomber detonated his explosives on the second floor of a restaurant in Kuta. Twelve people died, and 50 were injured. Husin, again, had constructed the bombs. The attacks killed four Australians, one of whom was a 16-year-old boy.

Following these bombings, efforts were renewed to catch Husin, but he had sworn he would not be taken alive. Late in 2005, Indonesian and Australian officials were closing in on his location. Rather than face arrest, Husin detonated explosives, which killed himself and several others in the room with him, although it was also reported that there was an exchange of gunfire, and that he may have been simultaneously shot by a sniper deployed by Indonesia's Counterterrorism Special Detachment 88. He was identifiable only by his fingerprints. Although Husin was confirmed dead, JI had long demonstrated the ability to regroup and regenerate after the loss of key personnel. Within a few years, they were operational again.

In 2009, JI was suspected of an attack against two hotels in South Jakarta. Shortly before 8.00 a.m. on 17 July, in peak tourist season, a man loitered in the foyer of the JW Marriott Hotel. He had checked in several days beforehand, claiming to be a traveller. There, in his room, he constructed the bombs that he would wear into the foyer: from there, he went to a function room rented by affiliates of the US Chamber of Commerce. A CEO breakfast was occurring, attended by Australians, New Zealanders and businessmen from the Netherlands. He detonated the explosives, killing himself and others in the room, with the blast projecting into the lobby of a nearby hotel.

Five minutes later, a second suicide terrorist walked into the second-floor restaurant of the Ritz-Carlton Hotel. He detonated his explosives, killing himself and blasting through the windows and part of the hotel façade. In all, nine people died, three of them Australians, while another 50 people were injured. Noordin Top, the logistic chief of JI who had evaded authorities since the first Bali bombings, was believed to be responsible. He was finally tracked down by Indonesian forces and killed in a gun battle at his central

Java hideout on 19 September 2009. Indonesian police confirmed his death with a DNA test.

This was not to be the end of JI's violence in Indonesia. Even as key players were removed from the field by Detachment 88, new players joined the game. Australians, who had so many times been targeted as white meat, remained in the firing line of a now significant international network of Salafist terrorists. New groups emerged, such Jemaah Ansharut Tauhid, founded by Ba'asyir and supported by Al-Qaeda; and in time Islamic State would foster a new group, Jamaah Ansharut Daulah, to support its bloody goals in South-East Asia.[29] While Al-Qaeda and the Taliban fought Western armies in the Middle East, Indonesian extremists continued to hunt Western holiday-makers in South-East Asia.

Many Australians travel to Bali seeking relaxation and rest, or adventure. Some, however, find bloodshed, pain and death at the hands of terrorists with utopian goals beyond their understanding. Human lives are nothing more to such terrorists than pieces on a chessboard, to be sacrificed or manoeuvred to achieve obscure—and impossible—goals. Some pawns are sacrificed strategically: because of their nationality, the threat that can be conveyed through their loss, and because of the sense of entitlement of the chess players. That is why Australians have died in Bali: for what they represent, not for who they are, and what that means to others.

Australian tourists still flock to the islands. The Balinese people still share their culture and their ways with foreigners. And kites still fly above the skies of Bali, earthly messages of thanks to the gods for a bountiful harvest. But now, the promise of joy is mingled with the threat of violence. The War on Terror, being conducted thousands of miles away in Afghanistan, and later Iraq and Syria, would touch the island of Bali and countries around the world, including Australia. Terrorists would continue to overcome borders and boundaries, evade the unseen picket lines between war and peace, and conduct attacks in the homelands of their enemies.

10

Caliphate dreaming: the Al-Qaeda franchise

In the early hours of 8 November 2005, heavy rain fell over parts of New South Wales and Victoria. Despite the miserable weather, around 400 federal and state police officers were quietly preparing to conduct pre-dawn raids against locations in both Sydney and Melbourne. The suspects were violent Salafists, ready to engage in jihad to testify to their purity and their devotion to their god. The suspects had stockpiled weapons and ammunition, and had been training for months. There were rumours—suspicions—that a large-scale chemical terrorist attack was being plotted. Since May 2004, counterterrorism authorities under Operation Pendennis had been watching two cells in two cities, both inspired by the deadly creed of Al-Qaeda.

Now, finally, after long months of monitoring and assessment officers swooped on target locations in the largest terrorism raids in Australia's history to that point. In one case, a suspect engaged in a gunfight with officers and was shot and wounded in the neck. In all, the officers arrested seventeen terror suspects: nine in Melbourne and eight in Sydney. Both cells were linked to Al-Qaeda, the most recent realisation of the terrorist network's reach into far-flung democracies such as Australia. In so doing, Pendennis thwarted an Al-Qaeda–inspired terrorism in Australia by cells largely comprising Australian citizens.

With the attack on 9/11, Al-Qaeda had become the greatest terrorism menace of the modern world. The quiet threat that had been developing in the forgotten deserts of the Middle East and had consolidated in under-governed regions of Africa suddenly manifested as a powerful global network. Al-Qaeda had demonstrated its power to strike in the heartlands of the West, and to mobilise Westerners to their cause even as they wreaked havoc and violence in their nations. Much like the terrorist networks before them, Al-Qaeda developed the terrible power to motivate sympathisers around the world, including Australia.

The gloves were off: where once it was common for international terrorist organisations to accept that not all supporters could be violent operatives, this was no longer the case. Al-Qaeda demanded its followers engage in jihad as a testament to their faith, the strength of their commitment to Allah, and their purity as Muslims. It disseminated this message using both online and offline information networks. This transnationalism saw Al-Qaeda inspire or assist Australian citizens on a quest for terror.

Ambitions in blood

Al-Qaeda follows an ideology of violent Salafism (also known as Salafi-jihadism). This means that at the heart of Al-Qaeda's dark ideology lies a rejection of democracy and democratic processes in favour of a religious dictatorship in which a fundamentalist interpretation of Islam is the desired form of government. Violent Salafism originated with Egyptian jihadists in the mid-twentieth century who became obsessed with the notion of *jahiliyyah* (Age of Ignorance). *Jahiliyyah* refers to a state of human barbarity and ignorance that Muslims believe preceded the enlightenment of Islam in 610 CE. Modern Salafis, however, believe that *jahiliyyah* is a modern condition, a pandemic that has seized the modern world, sickened the faithful, and led people away from Islam.

Salafis seek to purify Islam and restore Islamic life to a heavily romanticised golden age known as Dar al'Islam, through a strict observance of their interpretation of the Quran. In this interpretation, Muslims may only be legitimately governed by a caliph who has combined powers of both religion and state. Only under the reign of the caliph can Muslims truly experience *tawhid*: the oneness and unity of life under Islam. In this worldview, many regional regimes were therefore declared apostate and rejected as corruptions of Islam. Violent Salafists believe that the only way that apostate regimes can be destroyed and the caliphate achieved is through violent jihad, directed at the enemies of Islam and in defence of Islam.

Osama bin Laden believed that the United States upholds these apostate regimes in the lands of Islam, its great power buttressing corrupt religious practice. It was for that reason that Al-Qaeda ultimately targeted the United States—declaring it the Great Satan—and beyond it, its allies such as Australia. As time went on, Western democracies also came to symbolise *jahiliyyah*: nations perceived as ignorant barbarians (or *kuffar*, meaning unbeliever). The duty of the Salafi Muslim, then, became *al-wala' wal-bara'* (loyalty and disavowal): demonstrating their loyalty and religious purity through a rejection of *shirk* and *bidyah*—the innovation and corruption of Western nations. The struggle for purity and authenticity was seen as a great cosmic battle between the supposedly righteous Salafi Muslims and the decadent, immoral crusaders of the West.

Emerging from the Soviet–Afghan War as self-titled victors, Al-Qaeda quickly leveraged its affiliate networks in Australia and South-East Asia, with organisations like Jemaah Islamiyah, even while it provided seed funding for other organisations such as Lashkar-e-Taiba (LeT) in Pakistan. LeT was also a Salafist group, but it focused on the ejection of Indian forces from Kashmir in favour of an Islamic state. Such distinctions in goals did not limit Al-Qaeda, which did not entirely rely on offline networks. Across the dark online spaces, through chain messaging and media, it issued the clarion call of jihad. The Muslims of the world were exhorted to revolt, to throw off the unclean ways of the *kuffar*, and to demonstrate their allegiance to Allah. The practice of democracy, Ayman al-Zawahiri (second-in-command of Al-Qaeda) taught them, was incompatible with Islam: democracy allowed for the people to take part in their own rule, but only Allah had lordship and dominion over humanity. For the most part, the calls from Al-Qaeda fell on sceptical ears as mainstream Muslims recognised its interpretations were uninformed and that Al-Qaeda's members did not actually have the necessary mandate to re-interpret the Quran and its teachings, and were thus distorting its conventional meaning.

The messages of Al-Qaeda were, however, well received by a small number of people. These followers were inflamed with dreams of a caliphate, and of achieving *tawhid* and, beyond it, a place in Jannah—paradise. Al-Qaeda's terrorism was global, and sympathisers were rising from torpid slumber in the West and preparing to act in its name.

Transnational wanderers

Even before the attacks on 11 September 2001, Australians had some measure of acquaintance with Al-Qaeda, which was then a little-known and underestimated band of mujahideen in an unstable and war-torn region of Afghanistan. One such Australian guest to the desert camps of the mujahedeen in the late nineties was Jack Roche, who travelled on the behest of JI. But he was not the only one: Joseph Thomas and David Hicks both became household names for travelling to the Middle East and engaging in actions in conjunction with Salafist forces. Both cases, too, are indicative of the seductive nature of Al-Qaeda ideology, transcending borders and beliefs.

Joseph 'Jack' Thomas was from Williamstown in Melbourne, where he worked numerous jobs including as a milkman, a chef and a taxi driver. He converted to Islam in 1999 and travelled to Afghanistan in March 2001. His intention was to join the Taliban in its civil war against the Northern Alliance for control of Afghanistan and install an Islamic state. He received a visa from members of the Taliban (which was deemed the legitimate government of Afghanistan at the time) and travelled to the front line, where he fought alongside Taliban forces for a week.

It was also alleged that Thomas had contact with Al-Qaeda and was confirmed to have attended the terrorist training facility, Al Farouk camp. The camp was well known for teaching fighters how to manufacture explosives, conduct surveillance, and engage in warfare. After training, Thomas returned to Pakistan and stayed in safe houses affiliated with either Al-Qaeda or the Taliban. He attempted to return to Australia on three occasions: after 9/11, after the Bali bombings, and after an earthquake in 2002. Fearing that his passport would be his one-way ticket to Guantanamo Bay, Thomas tried to modify it and hide the Taliban visa, although it was also suggested that Al-Qaeda forced these modifications.

Eventually, high-ranking Al-Qaeda operative Khaled bin Attash gave Thomas a ticket home and US$3800 to get him there. The money supposedly came with a request from Osama bin Laden that Thomas consider working for Al-Qaeda in Australia, and there were rumours that he was to set up a sleeper cell in Melbourne. Thomas did not make it so far: he was arrested in the airport in Pakistan on 4 January 2003, where he was blindfolded and hooded by men carrying assault rifles. He was detained in custody for more than five months, where he initially told his American and Pakistani interrogators that he was in Pakistan as a student. He was taken to a different location and locked in a cell he described as a 'dog kennel'—open to the elements and the size of a toilet cubicle.[1] During subsequent interrogations, Thomas maintained the student story. His interrogators soon resorted to threats, including one to electrocute him to death.

'We are outside the law,' a Pakistani interrogator allegedly told him. 'No one will hear you scream.'[2]

After violence and threats, Thomas eventually told the truth. He was removed to a different location, this time in Islamabad, where he finally received a visit from the Australian High Commission and was allowed a phone call with his family. Pakistani officials continued to make threats to send him to the infamous US offshore prison Guantanamo Bay. Throughout his detention, he was frequently denied legal representation, and when he was finally interviewed by the AFP and ASIO, it was presumed that the circumstances of his detention implied a measure of duress in obtaining his confession. He was then removed to Lahore, where interrogation by American and Pakistani officials continued, and back to Islamabad for more interviews with the AFP.

When Thomas finally returned to Australia in June 2003, the Australian press nicknamed him 'Jihad Jack'. He was charged with terrorism offences, and subject to the nation's first control order, which restricted his movements, imposed a curfew and controlled his contacts.

'I am not a dickhead who will help to hurt innocent people, which those people [the Taliban] have shown is their tactic,' Thomas told *The Age* before his trial.[3] While he admitted that he trained with the groups, he said he did not agree with their methods. His trial was plagued by issues regarding the nature of his confession, access to a lawyer, and his treatment while in custody. On 26 February 2006, Thomas became the first person to be convicted under the Australian Anti-Terrorism Act. The conviction was thrown out after an appeal—based in part on the distressing circumstances in which his confession was obtained. He faced a retrial in 2008 and was cleared of terrorism-related charges. Thomas has since become a keen opponent of Taliban violence, as he told ABC Radio: 'I'm not saying that all of the Taliban are wonderful characters, but unfortunately what happens . . . when people come to power you get a lot of . . . as the old chefs used to say to me when I was a chef, that like a stock pot, in life the scums seem to rise to the top, so there was unfortunately and there still is.'[4] Such people had indeed risen to the top and were not averse to leveraging international wanderers for their cause.

The other man caught early in the nets of transnational terrorism—and counterterrorism excesses—was David Hicks. Born in Adelaide, Hicks spent his early life working as a jackaroo in the cattle-rich regions of Queensland and the Northern Territory. His equestrian interests eventually saw him decide to travel the Silk Road on horseback, but he put this plan on hold when he discovered Islam in 1999. Instead, he converted to Islam and travelled to Kosovo to fight with the Kosovo Liberation Army in the war against the Serbians.[5]

When Hicks returned to Australia, he attempted to join the ADF. When this failed, he travelled to Pakistan, where he trained with the bin Laden–backed LeT. During his two-month stay, Hicks was operational and participated in a firearms attack on an Indian Army bunker.[6] Eventually, he moved on to camps in Kandahar, Afghanistan. At Al Farouk camp Hicks was rumoured to have met Osama bin Laden. He moved on to Tarnak Farm in Afghanistan to learn surveillance, and then went on to Pakistan to visit a friend in September 2001. He was there when the September 11 attacks occurred, after which he immediately returned to Kandahar.

It was contended that Hicks returned to Kandahar to fight with Al-Qaeda and the Taliban. He joined a Taliban group near Kandahar airport, and, armed with an AK-47, guarded a Taliban tank. In November 2001, he was sent to the front line at Konduz in northern Afghanistan. After Coalition forces overran the Taliban position, Hicks sold his AK-47 and was fleeing towards Pakistan when he was captured by Coalition forces and handed over to the US military, which moved him to Guantanamo Bay on 11 January 2002. Hicks, still an Australian citizen, was kept in isolated detention for three years without charge. The US military classified him as an enemy combatant, and eventually charged him with conspiracy, attempted murder and aiding the enemy. Before his case even got to trial, it was dismissed because the US Supreme Court found the military processes to be unlawful.

Hicks remained in detention for another two years until 2007, when he was again charged and committed to trial. There, he pleaded guilty to the single charge of providing material support to terrorism. He received a seven-year suspended sentence, with the final nine months to be served in Australia. When he arrived back in Australia, he was subject to a control order. In 2014, he appealed his conviction and in 2015 it was dismissed; the unlawful processes used by the US military were an important consideration.

'It's not so much about me,' Hicks told *The Guardian*. 'It's about being an Australian citizen, a human being. Torture should never be used under any circumstances. The law should not be tossed aside.'[7]

Neither Hicks nor Thomas had been convicted of any offences before their involvement with transnational Salafists such as the Taliban and Al-Qaeda. A key element of the Hicks affair was that it exposed the ambiguity of moral boundaries on the one hand, and ever-changing operational boundaries on the other. Security postures, laws and legislation changed frequently, all underpinned by a zealous desire to prevent another 9/11.

Domestic intervention

This hypervigilance was not only evident in international domains and in the context of the War on Terror, but also proved a domestic complication. A key example is the Zaky Mallah affair of 2003. Mallah was the first person to be charged under Australia's newly enacted post-9/11 terrorism laws. He was nineteen years old, Australian-born and living in Sydney, where he was active in an Islamic youth group. In May 2002, he decided to travel to Lebanon to visit his brother and meet a prospective wife of his own, so he applied for a passport. Instead, Mallah received an email from ASIO refusing his passport on the grounds of an assessment suggesting that he might engage in activity that would prejudice Australian security. Mallah, in response, requested the assessment review, with little success. In mid-2003, Mallah videotaped a suicide message and bought a gun and ammunition. He also wrote a manifesto explaining his grievance (especially against ASIO) and a will, and obtained a document titled 'How can I prepare myself for Jihad'. His plan involved storming Sydney's ASIO or DFAT offices and killing staff—an attack he did not expect to survive. During one phone call, he said that he would kill the ASIO officer responsible for his situation. His house was raided, and the rifle and ammunition were seized from under his couch. Mallah was then charged with firearms offences.

The Counter Terrorism Command allegedly arranged an undercover operative to contact Mallah, masquerading as a journalist attempting to acquire a suicide video from him. Mallah took the bait and tried to sell his written manifesto and video to the agent for $3000. He also boasted to the operative about his plans for an attack. Mallah was subsequently arrested and charged with planning a terrorist attack.

'I was subject to solitary confinement, a 22-hour lockdown, dressed most times in an orange overall and treated like a convicted terrorist while under the presumption of innocence,' Mallah later said. 'I had done and said some stupid things including threatening to kidnap and kill . . .'[8]

He spent two years awaiting trial in a maximum-security prison under continuous video surveillance and moved only under escort by an armed tactical team. Mallah's lawyer, Phillip Boulten, SC, denied that Mallah's video preceded a genuine attempt at terrorism. His client was simply a nuisance, a 'publicity-hungry' orphan, as Boulten described him; Boulten challenged the jury to decide whether Mallah was a terrorist or just a ratbag.[9] The jury acquitted Mallah of terrorism charges early in 2005. He pleaded guilty to the charge of threatening Commonwealth officials and was sentenced to two and a half years. This high-profile media trial was but one of a string of incidents that became heavily politicised when public interest in Al-Qaeda terrorism was soaring.

In other cases, the threat of Al-Qaeda–inspired or –assisted terrorism in Australia was far more severe. The first brush with a real threat was the case of Faheem Khalid Lodhi in 2003. Lodhi, a Pakistani-born Australian, migrated in 1998. He had studied architecture for five years at Lahore University, and he continued these studies at the University of Sydney, graduating with a Bachelor of Architecture in 2000. Despite this focus on study, it is possible that Lodhi had existing ties to militant jihadi groups in Pakistan, including LeT, an Al-Qaeda ally. Lodhi returned to Pakistan in October 2001, less than a month after 9/11, ostensibly to look for import–export opportunities.

Instead, it was alleged that he was acting in an official capacity at LeT camps in Lahore. These camps provided military instruction, terror manuals and ideological education to fundamentalist Muslims, with the expectation that graduates would, upon returning to their own countries, continue the fight. While at the camps, it is likely that Lodhi met French jihadist Willie Brigitte, who was also there that month; and on a later trip to the camps in early 2003, he crossed paths with an Australian medical student, Izhar ul-Haque, with whom his future would be inextricably linked. Lodhi was believed to have maintained connections with LeT, including an operative called Sajid Mir. Mir also had connections of his own with Brigitte.

In May 2003, Brigitte travelled to Australia, and it is likely that Mir connected him with Lodhi in an operational capacity. Lodhi helped Brigitte secure accommodation in Sydney, and registered Brigitte's pre-paid mobile under a false name. Brigitte himself did not arrive empty-handed; he had in his possession a map of Australian nuclear sites, which Lodhi was believed to have borrowed. Brigitte's three-month visa expired and, having overstayed his visa, he was apprehended and deported in October 2003.

Several days before Brigitte's deportation, Lodhi was suspected of purchasing two restricted-access maps of the Australian electricity network under a false name. He also investigated power stations, critical infrastructure, and military bases such as Holsworthy Barracks, Victoria Barracks, and HMAS *Penguin*. He compiled 37 aerial photographs, downloaded literature on making poisons and explosives, and began to stockpile items that could be used in the manufacture of bombs. This included toilet paper, which, when added to a nitrate mix, can produce a low-grade explosive called nitrocellulose. Nitrocellulose can ignite when subjected to pressure, essentially causing an explosion without a detonator.

Under an assumed name, Lodhi also sought to acquire chemicals that could be used to produce explosives.[10]

Unbeknown to Lodhi, he had been under ASIO's scrutiny for six months as part of Operation Newport. In October 2003, shortly after he acquired the restricted maps of the Australian electricity network, his Lakemba home was raided, as was his office. Officers seized the photographs, maps and plans, the literature on poisons and explosives, and terrorist training and doctrine DVDs and CDs, including those of the Lions of Allah. Investigators believed that Lodhi had planned to bomb either the electricity network or ADF installations on behalf of LeT and, by extension, Al-Qaeda. Shortly after Lodhi's arrest, Izhar Ul-Haque was detained in November 2003.

Ul-Haque was a 21-year-old student at the University of New South Wales. He had spent his day on campus before boarding a train home with his younger brother around 6.30 p.m. As they disembarked, Ul-Haque was met by three ASIO agents. Leaving his brother in the car (which he could not legally drive) at the train station, Ul-Haque went with the officers for questioning in a nearby park, while another team of twenty ASIO agents and five police officers searched his family home. Ul-Haque was then taken home, leaving his brother stranded in the carpark for the next two hours before anyone thought to collect him. The interviews with Ul-Haque centred on his relationship with Lodhi, and any terrorist plans Lodhi may have been involved in. The interviews began with first contact around 7.00 p.m. and did not finish until 3.45 a.m. All the while, another brother of Ul-Haque was not allowed to contact him and was made to sit at the table in his own kitchen.

In the words of the judge: 'To my mind, to conduct an extensive interview with the accused, keeping him incommunicado, under colour of the warrant, was a gross breach of the powers given to the officers under the warrant.'[11] These interviews, and others, were subsequently found to be inadmissible. Ultimately, Ul-Haque was charged with receiving combat and weapons training from the terrorist organisation LeT between 12 January and 2 February 2003—although LeT had not yet been designated a terrorist organisation. Ultimately, the case against Ul-Haque was abandoned.

He was, however, expected to be a witness in Lodhi's trial, given that authorities suspected the two used a secret method of communication. He refused, and this refusal was permitted. Lodhi was tried without Ul-Haque as witness and faced four major charges pertaining to planning to commit terrorist acts. He was convicted of three: obtaining the electricity network maps in preparation for a terrorist act; seeking explosive materials in preparation for a terrorist act; and possessing literature for use in the preparation of a terrorist act—namely, the production of poisons and explosives. For these charges, he was convicted and sentenced to fifteen years in prison.

Lodhi was not the only active operative in Australia during 2003 with demonstrable links to the global Salafist network. Another was Bilal Khazal, a Lebanese-born Australian who was part of the Global Islamic Youth Movement and worked for a time for Qantas. As early as 1998, the CIA believed that Khazal had travelled to Afghanistan and trained with Al-Qaeda. In the lead-up to the Sydney Olympics in 2000, Khazal was scrutinised by authorities, even while he was an informer to ASIO. There were rumours that he had met Osama bin Laden, who had delegated to Khazal responsibility for Al-Qaeda in Australia and made him the 'man on the ground'.[12]

In 2003, Khazal became the editor for a radical magazine that regularly praised bin Laden. He was soon considered the author of a particularly incendiary document written in mid-September, entitled the *Provision in the Rules of Jihad—Short Wise Rules and Organisational Structures That Concern every Fighter and Mujahid Fighting against the Infidels*. Writing under the alias Abu Mohamed Attawaheedi, Khazal discussed assassination, booby trapping, bombing, sniping and ideal targets (Australia came fifth in a list of nine countries). It would soon transpire that Khazal had plagiarised much of the document, merely editing certain parts and adding a dedication and preface. He then submitted it as an eBook to the Al-Qaeda–affiliated Almaqdese website, where it remained until 2004.

Khazal was charged with creating a document likely to facilitate terrorist acts, although he argued that he had only compiled the document. He was convicted and sentenced to twelve years. Khazal also was convicted in absentia by Lebanese Courts and sentenced to fifteen years for financing terrorism. According to the Lebanese authorities, Khazal funded a terrorist group, Khaliyat Trablus, which attempted to bomb a Beirut McDonald's. Amid this scrambled, disjoined activity, other Al-Qaeda threats were coalescing in Australia.

Australian cells emerge

With Australia's military engagement in Afghanistan and Iraq came the chilling desire for retribution from Al-Qaeda. The previous incidents were not only linked to or inspired by Al-Qaeda, they were also directly encouraged by the organisation. On July 2004 Al-Qaeda in Europe issued the following threat to Australia:

> ... Crusader Australian Government: We demand that you depart from Iraq, before your country is transformed to pools and baths of blood. Australian people: Your interest is in the hands of your Government. If it chooses not to answer our demand to withdraw, we shall make the earth quake under your feet, just as we did in Indonesia. God willing, lines of booby-trapped cars will not stop. Enemies of God, you will have the same fate as the Americans, if you don't respond to our demand. We will turn your nights and your days into hell, as we previously did in Indonesia and other countries. You have come to our country wanting to steal our wealth. With God's permission, we will divert the battle course and shift it to your country, as you brought the battle to our country. Our arms are long and capable of reaching you not only in Australia, but

in all Arab and Islamic countries. We can get to anyone, at the time of our choice . . .[13]

The declaration of jihad was not without significance. Leading into 2004, it became apparent that Australian Salafist cells were forming in Sydney and Melbourne that could be linked to Bilal Khazal (although he by no means controlled them).

What started with a tip-off from a concerned member of the Muslim community soon involved an undercover agent, telephone intercepts and over 400 hours of surveillance in the largest counterterrorism investigation of its time. Victoria Police launched Operation Pendennis, and were quickly joined by NSW Police, the AFP and ASIO. The operation lasted seventeen gruelling months and investigated two terror cells that, initially, evolved separately but were inspired by Al-Qaeda. As time went on, however, they connected and began plotting together.

The first cell comprised people with both familial and ideological connections. The Elomar family lived in Sydney; the head of the family was Mohamed Ali Elomar Sr, whose brothers ran a successful construction business. Unlike his brothers, Elomar Sr spent his time exploring Sydney's criminal underworld. Soon, he drew his two nephews, Mohamed Ali Elomar Jr and Ahmed, into the fold. The two young men were rising stars on Sydney's boxing circuit. In time, they also began attending the Global Islamic Youth Centre, which was affiliated with Bilal Khazal, and run by the radical Sheikh Feiz Mohammad, connections that exposed them to Salafist interpretations of Islam.

Feiz Mohammad was born in southern Sydney to a Lebanese migrant family. He left school early to become a carpenter and became involved in boxing, winning the NSW amateur welterweight championship in 1987. He turned to Islam at nineteen and followed a radical Muslim cleric, Sheikh Mohammed Omran, who sent Feiz to Saudi Arabia in 1990 to study Islamic law. Feiz returned in 1997 as a sheikh and in 2000 set up the Global Islamic Youth Centre. His activism also saw him develop links with JI through

Jack Roche, the Ayub brothers and Rabiyah Hutchinson. Oddly enough, he also informed on his congregation to ASIO, while calling for the killing of unbelievers.

Feiz and the Elomars were close friends with the Cheikho family. Khaled Cheikho is the head of the family and his wife is Rahmah Wisudo, the daughter of Rabiyah Hutchinson. Khaled, his nephew Moustafa and Elomar Sr had all trained with LeT in Pakistan sometime between 1990 and 2002. Their close friend and cell member Abdul Rakib Hasan also trained with LeT, in 1999–2000. Bangladeshi-born Hasan arrived in Australia in 1989 and lived a relatively secular lifestyle in Bondi, complete with alcohol, drugs and sex, before recommitting to an austere and fundamentalist interpretation of Islam in connection with his new contacts.

The Jamal family was also connected to the budding cell. Mohammed Omar Jamal became involved first, and soon drew in his brother, Saleh Jamal. The Jamal brothers became intrinsic to the coordination of the Sydney cell's activities. Saleh was also an acquaintance of Bilal Khazal and believed to be involved with a street gang called DK's Boys. Other cell members included Khaled Sharrouf, who was known to be a petty criminal and drug taker—rather at odds with the strict observances of Salafist Muslims; Omar Baladjam, an actor on the soap *Home and Away* in 1998 before becoming a spray painter; and Mazen Touma. In another stark contrast to Salafist Islam, Omar Baladjam and Abdul Rakib Hasan began selling drugs such as steroids in Kings Cross to finance terror activities.

In time, the Sydney cell connected with a like-minded cell in Melbourne led by Abdul Nacer Benbrika, a radical preacher who espoused the teachings of Osama bin Laden. Benbrika, born in Algeria, had overstayed his tourist visa and fought to become an Australian citizen in the late 1990s. Much like Sheikh Feiz, Benbrika developed connections with Sheikh Mohammed Omran, although he soon splintered from him as well. In August 2004, Benbrika appeared on ABC's *7.30* under the name Abu Bakr, telling interviewers:

Osama bin Laden was a great man before 11th September, which they said he did it. Until now, nobody knows who did it. What you have to understand that anyone who fights for the sake of Allah, the first—when he dies, the first drop of blood that comes from him out, all his sin will be forgiven.[14]

Such sins could include drug dealing, pre-marital sex, and drinking alcohol. Benbrika began preaching his extreme Salafist views to a small group of students, adopting his plan for revolution from Al-Qaeda strategist Abu Musab al-Suri and his book *Call to Global Islamic Resistance*.[15] After the September 11 attacks, Al-Qaeda faced internal reflections about whether it had overreached itself strategically, and what it should do next. Al-Suri suggested that the movement had to decentralise into small, autonomous cells, and engage in low-level attacks to better survive counterterrorism efforts from the Coalition. Al-Suri's writings, with their dangerous strategies and complete commitment to jihad, were adopted haphazardly by Benbrika.

Benbrika's two most committed followers were Aimen Joud and Fadl Sayadi. These two became his deputies in the Melbourne cell, acting as leaders and group administrators. Ahmed Raad was his treasurer and chief fundraiser. Other key members included Raad's brother Ezzit Raad, Shane Kent, Amer Haddara, Abdullah Merhi and Izzydeen Atik. In total, there were fifteen members of the Melbourne cell, which, much like the Sydney cell, devolved to criminality to raise the funds for jihad. Members stole cars and sold them to chop shops for parts. The Melbourne cell also amassed a large amount of extremist literature (and, in Shane Kent's case, created literature) and bomb-making manuals, and were attempting to acquire firearms and other materials on the black market. This included the laboratory equipment and chemicals required to make the 'Mother of Satan' explosive compound, known as TATP. Surprisingly, Benbrika wanted the group to engage in a spectacular attack, more consistent with Osama bin Laden's strategies than al-Suri's. The group discussed many targets, including the Melbourne Cricket Ground during the AFL Grand Final, or Crown Casino during the Grand Prix weekend, and even assassinating Prime Minister John Howard.

Despite these violent fantasies, the Melbourne cell lacked operational expertise, only two of its members having trained at an overseas camp: one at Al Farouk in Afghanistan and the other with Jaish-e-Mohammed in Pakistan. They sought to upskill other members and prepare for jihad by running training camps on rural NSW cattle farms. They also brought in an outsider: an explosives expert to assist them with their bomb-making abilities. Unbeknown to the Melbourne cell, this expert, codenamed SIO39, was a special intelligence officer with Victoria Police.

The two cells, while still largely separate, established a kind of mutual dependency through a series of visits. Benbrika was the spiritual anchor in Melbourne, while the Sydney families had more operational skills and training. The Sydney cell managed to amass twelve firearms, 10,000 rounds of ammunition, detonators, chemicals, laboratory equipment, and bomb-making manuals. In September 2005, Abdul Rakib Hasan, using a false name, attempted to purchase chemicals in bulk, including acetone, glycerine, citric acid, methylated spirits, and battery acid: all of which can be used in manufacturing explosives. Other chemicals the cell did manage to purchase include hydrogen peroxide and hydrochloric acid. Khaled Sharrouf obtained six clocks and 140 batteries for use in bomb-making. Elomar Sr was also rumoured to have purchased five rocket launchers from Taha Abdul-Rahamn that had been stolen from the Australian Army, although they were never recovered.

Their plot was not yet clearly defined, although they did discuss using the weapons against the Lucas Heights nuclear reactor. Three cell members, Touma, Hasan and Elomar, were later caught trespassing in the restricted zone of the nuclear facility. The Sydney cell was also accessing Al-Qaeda material on waging jihad. For example, *In Defence of Muslim Lands* by Osama bin Laden's mentor Abdullah Azzam was found on Hasan's computer, along with nearly

200 other pieces of extremist literature. They also became paranoid about discovery, hiding materials and weaponry underground. Some was also hidden at Mazen Touma's house, where 165 railway detonators and ammunition were later discovered.

Operation Pendennis continued its monitoring, amassing more than 16,400 hours of recordings and intercepting 98,000 text messages for the Melbourne cell alone. Eventually, the raids were planned for the early morning of 8 November 2005: the biggest terrorism raids in Australia to that point. Most were arrested without violence except Omar Baladjam, who carried a firearm and shot and wounded a police officer before being shot in the neck himself. He survived the injury. The two cells were charged with terrorism offences but tried separately, the Sydney cell in the NSW Supreme Court and the Melbourne cell in the Victorian Supreme Court.

The senior members of the Sydney cell received the longest sentences: Elomar Sr was sentenced to 28 years; Khaled Cheikho 27 years; Moustafa Cheikho 26 years; Abdul Rakib Hasan 26 years; and Mohammed Omar Jamal 23 years. Saleh Jamal had fled Australia before the raids, after he was alleged to have been involved in a shooting at the Lakemba police station; while Khalid Cheikho's wife, Rahmah Wisudo, absconded to Jordan and is believed to have continued her relationship with Al-Qaeda. Omar Baladjam and Mazen Touma pleaded guilty and received lighter sentences. Khaled Sharrouf claimed mental illness and also received a lighter sentence. He and his family later went to Syria, where he joined Islamic State. Mohamed Ali Elomar Jr joined Sharrouf there.

The Melbourne cell had its conspiracy charges quashed, resulting in charges for lesser offences. Benbrika was sentenced to fifteen years, while his deputy, Aimen Joud, and treasurer, Ahmen Raad, were sentenced to seven and a half years each. The other deputy, Fadl Sayadi, received a six-year sentence, and Ezzit Raad five years and nine months for his fundraising role. Kent pleaded guilty for his propaganda role and received a sentence of three years and nine months. Other members, such as Amer Haddara and Abdullah

Merhi, received around four and a half years each, while Izzydeen Atik was given a four-year sentence. Despite the disparate outcomes, Operation Pendennis was a success, having effectively and lawfully prevented two ideologically motivated, armed and dangerous Salafist terror cells from consolidating their plans and engaging in acts of terrorism.

False alarms

While Operation Pendennis was evidence of counterterrorism mechanisms functioning as intended, the operating environment was often complicated by false flags and false alarms. In May 2006, for example, Queensland Police's counterterrorism unit received two emails from the Hotmail account qld.jihad. The author claimed to be a member of Al-Qaeda and had attached photos of IEDs with a threat to target populated areas. The author was not a member of Al-Qaeda: John Howard Amundsen was actually a Brisbane high school teacher.

The IEDs, however, were very real. Amundsen had emailed Queensland Police to divert their attention towards Al-Qaeda so that he could detonate his bombs in a public carpark 50 metres from his girlfriend's parents' house in order to threaten them. Queensland Police identified Amundsen and arrested him on 9 May 2006. He was in possession of two plastic containers full of power gel and studded with 15-centimetre-long nails, detonators, transmitters and gas canisters. Fifty-three kilograms of explosives were uncovered, in addition to fake passports and counterfeit cash. He was initially charged with terrorism offences, although these were later dropped in favour of other charges. This incident is noteworthy not as a terrorist plot, but for the appropriation of terrorism to obscure acts of criminality. Anxious to prevent loss of life, counterterrorism authorities were left with little choice but to treat hoaxes as serious until proven otherwise.

The operating environment was also complicated by international events with domestic repercussions. In London on 29 June

2007, unexploded car bombs were discovered: one in Haymarket and the other near Trafalgar Square. While the bombs were discovered and defused, the following day a Jeep Cherokee attempted to ram an airport terminal at Glasgow International Airport. The attackers, Bilal Abdulla and Kafeel Ahmed, hoped that the Jeep would explode on impact. When it didn't, Ahmed doused it in petrol and set it (and himself) on fire while Abdulla threw petrol bombs. The car bombs were linked back to Abdulla and Ahmed, who were both arrested and charged. Two days later, however, the London Metropolitan Police Service Counter Terrorism Command, believing there was an Australian connection, contacted the AFP. From then, Operation Rain was born. At its peak, Operation Rain required the support of hundreds of officers, including: 249 from the AFP, 225 from Queensland Police, 54 from Western Australia Police, 40 from NSW Police, two from Northern Territory Police, one from Tasmania Police, twelve Attorney-General's Department staff, six translators, six Custom officers, two British police, and four other personnel. The cost of the operation was about $8.2 million dollars.

In the immediate aftermath of the attack, British authorities kept Abdulla in custody and took Ahmed to hospital with burns to 90 per cent of his body, where he died about a month later. Ahmed had a second cousin who lived in Australia, Dr Mohamed Haneef. Haneef was a doctor from Bangalore, India, where much of his family remained, and in July 2006 he had travelled to the United Kingdom. While there, he applied for and secured a position as senior house officer at the Gold Coast hospital. Upon departing the UK, he gave his SIM card to his cousin, Sabeel Ahmed, as it was going to expire in a month, cancelling his direct debit payments soon afterwards. The same day that Operation Rain was launched, Haneef was arrested on the Gold Coast in relation to the London car bombs.

Sabeel was the brother of Kafeel Ahmed. British counterterrorism agents contended that the SIM card was found in the Jeep that Kafeel used to ram the airport terminal. Sabeel was arrested in Liverpool, while Haneef was arrested in Australia. Haneef was detained for twelve days under counterterrorism provisions, and his visa was cancelled on character grounds. On 14 July, he was charged with recklessly providing resources to a terrorist organisation by way of the SIM card. Four weeks later, the charges were dropped; the SIM card had not been found in the Jeep at all, but in the house of Sabeel who, it transpired, was ignorant of his brother Kafeel's attack until after it happened. The SIM card was never used to support a terrorist organisation, nor was there any evidence to support the charges against Haneef.

This represents a different complication to that of the Amundsen case. The Haneef case instead exposed the damage that hypervigilance can wreak on innocent people. For Australian Muslims, the Haneef case, in addition to the Mallah case, likely created the perception that counterterrorism laws were not being appropriately applied, and that procedural fairness and evidentiary expectations were not being met in relation to Salafist terrorism.

Bushfire jihad

In the interim, Australia was still included in Al-Qaeda's exhortations as a target for terrorist violence. This permeated its rising franchises, including Al-Qaeda in Iraq (AQI), which coalesced following the invasion of Iraq by Coalition forces. In 2005, the leader of AQI, Abu Musab Zarqawi, issued a message to the mujahideen of the world, encouraging them to continue the war of attrition on the United States and its allies, to drain their resources through ongoing war. Eventually, Zarqawi believed, the loss of life and money would be too great, and the Coalition would have to concede defeat. In a communiqué from 30 March, he claimed that America was made strong by allies such as Australia. These allies had to be targeted, weakened and eventually overthrown. 'Attack everyone from the head of the snake, America, and the old wretch, Britain, to the tail of the snake, Australia,' Zarqawi told his followers.[16]

Al-Qaeda central also continued its propaganda campaign, exhorting Western Muslims to rise up against their own societies and engage in violence. A key propaganda outfit for this move was its *Inspire* magazine, aimed quite literally at inspiring Western Muslims to engage in jihad against Western nations. Editions commonly came with instructions on how to construct and use bombs and firearms, choose targets, and plan attacks. The likes of Al-Suri had also encouraged sleeper cells in the West to awaken, arm themselves, and strike at the West. This was all for a specific purpose: Al-Qaeda sought to erode the political will of Coalition partners to continue the War on Terror in the Middle East. To do this, they tried to circumvent the rules of the game by breaching the front line and exploiting sympathisers in countries such as Australia to attack from within—to bring the war home. The key objective for Al-Qaeda was to leverage this as a propaganda victory, whereby it could magnify recruitment outcomes and expand its power and influence.

In one case, *Inspire* proved somewhat problematic in the Australian context. A Melbourne man, Adnan Karabegovic, was accused of downloading the 2012 edition of *Inspire* in connection with preparation for engaging in a terrorist act. This edition, looking back on the extensive bushfire crisis experienced in 2002–03, had a special section on igniting firebombs in Australia. That particular bushfire season claimed seven lives and destroyed more than 40 houses in Victoria. *Inspire* magazine noted that 500 homes were lost in the ensuing firestorm, as occurred in the ACT. It instructed its readers to construct an ember bomb, wait for dry and windy conditions, ask Allah for assistance, and light the bomb. Possession of *Inspire* was not a crime, and it took a jury only a few hours to find Karabegovic not guilty of the charges.

Hardest of targets

Part of the difficulty in countering Al-Qaeda was its advanced network, which on the one hand used modern information highways to disperse instructional manuals and propaganda such as *Inspire*, and on the other mobilised sympathisers through allied organisations. It was not only Al-Qaeda's close associates JI and LeT that had a presence in Australia. Al-Shabaab, another close associate, also had supporters mobilise in Australia and seek to perpetrate violence against high-profile targets.

Al-Shabaab ('The Youth') was formed in December 2006, and was the newest iteration of a decade of violent Salafist politics in Somalia. Al-Shabaab seeks to oust the Somalian government and establish an Islamic state in Somalia, governed by the organisation's harsh interpretation of Islam. It made its name initially by killing international aid workers, but primarily targeted Somalis, Kenyans, Ethiopians and other members of the African Union. From early on, it had close ties to Al-Qaeda, which was demonstrated by their joint training and resourcing, and public praise of each other following successful attacks. With that relationship came an expansion in Al-Shabaab targeting to include US and United Nations targets. Within a year, the AFP launched Operation Rochester to investigate claims that Australians supported Al-Shabaab, but it came to little.

There were, however, Australians who sympathised with the Al-Shabaab cause. One of these was Saney Aweys, a Somali refugee who fled the violence and civil war in the 1990s to seek safety in Australia at the age of fifteen. He left school early to take up a trade and support his family. He also began attending Preston Mosque, where he met a number of men who shared his religious and political views. Wissam Fattal was one of them. He was born in Tripoli, and left school at fourteen to pursue a career in kickboxing. He was very successful and won the Lebanese Kickboxing Championship three times. He came to Australia when he was 27, married, separated, and worked as a bricklayer.

Another Preston Mosque regular was Nayef el Sayed, who was born in Lebanon and came with his parents to Australia during Lebanon's civil war. He returned to Lebanon for six years and did compulsory service in the Lebanese Army. When Sayed returned to Australia in 2006, he also worked as a bricklayer, which brought him into contact with Fattal and a young man called Yacqub Khayre. Born in Somalia's capital Mogadishu, Khayre came to Australia with his family as a child. From the age of sixteen, he was well known to the juvenile justice system. As a prolific user of methamphetamine, he was in and out of correctional facilities, racking up more than 40 offences. He too began to attend Preston mosque, where he met the other men and Abdirahman Ahmed, another Australian of Somali descent.

The Preston cell members were fascinated by Al-Shabaab. Aweys had many phone calls with Sheikh Hayakallah, a Somali cleric who advocated jihad, to learn more about the group. Sheikh Hayakallah had made international news headlines in 2008 when he and an Islamic Court sentenced a woman to death by stoning for adultery. She was buried up to her neck and 50 men threw stones at her until she was dead. Aweys also contacted Walid Mohamed, an acquaintance who had travelled to Somalia to train and fight with the terrorist group. It appears that the goals and ambitions of Al-Shabaab resonated with the cell members, who began to raise funds and send money to Al-Shabaab from early 2009.

The Preston cell members were not content with fundraising: they wanted to engage in violent jihad in Australia on behalf of Al-Shabaab. They made some attempts to have leading Somali sheikhs pronounce a fatwa justifying violence in Australia, but this was met with refusal. The cell then decided they would send one of their own to request a fatwa in person from the sheikhs of Al-Shabaab, and, while there, train with the organisation. Only one of their number could go and they chose Yacqub Khayre. After two weeks, however, Khayre fled and begged for money for an early flight back to Australia, which was provided to him. He brought no fatwa back with him and little training. The cell decided to progress without either.

They took inspiration from Al-Shabaab's early operations against Ethiopian military forces and looked to the hardest of targets—military installations—rather than civilian targets. In March 2009,

Fattal caught the train from Lakemba to Holsworthy, where he performed reconnaissance on Holsworthy Barracks military base. As one of the few Australian military bases focused on domestic counterterrorism, Holsworthy Barracks is arguably one of the hardest targets in Australia. It is home to the 2nd Commando Regiment, an elite Special Operations team constituting some of Australia's most hardened, battle-ready and well-trained soldiers.

Fattal saw none of this. He returned to Sayed, and the two spoke in code, discussing the possibility of targeting Holsworthy Barracks. Fattal assured Sayed that he had visited the barracks, and he described an attack as 'something that is very easy'. When Sayed asked for more confirmation, Fattal extrapolated, saying, 'It's nice, the stroll is nice and there is work and so on. Do you understand what I mean?'[17] Bizarrely, the Preston cell would refer to Holsworthy Barracks as a 'soft target'.[18]

So the target was chosen. All the plotters needed now was permission from a sheikh. Over numerous telephone calls throughout June with Sheikh Hayakallah, Aweys attempted to get a fatwa to permit the attack. Hayakallah did not want to imperil Muslims in Australia, and by 5 July his answer was a definitive no, as it was from other Somali sheikhs. This suited Ahmed, who opposed the operation, saying that it would be a 'catastrophe' if they were given the go-ahead by Al-Shabaab sheikhs.[19] But the rest of the Preston cell would not take no for an answer. They were committed to the plot, and all they needed was weapons. Once armed, they would storm Holsworthy and kill as many as they could before dying a martyr's death. A suicide attack was in the works.

Little did the cell know that from the moment they began sending money to Al-Shabaab Operation Neath was launched. It became a seven-month investigation with heavy use of surveillance, and required the help of 400 officers from the AFP, Victoria Police and NSW Police. Of that number, twenty officers were from the NSW Police Counter Terrorism and Special Tactics Command. An undercover operative codenamed Hamza contacted the men and befriended Fattal and some of the others. When the cell began preparing for the base assault in earnest, Operation Neath moved. At 4.30 a.m. on 4 August 2009, it executed nineteen search warrants in Victoria and New South Wales. Saney Aweys, Abdirahman Ahmed, Yacqub Khayre, Nayef el Sayed and Wissam Fattal were arrested.

The Preston cell went to trial in 2010. A line was drawn between Khayre and Ahmed, and their more senior fellows Aweys, Fattal and Sayed. These three were convicted and each sentenced to eighteen years for the plot. Ahmed, given his reluctance to be involved, was found not guilty of terrorism offences. Khayre, the one member who had travelled to Somalia with the clear intention of contacting and training with one of Africa's most dangerous terrorist groups, was also found not guilty. This verdict left AFP officers 'grim-faced'[20] and would have dire consequences in the years to come, when Khayre would act again, this time in the name of Islamic State.

Enter player two

Although international terrorist organisations had shown an interest in using Australia as a theatre for terrorism, Al-Qaeda's strategy against the West had seen Australians targeted as victims of terrorism on a scale never before seen. The campaigns of left-wing extremists, Ustaša terrorists, the Palestinians, the Ananda Marga, Armenian terrorists, and even the extreme right to this point appeared to pale in significance—even though to date Al-Qaeda had accrued fewer domestic fatalities or successful operations in Australia. What began with 88 dead Australians in Bali continued with various plots in Australia, in some cases resulting in the identification and apprehension of Al-Qaeda–inspired terrorist cells, and in others, catching other citizens in the crossfire of counterterrorism practice.

Osama bin Laden was killed on 2 May 2011 in Abbottabad, Pakistan, at the hands of a US Navy Seal team. Despite his death, Al-Qaeda was too well established for decapitation strategies to set the network back in any significant sense. Al-Qaeda central had developed strong links and affiliations beyond Jemaah Islamiyah and LeT. Al-Qaeda in Yemen had merged with Al-Qaeda in the Arabian Peninsula and conducted attacks around the world. Al-Qaeda in the Islamic Maghreb developed into a strong regional player and filled a power vacuum in North Africa. Al-Shabaab pledged allegiance to Al-Qaeda in 2009, and the Islamic Movement of Uzbekistan continued to support both Al-Qaeda and the Taliban operationally and ideologically.

For Al-Qaeda in Iraq (AQI), however, a different fate was in store. Under the leadership of Abu Musab Zarqawi, the group lost the support of Al-Qaeda central through its frequent deviations from strategic targeting and its publicity-hungry antics. With bin Laden's death, the new leader of Al-Qaeda was Ayman al-Zawahiri, who even publicly reprimanded AQI to no avail. AQI continued to alienate Al-Qaeda, mostly through targeting fellow Muslims (Sunni and Shia alike) instead of the United States and its allies. When Zarqawi was killed in a US airstrike in 2006, it was expected that AQI would scatter among the rubble of the Iraq insurgency. For a time it did, as its fighters were targeted by Iraqi forces and local Sunnis, and much of its leadership decimated.

But then, like a snake shedding its skin, AQI was reborn as Islamic State under the leadership of Abu Bakr al-Baghdadi. Its venom would reach the far corners of the world, claiming the lives of hundreds of thousands of people in Syria and Iraq; attempting the genocide of the Yazidi people; enslaving, murdering and torturing fellow Muslims; and inciting sympathisers in the West to violence. This would encourage terror in Australia on a scale beyond anything Al-Qaeda had attempted. Al-Qaeda may have created the spark for Salafist terrorism, but it would be Islamic State that would set the world on fire.

11

Civilisation burning: the Islamic State network

It was quiet in the Lindt Café on the morning of 15 December 2014—the lull before the storm of Christmas activity. Sydney's Martin Place was usually busy at that time in the morning, and across the way the Seven Network's city office was already a hive of activity. The seven staff of the Lindt Café went about their work, managed by Tori Johnson. A pregnant barista was stationed on the coffee machine, and ten customers were scattered about the store. Among them were three commercial barristers, including Katrina Dawson, who was also pregnant; four staff from Macquarie and Westpac banks; an 82-year-old retiree on the way to a doctor's appointment; and two women sharing breakfast before facing the day.

Around 8.30 a.m., a man entered the café carrying a black backpack. He took a seat and ordered black tea and cakes. He asked staff to watch his bag while he went to the toilet, which they did. Unbeknown to them, inside his backpack was a sawn-off, 12-gauge pump-action La Salle shotgun manufactured in the 1960s. A cartridge was already chambered, and three more were in the magazine. He also had 24 more cartridges in his backpack, along with a stereo speaker rigged with wires to look like an IED, a handwritten note warning of bombs hidden around the city, and a mobile phone.

At 9.40 a.m., after 70 minutes in the café, the man asked to see the manager. Tori Johnson immediately went to see what was wrong. The staff watched the interaction uneasily: something seemed off. Johnson beckoned a staff member and instructed them to lock the café doors and remain calm. The man passed his phone to Johnson, who rang 000. 'Australia is under attack by the Islamic State,' Johnson told the operator. 'There are 3 bombs in three different locations Martin Place, Circular Q [sic] and George Street.'[1]

The siege of Lindt Café had begun. The distant terrorist network of Islamic State had finally inspired a seemingly complex terrorist attack in Australia.

Origins of Islamic State

On 20 March 2003, US president George W. Bush declared war against Iraq, based on false claims of weapons of mass destruction. As far as military campaigns go, the invasion of Iraq was considered a textbook success. Mission success was well defined and achieved within weeks. By 9 April 2003, the dictator Saddam Hussein had been deposed, and in the political vacuum the United States installed career diplomat Paul Bremer to handle the Coalition Provisional Authority. Bremer's task, in essence, was to put the shattered pieces of Iraq back together in such a way as to allow it to transition to a modern nation-state. His strongest move was to disband the two mechanisms that had maintained Saddam's power: his Ba'ath Party, and the army. In the single stroke of a pen, Bremer effectively made 400,000 men with military training unemployed in Iraq.

Despite Afghanistan functioning as an estuary of mujahideen, Iraq also had a number of fighters who had trained in those early days of the Afghan camps. One such man was Ahmad Fadhil Nazzal al-Kalaylah. Born in Jordan, he was a barely literate petty criminal, a heavy drinker, and a drug user. He was rumoured to be involved in a violent robbery in which a relative was killed, he regularly brawled, and at one time he was a pimp. He was in prison when he truly became involved with Salafi Islam. Upon his release, Kalaylah joined the war in Afghanistan against the Soviets, but by the time he arrived in 1989 the war was over. Nonetheless, in the camps he met the radical preacher Abu Mohammed al-Maqdisi. They made their way back to Jordan, where they were welcomed as returning heroes, and formed their own terror cell: Bayaat al-Imam (Pledge of Allegiance). They were both arrested and imprisoned again in 1995, during which time al-Maqdisi continued Kalaylah's religious education.

Kalaylah returned to Afghanistan before 9/11, assumed a new name—Abu Musab Zarqawi—and started a new group, Jama'at al-Tawhid wa'al-Jihad (Organisation of Monotheism and Jihad; JTJ). While Zarqawi was not involved with Al-Qaeda before 9/11, they soon joined forces during the US-led invasion. Although Osama bin Laden did not like him, Zarqawi rose to be one of his trusted fighters. Bin Laden took him to the Battle of Tora Bora, after which Zarqawi fled to Iraq. He was there, transforming his JTJ network into Al-Qaeda in Iraq (AQI), when Bremer created the power vacuum that Zarqawi would so notoriously exploit. He became a significant player in the Iraq insurgency, and maintained this power in part through his media campaign. He started by capturing Westerners, dressing them in orange jumpsuits reminiscent of Abu Ghraib prison, and filmed himself beheading them; US contractor Nicholas Berg was one such victim. Zarqawi also instigated suicide bombing campaigns and encouraged Sunni and Shia to turn on each other in a mass of violence.

While he was still technically a Salafi jihadist, Zarqawi began to diverge from the Al-Qaeda script by targeting Shia Muslims and some Sunnis, declaring them apostates. Under Maqdisi's teachings, Zarqawi questioned what it meant to be an authentic and pure Muslim and set about slaughtering those he did not think pure enough. When he was scolded by Maqdisi for his violent excess, Zarqawi split from his ideological mentor. The only true Muslim, he argued, was one who wielded a sword. Soldiers, then, had more legitimacy than armchair ideologues like Maqdisi. Al-Qaeda sought to restrain Zarqawi's wanton brutality against Muslims (wanting him to focus his efforts on the United States), but to no avail.

At the same time, many fighting-age men in the region were rounded up by US forces and detained in Camp Bucca. There, the innocent and the terrorist were stabled together, and new networks formed. One such detainee was Abu Bakr al-Baghdadi. When he left the camp in 2004, he immediately joined AQI, and Zarqawi's power continued to grow. While the United States pursued a (non-literal) decapitation strategy against Zarqawi's growing network, his trusted lieutenants, who were former Iraqi military and intelligence officers, could be readily replaced. Eventually, Zarqawi himself was killed in a US airstrike, but despite this neither his organisation nor his network collapsed. AQI maintained momentum for a short time, but then began to fail as the United States engaged Sunni tribes in the fight. AQI floundered for a time under numerous leaders and organisational names until al-Baghdadi assumed control in 2010.

In the chaos that came with the Arab Spring and the revolution in Syria, the insurgencies of Al-Qaeda and AQI flourished. In 2012, Al-Qaeda's new commander in chief, Ayman al-Zawahiri, who had assumed control of Al-Qaeda shortly after the death of Osama bin Laden, ordered the Muslims of the world to stand with the civilians of Syria and fight to bring down President Bashar al-Assad, whom they viewed as an apostate Muslim. AQI also capitalised on the disturbances, sending an operative into Syria to set up a terror group, Jabhat al-Nusra (JaN), to masquerade as independent of both Al-Qaeda and AQI. JaN subsumed smaller groups, destroying moderate Syrian organisations in the process.

In 2012, AQI initiated its 'Breaking the Walls' campaign, freeing prisoners and recruiting them in its army. The next year it ran a new campaign, 'Soldiers Harvest', and evolved from a simple terror group into one that controlled territory, with light and motorised infantry, and a considerable bureaucracy. In 2013, when AQI announced a merger with JaN to control the Syrian groups as well, JaN resisted and instead tried to align itself with Al-Qaeda. Following this dysfunction, Al-Qaeda renounced its ties with AQI in

2014, the same year al-Baghdadi renamed his group and declared an Islamic State of Iraq and Syria (ISIS). His new group became known more simply as Islamic State (IS).

City after city fell to IS control: Ramadi, Raqqa, Mosul and Tikrit. In Tikrit, IS slaughtered over a thousand Iraqi cadets in a single day, a massacre so vast that the site could be seen from space. A single man survived—left to tell the tale. All civilians deemed false Muslims by IS were put to death: men, women, and children. Entire ethnic minority groups were surrounded and faced with either death or slavery. By late 2014, IS had established its headquarters in Raqqa and controlled more than 100,000 square kilometres of territory, governing 11 million people, and operating the oilfields. There, in Raqqa, al-Baghdadi realised the dreams of Zarqawi and Al-Qaeda: he declared a Caliphate and named himself caliph.

Going viral

IS went viral. Under Zarqawi, the group had early on demonstrated its willingness to engage in brutal and gratuitous violence on camera. Al-Baghdadi pursued the same policy: his fighters exploited social media channels, including Twitter, to share propaganda calling on Muslims to act in the name of IS. This call to action, also known as *qital fi sabil Allah* (combat on the path to Allah), is a more simplified (and debated) version of jihad.[2] IS contextualised it as a battle between a Muslim tribe and a non-Muslim army. When the US began airstrikes in late 2014, it played right into the IS narrative. IS believed themselves to be engaged in an apocalyptic battle against the West, against the Crusaders, against the unbelievers and against the Jews. This battle, they claimed, would last forever.

IS created a new magazine, *Dabiq*, that spread IS ideology using dramatic imagery, spiritual annotations and interviews from the front line. It shared its worldview and its purpose with followers, and framed the Caliphate as a promised utopia. It was depicted as a sunny, perfect land, cleansed of all impurities: Dar al'Islam, the Abode of Peace. *Dabiq*, alongside social media videos, invited Muslims from around the world to travel to the Caliphate and be part of history in the making. The content showed the Caliphate joyfully welcoming Muslim arrivals on the one hand, and indiscriminate slaughter of non-Muslims on the other. Those who could not travel to the Caliphate were exhorted to join the cause from afar, by perpetrating violence against their home countries.

Australia was not irrelevant to IS and its propaganda machine. Australian Neil Prakash, known as Abu Khalid al-Kambodi, was the star of the IS video *Stories from the Land of the Living*, presented by Al-Hayat Media Centre. A Sydney native, Prakash arrived in Syria as a foreign fighter in 2013. With his heavy Australian accent, he was able to talk to Western audiences and perpetuate a narrative of life in the Caliphate: a life that was presented as being in conformity with the will of Allah, rejecting corruption and innovation, the worship of false idols, and democratic tyranny. This utopia was promised to the viewer: the doors to the Caliphate were open.

In an attempt to undermine the seduction of IS's narratives and fictionalised portrayals of the Caliphate, Australia's Prime Minister Tony Abbott began to refer to IS as a 'death cult'. He used this term no less than 346 times over an eight-month period, although it ultimately failed to delegitimise the IS narrative.[3] Instead, some Australians were inspired by the IS narrative, and sought to travel to the Middle East and join the Caliphate. Those who could not travel channelled their inspiration into terrorist attacks—as instructed by IS—in the name of Allah and IS.

Inspired by IS

Most of the Western attacks inspired by IS were lone terrorist attacks, conducted by individuals who believed themselves to be part of the IS community without having any direct link to it. Because ideologies cannot be stopped at the border, they have the clear and demonstrable power to motivate sympathisers to violent action, even when they have had no actual contact with the progenitor of the ideology. As a result, such attacks are generally lacking in capability, poorly planned or opportunistic. By adopting the ideology of IS, however, these individuals feel like they are part of a transcendental movement, joining a legion of faceless fighters in pursuit of a sacred cause. This was fostered by IS, which, in September and October 2014, encouraged every Muslim to travel to the Middle East to join its quest. If travel to the designated zone was not possible, IS exhorted its followers to kill crusaders and declare it in IS's name. In the words of a senior IS leader:

> If you can kill a disbelieving American ... or an Australian ... or any other disbeliever from the disbelievers waging war, including the countries that entered into a coalition against the Islamic State, then rely upon Allah, and kill them in any manner or way however it may be. Smash his head with a rock, or slaughter him with a knife, or run him over with your car, or throw him down from a high place, or choke him or poison him.[4]

Such was the case with the first IS-inspired attack in Australia. Abdul Numan Haider was born in Afghanistan in 1997 and migrated to Australia with his family as a child. At the age of fifteen, he began attending the Al-Furqan Mosque in Springvale, Melbourne, and associating with radical religious groups. Aged seventeen when IS declared its Caliphate, Haider expressed a desire to travel to Syria to fight with IS. This brought him onto the radar of authorities; his passport was cancelled and his house searched. He was also the subject of a telephone intercept, in which counter-terrorism authorities overhead him confiding to a friend a plot to stab police officers. This information was not transcribed and, as a consequence, not shared.

Haider also attracted attention through social media posts making threats on Prime Minister Tony Abbott's life. On 18 September 2014, Haider posted a photo of himself wearing a black balaclava and a camouflage-patterned shirt, and holding the black shahada flag (a declaration of faith used across Islam and perverted by IS). The post also criticised both ASIO and the AFP. He was interviewed by police, and ASIO assessed that he adhered to extreme ideology. On 23 September, Haider was summoned for an interview at the Endeavour Hills Police Station in Melbourne's south-east as part of an investigation linked to his cancelled passport.

En route, Haider dropped a friend, Omar Sakejha, at Melbourne International Airport; Sakejha was going to fight for IS in Syria. Haider continued to the Endeavour Hills station but refused to enter the building. Instead, he requested that the two officers of the Joint Counter Terrorism Team, one an Australian Federal Police officer and the other a Victoria Police officer, meet him outside. As the Victoria Police officer attempted to shake Haider's hand, Haider drew a knife and stabbed him in the arm, then turned to the AFP officer and stabbed him three or four times in the head and body. The wounded Victorian officer shot Haider dead.

It was rumoured that Haider had planned to behead the officers, drape the shahada flag over their bodies, and post the image online to testify to his allegiance to IS. In any case, his attack was celebrated by IS, and in particular Prakash. He told his audience that Haider had been denied the opportunity to join the Caliphate: 'You must start attacking before they attack you,' Prakash declared.[5]

Haider was not the only IS sympathiser in Australia. A number of citizens were believed to support the Caliphate and had formed cells plotting to behead Australians on camera. Operation Appleby was launched in 2014 to monitor these individuals and groups. Several days before Haider's attack, more than 800 officers raided 25 Sydney properties. Another 70 Queensland Police officers searched properties in Brisbane as part of a separate investigation. Fifteen people were detained by Operation Appleby and charged with a variety of offences—with their trials going on for years.

One of the major arrests was Omarjan Azari, who was in contact with an Australian IS recruiter, Mohammad Ali Baryalei. During Azari's trial, the court heard that Azari planned to kill six or seven Australians a month in the name of IS. His trial was aborted in

May 2017, due to fears of prejudice, although he was retried and convicted in 2019. Eighteen-year-old Sameh Bayda was also arrested and charged with collecting documents to facilitate a terrorist act, along with his wife, Alo-Bridget Namoa. Similarly, Mohammed Almaouie was arrested in December 2015 for conspiracy to undertake a terrorist act. Another arrest was Maywand Osman, who was charged with terrorism act offences and held in Goulburn Supermax prison for eighteen months before the charges were withdrawn in June 2016. On 22 March 2016, two more people targeted in Operation Appleby were arrested by the Joint Counter Terrorism Team Sydney, this time as part of Operation Peqin. A man, Milad Atai, and a sixteen-year-old girl were charged with funding, or receiving funds from, terrorist groups. Atai would later face other charges in association with another terrorist attack inspired by IS.

For all of this activity, one fish slipped the net.

Lindt Café siege

In 1996, Iranian Mohammed Hassan Manteghi travelled to Sydney on a business visa. From what can be gathered, Manteghi was a privileged Shia, part of an affluent family that enjoyed access to tertiary education and the favour of the Iranian regime—at least initially. When he embezzled his own travel agency, he abandoned his family and went on the run from Iranian authorities (even though it was rumoured that he was an Iranian intelligence agent). Within a month of landing in Australia, he claimed asylum. Initially, the Department of Immigration rejected his protection visa because ASIO considered him an indirect security risk. That was later overturned and Manteghi was granted a visa and, in 2004, Australian citizenship. He then changed his name to Michael Hayson Mavros.

He shed occupations frequently. First he worked as a security guard, and later a retail salesman. Mavros then decided to go by the name Hayson, and began work as a self-accredited 'sexual healer', which involved him rubbing oil on people and sexually assaulting them. He also photographed and filmed some of these assaults, which led police to form a strike force and charge him with 43 counts of aggravated sexual assault, sexual assault and indecent assault. He married an Australian woman and had two children, divorced her, and then married another woman. His Australian ex-wife was stabbed eighteen times and set alight by Hayson's new wife, Amirah Droudis, in order to gain custody of the children; Hayson was considered an accessory to the murder.

Hayson changed his name again to Man Haron Monis, and around 2008, began to channel his efforts into political activism. Between 2007 and 2009, he dispatched numerous offensive letters to the families of ADF personnel killed in the War on Terror, likening the deceased to Hitler and saying they would go to hell, and to the family of an Australian Trade Commission official who was killed in the Jakarta bombing. He also sent copies to the prime minister, the Minister of Defence, the chief of the ADF and the AFP commissioner. He signed all the letters as Sheikh Haron, and published copies on his website, sheikhharon.com. Despite being charged with using the postal service to menace and harass, Monis continued his letter campaign, and began posting fatwas to his website praising Al-Qaeda and Jemaah Islamiyah. He converted from Shia to Sunni Islam, aligning his views with violent (Sunni-derived) Salafist groups.

In 2012 and 2013, he attempted to join the 1%er (one per center) outlaw motorcycle gang, but the gang rejected him and took his bike. In January 2014, Monis escalated his political activism, becoming involved with radical Islamist organisation Hizb ut-Tahrir, and with opposing counterterrorism raids. In December 2014, he set up a Twitter account under the handle @sheikh_haron and began posting graphic images of dead children, blaming their deaths on the US and Australian engagement in the War on Terror. Due to these posts, several people made complaints to the National Security Hotline in the weeks before the Lindt Café siege. The complaints were reviewed by NSW Police, ASIO and the AFP. By 13 December, ASIO assessed that Monis did not have the desire or intent to engage in terror. The very next day, Man Haron Monis published a manifesto on his website, sheikharon.com, alleging that Australian and US forces were responsible for killing children in the Middle East.

He was still on bail when he methodically prepared for the Lindt Café siege. He bought a SIM card as early as October, registered it under someone else's name and inserted it into a second mobile phone. He activated it, then switched it off until 13 December. When he turned it back on briefly, he went to several banks and emptied his accounts of over $600. He then purchased a $70 backpack, while the remaining cash vanished, likely invested in the old, grey-market shotgun and ammunition. The next day, he attended the Campsie Police Station at 5.00 p.m. in accordance with his bail conditions and made his final post to his website. At 8.21 a.m. on 15 December, Monis switched on his second mobile phone. He was in the Haymarket area.

He went to Lindt Café, arriving sometime after 8.30, and seemed for all the world like a relatively normal customer, despite his heavy backpack. The siege of the café began at 9.40, when Monis finally beckoned manager Tori Johnson over and made him call Triple Zero. Monis drew the shotgun from his bag and forced everyone to the front of the café, blocking the windows. He put on a black headband with Arabic shahada inscriptions (normally used to testify faith to Islam), a black vest and a wristband. Among his demands, relayed in a scrambled manner to the Triple Zero operator, was a live debate with Prime Minister Tony Abbott. If police attempted to rescue the hostages, Monis claimed his allies around the city would detonate bombs while he himself would kill the hostages. All this activity, according to Monis, was in the name of IS. He forced his hostages to hang the shahada flag in the windows of the café.

Police soon arrived at the scene, and a hostage covertly shared hand signals with a responding officer: one gunman and eighteen hostages. Police cordoned off the area and began evacuating neighbouring buildings while the tactical teams and a negotiator arrived.

A detective watching the live media coverage of the siege identified Monis, having engaged with him in the case related to the violent homicide of Monis's ex-wife. Monis forced the hostages to make calls to various media stations and he dictated their social media posts. As the siege dragged on, Monis continued to make demands, including the supply of an IS flag, and threatened to kill the hostages.

At 3.35 p.m., after six hours under threat, three male hostages escaped, opening the front and side entrances and fleeing into the streets, where they were immediately secured by tactical unit officers. Back inside the café, Monis threatened to kill hostages if any more attempted to escape. He forced them to build barricades in the event of police entry. He had Fiona Ma, a café staff member, shifting hostages from one window to the next, or escorting them on toilet breaks. She was encouraged to escape due to her freedom of movement, but she refused to abandon the other hostages.

While Monis was distracted, two female staff members slipped out of the café, having covertly unbolted the doors while other hostages muffled the sound with coughs. Monis did not notice their escape. Another male staffer, Jarrod Morton-Hoffman, initially tried to conceal it from Monis, given he could have started following through on his threats to kill them. It appeared Jarrod was successful—until the media began reporting that five hostages had escaped, which Monis saw on television. Jarrod convinced him that the media were lying, and in doing so likely saved the lives of his fellow hostages for a time at least.

As the siege continued, Monis became increasingly agitated that his demands were not being met. When night fell, he began overreacting to the slightest noise around the café, and he forced the hostages to gather around him as a shield. Negotiators still hoped for a peaceful outcome, and although sniper opportunities were identified, they were not pursued. Investigators raided Monis's property, and the hunt for the promised IEDs continued. At 11.00 p.m., Monis permitted the hostages to call their loved ones, and then tried to contact the negotiators again to have the Martin

Place lights turned off. Four calls to the negotiators went unanswered, as they were made during the handover meeting for the new team. Jarrod and Fiona continued their efforts to keep Monis calm—a task that became increasingly difficult as his behaviour became more erratic and dangerous.

Around 2.00 a.m., a strange calm fell over Monis, and he instructed the hostages to build new barricades around the other exits. While he was distracted, six more hostages seized the opportunity and fled—but they broke a glass in the process, which drew Monis back to the room. He fired a shot towards the fleeing hostages, then turned to Tori Johnson, the manager of the café, and forced him on his knees with his hands behind his head. Monis fired a shot into the ceiling and Tori flinched. Another hostage fled: Monis did not even notice. Several minutes later, Monis fired again, this time at Tori Johnson at point-blank range, killing him instantly.

The words 'hostage down' echoed across the radio, and tactical teams acted: they breached the Lindt Café from both sides. As police stormed the room, Monis was shot and killed almost immediately. In the ensuing chaos, seventeen bullets were fired, creating shrapnel that cut through the room. Once the dust settled, Katrina Dawson was found half hidden by the furniture and bleeding heavily. Shrapnel from police gunfire on entry had struck her in her back, neck and shoulder. A single fragment of a bullet had caused catastrophic damage when it perforated her heart. Emergency resuscitation was attempted as paramedics raced her to hospital, but they were unable to save her life. Three other hostages were also wounded.

The Lindt Café siege was finally over, but criticisms about how it was managed soon began. These spanned the lack of experience of negotiators, missed opportunities of the sniper team, debriefing of escaped hostages, lack of facilities available to first responders, and more. The criticisms became focal points of the subsequent coronial inquest, which identified areas for improvement while nonetheless stating: 'the deaths and injuries that occurred as a result of the siege were not the fault of police. All of the blame for those rests on Monis.'⁶ The families of Katrina Dawson and Tori Johnson, however, were far from satisfied with the outcomes.

Beyond the heroism of Tori Johnson, who had refused to leave any of the hostages at the mercy of Monis, two other heroes emerged: Fiona Ma and Jarrod Morton-Hoffman. Both were full-time university students and casual employees of Lindt Café. Over the extended period of the siege, they mollified Monis, made attempts at de-escalation whenever his sudden and unpredictable rages came upon him, and engineered the escapes of others. Ultimately twelve of the eighteen hostages managed to flee the terrorist: those left were two pregnant women including Katrina Dawson, two elderly women, café manager Tori Johnson, and one other.

Monis was not a member of IS, but he wanted to be. His history of criminality, political activism and violence, and his flailing attempts to emulate clerics and bikies, speak of an individual seeking to achieve significance. Subsequent investigations found that he had no contact with IS, although he had made significant effort to align his cause with theirs. He relentlessly told the hostages that he conducted the attack on behalf of IS, and in his final manifesto he allegedly swore *bay'ah* (allegiance) to IS—exactly as IS had instructed in its 2014 issues of *Dabiq*. IS claimed responsibility for the attack.

* * *

Monis was not the only IS-inspired threat during this time. IS proved to have a long arm, as readily observed in the Western world through the number of attacks disrupted by counterterrorism authorities. At exactly the same time the siege was occurring, counterterrorism authorities had been monitoring another cell. The conspirators were all young men, and included Sulayman Khalid, Ibrahim Ghazzawy, Jibryl Almaouie, Mohammed Almaouie, Farhad Said, and a fourteen-year-old boy. They spoke in code and were planning to obtain firearms and either kill members of NSW Police and the AFP or attack government buildings, when they were apprehended and charged. This sort of case fast became a feature of the threat landscape: in 2016, an unnamed adolescent was found to have been planning an IS-inspired stabbing spree in Sydney, while another youth in Sydney planned an attack on Anzac Day commemorations using both explosives and firearms. Both plots were successfully disrupted by authorities.

Assisted by IS

From November 2014, the US commenced airstrikes against IS positions in Iraq and Syria, and began to arm Kurdish groups with weapons and ammunition. IS, despite this pressure, continued to expand and affiliate with terror groups around the world, including Boko Haram in Nigeria, Abu Sayyaf in the Philippines, and groups in Libya and Egypt. The IS propaganda machine also escalated its activities, and continued to encourage its followers in the West and all over the world to launch terror attacks in its name. IS was not unique in seeking to mobilise followers in this fashion. Abu Musab al-Suri, a Syrian strategist with Al-Qaeda, had encouraged such activity since the early 2000s: 'the basic axis of the Resistance's military activity against America and her allies now, must lie within the framework of "light guerrilla warfare", "civilian terror", and secret methods, especially on the level of individual operations and small Resistance Units completely and totally separated from each other'.[7]

Al-Suri envisaged small secret terror cells and lone actors conducting international attacks on behalf of a managing organisation they had never met, or with the advice of an operative through encrypted apps. IS advised cells and individuals around the world on who to target and how. Because the attackers were often untrained and lacked technological capability, they were encouraged to use basic weapons such as knives or cars. Some in Australia received such assistance.

In early 2015, two Sydney-based IS supporters, Omar Al-Kutobi and Mohammad Kiad, were found in possession of homemade napalm in a jar, the equipment to make an IS flag, IED instructions and materials, and a hunting knife. They had sworn allegiance to IS and were receiving instructions from an IS controller called Rahman, located around Syria, who was assisting with their plot. Al-Kutobi wrote in his phone: 'We are now in the heart of the homeland of the infidels, we can hit at any time we want and we will not let them live in peace before we can live in peace in the land of Muslims.'[8]

As their plot progressed, they became subject to investigation under Operation Castrum. The two men planned to attack a Shia mosque—inspired by IS and its slaughtering of Shia Muslims in the Middle East as so-called apostates of Islam. They were disrupted by counterterrorism forces, and ultimately convicted of Terrorism Act offences. This was not the only attempt to target Australia's Shia Muslims. In another incident, nearly two years later, a group of three men—Ahmed Mohamed, Abdullah Chaarani, and Hatim Moukhaiber—committed arson attacks against a Shia mosque in Melbourne and claimed it for IS.

The first successful terror attack in Australia assisted by IS was by Farhad Khalil Mohammad Jabar. Born in Iran, he migrated to Australia with his family when still young. Around 2015, when IS was dominating headlines, Jabar began to skip school in favour of attending his mosque. Late in September, a friend of Jabar's saw him sitting on the mosque floor with four unknown men. When he approached Jabar, Jabar gave his friend the cold shoulder. 'I got the sense he didn't want the others to know we had an interaction going on,' the friend recalled.[9]

On 1 October, Jabar's sister, Shadi, left Australia to join IS and support the so-called Caliphate. The next day, Jabar missed school again to pray at the mosque for 40 minutes. As he departed, he gave the IS salute to a CCTV camera in the mosque entrance. Later that day, Milad Atai handed Jabar a .38 Smith and Wesson revolver. Atai was later convicted of membership of Islamic State, among other charges. Jabar then walked to the police station in Parramatta, where he took aim, fired and killed the first person he saw exiting the building. That person was Curtis Cheng, an accountant and father of two. The special constables on duty returned fire and killed Jabar. A suicide note was found on his body: 'Soon by the will of God ... your nights will turn into nightmares, your days into hell ... By the will of Allah I have come today to put terror into your hearts and soon the majahideen [sic] will do the same, by the will of Allah.'[10]

An identical note was found by investigators in the handwriting of Jabar's sister, Shadi, in the wastepaper basket in his bedroom. Four people besides Shadi supported Jabar's attack: Raban Alou, Talal Alameddine, Mustafa Dirani and Milad Atai. They had sworn membership to IS and had donated to the IS cause. All except Shadi, who was killed in an airstrike in Syria a year later, would face charges in relation to the killing of Curtis Cheng.

Jabar was young at the time of his offence, and this trend was to continue with eighteen-year-old Sevdet Ramadan Besim. Born in Melbourne, he began attending the Al-Furqan Islamic Centre and, while there, encountered Abdul Numan Haider, Neil Prakash and Irfaan Hussein, another Australian fighting for IS. Following the deaths of Haider and Hussein, Prakash contacted Besim and urged him to join the fight in Syria. When Besim's application for a passport was refused, Prakash suggested that he launch an attack in Australia, putting him on to an online Islamic State planner known simply as 'S'.

S was actually a fourteen-year-old boy masquerading on the internet as an old married man, with an imaginary son the age of Besim. Using encrypted communication platforms, S acted the part of an experienced terrorist. Under the guidance of S, Besim began to consider targets in Australia, including Anzac shrines, police stations and shopping centres. Besim considered making a false police report and ambushing the officers that attended the scene, but eventually he dismissed the idea. In another plot, they considered packing the pouch of a kangaroo with C-4 and setting it loose in Sydney. After much discussion, they decided that Besim should run over a police officer with a car on Anzac Day, steal their gun, and shoot people until he himself was killed. When S was arrested in the UK in relation to a different investigation, the UK police obtained the messages between the two. The information was passed to Victoria's Joint Counter Terrorism Team, which arrested Besim on 17 April 2015.

Although four others were also arrested, only Besim was formally charged. Subsequently, internet searches about Anzac Day and the Dandenong RSL were found on his phone, and it transpired that he'd chosen Anzac Day because he wanted 'to make sure the dogs remember this as well as their fallen heroes on Anzac Day'.[11] There were also notes on Besim's phone: 'a growing feeling inside me has led me to decide to carry out my own. To establish my Jihad in Australia . . . and to put fear into those who are enemies to Allah.' When his plans to join IS overseas were thwarted, he wrote: 'I started to prepare myself for my attack against the enemies of Islam.'[12] Besim was charged with terrorism offences and pleaded guilty. He was sentenced to ten years in jail, but when he appealed the original sentence, the Court of Appeals re-sentenced him to fourteen years due to the gravity of his offences.

Another person in contact with IS was even younger than Jabar, Haider and Besim. In 2015, a Melbourne teenager codenamed MHK began posting comments online in support of IS. These were reported to the National Security Hotline and came under the attention of ASIO. It soon transpired that MHK was talking to an older British, Raqqa-based IS recruiter, Junaid Hussein, via Facebook. When the recruiter realised that MHK was too young to obtain a passport and fight in Syria independently, he instead goaded MHK into engaging in terrorism in Australia. He sent MHK links to articles with instructions on how to build IEDs. MHK partially built three pipe bombs, which he planned to detonate at a crowded event. His house was raided in May, and the bombs and materials seized. It was suspected that he planned to detonate them in a public place on Mother's Day—in Melbourne's CBD, on a train or at a police station. MHK was charged in County Court with preparations for an act of terrorism. He pleaded guilty and was sentenced to seven years.

Of course, this is not the sum of attacks potentially assisted by IS. On one occasion, Australians helped IS more than IS helped them. Haisem Zahab, a resident of Young, New South Wales, was found to have assisted IS by engaging in research and development on its behalf, working with rockets, lasers, guidance systems and receivers. He received a nine-year sentence for this activity. By contrast, Tamim Sahil Khaja thought he was receiving assistance from an IS operative called Abu Baraa, but was in fact talking to undercover officers about his plot to obtain weapons and conduct an attack. He, too, was apprehended, charged with terrorism offences and received a long prison sentence.

Violent rampages

As the IS propaganda machine continued to incite action in the West, more and more people sought to conduct violence in its name. One such terrorist was Australian-born Ihsas Khan, who on 10 September 2016 attacked grandfather Wayne Greenhalgh with a knife as he walked past him on the street in Minto in Sydney's west. While significant mental health issues were suggested to be at play, and there was no evidence of direct contact or links with IS, NSW Police believed Khan was a sincere IS supporter. During the violent attack on Greenhalgh, Khan yelled 'Allah Akbar' and accused Greenhalgh of being complicit in Western crimes in Iraq and elsewhere as part of the War on Terror.

Greenhalgh escaped to a nearby hairdressing salon, where a civilian armed with a fence paling fended Khan off until police arrived and subdued him. Greenhalgh was grievously injured, with cuts to his arms and a punctured lung, and required litres of blood transfusions to save his life. Khan told police that he attacked Greenhalgh because his victim had been wearing an American T-shirt, which he claims triggered him. Greenhalgh clarified the nature of his T-shirt in the ensuing trial: it was emblazoned with the words 'World's greatest farter ... I mean father'. Khan was charged with Terrorism Act offences and attempted murder, and given a 36-year sentence.

Another episode of expressive political violence occurred in 2017, when Yacqub Khayre went on a violent rampage in the Melbourne beachside suburb of Brighton, an event now known as the Brighton siege. Khayre, as mentioned in the previous chapter, had attended Al-Shabaab camps and was once inspired by Al-Qaeda. He had served sixteen months in prison while on trial for terrorism offences, although he also engaged in ordinary crimes. In 2012, for example, he broke into a home to commit burglary when he was discovered by the occupants. He assaulted three men before police arrived, where they found him high on ice. He pleaded guilty to the break-in and assault, and was sentenced to five and a half years. While on parole for this crime, Khayre orchestrated the Brighton siege.

Sometime in early June 2017, Khayre tampered with the ankle bracelet that was a condition of his parole. He purchased a sawn-off double-barrelled shotgun, allegedly from a Melbourne man, George Matte-Hado, in a carpark. On 5 June 2017, Khayre arrived at the Buckingham Serviced Apartments in Brighton. On the way in, he shot and killed the receptionist, Nick Hao, who had been married for only fifteen days. He ordered a female escort to his unit, whom he then took hostage, tying her up and locking her in the bathroom. At 4.00 p.m., Victoria Police were called to the apartments, drawn by reports of an explosion—which was actually gunfire. On arrival they found Hao dead, and at 4.10 p.m. Triple Zero received a distress call from the escort, who had managed to free her hands in the bathroom. She informed authorities that she had been taken hostage by an armed man.

Around 5.30 p.m. Khayre used the same mobile phone to call Channel Seven, claiming the attack in the name of Al-Qaeda and IS—apparently ignorant that the two organisations had denounced each other. He also claimed to have a bomb, and said that if anyone attended the unit he would kill the hostage. Around 6.00 p.m., Khayre exited the apartment and fired at members of the Special Operations Group, who shot him dead. The hostage was freed, and the apartment cleared of any bomb. IS claimed responsibility for the attack through its propaganda mouthpiece Amaq, although subsequent investigations found that Khayre had no links with Al-Qaeda or IS.

Between 2016 and 2017, IS began to suffer territorial losses as a result of offensives in both Syria and Iraq. In Syria, the Syrian Democratic Forces, the Assad regime and its Russian allies chipped away at IS-held provinces; while in Iraq, the Coalition, the Iraqi Army and local Shia militias took and held former IS territory. Finding themselves besieged on all sides and failing to secure the Caliphate, IS put out a clarion call for attacks in the West, to disincentivise Western action and to distract Westerners on the home front. IS abandoned its earlier propaganda outfit, *Dabiq*, and instead began to produce the magazine *Rumiyah*, which encouraged lone-actor attacks in the West:

> Stationed behind enemy lines, the just terror mujahid has at his disposal a multitude of weapons and techniques that he may employ at any given time to inflict misery and destruction upon the enemies of Allah, demonstrating by his actions an unforgettable lesson for every hardheaded, obstinate kafir nation that wishes to engage in war on the Islamic State. Allah said, 'Through them, disperse those behind them, that they might take heed' (Al-Anfal 57).[13]

To do this, Islamic State advised lone terrorists to launch vehicle attacks against the general public in crowded spaces such as parades. Such attacks then occurred around the world, the deadliest of them in Nice, France, killing 87 and injuring more than 400 on Bastille Day, 14 July 2016.

In Australia, a man named Hassan Khalif Shire Ali noticed this attack, if not the words of IS. Married with one child, he was born in Somalia and migrated to Australia as a boy. At some stage in 2015, he attracted the attention of counterterrorism authorities and his passport was cancelled in October on the suspicion that he would travel to Syria or Iraq with the intention of becoming a foreign fighter for IS. He was categorised as a low-level threat and not actively monitored. Much like Khayre, he had a criminal record for drug possession and use, as well as receipt of stolen goods and burglary offences. He regularly breached orders and bail conditions. In February 2017, he was charged with driving offences on three separate occasions. When he failed to attend court in August 2017 to answer these charges, his bail was forfeited. By October 2018, Shire Ali's friends and family claimed he had mental health issues and was becoming increasingly delusional. His substance-abuse problems had persisted, and he had been kicked out of the family home. He moved back in with his wife several months later.

After two months back with his family, Shire Ali acted on 9 November 2018. He stacked several gas cylinders in his ute cabin. He drove to Bourke Street in Melbourne, where he opened the cylinders and set them alight, hoping they would cause the vehicle to explode. He then drew a knife and began stabbing members of the public. He stabbed a security guard, Shadi Helal, in the neck, and Rod Patterson in the head. Sisto Malaspina, the co-owner of Pellegrini's Espresso Bar, was stabbed and killed. Police arrived within minutes of the attack, and a civilian called Michael Rogers used a shopping trolley to hold Shire Ali at bay. Responding officers were forced to shoot Shire Ali in order to subdue him, and he died on his way to hospital. The following day, police raided Shire Ali's parents' house and found evidence to indicate that his attack had been inspired by IS, although he, too, had no direct contact with the terror group.

The Melbourne community mourned Sisto Malaspina and lauded the heroism of Michael Rogers. The solidarity, however, was not without disruption, as Prime Minister Scott Morrison told Muslim leaders they needed to take 'special responsibility' for extremism in their communities.[14] Exactly how religious leaders were supposed to make better terrorism threat assessments than the combined powers of ASIO and the Victorian criminal justice system was not made clear.

Of course, behind this seemingly chaotic violence lay the cold, strategic instructions of IS, and its proven power to mobilise supporters around the world. Another of those supporters was a young woman by the name of Momema Shoma, a citizen of Bangladesh who sought to travel to Syria via Turkey in 2017, following calls from IS for women to engage in jihad. She failed in this endeavour and instead decided to demonstrate her fealty by conducting attacks in the West. To that end, Shoma applied for and received a scholarship to study at La Trobe University. She packed a knife and flew to Australia.

After arriving at the home of her host family, she purchased night-vision goggles from Amazon, and steadily consumed IS propaganda. A week later, she took her knife and rehearsed a stabbing: stabbing the mattress of her hosts up to nine times while they were out of the house. When the host family saw the damage to the mattresses and reported it, Shoma was removed and placed in the home of a new host, Roger Singaravelu, who had a five-year-old daughter. Singaravelu and his daughter took afternoon naps each day. This gave Shoma a new idea.

Shoma observed the routine and told a contact over an encrypted application that she would 'gather more courage'.[15] On 9 February 2018, while Mr Singaravelu was having his afternoon nap with his young daughter beside him, Shoma took her knife and stabbed him in the neck. The blade hit his spine and fractured it, becoming lodged in his neck. Singaravelu woke up and struggled with Shoma, then gathered up his young daughter and fled. When the police apprehended Shoma a short time later, she claimed the attack was in the name of IS. She was arrested and charged, and pleaded guilty to the act. She showed no contrition and regretted only that she had not killed her victim. In the words of Justice Taylor: 'You have achieved nothing except . . . to make yourself an insignificant criminal of transitory notoriety, notwithstanding your adherence to a now defunct caliphate and its unmasked falsehoods.'[16] She received a 42-year sentence, although appeals continue.

In another case inspired by IS, Ali Khalif Shire Ali, the twenty-year-old brother of the Bourke Street terrorist Hassan Shire Ali, sought to acquire a fake passport to travel to Syria, join IS and pursue martyrdom. When his international travel plan was frustrated, Ali sought to acquire an automatic firearm and some 200 rounds of ammunition. He planned to conceal them in a bag as he approached the New Year's Eve celebrations held each year in Federation Square, Melbourne. From there: 'As soon as the countdown finishes I'll be in the middle of the, you know, the audience or the whatever, the people . . . And just from then on I just start going off at it . . .'[17]

Ali planned to start shooting, seize hostages from a nearby club and force them to hold the IS flag in the windows, much like at the Lindt Café. His initial plan also included a truck attack, similar to Nice, but the cancellation of his licence derailed that component. His plot was thwarted by undercover officers, and he was ultimately convicted of terrorism offences.

The Etihad plot

Since late 2014, both the US and Russia had been intervening in Iraq and Syria (and Iran had also allegedly been operating in the region for a while). Unfortunately, the two superpowers were hardly united in their goal, and IS offered them the convenient opportunity to test new weapon systems. The conflict zone became a quagmire of contending superpowers, and fractious micro-powers of Kurdish, Shia and Sunni disposition. The US-led effort, known as Operation Inherent Resolve, was largely an air campaign, aiming to reduce IS's area of influence through airstrikes and surgical drone strikes. Australia's contribution to this effort was Operation Okra, centred on RAAF capabilities.

RAAF personnel, however, were not the only Australians involved in the conflict. Others were Australian citizens who had travelled to the region to become foreign terrorist fighters (FTF). While, as mentioned above, many Australians were prevented from travelling due to passport cancellations, hundreds would successfully make the journey and join IS. While they sought to build and defend the Caliphate on the one hand, they plotted revenge on their homelands on the other. One of the most significant plots disrupted in Australia began in Syria and Lebanon with Australian FTF. It was planned to detonate—quite literally—in the sky above Sydney, claiming some 400 lives and becoming the first mass casualty terrorist attack on Australian soil.

It started with Tarek Khayat, a Sunni sheikh who lived in Tripoli, Lebanon. He became a Salafist, and routinely called for public executions. At one point, he attracted a number of followers and successfully incited a riot against the Lebanese Army in a poor neighbourhood in Tripoli that killed or injured 400 people. He fled Lebanon in 2014 and joined IS in Syria, fast becoming a senior commander. Within two years, he had assumed a command position in Raqqa, and was involved in the lengthy Northern Raqqa Offensive, defending the city from Coalition forces (spearheaded by the Syrian Democratic Forces), which sought to isolate the IS headquarters. As the fighting continued, one of Tarek's teenage sons was killed. Tarek made a martyrdom video memorialising his death, which was shared with his family—including those in Australia.

Following the deaths of his son, Tarek began to formulate a plot against the West, aided and abetted by another career terrorist, Basil Hassan. As fortune would have it, three of Tarek's brothers had long since left Lebanon and moved to Sydney: Khaled Khayat, an electrician based in Lakemba; Mahmoud Khayat, who lived in Punchbowl, and Amer Khayat. Tarek reached out to his brothers in Australia and convinced them to help him exact revenge. This did not come out of the blue: two of the brothers had maintained steady communication via encrypted apps over the years. Amer Khayat was not part of these conversations. Amer's alleged drug and alcohol use and his homosexuality were seen as decadent and shameful. He was estranged from Tarek, but that, in itself, would not spare him.

Khaled and Mahmoud appeared to support IS. They shared photos with Tarek of themselves doing the IS salute on the banks of the Georges River in November 2016, as well as pictures of their children in headscarves with IS symbols. Their wives, Dianne and Rana, were also sisters, and the two families were close. On 21 January 2017, Tarek messaged Mahmoud, asking for the address of Dianne and Rana's brother, Abdul-Karem Merhi, so he could send a package. On 13 April, a package left Turkey destined for Merhi's house—Tarek even took a photo as proof of its departure.

Three days later, the parcel arrived in Sydney—but no one was home to accept it. After scrambling by Mahmoud, it was redelivered to Merhi's house. On 21 April, Khaled opened the package, which contained a welder, and began stripping elements out of it, such as copper wire, to make a device. He regularly sent pictures back to Tarek and his associates, who replied with further instructions. Over the course of weeks, he constructed the IED and rigged it with a timer. At the same time, Khaled was also receiving instructions on the manufacture and dispersal of a lethal gas.

Khaled learned that his brother Amer was about to travel to Lebanon, which Amer did frequently to stay in touch with family. Khaled and Mahmoud conspired to exploit Amer's trip and place the bomb in his cabin luggage, hidden in a meat grinder. The timer was set to detonate midair, killing everyone aboard—including their own brother, who had no notion of their murderous plot. On the day of the flight, 15 July, Khaled and Mahmoud collected Amer and drove him to the airport. Amer still had no idea that his brothers planned to kill him on the instructions of another brother.

Mahmoud sat in the car while Khaled went with Amer to check in. During the process, the airline agent Justine Browning noted that Amer's cabin luggage was overweight. When Khaled and Amer returned to the car to rearrange the luggage, Khaled was spooked and removed the bomb. Amer, still oblivious, returned to the terminal and successfully checked in. His flight departed and landed safely in Beirut. Khaled and Mahmoud, meanwhile, raced home to disconnect the timer and prevent the detonation of the bomb. They partially dismantled it and hid it in Khaled's garage.

When contacted by IS, Khaled lied about why the bomb wasn't on the plane, blaming Amer.

The IS operatives encouraged Khaled to continue with the gas plot instead and gave him direct and functional instructions on its manufacture. Khaled wrote them down and kept them in his wallet. From 27 July, he was told his focus was to be on the poison gas. Unbeknown to Khaled and Mahmoud, eight police operatives had Khaled under surveillance. On 29 July, they observed the brothers testing the poisonous gas near a public barbecue area. Both were arrested that afternoon, and their homes raided by NSW Joint Counter Terrorism Team officers.[18] In time, both brothers were tried together, although Mahmoud requested to be tried separately.

Amer Khayat was arrested in Lebanon ten days after his brothers and was held in an east Beirut prison for terrorists. After he'd spent two years in custody, a military court found he was innocent of involvement. He returned to Australia and was required to testify at the trial of his brothers. The trial was difficult: jurors were worried about strange people in the courtroom, being followed onto trains, and having their photos covertly taken. In one case, the jurors were also rumoured to be fighting among themselves so much that the judge reminded them to be courteous. Eventually, a guilty verdict was returned for Khaled, who was handed a 40-year sentence, while no verdict could be reached on Mahmoud. He was retried twice and found guilty at the end of 2019. He received a 36-year sentence.

The question remained as to how the brothers had come onto the radar of counterterrorism authorities. Some alleged that the original tip-off had come from the United States or the United Kingdom, while Israel also asserted that its intelligence unit, known as 8200, provided intelligence that led to the arrest of IS operatives working on the attack. Lebanese authorities also released a statement claiming that they had been monitoring the Khayat brothers for more than a year and been coordinating with the Australian government for a long time. Tarek Khayat was caught in Iraq in April 2018, tried and sentenced to death by the Al-Rusafa Central Criminal Court in Baghdad. Such sentences are normally carried out by hangings, not unlike the executions Tarek himself used to demand. It is not known whether it actually took place.

Foreign flags

IS had sown international seeds, popularised a movement and demonstrated that it was an adept recruiter. All over the world, people decided to join their cause and travel to Syria and Iraq to become citizens of the Caliphate. Foreign Minister Julie Bishop claimed in 2014 that 185 Australians were involved with extremism in the Middle East, while a 2019 report by Rodger Shanahan of the Lowy Institute found that some 173 Australian citizens answered the call of IS and made their way to the conflict zone.[19] According to Shanahan, some 85 per cent of the travellers who became known as FTF were male. While the average age of FTF was around 25, some were younger than eighteen and others older than 35. The majority (66 per cent) were born in Australia but made the decision to leave and swear allegiance to a foreign flag emblematic of wanton slaughter and genocide.

Once they arrived, they provided IS with a broad variety of services. A very small number of Australians assumed leadership roles in IS of considerable importance. One such FTF was Sheikh Abu Sulayman al-Muhajir, also known as Mostafa Farag, a Sydney-based Muslim cleric, preacher and bookstore owner. Sulayman travelled to join JaN in 2012 and was immediately given a senior role in the high council. This quick rise through the ranks was suspicious, leading US Counterterrorism analyst Thomas Jocelyn to suggested that Sulayman may have been involved with Al-Qaeda even before he left Australia. When Al-Qaeda and IS came into conflict over JaN, al-Zawahiri chose a team of scholars, including Sulayman, to mediate the disagreement. Sulayman also played a key role in recruiting other Australian Salafists and leading fundraising efforts.

Sulayman is not the only leader still alive. Neil Prakash, who travelled to support IS in 2013, grew up in Melbourne and attended the Al-Furqan Mosque after converting to Islam. It appears he worked his way up through the group to become a senior IS official and was on a US kill list. From there, he was involved in several complex terrorist plots, including the Statue of Liberty plot, the plot to behead a Melbourne police officer, and the double stabbing outside a Melbourne police station, and he frequently appeared in propaganda videos encouraging lone-actor attacks. He was thought dead following a US airstrike in 2016, but made it to Turkey, where he was apprehended. While awaiting trial in Turkey, he was stripped of his Australian citizenship.

More senior than Prakash was Mohammed Ali Baryalei. A former actor and Kings Cross bouncer, Baryalei joined JaN sometime in April 2013. After two months, he switched sides to IS. He is believed to have convinced nearly 30 Australian men to join IS. Some suggest that Baryalei was the most senior Australian operational commander of IS until he was killed in 2014. Another leader was Abraham Succarieh. The oldest of the three Succarieh brothers to become FTF, Abraham took on an operational leadership role with IS, while his brother Omar assisted with financing and Ahmed became a suicide bomber, the fate of many Australian FTF. Ahmed launched his attack shortly after arriving in Syria, driving a truck bomb laden with explosives to a Syrian checkpoint, killing 35 people.

Jake Bilardi, a Melbourne teenager, travelled to Iraq in August 2014 and contacted IS. He attempted a suicide attack at Baiji, which failed, so he made a second attempt in Ramadi, which although successful only killed himself. After his death, IS mocked Bilardi, saying he was weak and sold 'his soul to Allah for a cheap price'.[20] Another teenage suicide bomber was Adam Dahman, who travelled to Iraq in November 2013. His sister, Maryann, was married to Ahmed Raad, a senior member of the Benbrika group. On 17 July 2014, after nearly half a year in the Middle East, Dahman wore a belt bomb to a marketplace near a Shia mosque in Baghdad. He detonated it, killing five.

Other FTF took on more conventional fighting roles on the front line. A sizeable number died within their first two years, all aged between twenty and 30, and running the gamut from university students to kickboxers, aspiring clerics and imams, and tradesmen. One was formerly in the Australian Army, another was a council worker, while Sharky Jama was a model. A friend of Abdul Numan Haider, Irfaan Hussein died fighting on behalf of IS. Abu Ousama—the so-called 'Coco Pops Jihadi'—survived for nearly three years before being killed. Other FTF may have survived longer, although it may well be that they perished in any of the numerous offensives surrounding the fall of the Caliphate in late 2018. Abu Ubaida al-Lubnani, an IT technician who joined the conflict in 2013, is presumed to still be alive. The four Elbaf brothers, Taha, Hamza, Bilal and Omar, are all thought to still be alive, as is Yusuf, a former university student. Countless others remain in Iraq and Syria, but their names are not so well known and information on them is not publicly available.

Alongside FTF, many Australians served IS in support roles. One notable example is paediatrician Tareq Kamleh (also known as Abu Yousef al-Australie), who starred in an IS propaganda video enticing others to join Islamic State and assist in building a caliphate. Numerous women who travelled also provided healthcare services to the fighters, cooked for them, married them, and managed their Yazidi slaves. Some did not last long. Shadi Jabar, the sister of Farhad, died soon after arrival, as did Amira Karroum. Tara Nettleton, the wife of Khaled Sharrouf, travelled to Syria to join her husband in 2013 and died of appendicitis two years later. Zehra Duman, a 21-year-old Melbourne woman, married Australian fighter Mahmoud Abbullatif, who was later killed. Duman allegedly helped to recruit and run online campaigns. Another two women who went to Syria together, Hodan Abby and Hafsa Mohamed, are thought to still be alive and living with IS supporters in Syria. Little is known of other potential female FTF, such as Dullel Kassab and Zaynab Sharrouf (Zaynab was taken to the Caliphate by her father Khaled while still a child).

A few Australians have become propagandists for IS, weaponising social media to lure more people into the fight. Mohamed Ali

Elomar Jr, the nephew of Mohamed Ali Elomar Sr identified in Operation Pendennis, became a notorious propagandist. Alongside Khaled Sharrouf, who was also charged under Operation Pendennis, he frequently generated and shared IS propaganda. They were heavily involved in the Yazidi slave trade, and purchased Yazidi women and raped them. Sharrouf tried to forbid the enslaved women from crying and threatened to sell or kill them if they spoke to his wife. His children, too, were implicated in the torture of the Yazidi women, and the murder of soldiers. In August 2014, Sharrouf shared photos on Twitter of his eldest son holding the severed head of a Syrian soldier in Raqqa. This was propaganda gold for IS and attracted international media attention, the image emblazoned on the front page of the news.

Another propagandist was Abdullah Elmir, a butcher from Bankstown. At the age of seventeen, he and a friend decided to join IS.[21] While his friend ultimately decided not to go, Elmir went on ahead and starred in an IS video in October 2014, where he proclaimed:

> ... I deliver this message to you, especially the people of Australia, and I say this about your Coalition ... bring every nation that you wish to us, that you want to come and fight us. It means nothing to us. Whether it is fifty nations, or fifty thousand nations, it means nothing to us ... We will not stop fighting, we will not put down our weapons until we reach your lands. Until we take the head of every tyrant. And until the black flag is flying high in every single land.[22]

Elmir married a sixteen-year-old British schoolgirl, Amira Abase, who had joined IS a year earlier and then groomed other young women to join. In June 2015, the ABC reported that Elmir tried to infiltrate youth welfare groups in Sydney in order to recruit young people to his cause before his departure to the Middle East.[23] Both were killed by an airstrike in December 2015.

Other propagandists included Abu Nour al Iraqi, Mounir Raad and Abu Mansour al-Lubnani. While little is known about Abu

Nour al-Iraqi, including his real name, he appeared in a significant propaganda video titled 'There is No Life without Jihad'. Mounir Raad (alias Abu Yahya ash Shami and Abu Adam) issued calls in August 2017 for Australians to carry out attacks at home, using trucks and nail guns.[24] Not all had to travel to the conflict zone to assist the IS effort. Hamdi Alqudsi of Sydney became the first person to be charged for assisting people (in his case, seven men) to travel to the Middle East to become FTF. To do so, he liaised directly with an Australian IS leader, Baryalei. He was arrested in December 2013 and sentenced to eight years in prison.

The Caliphate burns

IS, with its fledging bureaucracy and light infantry, did not withstand the offensives launched by the United States on the one hand, and by Russia on the other. Piece by piece, the Caliphate crumbled, losing city after city, province after province in Iraq. It was cut off from its main supply route to Turkey, and from the porous border regions it had exploited. The airstrikes continued, and in late 2016, Coalition forces commenced a nine-month siege of Mosul, which ended in IS's defeat on 10 July 2017. The battle for Raqqa was similarly complex, requiring two separate offensives spread out over nearly a year. In the ruins of IS cities and towns, IEDs were everywhere. The cities may have been lost to IS, but they made sure that no one else could have them either. The refugee camps swelled.

Many of the Australian FTF likely died in the subsequent offensives across Iraq and Syria. According to Australian Defence minister Marise Payne, killing them overseas was preferable to prosecuting them in Australia.[25] By December 2017, 40 of the FTF had returned home and faced the new FTF legislation, which made it an offence to enter a foreign country with the intent of hostile activity (excluding in the service of a government military), to assist in preparations, and to recruit others to the task. Those who do so face a ten-year jail sentence on their return. Those who are found to have links to registered terrorist organisations face a 25-year jail sentence. The collection of evidence from foreign conflict zones, however, has made prosecution difficult in some cases.

Exhortations against Australia by IS propagandists, strategists and leaders continue, and a small number of IS sympathisers in Australia continue to face prosecution for the glorification of terrorist acts. In other cases, IS seeks to exploit Australian tragedies and twist them to its own purposes. In 2018, for example, a disgruntled strawberry farm employee began inserting needles in fruit. The strawberries were dispersed around the country with their dangerous additions. While ultimately the perpetrator was discovered and had no relationship with IS, IS supporters sought to capitalise on the event. They published a number of media items with photos of strawberries behind words of threat. One such item, which suggested that while Australian planes dropped bombs on Iraq and Syria the Australian people could never be safe in their own homes, featured a bloody smear in the foreground and an IS militant meddling with strawberries in the background.

Since the last IS-held territory was taken in 2019, it has retained its wealth and its network endures in Egypt, Afghanistan, Pakistan and scattered across the greater Sahara. Without a Caliphate and its territorial gains, it is possible that IS will revert to terror attacks in Western jurisdictions—even with the withdrawal of Western militaries from Afghanistan in September 2021. With its host of digital natives and original content creation, the IS narrative is an easy sell—and it has proven its capability in the dark marketing of terror. Tens of thousands of people remain in refugee camps, most of them victims of IS terror, others former IS operatives. Time will tell if these operatives will rise again and more bloodshed will fall upon the grey ashes of a false Caliphate.

12

Darkest of hours: the extreme right

In a sparsely furnished house in Dunedin, New Zealand, a man finalised his preparations. He had spent the past two years training and plotting. His firearms were inscribed with ideological symbols that he exploited to communicate his commitment to the race war that would bring with it the complete destruction of Western civilisation. His other preparations included a helmet camera, with which he would livestream his attack and secure his own notoriety, and a 74-page manifesto extolling his beliefs and justifying his violence. He believed society was irreparably degenerate and corrupt, besieged by enemies inside and out. His strategy was to destabilise society, accelerate its destruction and ultimately bring about its ruin. To achieve this, his tactic of choice was terrorism.

On a busy thoroughfare in the city of Christchurch, New Zealand, lies the Al Noor Mosque. The mosque is open to the community, and the Muslims who prayed within those walls gladly welcomed guests. Sometime in January, the community welcomed in a visitor who hid his malevolent intentions: he was not there to share in Muslim culture but to engage in reconnaissance. He had also flown a drone over the building to ascertain the entry and exit points. Anyone else would see the main prayer hall as large and beautiful, with an arched ceiling and large windows to let in the light. The primary access to the hall is a single corridor that opens up onto the mosque foyer. Mosques are not simply places of prayer and worship, but hubs for the community: places where experiences and friendships are shared, safety and security sought, and peace found. At the rear of Al Noor is a flower garden: the product of love and toil from a worshipper. He also grew vegetables and planned to use them in a banquet for all of the community to share. He would not live to see the fruits of his labours.

As the sun rose on 15 March 2019, the city came to life: people went to work, opened their businesses or attended to their devotions. For some, this would be their last day. Sometime that morning, a car departed Dunedin for Christchurch. Around five hours later it arrived. At 1.28 p.m., the man went online and logged on to one of his usual forums, 8chan—a cesspool of trolls, Nazis, fascists and misogynists of every stripe. There, he made his final post:

> Well lads, it's time to stop shitposting and make a real life effort post. I will carry out and [sic] attack against invaders, and will even live stream the attack via facebook . . . It's been a long ride and despite all your rampant faggotry, fecklessness and degeneracy, you are all top blokes and the best bunch of cobbers a man could ask for. I have provided links to my my [sic] writings below, please do your part by spreading my message, making memes, and shitposting as you usually do. If I don't survive the attack, goodbye, godbless and I will see you all in Valhalla![1]

Four minutes later, he emailed his manifesto to the New Zealand prime minister, Jacinda Ardern; the leader of the National Party opposition, Simon Bridges; Speaker of the House of Representatives Trevor Mallard; and a number of domestic and international media outlets. He got in his car, turned on music, initiated the livestream from his helmet camera, turned on a disorienting strobe light attached to a rifle, and drove.

Several minutes later, he parked outside the Al Noor Mosque. It was shortly after the *salat al-zuhr* prayers, which occur just after the sun passes its midday peak. Some 190 worshippers—men, women and children—were in the mosque. He was met at the door by a Muslim who welcomed him with the fateful words: 'Hello, brother.' He was answered with gunfire. The man stormed the mosque, shooting as he went. The light-infused main prayer hall had no back door, the windows did not open, and the emergency exit was jammed. Nearly 120 worshippers were in the hall as he entered. As he raked the room with bullets, the worshippers were trapped, unable to escape en masse. He shot and killed the unarmed and innocent people—the men, women and children—systematically, returning to murder the wounded in cold blood. When he ran out of bullets, he went back to his car, checking that prone victims were dead as he went, and rearmed himself. He returned and continued his massacre of a community that—merely months before—had welcomed him as a guest. He killed the injured and the trapped, inside and outside the mosque.[2]

From Al Noor, he drove to Linwood Islamic Centre, shooting people on the street as he went. Linwood mosque is a small building, barely visible from the verge of a quiet street. It, too, was for the most part a large prayer hall, with high-set windows and white walls. It, too, was a place of peace and sanctuary for its worshippers. At 1.52 p.m., the gunman began shooting into the mosque from outside, aiming at worshippers in the driveway, and through the windows of the mosque. He returned to his vehicle and rearmed, this time to continue the assault from within the mosque, where worshippers huddled in the corners of the hall. Some worshippers sought to shield their Imam, while others challenged or attempted to distract the shooter. He withdrew to his vehicle, and as he went, a worshipper seized one of his discarded weapons and pursued him, forcing him to flee. He fled Linwood and was en route to a third mosque, Ashburton, when his vehicle was rammed by armed police. He surrendered immediately to the New Zealand police officers, worried he would be shot. Around twenty minutes had elapsed since the first attack was reported.

Ambulances raced to the site, and the Canterbury District Health Board activated its mass-casualty plan. Some of the victims died at the scene; others passed away in the backs of ambulances while paramedics worked feverishly to save them. In the weeks that followed, we would learn that 51 people had been killed, and another 49 injured. One of the victims was a three-year-old child. Others had only just gained citizenship, excited to start their new lives in New Zealand.

This was the worst massacre in New Zealand's modern history, and it was perpetrated by an Australian terrorist. Brenton Tarrant had moved to New Zealand in 2017 for a single purpose: to train for his attack. As time went on, he decided the country was just as good a target as it was a training ground. A single choice by the perpetrator—driven by convenience—is what led the attack to occur in New Zealand rather than Australia. Tarrant did not emerge from a void; his ideas were no strangers to his fellow Australians. His attack was international, but his ideas were embedded and influenced by the domestic Australian extreme right.

Threat emergent

The arrest and imprisonment of the extreme-right figures in the 1990s, discussed in Chapter 7, may have quelled the movement's activities but it did not dispel its communities. The ideas and ideologies persisted, undisturbed by government disengagement or community-building initiatives. From this time onward, the various subcultures and communities of the extreme right were left to their own devices. Deprived of the strong leaders of the 1980s, these subcultures were, to an extent, a rudderless ship—they existed but lacked direction. They were subject to fragmentation in some ways, and expansion in others.

Numerous groups and movements had arisen throughout the 1990s, and many persisted well into the 2000s. Many were fundamentally transnational in nature, such as the Women for Aryan Unity (WAU), a female-driven white supremacist network that was originally formed in Belfast, Ireland, before establishing chapters around the world. In 1992, it established an Australian chapter called Women of the Southern Legion, which devoted much of its energy to creating a magazine of the same name. The magazine dispersed the group's ideology, which discouraged racial mixing and celebrated Aryan greatness on the one hand, and shared conspiratorial beliefs that Jews were responsible for the destruction of Western civilisation on the other. This magazine became a vehicle for disseminating the prison writings of white supremacists such as David Lane, a member of US terrorist group the Order. In time, WAU connected with Jack van Tongeren (see Chapter 7) while he was in prison, and soon came to share his book *The ANM Story*, essentially becoming a distribution point for both Australian and international extreme-right ideology and writings.

The Women of the Southern Legion directly fostered engagements in Australia with Blood and Honour (B&H), formed in the United Kingdom in the late 1980s by British white supremacist and musician Ian Stuart Donaldson. He was a member of the white power punk band Skrewdriver, whose lyrics were loaded with extreme right ideology. Their song 'Blood and Honour' became the anthem for white resistance, the lyrics detailing what they believed was the left-wing threat to society. B&H proliferated in the white power music scene, and soon gave rise to an offshoot known as Combat 18 (C18) in 1992. Both B&H and C18 continued to expand, exploiting the developing white power music networks, and became well established in Australia, where membership between the two was largely interchangeable. B&H Australia coordinates yearly concerts in memory of Ian Stuart Donaldson, events cloaked in swastikas and awash with references to Valhalla, Ku Klux Klan hoods, and other Nazi symbols such as the *Totenkopf* (the death's head).

B&H, in turn, developed a direct relationship with the Hammerskins, a white supremacist network that formed in Dallas, Texas, in the later 1980s and quickly established chapters throughout the United States. It soon spread to Australia, New Zealand and the

United Kingdom. There were two primary chapters in Australia: the Australian Hammerskin Nation (AHSN) and the Southern Cross Hammerskins (SCH). Between 1997 and 2005, the Hammerskin Press also published eleven magazines, three of which spoke directly to AHSN and once to the SCH chapter, while the New Zealand chapter figured prominently in half of all editions. These magazines were the spearhead of ideology on one hand, labelling political enemies as traitors and sharing content regarding white resistance, and community-building on the other, promoting white power music events and materials. They even shared content regarding WAU, B&H and C18, which shared their materials in turn.[3]

In 2002, the old denizens of Australia's historical extreme right were released from prison, Jack van Tongeren having served twelve years of his sentence. He immediately reconnected with his old comrade John Van Blitterswyk. The two men, in addition to existing ANM members Daniel Tyrone Klavins and Matthew Billings, formed a new plot. They started with a racist sticker campaign; graffiti attacks on a synagogue, a police station and a restaurant; and a plot to firebomb four more Chinese restaurants in Perth. While these actions and activities were aimed at promoting van Tongeren's re-released book, *The ANM Story*, they were also perpetrated in pursuit of a political program that sought to realise its goals through coercive violence. The former leaders of Australia's extreme right, however, continued to lack relevance and public interest was limited. Through their magazines, activities and events, subcultural communities like WAU, B&H and C18—more so than the Australian Nationalist Movement—kept the fire of the extreme right burning, and its ideas alive.

The landscape changed, however, with the attack by Al-Qaeda on 9/11 and Australia's engagement in the War on Terror. Up to this point, the main enemies of the extreme right were Jews; left-wing political opponents, who they saw as traitors; the LGBTIQ community; and, of course, migrants. In Australia, the anti-immigration sentiment was primarily aimed at the Asian community. This changed with 9/11: suddenly the enemies of the extreme right expanded to include Muslims, and narratives began to develop in many Australian communities that all Muslims, or people of Middle Eastern or Mediterranean appearance, were terrorists and an immediate threat to Western society and the broader survival of the 'white race'.

Society divided

As the War on Terror dragged on and more lives were lost, community tensions continued to rise. Then, in an uncontrolled outburst, there was a physical altercation on Sydney's Cronulla beach between white Australian lifeguards and Australians of Middle Eastern appearance on 4 December 2005. A series of text message chains became central to a plan to gather at Cronulla beach—a show of force by white Australians against ethnic Australians. The planned event was magnified by the media and radio shock jocks such as Alan Jones, who read some of the text messages aloud on air, one of which stated 'Come to Cronulla this weekend to take revenge. This Sunday every Aussie in the shire get down to North Cronulla to support the leb and wog bashing day . . .' Jones claimed to discourage his listeners from taking the law into their own hands, and yet inflamed the situation by calling Middle Eastern Australians 'grubs', saying 'we don't have Anglo-Saxon kids out there raping women in Western Sydney', and lauding callers who planned vigilante action.[4] On 11 December, a week after the first fight, 5000 people gathered on Cronulla beach, and violent clashes occurred between the white Australian and ethnic Australian communities, spreading to surrounding suburbs over the next several days, incurring numerous injuries and extensive damage to property.

This event highlighted the increasing hostility towards Australians of Middle Eastern appearance. Islamophobia scholar Professor Scott Poynting likened the event to a pogrom: an attempt by Australia's white majority to subdue ethnic minorities and 'put them back in their place'.[5] His study found that tabloid media and radio shock jocks were central to whipping up hysteria in the time between the assault and the riot; but that the riot itself was also encouraged by white supremacist groups, such as the Patriotic Youth League, which was committed to a white Australia. Attendees at Cronulla even wore T-shirts with the slogan 'ethnic cleansing units'. The Howard government refused to recognise that racism may have been a factor in the riots, and the white supremacist contribution went largely unaddressed at a federal level. Subsequent studies found that interest in extreme-right subcultures like SCH and B&H likely peaked between 2004 and 2006—and so can hardly be disassociated from these events.[6]

The vilification of Muslim Australians did not discontinue after the Cronulla riots, nor did the extreme right stop targeting its other enemies. Skinhead gangs randomly bashed people in Hyde Park, Sydney. Arson attacks against synagogues continued, and rumours of an Australian Ku Klux Klan persisted. Other groups began to develop, such as the Southern Cross Soldiers, whose member Tyler Cassidy was shot and killed by police when he advanced on them armed and intoxicated. The white power Creativity Movement stickered the place of his death in his memory. Catch the Fire Ministries, a Melbourne-based church, was charged with racial vilification against Muslims—a charge it appealed successfully. Extreme-right sentiment, attitudes and beliefs remained a feature of certain Australian subcultures, but their violence was still largely expressive and opportunistic. James Dean-Willcocks, for example, randomly assaulted an elderly Japanese man, occasioning his death, while screaming racial abuse. This was undoubtedly a hate crime, but the attack lacked the premeditated and political nature that would qualify it as an act of right-wing terrorism.

By 2009, SCH, B&H, C18, and WAU were grudgingly making way for new groups that shared the same ideas, while still seeking to retain their market share of members. The Crazy White Boys, a neo-Nazi skinhead gang, formed in Melbourne and targeted Jewish, Asian and African Australians. A year later, two members, Wayne O'Brien and Shannon Hudson, launched an unprovoked attack on a Vietnamese international student, Minh Duong, assaulting him with a brick and stabbing him twice. Duong suffered significant injuries, including a fractured skull and swelling on the brain, and was hospitalised for seven days. They were convicted, and Hudson was sentenced to more than ten years in jail, while O'Brien received a four-and-a-half-year sentence. The Australian Defence League also formed around 2009, under Ralph Cerminara, inspired by the English Defence League in the United Kingdom and motivated primarily by anti-Muslim beliefs; its activities were largely related to harassing Australian Muslims.

Over the following years, Muslims were cemented as new targets of the Australian extreme right, joining other commonly targeted ethnic, cultural and sexual minorities. Muslims were portrayed as a foreign, dangerous and subversive threat: deliberately migrating to white-majority countries and seeking to bend them to their will. This developed into the Eurabia conspiracy theory, which was prominent on European websites and blogs. The theory went that Muslim countries were using their vast oil wealth to purchase traitorous politicians who, in turn, would support unlimited Muslim migration to Western countries. Many in the extreme right believed that this secret plot was part of a greater conspiracy aimed at the subjugation and enslavement of the so-called white race to Muslim overlords. In sum, elements of this extremist community began to believe that their entire civilisation was under direct and immediate threat from Muslim migrants.

On 4 February 2010, this anti-Muslim sentiment was expressed quite clearly by two B&H and C18 members, Bradley Neil Trappitt and Jacob Marshall Hort. In the early hours of the morning, these two men went to the Suleymaniye Mosque in Queens Park, Perth, and discharged a firearm at the domed roof. In the months that followed, they were arrested and charged with the shooting, and Western Australia Police believed it had eliminated the neo-Nazi chapter. They pleaded guilty to the charges and received suspended sentences and substantial fines. The chapter may have been dismantled, but such sentiment persisted in Australia and elsewhere in the world.

In Oslo the following year, this sentiment catalysed in a much more serious way: Anders Breivik, a white supremacist who avidly believed in the Eurabia conspiracy and feared white Norwegians were being overwhelmed and replaced by migrants, conducted a highly lethal, dual-phase right-wing terrorist attack in conjunction with the release of his manifesto, '2083'. Breivik car-bombed the Norwegian prime minister's office in Oslo, killing eight people and injuring more than 200. He then travelled to the island of Utøya, where a youth camp affiliated with a left-wing political party was taking place. He donned a makeshift police officer's uniform and gathered the young people around, pretending to be informing them of the bombing. Instead, he opened fire on the teenagers, and spent the next 90 minutes systematically hunting and executing them around the island. Some of the teenagers were only wounded in the initial onslaught and feigned death, but Breivik returned to shoot and kill them. The attack only ceased when police arrived. Dozens of young people were injured, and 69 were killed. While broadly condemned, the attack was nonetheless celebrated by the extreme right around the world, who continued to share Breivik's manifesto and propagate his beliefs online. Australians were among Breivik's avid admirers.

Hate and violence

The next several years were tumultuous. The War on Terror continued, lone-actor jihadist attacks began in the West, and IS arose in the under-governed spaces of Syria and Iraq. Anti-Muslim sentiment featured in both the extreme right and in the mainstream, which in turn led to the development of anti-Islam micro-parties such as Restore Australia (now Advance Australia), founded by Mike Holt in 2012 (himself a British migrant to Australia), which sought to outlaw the practice of Islam in Australia and end Muslim migration.[7] The real driver for the galvanisation of new nationalist movements, however, was the 2014 Lindt Café Siege, carried out by Man Haron Monis (see Chapter 11). Following the siege,

Wanda Marsh, John Oliver and Catherine Brennan founded a grassroots organisation in 2015 called Reclaim Australia, modelling themselves as concerned citizens worried about Islam in Australia. Their original manifesto, however, was focused on maintaining the hegemony of a white, Christian Australia, seeking to 'expel unsuitable immigration candidates and traitors', revoke citizenship for people who do not swear allegiance to Australia, and compulsory singing of the Australian anthem.[8]

Online, Reclaim Australia perpetuated hate narratives about Islam. Scholars Lella Nouri and Nuria Lorenzo-Dus found that the combined 1,015,000 words posted by Reclaim Australia on Twitter and Facebook were largely focused on opposing Muslims, immigration and halal certification, and arguing that migrants posed a health risk to the rest of society.[9] Offline, Reclaim Australia engaged in a number of rallies and protests based on these issues. This is the true significance of Reclaim Australia: it provided a point of gravity around which other small organisations would come to orbit. One unlikely location for this activity was Bendigo, Victoria, where the local Muslim community had recently proposed to construct a mosque. In response, anti-Islam groups affiliated with Reclaim Australia would travel from all over the country to congregate in Bendigo to protest—but also to recruit and network.

Among those smaller organisations was the True Blue Crew, founded by Kane Miller around 2015, which splintered off from Reclaim Australia. Its members were present at the Bendigo protests, but their primary action was opposing a housing project in Melton, Victoria, because they believed it would be only for Muslims. Interestingly, they clashed with like-minded groups such as the Soldiers of Odin (SOO), which formed in Australia in 2016, emulating the Finnish group of the same name formed after a series of sexual assaults on women in Finland on New Year's Eve, 2015. SOO members saw themselves as vigilantes: the last line of defence for white women against brutal ethnic attacks. In Australia, SOO largely patrolled Melbourne's streets at night, claiming to be defending its communities from ethnic gangs. As well as this offline mobilisation, there was also online activity, such as the formation of Battalion88, a white supremacist and neo-Nazi site developed in February 2016. It was quickly deplatformed due to swift action by the Online Hate Prevention Institute.

A more unusual group was also seeking to establish itself in Australia—Right Wing Resistance (RWR), an extreme-right organisation located in New Zealand. Between 2015 and 2016, it approached a man affiliated with B&H Australia, Ricky White, and asked him to lead an Australian chapter. He did so, and a fledgling cell began in rural Australia. A white supremacist but also a follower of Odinism, White believed that Christianity is responsible for the decay of the West through encouraging the 'mongrelisation' of the white race. In August 2016, White was convicted for setting fire to Destiny Church in Taree. He was assessed to be a threat to the community on the basis of his beliefs and became subject to a terrorism supervision order while in prison. Other members affiliated with RWR Australia, such as Ethan Tilling, developed transnational connections with other elements of the extreme right and travelled to the Ukraine to fight Russian-backed left-wing separatist forces. Many of these foreign fighters had previous military experience and have since returned home to Australia.

The most prominent of these groups, however, was the United Patriots Front (UPF) founded by public figures such as Blair Cottrell, Neil Erikson and Chris Shortis around May 2015. Tom Sewell would also later emerge as a leading public figure. The UPF Facebook page, which garnered some 18,000 followers, claimed to be 'Australia's political resistance against the spread of Islam and far-Left treason', effectively uniting new and old enemies in a single sentence.[10] The UPF became a prominent feature of the Reclaim Australia rallies, with each of its leaders developing a cadre of admirers. The ideology of the movement was soon twisted in numerous directions, as Cottrell, Erikson and Sewell each pursued their own agendas and sought to expand their own power bases. In the short term, Cottrell was particularly successful, using online communication apps like Gab to preach to his followers that racial mixing was responsible for the degeneration of Australian society; that Muslim immigration was leading to the genocide of the white race; and that white men were too effeminised to do anything about it.[11]

The UPF included members who were ready for violence. In July 2015, a UPF passenger aboard a bus en route to a Reclaim Australia rally in Melbourne was found to be in possession of firearms. Another UPF member, Nathan Davidson, was arrested for possession of firearms, steroids and drugs. He had tattoos testifying to white supremacist ideas, including '1488'—the '14' signifying his support for the neo-Nazi mantra known as the 14 Words ('We must secure the existence of our people and a future for white children'), and the '88' alphanumeric code for 'Heil Hitler'. Three of the leaders of the UPF, Cottrell, Erikson and Shortis, were convicted of inciting contempt against Muslims after staging a mock beheading in imitation of IS as part of their campaign against the Bendigo mosque. In time, the UPF fragmented due to leadership infighting, and Erikson split from the group and established Cooks Convicts.[12]

Terror manifests

Group fragmentation and discord can relegate committed members to the fringes of even their own communities. In 2016, a man who ardently followed Reclaim Australia, the True Blue Crew, and the UPF was apprehended by Victoria Police. His name was Phillip Galea, and he had spent a significant amount of time immersing himself in these protests, movements and activities. He had also begun writing a terrorism manual he called 'The Patriot's Cookbook' and started plotting attacks. Surprisingly, given Galea's engagement with anti-Islam groups, he did not choose to plot against Muslim targets. Instead, he, much like Breivik, sought to strike against more immediate enemies: anti-racism counterprotesters and left-wing political opponents who opposed Reclaim Australia at rallies, and whom he saw as a threat to himself and to Australia. Galea planned to attack prominent left-wing premises in Melbourne, targeting a number of prominent anti-racism activists. His goal was to use violence to incite people to rise up against leftists and Muslims. Fortunately, he was prevented by Victoria Police, and became the first member of Australia's extreme right to be convicted of terrorism offences. He was sentenced to twelve years in prison. Of all the leaders of UPF, only Erikson attended Galea's trial, marking the end of a fickle friendship.

In 2017, the UPF reformed as the Lads Society: an outwardly white nationalist organisation emphasising white identity, brotherhood and community.[13] Central to the Lads Society was Cottrell and Sewell's increasingly cohesive ideology. They opposed modern society, which they saw as decayed and degenerate, the corruption and perversion of their people, and what they saw as the replacement of their 'race'. They challenged their followers to exercise, to purify their minds and bodies, and to train in martial arts—to which end they established a fight club. In 2018, the Lads Society coordinated with Antipodean Resistance, another emerging neo-Nazi group. Antipodean Resistance identifies outwardly with Nazism, and continues propaganda campaigns against the homosexual community, Jewish community, and left-wing groups. Its members believe that society is disintegrating due to modern promiscuity, interracial coupling and homosexuality. Their anti-modernist ideology is reactionary, based on the belief that their way of life, values and security are imperilled. Together, the Lads Society and Antipodean Resistance launched a covert infiltration of the Young Nationals in New South Wales, mimicking earlier tactics used by the Australian League of Rights. Once at the Young Nationals conference, the infiltrators engaged in branch stacking to push an anti-immigration agenda, essentially testing how much Australia's democratic system could be exploited and perverted. It was only an investigation by ABC News that exposed the extent of their activity.

The activities of the UPF–turned–Lads Society attracted the attention of Brenton Tarrant. He was one of many who admired Cottrell, whom he called his 'Emperor'. When the UPF was criticised on Facebook, Tarrant defended the group, describing it as 'the leading ethno-nationalist group within Australia'.[14] He was deeply invested in the Reclaim Australia movement and anti-Islam protest activity within Australia, and engaged with the increasingly extreme ideas being perpetuated by these figures and groups. Following the death of his father in 2011, Tarrant inherited nearly half a million dollars. Some of this money he donated to the extreme-right cause domestically, such as the UPF (although he declined Sewell's invitation to join the nascent Lads Society), and some to the extreme right internationally, specifically the German and Austrian Identitarian Movement led by Martin Sellner.

Tarrant also used this money to travel the world, opting to adventure into less-travelled authoritarian hotspots such as North Korea, Russia and the Ukraine. At some time in January 2017, Tarrant moved to Dunedin. The authorities there believe that he began his plotting either shortly before or after his arrival. He didn't need a job and didn't seek to acquire one. All his efforts, from the time of his arrival, were focused on preparing for his attack, including the acquisition of a firearms licence, weapons and ammunition. A fellow white nationalist in New Zealand helped him with the firearms licence. From there, he acquired more than 7000 rounds of ammunition, in addition to military-style semi-automatic rifles such as two AR-15 .223 calibre rifles, and shotguns.[15] Tarrant's immersion in the ideas and activities of the domestic and international extreme right guided his activities. He admired Australian leaders and groups, but beyond all else the man he really worshipped was Anders Breivik, the Oslo terrorist. It was Breivik and his manifesto '2083' that would influence Tarrant's own attack, manifesto and ideology.

Twisted ideas

The simplest explanation offered in the early days after the Christchurch attack was that Tarrant's ideology was something foreign, acquired during his travels or his online interactions. This is highly unlikely; what is more likely is that Tarrant's ideology was developed domestically, expanded online, and confirmed internationally by his travels. This is the same pattern demonstrated by Rosemary Sisson (see Chapter 7), who had travelled to South Africa, the United Kingdom and Europe before returning to Australia to lead her racist group National Front. Overseas adventures may introduce people to new ideas, but they can also work to confirm and validate their pre-existing beliefs and direct the path they take. The domestic influence on Tarrant's beliefs can be seen clearly in his manifesto, which carries on the same trends and ideas of the Australian extreme right. What Tarrant did far more effectively than all of these people and movements, however, was concisely describe a set of theories that he believed explained the current degeneration of the West: ecofascism, accelerationism and replacement theory.

At the core of Tarrant's belief system is ecofascism, a worldview that unites white nationalism with privileged white claims on territory, based on an imagined natural order in which ethnicities should be segregated to maintain racial purity and ecological harmony.[16] Ecofascists believe that nature has shaped people and been shaped by people in turn, creating an unbreakable bond that they call the 'natural order'. Ecofascists argue that this sacred unity of humanity and nature has been disrupted, corrupted by the decadent forces of modernity such as uncontrolled population growth (especially of ethnic populations), environmental destruction caused by urbanisation and industrialisation, and immigration leading to multi-ethnic (and therefore 'unnatural') relationships. Ecofascists believe that as the environment has degraded, so too have the people—disconnected from the natural order and engaged in a desperate scramble to survive in an overpopulated world. This situation, they believe, is unsustainable; the only solution is a return to the natural order, whereby people are divided by ethnicity, and relegated to their 'natural' environments. In such a way, 'native' populations would be best positioned to salvage the natural world. In rescuing nature, they rescue the people. All other people, especially migrants, are rejected as an invasive species, accused of disrupting the delicate balance of the ecosystem.

The great illogicality of ecofascism, and its adoption by Tarrant, is that white Australians are of course not native to Australia, in the same way that white New Zealanders are not the native population of New Zealand. This is where the fascism shines through: ecofascists believe that the indigenous populations of settler societies such as Australia, New Zealand and the United States failed to manage and defend their land. Because these lands were successfully taken, often through force or guile, the indigenous populations are seen as weak and having surrendered any right to the land. Instead, ecofascists make exclusive claims to the land by right of conquest. They extol the legends and myths of the frontier—of pioneers battling the primordial forces of nature and subduing the bush, of bushrangers and their daring exploits in the wild reaches—creating the basis of memories and entitlement to nature, gradually shaping the land and being shaped by it in turn. In that way, they make privileged and racial claims to territory.

While indigenous populations feature little in ecofascist stories, other enemies are subject to much more scrutiny. Ecofascists often believe that their separation from nature has been deliberately constructed—the product of some malevolent plot. While this is often believed to be engineered by Jews, Muslims are also frequently targeted as a visible migrant minority population whom the ecofascists believe have children younger and at a greater rate than white people. This means that ecofascists, much like Tarrant, are likely to subscribe to replacement theory. Replacement theory, or white genocide, is the enduring belief that white peoples are being bred out of existence by ethnic populations—who either mix with whites and 'contaminate' their bloodlines, or simply reproduce at a greater rate. This belief is popular within Aryan Nations and the Ku Klux Klan in the United States, and leaves adherents feeling besieged. They begin to believe that the fate of their entire race is directly imperilled by the presence of migrants. Immigration becomes a silent invasion, and migrant families are seen to be slowly and incrementally replacing the 'white race'.

This perilous worldview flows directly into accelerationist thought. Within the extreme right, accelerationism is sometimes interpreted in an ideological sense, while for others it is a tactic to achieve victory. As an ideological component, accelerationism is derived from US neo-Nazi James Mason, who wrote a series of newsletters throughout the 1980s for National Socialist organisations that were later merged into his book *Siege*. The book has enjoyed fringe popularity in recent years within the online extreme right, and specific offline groups such as Mason's Atomwaffen Division and the Base—both of which subscribe to his accelerationist beliefs. Both also have admirers in Australia, and, it is rumoured, secretive cells. They perpetuate Mason's work, and his accelerationist belief that 'the country isn't going but has gone MAD; that the final END of society is accelerating; that the entire foundation itself is so thoroughly corroded; and that there is no longer any place to go to hide . . .'.[17] Mason wrote that current society is unsustainable and doomed to collapse, and the role of the individual is to hasten that collapse. Because the notion of acceleration includes an interpretation of current events, it becomes part of an ideological perspective held by numerous neo-Nazis around the Western world.

Despite this, others in the extreme right believe that accelerationism is a tactic by which the final destabilisation of society can be achieved. Individual acts, great and small, violent and non-violent, that would work to destabilise the status quo are believed to be essential in order to catalyse the revolution. Tarrant subscribed to this interpretation, explicitly championing accelerationism as a tactic for revolution, as 'only in times of radical change and social discomfort can great and terrific change occur'.[18] Tarrant preached violence to create this discomfort; his manifesto encourages assassination, poster campaigns, exacerbating societal conflicts, voting for destabilising radicals even if you disagree with their politics, and, above all else, inciting conflict. 'Destabilize, then take control,' Tarrant wrote. At its core, then, accelerationism is a tactic by which terrorists seek to increase their own power, reduce the democratic powers of the people, and destroy the democratic order.

Ecofascists and accelerationists alike believe that society is rotten to its core, beyond salvage or redemption. The entire order must be destroyed. From the ashes of the old world, the new order will be born. But for that to occur, many in the extreme right believe they must accelerate society's demise through individual acts of disruption, targeted violence and terrorism. This, and only this, can incite the final race war required to purge the world and purify the people. Only with this purge can their 'natural order' be realised: a world divided by superficialities such as skin colour, where only people of a single ethnicity can exist in a supposedly pure state. None of these ideas or theories is original, or indeed unique to Tarrant. They are common components of white nationalist and white supremacy expressions in Australia and around the world. Tarrant aimed, however, to energise them with his Christchurch attack, and in this he was, unfortunately, successful.

Inspiration is born

While Tarrant was handcuffed in the back of the police car, the dark online world of 8chan watched his assaults over and over. Even after the Facebook livestream had been removed, they ensured it was archived and shared on other streaming sites. It was watched millions of times. Their response was sickening: they celebrated the murders and gloried in the lives lost. In a matter of weeks, Tarrant was deified as a saint. It was also watched by counterterrorism personnel, who anticipated that they were witnessing an event that would fundamentally change the existing threat landscape.

Tarrant inspired copycats both internationally and domestically. Five months after Christchurch, an attack occurred in El Paso, Texas. On 3 August 2019, Patrick Crusius drove ten hours across Texas from the Dallas suburb of Allen to El Paso, and arrived in the carpark of a Walmart supercentre shortly after 10.40 a.m. He began shooting on his approach to the door. The store manager initiated the active-shooter response, and employees and customers inside the Walmart began to flee or hide. Crusius continued into the store, shooting and killing 23 people, and injuring another 23. One of the deceased was only fifteen years old. After the shooting stopped, Crusius drove to a nearby intersection and surrendered to Texas Rangers. The incident has been described as the deadliest against Latino Americans in the recent history of the United States.[19] In his manifesto, also posted to 8chan, Crusius flagged his commitment to the ideas championed by Tarrant, including replacement theory:

> In general, I support the Christchurch shooter and his manifesto. This attack is a response to the Hispanic invasion of Texas. They are the instigators, not me. I am simply defending my country from cultural and ethnic replacement brought by an invasion ... My motives for this attack are not at all personal. Actually the Hispanic community was not my target before I read The Great Replacement.[20]

He also showed adherence to ecofascism, describing the environmental destruction caused by modern American ways of living. But it did not end with El Paso.

Scarcely a week later another incident occurred, this time in the Oslo suburb of Bærum, Norway. Already a neo-Nazi, Philip Manshaus had read Tarrant's manifesto eight days earlier, and been inspired to conduct an attack of his own.[21] On the morning of 10 August, he logged on to Endchan (another online message board) and made his final post. Like Crusius, he showed his admiration for Tarrant and his commitment to the same universe of ideas: 'Well cobbers it's my time, i was elected by saint Tarrant after all. We can't let this go on, you gotta bump the race war thread irl [in real life] and if you're reading this you have been elected by me. Stream: stupid shit wont work. It's been fun, valhall venter [sic] [Valhalla awaits].'[22]

He tried and failed to set up a reliable livestream but went ahead with his plans anyway. First, he went into the bedroom of his sister, adopted from China. While she slept, he shot her three times in the head and once in the chest. He would later justify this murder by claiming it was because of her ethnicity. Manshaus then travelled to Bærum's mosque, the Al Noor Islamic Centre, arriving around 4.00 p.m., and shot his way through the locked front door. He gained access just as prayers had ended, and began shooting at the mosque elders who had remained behind in the prayer hall. The elders approached Manshaus and managed to disarm him, then, following a brief scuffle, subdue him entirely. He is currently awaiting trial on terrorism and murder charges.

Other attacks have demonstrated the persistence of these ideas, including the belief that extreme-right fighters will go to the hall of heroes in Valhalla if they are martyred. On 9 October 2019, only two months after Bærum, Stephan Balliet switched on his livestream, this time on Twitch, then attempted to enter a synagogue in Halle, Germany, during the Jewish holiday of Yom Kippur. His purpose was to kill as many Jews as he could, which he believed would weaken the power of the 'Zionist Occupation Government' and boost the morale of white men everywhere. 'If every white man kills just one [Jew], we win,' he wrote in his manifesto. Much like Tarrant, he invoked Valhalla: 'Repeat until all jews [sic] are dead or you prove the existence of *Waifus* in Valhalla, whatever comes first.'[23] (*Waifus* refers to a fictional female anime character that a fan believes is his one and only love—meaning that Balliet expected to discover whether the object of his desire would be present in the afterlife.) Balliet failed to gain access to the synagogue and instead shot and killed a German woman on the street before he drove to a Turkish kebab shop and fired into the store. He led police on a car chase before being arrested. In total, two people were killed and another two were injured.

Our darkest of hours

Numerous other attacks have been thwarted or prevented since Christchurch, including at least seven separate plots in the United States alone between the Christchurch and El Paso attacks.[24] Around the one-year anniversary of the Christchurch attack, a nineteen-year-old man photographed himself outside Christchurch's Al Noor Mosque. He was sitting in a car and wearing a *Totenkopf* skull mask, as is common among US and Australian neo-Nazis aligned with James Mason and Atomwaffen Division. He posted the picture to an encrypted communication app, along with a gun emoji and a message, in both English and Ukrainian, intimating that the mosque worshippers would be meeting for the last time. He was arrested and is awaiting charges. The national coordinator of the Islamic Women's Council told the media that this was the fourth threat made on the mosque since Tarrant's attack.[25]

In Australia, the threat from the extreme right persists. The Lads Society reformed again, this time as an outwardly neo-Nazi organisation called the National Socialist Network (NSN). Led by Sewell, the NSN demonstrates strong engagement to the ideas of Tarrant and Mason, opposing modern society as a degenerate departure from the natural order, subscribing to anti-Semitic and demographic conspiracy theories such as the great replacement. They oppose immigration, multiculturalism and any form of left-wing politics. The goal of the organisation is to provoke race war in Australia, to make way for a pure and ethically white nation—which they believe (erroneously) once existed and has since been lost. According to an investigation by journalists from *The Age*, their membership includes individuals with links to skinhead prison gangs, outlaw bikie clubs, employed professionals, tradesmen, and teenagers.[26] NSN also maintains links with other domestic organisations such as the European Australia Movement, C18 and numerous other groups with a presence on Telegram, in addition to American organisations such as the Base.

In March 2020, terrorism investigators with NSW Police executed two arrest warrants against suspected right-wing extremists on the South Coast of New South Wales. Raids of the suspects' homes yielded caches of weapons, extremist literature and a potential plot. In December, a teenager from Albury was arrested for making comments online encouraging right-wing terrorism and high-casualty events against Jews, Muslims and other minorities.

In February 2021, members of the Proud Boys—also from the Albury-Wodonga region—harassed people who had engaged with alleged Antifa (antifascist) posts on Facebook. That same month, a man in Western Australia was arrested after he painted a swastika on his head and tried to attack an Indigenous woman in Perth with a makeshift flamethrower. In March, a member of NSN made racist slurs against a security guard at Channel Nine in Melbourne, while Sewell violently assaulted the guard in full view of CCTV cameras, leading to his arrest. Since then, a number of arrests have been made in association with incidences and preparatory activities connected to extreme right-wing beliefs.

Nor are law enforcement agencies the only ones expanding their coverage of the threat. In 2020 alone, ASIO made two separate statements confirming that the threat is growing, requiring some 40 per cent of its counterterrorism resources, and that members of such groups are becoming more organised and sophisticated. In 2021, Burgess revised this number, stating that upwards to half of the significant counterterror probes were examining extreme-right wing threats. The same threat consumes 15 per cent of Australian Federal Police counterterrorism operations, to say nothing of state-based law-enforcement operations. Despite this activity, in December 2020, incumbent Home Affairs minister Peter Dutton labelled calls for extra resourcing as 'silly, stupid, petty'.[27]

The danger endures. Numerous groups championing extreme-right ideology continue to engage with each other domestically and internationally, both online and offline. The extreme-right threat is, however, a moving target. Its nature is ever changing and reactionary, responding to real events and imagined perils with equal energy. The COVID-19 pandemic especially has stirred these particular subcultures. With rising opposition to COVID-19 countermeasures, they have entangled themselves with ideological strangers, such as anti-vaxxers and conspiracists like QAnon. Some, such as the sovereign citizen movement, have expanded their reach and recruitment markedly, while others have remained small and kept a low profile. Large or small, the groups that abide by such divisive and dangerous ideologies remain a threat to the Australian community and its citizens. The Christchurch terrorist may have pleaded guilty to his crimes, but his legacy endures beyond the prison walls, inspiring other right-wing extremists to acts of violence.

A more powerful legacy endures elsewhere. A new graveyard lies on a windswept hill above the city of Christchurch: every headstone is new, and nearly all feature the same date. On that date, the community gathered in peace for worship. They welcomed guests, supported and helped others, and honoured the liberties and freedoms of democratic society. It was their strength and their legacy that resonated with New Zealand prime minister Jacinda Ardern. In her address at the Christchurch Memorial, she asked what words could express the pain and suffering of her people, and found a message of peace:

> . . . I came here and was met with this simple greeting. As-salaam Alaikum. Peace be upon you.
>
> They were simple words, repeated by community leaders who witnessed the loss of their friends and loved ones. Simple words, whispered by the injured from their hospital beds. Simple words, spoken by the bereaved and everyone I met who has been affected by this attack.
>
> As-salaam Alaikum. Peace be upon you.
>
> They were words spoken by a community who, in the face of hate and violence, had every right to express anger but instead opened their doors for all of us to grieve with them.[28]

A year later, the mosques continue to welcome in guests, just as they welcomed me, and worshippers continue to tend the gardens at Al Noor, cultivating the flowers and vegetables to share with all. Once targeted in what Ardern described as New Zealand's 'darkest of hours', the mosque communities have become the envoys of a simple message—a poignant legacy—that rejects all the imagined perils, twisted realities and conspiratorial messages of the extreme right. It is the message of peace.

Epilogue

Terrorism endures in rich nations and poor, in Western democracies and conflict zones. Even ideologies seemingly so foreign to our liberal democratic order feasibly take root in our soil. In countering such terrorism, we must first accept that there is no easy solution for handling people inspired by extreme ideologies—especially those ideologies that evoke an imaginary glorious past, or promise a golden, utopian future. Nor are these ideologies merely static views of the world: as the world around us changes, ideologies adapt to explain those changes. The international ideologies can easily be adjusted to the domestic domain to inspire terror. Such terrorism is therefore a moving target: groups and organisations rise and fall, threats evolve and diminish, and yet our democracy must endure.

Many persist with the myth that terrorists are exotic strangers from foreign lands and can be stopped at the border. This fails to comprehend the domestic threat, the insidious nature of extremist ideologies and their seemingly omnipotent ability to transcend borders and oceans. Ideas are not, and have never been, constrained by geography. *Chasing Shadows* demonstrates that terrorism and extremism in Australia are represented by a dynamic variety of ideologies that have found supporters and operators among the Australian citizenry. Terrorism in Australia, and relating to Australians, has always been highly transnational, regardless of border-control mechanisms.

Australia might perceive itself to be isolated from the rest of the world, but in actuality, the nation's terrorism experiences demonstrate just how much influence international forces have on the domestic domain. Australia is a case study in international extremism, a microcosm of international extremist movements and forces that believe violent revolution is the panacea for societal disease. This is not to say that Australia is solely a theatre for international actors: it may be the theatre for an international playbook, but the actors are often local and sympathetic to international ideologies and incidences. Beyond all else, our record of terrorism demonstrates that terrorism is our problem as much as it is anyone else's. It is not an act of some imagined other, some masked stranger—it is an act of our people.

Governments can hold borders sovereign, but they cannot control the political will of their people. It is important to recognise this, as we conceptualise terrorism as *our* problem, not a problem that belongs to *someone else*, be it another nation or people. Australians, for all our happy-go-lucky and 'it'll be right' attitude, have a strong history of adopting political causes, whether domestic or international. For a time, political radicalism was an important part of university counterculture, and it has not lost its lustre over the decades. Australians will continue to become enamoured of foreign or domestic terrorists and their extreme ideologies, believing themselves to be the visionaries upon whose shoulders the righteous future rests.

In 1976, an ASIO official noted that 'Terror is still a growth industry'.[1] This hasn't changed in more than 45 years. Today, Australia must confront a two-faced terrorism threat: on one side, the significant danger posed by violent Salafists, and on the other, right-wing extremists and terrorists. Both are highly embedded in the global communities of like-minded people; both exploit modern information highways; and both show an intent to inspire and assist others to engage in lethal terrorist violence. Not only have both jihadists and right-wing terrorists proven successful in this, but their success can be clearly observed in the Australian domestic context. My hope is that this book will be the first of many that dispels the shadows around terror, which at first seems unknown and unknowable, to reveal its distinct—and anti-democratic—nature. Without looking backwards, we risk undermining our own freedoms moving forward.

Terrorists have the capacity to kill, to maim and to terrify. Terrorists have the ability to destroy infrastructure, cripple public services and damage our sacred spaces. Terrorists have the ability to create an atmosphere of enduring, oppressive fear. Terrorists have the intent to divide people and set citizens against one another. But terrorists cannot destroy our institutions. Terrorists cannot subvert our essential values. Terrorists cannot force us to trespass upon our own sacred principles. Terrorists cannot actually annihilate our freedom and close our open democratic societies. Only *we can do this* by overreacting to terrorism. Only we can do this by allowing the erosion of our fundamental freedoms.

Terrorists cannot take our freedom. Only we can do that through supporting government policies and actions that reduce our freedoms. Only we can do that through supporting the surveillance of peaceful citizens; supporting the prosecution of people for exposing government cruelty or illegality; and supporting measures that seek to control an open, accountable and transparent media. Terrorists want these events to happen because it will be proof of a malevolent, corrupt system. The task for the state, then, is not to prove them right.

Our task as citizens is to hold to our own values and principles as Australians, and as members of an open, democratic society while combating violent elements in political society. We must hold to our democratic principles and resist attempts to create suspect communities that divide our people by ethnicity or religion. We must hold to freedom of assembly and political participation, and resist attempts to erode our right to protest and securitise our legally protected right to peaceful activism. We must hold to the rule of law and resist the politicisation of the judicial system by ensuring that all people have the right to an open and fair trial whatever their crime—especially Terrorism Act offences.

The ultimate goal of terrorists, regardless of their creed, is not to destroy us, but to create the circumstances in which we destroy ourselves. It is to manipulate us into trespassing upon ourselves and our own values. The only way to triumph over terrorism is to refuse to fall into that trap, and to stand by the values that make our society fair and free. While they strike from the shadows, we stand in the open.

Acknowledgements

It takes a great deal of patience to support the obsessions of others. I was incredibly fortunate to have so many people willing in their unique and occasionally reluctant ways to support mine. To Curtis, thank you for 'getting it'—from start to finish. To Janine, thank you for again believing so strongly in this history—and in me. To Andrew, thank you for the discussions and occasional vagrancy into obscure philosophy. To Jamie, thank you for your constancy and encouragement (and, let's face it, the wine). Lastly, there is one person who has had the singular misfortune of reading each word, over and over since 2018. Thank you, Jack—not only did you have to read every word as I wrote it, but you had to hear every thought as I conceived it. I promise you won't have to read it again.

Notes

INTRODUCTION

1. The IWW case during World War I was plagued by doubt and rumours of a set-up; there was little in the way of hard evidence to prove that the arson committed in Sydney was in fact perpetrated by the IWW.

Shadows of Empire, 1868–1918

CHAPTER 1: THE FENIAN CIRCLE

1. Deborah Tout-Smith, 'HRH Prince Alfred, Duke of Edinburgh (1844–1900)', Museums Victoria, <https://collections.museumvictoria.com.au/articles/2056>, accessed 4 July 2018.
2. Catharina Japikse, 'The Irish Potato Famine', *EPA Journal*, vol. 20, nos 3–4, 1994, p. 44.
3. S.H. Cousens, 'Regional Death Rates in Ireland During the Great Famine, from 1846 to 1851', *Population Studies*, vol. 14, no. 1, 1960, p. 55.
4. Robert English, *Irish Freedom: The History of Nationalism in Ireland*, Oxford: Pan Books, 2006, pp. 169–70.
5. 'The Stephen Street Outrage', *Herald* (Melbourne), 16 December 1867, <http://nla.gov.au/nla.news-article244956970>, accessed 7 January 2021.
6. 'Trial of H. J. O'Farrell for the Attempted Assassination of the Prince', *Bega Gazette and Eden District or Southern Coast Advertiser*, 4 April 1868, <http://nla.gov.au/nla.news-article110318264>, accessed 18 July 2018.
7. 'Hector Bolitho Continues the Story of the First Duke of Edinburgh: How He Escaped the Assassin', *Sydney Morning Herald*, 4 February 1954, <http://nla.gov.au/nla.news-article18407713>, accessed 18 July 2018.
8. Ibid.
9. Robert Kee, *The Green Flag: A History of Irish Nationalism*, London: Penguin, 2000, p. 10.
10. J. Bartgen, 'The Rise and Fall of the Fenian Brotherhood', MA thesis, Roosevelt University, 2010, pp. 12–13.
11. 'The Confessions of Henry James O'Farrell, after His Attempt to Assassinate His Royal Highness the Duke of Edinburgh. I', *Cornwall Chronicle* (Launceston), 30 December 1868, <http://nla.gov.au/nla.news-article66466698>, accessed 18 July 2018, p. 3.

12 Ibid., p. 2.
13 Ibid., p. 2.
14 'The Trial of O'Farrell for the Attempted Assassination of the Duke of Edinburgh', *Express and Telegraph* (Adelaide), 11 April 1868, <http://nla.gov.au/nla.news-article207737592>, accessed 18 July 2018.
15 'Trial of H. J. O'Farrell for the Attempted Assassination of the Prince'.
16 'Execution of O'Farrell', *Express and Telegraph* (Adelaide), 2 May 1868, <http://nla.gov.au/nla.news-article207738016>, accessed 18 July 2018.
17 Ibid.
18 Ibid.
19 Michael Burleigh, *Blood and Rage: A Cultural History of Terrorism*, New York: Harper Perennial, 2009, p. 11.
20 'Convicts and the British Colonies in Australia', Australian Government, <www.australia.gov.au/about-australia/australian-story/convicts-and-the-british-colonies>, accessed 18 July 2018.
21 Chris Ashton, 'Fenian Tale of Derring-Do', *Quadrant*, June 2009, pp. 69–71.
22 'Story of the Catalpa: How Officialdom Was Bluffed When the Fenians Got Away from Fremantle', *Western Mail* (Perth), 30 October 1947, <http://nla.gov.au/nla.news-article52180463>, accessed 18 July 2018.
23 'Our Special Correspondence', *Advocate* (Melbourne), 14 April 1906, <http://nla.gov.au/nla.news-article170191986>, accessed 18 July 2018.
24 'The Catalpa Incident', *West Australian* (Perth), 30 October 1884, <http://nla.gov.au/nla.news-article2993030>, accessed 18 July 2018.
25 'Our Special Correspondence'.
26 Gilbert King, 'The Most Audacious Australian Prison Break of 1876', *Smithsonian Magazine*, 12 March 2013, <www.smithsonianmag.com/history/the-most-audacious-australian-prison-break-of-1876-1804085>, accessed 18 July 2018.
27 'An Episode in West Australian History', *West Australian* (Perth), 9 October 1895, <http://nla.gov.au/nla.news-article4542968>, accessed 18 July 2018.
28 'The Catalpa Incident'.
29 Ashton, 'Fenian Tale of Derring-Do', p. 71.
30 'Our Special Correspondence'.
31 'The Catalpa Rescue', *Southern Cross* (Adelaide), 6 June 1913, <http://nla.gov.au/nla.news-article167010851>, accessed 18 July 2018.
32 Kee, *The Green Flag*, p. 309.
33 Charles Townshend, *Easter 1916: The Irish Rebellion*, New York: Ivan R. Dee, 2006, p. 301.
34 Activities in the Commonwealth of Sinn Fein and Seditious Irish Societies, Papers Relating to the 'Irish Republican Brotherhood', 1918, National Archives of Australia (NAA), CP406/1, Bundle 1.
35 'Inquiry before Mr Justice Harvey Re Certain Internees, Irish Republican Brotherhood', c. 1920, NAA, A5522, M770.
36 Patrick O'Farrell, *The Irish in Australia*, New York: American Council of Learned Societies, 1987, p. 257.
37 Kee, *The Green Flag*, p. 137.
38 'Inquiry before Mr Justice Harvey Re Certain Internees, Irish Republican Brotherhood', p. 3.
39 Garrath O'Keefe, 'Australia's Irish Republican Brotherhood', *Journal of the Royal Australian Historical Society*, vol. 83, no. 2, 1997, p. 138.

40 *Inquiry into Regulation 56b of the War Precaution's Regulations (1915) before Hon Justice Harvey Re Irish Republican Brotherhood*, Supreme Court of New South Wales, 1918, NAA, A432, 1929/4572, pp. 11–14.
41 Sinn Fein—South Australia—General Reports on Organisation, 1918, NAA, A8911, 219.
42 *Inquiry into Regulation 56b of the War Precaution's Regulations (1915) before Hon Justice Harvey Re Irish Republican Brotherhood*, p. 6.
43 Papers Relating to the 'Irish Republican Brotherhood'.
44 *Inquiry into Regulation 56b of the War Precaution's Regulations (1915) before Hon Justice Harvey Re Irish Republican Brotherhood*, pp. 30–31.
45 Ibid., p. 48.
46 Papers Relating to the 'Irish Republican Brotherhood', p. 25.
47 *Inquiry into Regulation 56b of the War Precaution's Regulations (1915) before Hon Justice Harvey Re Irish Republican Brotherhood*, pp. 38–39.
48 'A Melbourne Arrest', Leader (Melbourne), 24 August 1918, <http://nla.gov.au/nla.news-article89068460>, accessed 25 June 2020.
49 *Inquiry into Regulation 56b of the War Precaution's Regulations (1915) before Hon Justice Harvey Re Irish Republican Brotherhood*.
50 O'Keefe, 'Australia's Irish Republican Brotherhood', p. 143. The Hansard publication was linked to both criticism of the Irish internees and the conscription debate.
51 Hansard Seizure Case—Commonwealth v. State of Queensland and Others—Supplement, 1918, NAA, A432, 1929/4567 Supplement.
52 Newspaper clipping, in 'Inquiry before Mr Justice Harvey Re Certain Internees, Irish Republican Brotherhood'.
53 O'Farrell, *The Irish in Australia*, p. 277.
54 Sinn Fein—South Australia—General Reports on Organisation, p. 2.
55 Ibid.
56 'Hymn of Fate', ibid.
57 British Government, *Outrages (Ireland), January 1919 to April 1920 and Outrages (Ireland), April to May 1920*, National Library of Ireland, Collection List A18, 1916–21, p. 2.
58 Ibid.
59 The Circumstances Leading to the Establishment of ASIO—Documents 1–24, 1947–74, NAA, A12389, A13 Part 1.
60 Ibid., p. 185.
61 Frank Cain, 'Venona in Australia and Its Long-term Ramifications', *Journal of Contemporary History*, vol. 35, no. 2, 2000, p. 234.
62 Ibid.
63 The Circumstances Leading to the Establishment of ASIO—Documents 1–24, p. 40.
64 Establishment of ASIO—Australian Security Intelligence Organization, 1949–95, NAA, A7452, A48.

The Revolution Generation, 1965–75

CHAPTER 2: A SOCIALIST UTOPIA

1 Communist Party of Australia, ASIO, Special Projects Branch, Documents 52–67, 1971, Terrorism its Nature, Objectives and Revolutionary Role; A Note on the Past, Present and Future Significance of Communism in Australia; Significant Demonstrations, Including Violent Incidents Claimed by or Attributed to Terrorist-type Groups Like the People's Liberation Army, Worker-Student Alliance, the Utashi etc; A Note on Terrorist Activity;

Trotskyism in Australia; The National Socialist Party of Australia (NSPA); Communist Party of Australia (CPA), Socialist Party of Australia (SPA), Comment on a Communist Party of Australia Discussion Document for its 23rd Congress (1971); A Note on Recent 'New Left' Trends in the USA and Their Significance for the 'Left' in Australia; A Note on the 'New Left' in Australia; Urban Guerilla Warfare Including Anarchist and Radical Violence; The Politically Motivated Act of Violence, NAA, A12389, A30, Part 14, pp. 59–67.
2   R. Law, *Terrorism: A History*, Cambridge: Polity Press, 2009, p. 263.
3   Karin Asbley et al., *You Don't Need a Weatherman to Know Which Way the Wind Blows*, New York: New Left Notes, 1969.
4   ASIO, Special Projects Branch, Documents 29–33, 1970, NAA, A12389, A30, Part 8, pp. 3.
5   Ibid., p. 3.
6   Ibid., p. 37.
7   Ibid., p. 11.
8   ASIO, Special Projects Branch, Documents 52–67, 1971, p. 2.
9   ASIO, Special Projects Branch, Documents 43–45, 1971, NAA, A12389, A30, Part 12.
10 ASIO, Special Projects Branch, Documents 52–67, p. 10.
11 'Advertising: Alice's Restaurant-Bookshop', *Tribune* (Sydney), 20 August 1969, <http://nla.gov.au/nla.news-article237506310>, accessed 22 July 2020.
12 ASIO, Special Projects Branch, Documents 52–67, p. 3.
13 'Telephone Threat to Wreck Mr Jones' Home', *Canberra Times*, 18 October 1969, <http://nla.gov.au/nla.news-article107898525>, accessed 5 October 2018.
14 ASIO, Special Projects Branch, Documents 29–33, p. 6.
15 ASIO, Special Projects Branch, Documents 52–67, p. 7.
16 Ibid., p. 8.
17 ASIO, Special Projects Branch, Documents 52–67, 1971, Politically Motivated Incidents of Violence, Intelligence Report, NAA, A12389, A30, Part 14.
18 ASIO, Special Projects Branch, Documents 43–45, p. 6.
19 ASIO, Special Projects Branch, Documents 43–45, p. 6.
20 ASIO, Special Projects Branch, Documents 52–67, p. 4.
21 ASIO, Special Projects Branch, Documents 43–45, p. 3.
22 Ibid., p. 3.
23 ASIO, Special Projects Branch, Documents 52–67.
24 ASIO, Special Projects Branch, Documents 52–67, p. 5.
25 ASIO, Special Projects Branch, Documents 43–45.
26 Ibid.
27 Ibid., p. 4.
28 'Shot holes in 14 Panes, Court Told', *The Mercury*, 1970, 3, MFM NX 237, National Library of Australia, Canberra, Australia.
29 ASIO, Special Projects Branch Documents 52–67, Significant demonstrations, including violent incidents claimed by or attributed to terrorist-type groups like the People's Liberation Army, Worker-Student Alliance, the Utashi etc, Intelligence Report, NAA, A12389, A30, Part 14, 1971, pp. 64–67.
30 'Students Seek Trial by Jury', *Canberra Times*, 4 February 1969, <http://nla.gov.au/nla.news-article107076488>, accessed 5 October 2018.
31 ASIO, Special Projects Branch, Documents 52–67, p. 9.
32 ASIO, Special Projects Branch, Documents 43–45.
33 Sean Ashton, 'Police Alert as New Firm Hit', *Herald*, 2 July 1970.

34 'Arsonists Hit Again', *Canberra Times*, 7 July 1970, <http://nla.gov.au/nla.news-article110330601>, accessed 12 April 2019.
35 'Casualty: Plain Australian', *Tribune* (Sydney), 11 February 1970, <http://nla.gov.au/nla.news-article237505182>, accessed 12 April 2019.
36 ASIO, Special Projects Branch, Documents 52–67, p. 7.
37 ASIO, Special Projects Branch, Documents 34, 37, 38, 1976, NAA, A12389, A30, Part 9.
38 ASIO, Special Projects Branch, Documents 43–45, p. 7.
39 ASIO, Special Projects Branch, Documents 43–45.
40 ASIO, Special Projects Branch, Documents 29–33, p. 36.
41 ASIO, Special Projects Branch, Documents 43–45, p. 6.
42 'Politically Motivated Violence by Local Groups and Individuals Not Associated with the Croatian or Palestinian Causes', ASIO Seminar, February 1976, NAA, Politically Motivated Violence and Terrorism, 1976, A12391, R86, pp. 97–98.
43 ASIO, Special Projects Branch, Documents 52–67, p. 10.
44 'Comment on a CPA Discussion Document for its 23rd Annual Congress', 1971, ASIO, Special Projects Branch, Documents 52–67, p. 5.
45 John Blaxland, *The Protest Years: The Official History of ASIO, 1963–1975*, Sydney: Allen & Unwin, 2016, p. 104.
46 'Politically Motivated Violence by Local Groups and Individuals Not Associated with the Croatian or Palestinian Causes', p. 96.
47 'Note on Terrorist Activity', ASIO, Special Projects Branch, Documents 52–67, pp. 62–67.
48 'The Politically Motivated Act of Violence', ibid., p. 4.

CHAPTER 3: A FASCIST HOMELAND

1 Ivo Goldstein, 'Ante Pavelić, Charisma and National Mission in Wartime Croatia', *Totalitarian Movements and Political Religions*, vol. 7, no. 2, 2006, p. 225.
2 Randall Law, *Terrorism: A History*, Cambridge: Polity Press, 2009, p. 156.
3 Nick Higham, 'Croatian Holocaust Still Stirs Controversy', *BBC News*, 29 November 2001, <http://news.bbc.co.uk/1/hi/programmes/from_our_own_correspondent/1673249.stm>, accessed 30 December 2020.
4 Yugoslavia—Foreign Policy—Relations with Australia—Extremism—Part 31, 1980–81, NAA, A1838, 73/1/3/13 Part 31, p. 146.
5 Ibid., p. 118.
6 Central Intelligence Agency, *Yugoslavia—the Ustashi and the Croatian Separatist Problem*, Washington, DC: Office of National Assessments, 1972. p. 2.
7 John Blaxland, *The Protest Years: The Official History of ASIO, 1963–1975*, Sydney: Allen & Unwin, 2016, p. 125.
8 'Croatians getting Australian aid', *Canberra Times* (ACT: 1926–95), 21 September 1972, p. 3. <http://nla.gov.au/nla.news-article102005232>, accessed 1 October 2021, Senate Official Hansard, no. 13, 27 March 1973, *Parliamentary Debates* (Hansard), Commonwealth of Australia, 'Croatian terrorism: ministerial statement' by Senator Murphy, p. 537.
9 Correspondence in Attorney-General's Department, Terrorist Activities—Ustasha, 1967–73, NAA, M132, 330, pp. 92, 98; Croatian Terrorism: Relations with Yugoslav Government—Part 2, 1975, NAA, A5034, 1973/2136, Part 2, p. 63.
10 Frank Cain, *The Australian Security Intelligence Organization: An Unofficial History*, Cass Series: Studies in Intelligence, Ilford, Essex: F. Cass, 1994, p. 206.

11 Senate Official Hansard, no. 13, 27 March 1973. *Parliamentary Debates* (Hansard), Commonwealth of Australia, 'Croatian terrorism: ministerial statement' by Senator Murphy, p. 537.
12 Yugoslavia—Foreign Policy—Extremism—General Part 25, 1979, NAA, A1838, 73/1/3/13 Part 25.
13 Correspondence in Attorney-General's Department, Terrorist Activities—Ustasha, 1967–73, NAA, M132, 330, p. 98.
14 Croation Terrorism: Relations with Yugoslav Government—Part 2, 1975, NAA, A5034, 1973/2136, Part 2, Annex A, p. 199.
15 Cain, *The Australian Security Intelligence Organization*, p. 206. Correspondence in Attorney-General's Department, Terrorist Activities—Ustasha, 1967–73, NAA, M132, 330, p. 99.
16 Towards 1975, leadership was assumed by Ante Butković, who was apparently wanted by Interpol for a mail-bombing attack in West Germany, as suggested in Croatian and Palestinian Extremism, Croatian Terrorism: Relations with Yugoslav Government—Part 2, 1975, NAA, A5034, 1973/2136 Part 2, p. 199.
17 Correspondence in Attorney-General's Department, Terrorist Activities—Ustasha, 1967–73, NAA, M132, 330.
18 David Horner, *The Spy-Catchers: The Official History of ASIO, 1949–1963*, Sydney: Allen & Unwin, 2015, p. 275.
19 Blaxland, *The Protest Years*, p. 125.
20 Correspondence in Attorney-General's Department, NAA, M132, 330.
21 'Terrorism Plans "Admitted"', *Canberra Times*, 6 September 1963, <http://nla.gov.au/nla.news-article131736822>, accessed 22 January 2021.
22 Cain, *The Australian Security Intelligence Organization*, p. 207.
23 Correspondence in Attorney-General's Department, NAA, M132, 330.
24 'Terrorism Plans "Admitted"'.
25 Department of Police, Ustashi—Alleged Croatian Terrorist Organisation, 1964–83, Queensland State Archives, Series 39, Item 37399.
26 'Terrorist Migrant Flare-up Fear', newspaper article, 1967, ibid.
27 Blaxland, *The Protest Years*, p. 126.
28 Jim Cairns, 'Appropriation Bill 1963–1964', *Parliamentary Papers*, 17 October 1963.
29 'Disabled Croat Demands "Rights"', *Canberra Times*, 16 August 1966, <http://nla.gov.au/nla.news-article107887189>, accessed 22 January 2021.
30 Ustashi—Alleged Croatian Terrorist Organisation, police report, 1964, Queensland State Archives, Series 39, Item 37399.
31 Ibid.
32 'Blasts Baffle Police', *Canberra Times*, 18 November 1966, <http://nla.gov.au/nla.news-article106947050>, accessed 22 January 2021.
33 Blaxland, *The Protest Years*, p. 136.
34 Ibid., p. 138.
35 Gough Whitlam, 'Suspension of Standing Orders', *Parliamentary Papers*, 19 September 1972.
36 Blaxland, *The Protest Years*, p. 141.
37 'Croatians Yugoslav Agents "Ordered Murder"', *Canberra Times*, 19 May 1972, <http://nla.gov.au/nla.news-article102022079>, accessed 22 January 2021.
38 ASIO, Special Projects Branch, Documents 52–67.
39 'Incidents of Violence Related to the Yugoslav Community in Australia', ASIO Seminar, February 1976, NAA, Politically Motivated Violence and Terrorism, p. 89.

40 Blaxland, *The Protest Years*, p. 149.
41 'Yugoslav Denies He Aided Nazis', *Canberra Times*, 14 April 1972, <http://nla.gov.au/nla.news-article102209679>, accessed 22 January 2021.
42 Interview transcript, Department of Police, Ustashi—Alleged Croatian Terrorist Organisation.
43 Senate Official Hansard, no. 13, 27 March 1973. *Parliamentary Debates* (Hansard), Commonwealth of Australia, 'Croatian terrorism: ministerial statement' by Senator Murphy, p. 543.
44 'Ustasha Trials in Sydney', *Tribune* (Melbourne, 28 May 1974); *Tribune* (Sydney, 1939–91), p. 2, <http://nla.gov.au/nla.news-article236855961>, accessed 1 October 2021; 'Croatian Youth Leader Gets Off', Tribune (Sydney, 1939–91), 3 December 1974, p. 12, <http://nla.gov.au/nla.news-article236857137>, accessed 1 October 2021; Croation Terrorism: Relations with Yugoslav Government—Part 2, 1975, NAA, A5034, 1973/2136, Part 2, p. 147.
45 Correspondence, Department of Police, Ustashi—Alleged Croatian Terrorist Organisation.
46 Croatian Extremism—Note from Yugoslavia to Australian Minister—Belgrade, 1972, NAA, A432, 1972/5905, p. 53.
47 Newspaper clipping, Department of Police, Ustashi—Alleged Croatian Terrorist Organisation.
48 'The Croatian Struggle', translated newspaper, 1972, Department of Police, Ustashi—Alleged Croatian Terrorist Organisation.
49 Ibid.
50 'Police Raid Croats', newspaper article, 1972, Department of Police, Ustashi—Alleged Croatian Terrorist Organisation.
51 Newspaper clipping, Police, Ustashi—Alleged Croatian Terrorist Organisation.
52 International Terrorism, 1972, NAA, A1838, 912/17 Part 2.
53 'Parliament: Senate Statement on Terrorism', *Canberra Times*, 28 March 1973, <http://nla.gov.au/nla.news-article136967973>, accessed 22 January 2021.
54 Blaxland, *The Protest Years*, pp. 330–33.
55 Tony Stephens, 'Raid on ASIO Headquarters Deeply Regretted', *Sydney Morning Herald*, 1 January 2004, <www.smh.com.au/articles/2003/12/31/1072546585642.html>, accessed 28 April 2021.
56 'Summary Statement of Matters Dealt with by the Special Interdepartmental Committee and Its Working Groups on Special Passport and Citizenship Cases in November 1975', Croatian Terrorism: Relations with Yugoslav Government—Part 2, pp. 199–197.
57 Ibid., p. 18.
58 International Terrorism.
59 Yugoslavia—Foreign Policy—Relations with Australia—Extremism Part 27, 1979, NAA, A1838, 73/1/3/13 Part 27.
60 Central Intelligence Agency, *Yugoslav Emigre Extremists*, Office of Political Analysis: National Foreign Assessment Center, 29 May 1980, p. 26, https://www.cia.gov/readingroom/docs/CIA-RDP85T00287R000101220002-6.pdf.
61 'Croatian and Palestinian Extremism: A summary statement on matters dealt with by the special interdepartmental committee and its working groups on special passport and citizenship cases in November 1975', Croation Terrorism: Relations with Yugoslav Government—Part 2, 1975, NAA, A5034, 1973/2136, Part 2, pp. 9, 199.
62 Croatian Terrorism: Relations with Yugoslav Government—Part 2, 1975, NAA, A5034, 1973/2136, Part 2, p. 199.

63 Croatian Terrorism: Relations with Yugoslav Government—Part 2, p. 225.
64 Ibid., pp. 216–215.
65 Croatian Terrorism: Relations with Yugoslav Government—Part 2, 1975, NAA, A5034, 1973/2136, Part 2, page 112.
66 Aide-memoire, Yugoslavia—Foreign Policy—Extremism—General Part 14, 1977–78, NAA, A1838, 73/1/3/13 Part 14, pp. 101–100.
67 Yugoslavia—Foreign Policy—Relations with Australia—Extremism Part 27, p. 70.
68 'Police Say Men Had Gelignite', *Canberra Times*, 5 January 1970, <http://nla.gov.au/nla.news-article131680738>, accessed 24 May 2019.
69 Yugoslavia—Foreign Policy—Relations with Australia—Extremism—Part 31, p. 136.
70 Ibid., pp. 116–114.

CHAPTER 4: QUEST FOR STATE
1 Palestinian Terrorism—Assam Abdulhamid Abdulla, 1973, NAA, A5034, SR1973/2135 Part 2, pp. 140–139.
2 W. Clifford, speech, ASIO Seminar, February 1976, Politically Motivated Violence and Terrorism, p. 22.
3 'Palestine Committee Favours Partition Plan', *Morning Bulletin* (Rockhampton), 27 November 1947, <http://nla.gov.au/nla.news-article56802566>, accessed 1 August 2018.
4 United Nations General Assembly, 'Resolution 181 (II). Future Government of Palestine', A/RES/181(II), 29 November 1947, at UNISPAL, <https://unispal.un.org/DPA/DPR/unispal.nsf/0/7F0AF2BD897689B785256C330061D253>, accessed 7 July 2019.
5 Ghazi Falah, 'The 1948 Israeli-Palestinian War and Its Aftermath: The Transformation and De-signification of Palestine's Cultural Landscape', *Annals of the Association of American Geographers*, vol. 86, no. 2, 1996, p. 261.
6 Yezid Sayigh, *Armed Struggle and the Search for a State: The Palestinian National Movement, 1949–1993*, Oxford: Clarendon Press, 1999, Chapter 2.
7 Memorandum No. 475—Pro-Palestinian Terrorist Interest in Australia, 1979, NAA, A12390, 475.
8 Palestinian Terrorism—Assam Abdulhamid Abdulla.
9 'Palestinian Support Groups in Australia', in Memorandum No. 475—Pro-Palestinian Terrorist Interest in Australia.
10 'Palestinian Terrorist Groups—Local Support and Operational Interest in Australia', ASIO Seminar, February 1976, Politically Motivated Violence and Terrorism, p. 55.
11 Operational Interests in Australia, Protective Services Coordination Centre Library—Pro-Palestinian Terrorism—The Threat to Australia—August 1976, NAA A432, SEC1989/12342.
12 'Reaction to Agreement: Palestinian Groups Call Sadat a Traitor', *Canberra Times*, 3 September 1975, <http://nla.gov.au/nla.news-article110656582>, accessed 7 August 2018.
13 'Palestinian Support Groups in Australia', in Memorandum No. 475—Pro-Palestinian Terrorist Interest in Australia.
14 'Palestinian Terrorist Groups—Local Support and Operational Interest in Australia', ASIO Seminar, February 1976, Politically Motivated Violence and Terrorism, p. 58.
15 'Palestinian Support Groups in Australia', in Memorandum No. 475—Pro-Palestinian Terrorist Interest in Australia. Cablegram, Israel Australian Embassy, Terrorist and Guerilla Activity and Organisations, 1975–85, NAA, A9180, 230/9/4 Part 1, p. 253.

16 Terrorist Movements in Australia—Group and Others, 1972–74, NAA, A432, 1972/5646 Part 2. Note that these figures are from September 1972. In addition, the Queensland community was estimated at 4000 people, South Australia at 1500, Western Australia at 4000, and Tasmania at 20; numbers in the ACT were unknown.
17 Terrorist Movements in Australia—Group and Others, p. 25.
18 Palestinian Terrorism—Assam Abdulhamid Abdulla.
19 Protective Services Coordination Centre Library—Pro-Palestinian Terrorism—the Threat to Australia—August 1976, p. 10.
20 'Jewish Threat to "Get Even"', *Canberra Times*, 7 September 1972, <http://nla.gov.au/nla.news-article102002935>, accessed 7 August 2018.
21 Interdepartmental Committee on Counter Terrorism—Part 1, 1973, NAA, A6980, S250111, p. 190.
22 'Statement by Postmaster-General's Department to Counter Terrorism Committee on 19 December 1973', in Terrorist Movements in Australia—Group and Others.
23 Craig Whitney, 'Israeli Embassy in Bangkok Held by Arabs 19 Hours', *New York Times*, 29 December 1972, <www.nytimes.com/1972/12/29/archives/israeli-embassy-in-bangkok-held-by-arabs-19-hours-6-hostages-then.html>, accessed 8 August 2018.
24 Palestinian Terrorism—Assam Abdulhamid Abdulla.
25 Letter, Central Office, Department of Foreign Affairs, Entry into Australia—Abdul Hamid Abdulla Azzam Al Fatah—Agent, 1973–74, NAA, A1838, 1453/4531 Part 1.
26 Department of Foreign Affairs cablegram, Palestinian Terrorism—Assam Abdulhamid Abdulla; Al Fatah—The Significance of the Azzam Case, Middle East Crisis 1967—Arab Terrorist—Abdul Hamid—Abdullah Azzam, 1967–73, NAA, A1838, 181/18/1 Part 2.
27 'Brief Case History', Middle East Crisis 1967—Arab Terrorist—Abdul Hamid—Abdullah Azzam.
28 Compol Summary, Middle East Crisis 1967—Arab Terrorist—Abdul Hamid—Abdullah Azzam, 1967–73, NAA, A1838, 181/18/1 Part 1.
29 Crown Solicitor's Office letter, Department of Foreign Affairs, Entry into Australia—Abdul Hamid Abdulla Azzam Al Fatah—Agent, p. 74.
30 Middle East Crisis 1967—Arab Terrorist—Abdul Hamid—Abdullah Azzam.
31 Outward cablegram, Department of Foreign Affairs, Entry into Australia—Abdul Hamid Abdulla Azzam Al Fatah—Agent, p. 33.
32 Palestinian Terrorism—Assam Abdulhamid Abdulla.
33 Foreign Affairs report, Middle East Crisis 1967—Arab Terrorist—Abdul Hamid—Abdullah Azzam.
34 Al Fatah—The Significance of the Azzam Case, p. 285.
35 Inward cablegram, Department of Foreign Affairs, Entry into Australia—Abdul Hamid Abdulla Azzam Al Fatah—Agent, p. 27.
36 J.B. Burrows, Compol report, Middle East Crisis 1967—Arab Terrorist—Abdul Hamid—Abdullah Azzam.
37 Foreign Affairs cablegram, ibid.
38 Terrorist Movements in Australia—Group and Others.
39 Minutes, Department of Foreign Affairs, Entry into Australia—Abdul Hamid Abdulla Azzam Al Fatah—Agent, p. 35.
40 Al Fatah—The Significance of the Azzam Case, p. 283.
41 Ibid, p. 283–282.
42 Appendix B, Protective Services Coordination Centre Library—Pro-Palestinian Terrorism—the Threat to Australia—August 1976.

43 An ASIO speaker later suggested that an assassination attempt on the Israeli ambassador was, in fact, planned by PFLP (ASIO Seminar, February 1976, Politically Motivated Violence and Terrorism, p. 5).
44 'Hawke Says Australia Disappointed Israel PM', *Canberra Times*, 27 November 1973, <http://nla.gov.au/nla.news-article131694649>, accessed 9 August 2018.
45 Protective Services Coordination Centre Library—Pro-Palestinian Terrorism—the Threat to Australia—August 1976, p. 15.
46 Interdepartmental Committee on Counter Terrorism 1974—Part 2, 1974, NAA, A6980, S250143, p. 30.
47 'PLO "Operating in Australia"', *Canberra Times*, 11 March 1975, <http://nla.gov.au/nla.news-article116337531>, accessed 7 August 2018.
48 Protective Services Coordination Centre Library—Pro-Palestinian Terrorism—the Threat to Australia—August 1976, p. 16.
49 'In Brief: Help Sought in Bombing Case', *Canberra Times*, 28 December 1982, <http://nla.gov.au/nla.news-article130839184>, accessed 10 August 2018.
50 'Man Charged over Bombing at Club', *Canberra Times*, 2 February 1983, <http://nla.gov.au/nla.news-article116447375>, accessed 10 August 2018.
51 Stuart Koschade, 'Constructing a Historical Framework of Terrorism in Australia: From the Fenian Brotherhood to 21st Century Islamic Extremism', *Journal of Policing, Intelligence and Counter Terrorism*, vol. 2, no. 1, 2007, pp. 61–62.
52 G.V. Halliday, 'Special Interdepartmental Committees—Counter-Terrorism and Domestic Violence', ASIO Seminar, February 1976, Politically Motivated Violence and Terrorism, p. 17.
53 Minutes from 21 November 1975, Interdepartmental Committee on Counter Terrorism, 1975—Part 3, 1975, NAA, A6980, S250788, p. 119.
54 Interdepartmental Committee on Counter Terrorism Part 1, p. 188; underlining in original.
55 'ASIO's Role in the Field of Politically Motivated Violence and Terrorism', ASIO Seminar, February 1976, Politically Motivated Violence and Terrorism, p. 41.
56 Protective Services Coordination Centre Library—Pro-Palestinian Terrorism—the Threat to Australia—August 1976.
57 Farah Najjar and Hosam Salem, 'From Wedding Dresses to Soap: Gaza Event Highlights Israeli Siege', Al Jazeera, 3 August 2018, <www.aljazeera.com/news/2018/8/2/from-wedding-dresses-to-soap-gaza-event-highlights-israeli-siege>, accessed 3 August 2018.

Southern Cross Terror, 1975–90

CHAPTER 5: SPIRITUAL ELITES

1 Michael Head, 'Thirty Years since Sydney's Hilton Hotel Bombing: Unanswered Questions', *Legal History*, vol. 12, 2008, p. 245.
2 '"Dead before They Hit the Ground"', *Canberra Times*, 14 February 1978, <http://nla.gov.au/nla.news-article131715742>, accessed 21 November 2018.
3 Helen Crovetto, 'Ananda Marga, Prout and the Use of Force', in James R. Lewis (ed.), *Violence and New Religious Movements*, Oxford: Oxford University Press, 2011, p. 28.
4 Raphaël Voix, 'Denied Violence, Glorified Fighting: Spiritual Discipline and Controversy in Ananda Marga', *Nova Religio*, vol. 12, no. 1, 2008, pp. 7–8.
5 Ananda Marga Report, March 1983, Ananda Marga—General Threats Volume 2, 1978, NAA, A6122, 2805, p. 183.
6 P.R. Sarkar, cited in Crovetto, 'Ananda Marga, Prout and the Use of Force', p. 26.

7   Ibid., p. 29.
8   Voix, 'Denied Violence, Glorified Fighting', pp. 9–11.
9   'Even with Baba out of Jail, Ananda Margis Press on with Their Campaign', *Canberra Times*, 17 October 1978, <http://nla.gov.au/nla.news-article110917006>, accessed 19 November 2018.
10 'Ananda Marga Leader, 4 Followers Guilty of Murder', *Canberra Times*, 30 November 1976, <http://nla.gov.au/nla.news-article131798368>, accessed 20 November 2018.
11 Ananda Marga—Organisation, Administration, Management and Control, 1975–90, NAA, A6122, 2420, pp. 115–114.
12 'Ananda Marga Pracaraka Sangha (N.S.W.) Constitution', ibid.
13 Assessment A, Terrorism—Ananda Marga—Submissions, 1978–80, NAA, 1838, 1652/3/3 Part 2.
14 Ananda Marga—Activities in New South Wales Volume 1, 1969–77, NAA, A6122, 2407, p. 302.
15 Rachel Landers, *Who Bombed the Hilton?*, Sydney: NewSouth Publishing, 2016, pp. 80–81.
16 Ananda Marga—Organisation, Administration, Management and Control, pp. 113–112.
17 Submission No. 1805: Interim Report on Commonwealth Recognition or Assistance to the Ananda Marga—Decision 4252(Is), October–November 1977, NAA, A12909, 1805, p. 13.
18 Ananda Marga—Activities in Australia, 1976–77, NAA, A6122, 2410.
19 Ananda Marga—Intelligence Briefs Relating to Investigations of Ananda Marga in Australia Volume 1, 1977–78, NAA, A6122, 2433, p. 83.
20 Ananda Marga—General Threats Volume 2, p. 181.
21 Ananda Marga—Activities in New South Wales Volume 1, p. 301.
22 Yugoslavia—Foreign Policy—Extremism—General Part 25.
23 Assessment A.
24 John Blaxland and Rhys Crawley, *The Secret Cold War: The Official History of ASIO, 1975–1989*, Sydney: Allen & Unwin, 2017, p. 85.
25 'Indian Envoy Tells Court of Stabbing', *Canberra Times*, 27 October 1977, <http://nla.gov.au/nla.news-article110874756>, accessed 20 November 2018.
26 *Duff v. The Queen* (1979), 39 FLR 315.
27 Ibid.
28 Ananda Marga—Organisation, Administration, Management and Control, p. 40.
29 Ananda Marga—Assault on Air India Official, Collins Street Melbourne by Activist of Ananda Marga, 19 October 1977, NAA, A6122, 2409.
30 Ibid., p. 17.
31 Ananda Marga—Organisation, Administration, Management and Control, p. 106; underlining in original.
32 Ananda Marga—Assault on Air India Official, Collins Street Melbourne by Activist of Ananda Marga, pp. 8–7.
33 'Man Stabbed, Note Left: Envoy', *Canberra Times*, 20 October 1977, <http://nla.gov.au/nla.news-article110873208>, accessed 20 November 2018.
34 Ananda Marga—Assault on Air India Official, Collins Street Melbourne by Activist of Ananda Marga, p. 7.
35 Submission No. 1805: Interim Report on Commonwealth Recognition or Assistance to the Ananda Marga—Decision 4252(Is), p. 6.
36 Ananda Marga—Assault on Air India Official, Collins Street Melbourne by Activist of Ananda Marga.
37 Ibid.

38 Ibid.
39 Blaxland and Crawley, *The Secret Cold War*, pp. 85–87.
40 Submission No. 1805: Interim Report on Commonwealth Recognition or Assistance to the Ananda Marga—Decision 4252(Is), pp. 8–10.
41 Memo 14/78, Ananda Marga—Intelligence Briefs Relating to Investigations of Ananda Marga in Australia Volume 1, p. 160.
42 Interdepartmental Committee on Counter Terrorism 1974—Part 2.
43 Ananda Marga—Assault on Air India Official, Collins Street Melbourne by Activist of Ananda Marga.
44 Ibid.
45 Ananda Marga—Intelligence Briefs Relating to Investigations of Ananda Marga in Australia Volume 1, p. 145.
46 Protection against Violence—Incident—Ananda Marga—Activities in Australia, 1977–78, NAA, A10500, S16, p. 157.
47 Ananda Marga—General Threats Volume 2.
48 Ibid., p. 191.
49 Terrorism—Ananda Marga—Submissions, p. 69.
50 ASIO Minute, Ananda Marga—Intelligence Briefs Relating to Investigations of Ananda Marga in Australia Volume 1, p. 143.
51 Ibid., p. 134.
52 'The Aftermath of the Hilton Bombing', *Canberra Times*, 15 March 1978, <http://nla.gov.au/nla.news-article110887579>, accessed 21 November 2018.
53 Damian Cahill and Rowan Cahill, 'The 1978 Military Occupation of Bowral', *Illawarra Unity*, vol. 6, no. 1, 2006, p. 24.
54 Attorney-General's Department, 'Commonwealth Initiated Call out of Defence Forces in Aid of the Civil Power—Terrorist Demands Upon the Commonwealth', 1985, NAA, A432, 1985/12455.
55 'Commonwealth Heads of Government Regional Meeting Helicopters Used to Take Leaders to Bowral', *Canberra Times*, 15 February 1978, <http://nla.gov.au/nla.news-article131715967>, accessed 21 November 2018.
56 'Department, Commonwealth Initiated Call out of Defence Forces in Aid of the Civil Power—Terrorist Demands Upon the Commonwealth', p. 12.
57 'Police Check Hilton Lead', *Canberra Times*, 6 March 1978, <http://nla.gov.au/nla.news-article110886125>, accessed 21 November 2018.
58 Protection against Violence—Incident—Ananda Marga—Activities in Australia, p. 158.
59 Ananda Marga—Intelligence Briefs Relating to Investigations of Ananda Marga in Australia Volume 2, 1978–87, NAA, A6122, 2434, p. 39.
60 Ananda Marga—General Threats Volume 2, pp. 53–50.
61 Blaxland and Crawley, *The Secret Cold War*, pp. 90, 93.
62 Ananda Marga—Intelligence Briefs Relating to Investigations of Ananda Marga in Australia Volume 2, p. 64.
63 Ananda Marga—General Threats Volume 2, p. 103.
64 Landers, *Who Bombed the Hilton?*, p. 248.
65 Ananda Marga—Organisation, Administration, Management and Control.
66 Ibid., p. 258.
67 Landers, *Who Bombed the Hilton?*, pp. 328–29.
68 Ibid., pp. 332, 346.
69 Ananda Marga—Intelligence Briefs Relating to Investigations of Ananda Marga in Australia Volume 2, p. 18.

70 Blaxland and Crawley, *The Secret Cold War*, p. 89.
71 Ibid., p. 92.
72 Ananda Marga—General Threats Volume 2, pp. 79, 128.
73 Telex, July 1978, Ananda Marga—Intelligence Briefs Relating to Investigations of Ananda Marga in Australia Volume 2.
74 Ananda Marga—General Threats Volume 2, p. 181.
75 Ananda Marga—Intelligence Briefs Relating to Investigations of Ananda Marga in Australia Volume 2.
76 Ananda Marga—General Threats Volume 3, p. 79.
77 Blaxland and Crawley, *The Secret Cold War*, p. 94.
78 Ananda Marga—General Threats Volume 2, p. 179.
79 Blaxland and Crawley, *The Secret Cold War*, pp. 95–96.
80 Ananda Marga—General Threats Volume 2, p. 167.
81 Duncan Campbell, 'Sir Robert Mark Obituary', *The Guardian*, 2 October 2010, <www.theguardian.com/uk/2010/oct/01/sir-robert-mark-obituary>, accessed 31 December 2020.
82 'Former British Police Head Says No', *Canberra Times*, 27 February 1979, <http://nla.gov.au/nla.news-article136982627>, accessed 24 November 2020.
83 'Post for Woods "Reeks of Colonialism"', *Canberra Times*, 7 June 1979, <http://nla.gov.au/nla.news-article110950674>, accessed 24 November 2020.

CHAPTER 6: PROMISE OF VENGEANCE

1 Assassination of the Turkish Consul General in Sydney by the Armenian Genocide Justice Commando 17 December 1980 Volume 2, 1980–81, NAA, A6122, 2885, p. 143.
2 Gerard Chaliand and Arnaud Blin (eds), *The History of Terrorism: From Antiquity to Al Qaeda*, Los Angeles: University of California Press, 2007, p. 194.
3 Dov Jacobs, 'Jumping Hurdles Backwards: The Armenian Genocide and the International Criminal Court', *International Criminal Law Review*, vol. 14, no. 2, 2014, <https://doi.org/10.1163/15718123-01401009>, accessed 11 November 2017.
4 David Minier, 'Armenian Genocide: How Valley Prosecutor Missed His Chance to Be "Immortal Symbol of Justice"', <https://www.fresnobee.com/opinion/readers-opinion/article196785924.html>, accessed 12 February 2019.
5 Assassination of the Turkish Consul General in Sydney by the Armenian Genocide Justice Commando 17 December 1980 Volume 2, pp. 139–40.
6 Laura Dugan et al., 'Sudden Desistance from Terrorism: The Armenian Secret Army for the Liberation of Armenia and the Justice Commandos of the Armenian Genocide', *Dynamics of Asymmetric Conflict*, vol. 1, no. 3, 2008, <http://dx.doi.org/10.1080/17467580902838227>, accessed 11 November 2017, p. 235.
7 Assassination of the Turkish Consul General in Sydney by the Armenian Genocide Justice Commando 17 December 1980 Volume 2, p. 139.
8 ASIO Submission to the National Intelligence Sub-Committee of the Cabinet on the Armenian Terrorist Threat, Armenian Terrorist Alert, 1983–85, NAA, A11116, CA1040 Part 1.
9 Briefing notes, 'Armenian Terrorism', Assassination of the Turkish Consul General in Sydney by the Armenian Genocide Justice Commando 17 December 1980 Volume 2, p. 141.
10 'Security Increase Wanted', *Canberra Times*, 24 December 1980, <http://nla.gov.au/nla.news-article126165919>, accessed 30 October 2020.
11 'Consul's Assassins Waited: Theory', *Canberra Times*, 19 December 1980, <http://nla.gov.au/nla.news-article126164967>, accessed 30 October 2020.

12 Police report, Assassination of the Turkish Consul General in Sydney by the Armenian Genocide Justice Commando 17 December 1980 Volume 2, p. 144.
13 'Assassins Reward $250,000', *Canberra Times*, 3 February 1982, <http://nla.gov.au/nla.news-article126875942>, accessed 30 October 2020.
14 Assassination of the Turkish Consul General in Sydney by the Armenian Genocide Justice Commando 17 December 1980 Volume 2, p. 139.
15 'Consul's Assassins Waited: Theory'.
16 Assassination of the Turkish Consul General in Sydney by the Armenian Genocide Justice Commando 17 December 1980 Volume 3, 1981, NAA, A6122, 2886, pp. 206, 84.
17 Ibid., p. 207.
18 Foreign Affairs document, Assassination of the Turkish Consul General in Sydney by the Armenian Genocide Justice Commando 17 December 1980 Volume 2, p. 82.
19 Assassination of the Turkish Consul General in Sydney by the Armenian Genocide Justice Commando 17 December 1980 Volume 3, pp. 196–193.
20 Assassination of the Turkish Consul General in Sydney by the Armenian Genocide Justice Commando 17 December 1980 Volume 5, 1983–91, NAA, A6122, 2888, pp. 63–62.
21 Assassination of the Turkish Consul General in Sydney by the Armenian Genocide Justice Commando 17 December 1980 Volume 4, 1981–83, NAA, A6122, 2887, p. 102.
22 Assassination of the Turkish Consul General in Sydney by the Armenian Genocide Justice Commando 17 December 1980 Volume 3, pp. 224, 157.
23 Ibid., pp. 220–21.
24 Assassination of the Turkish Consul General in Sydney by the Armenian Genocide Justice Commando 17 December 1980 Volume 4, pp. 173, 168, 115, 113.
25 Assassination of the Turkish Consul General in Sydney by the Armenian Genocide Justice Commando 17 December 1980 Volume 4, 1981–83, p. 173.
26 John Blaxland and Rhys Crawley, *The Secret Cold War: The Official History of ASIO, 1975–1989*, Sydney: Allen & Unwin, 2017, p. 132.
27 Scorpion Melbourne intelligence, Assassination of the Turkish Consul General in Sydney by the Armenian Genocide Justice Commando 17 December 1980 Volume 4, p. 182.
28 Ibid, p. 182.
29 Armenian Terrorist Alert, pp. 33–32.
30 ASIO, Cabinet Memorandum 303—ASIO Submission to the National and International Security Committee of Cabinet—on the Armenian Terrorist Alert—Decision 2053, 1983, NAA, A13978, 303.
31 Ibid, p. 2.
32 Activities of Armenian Terrorists Part 2, 1981, NAA, A1209, 1981/1871 Part 2, p. 134.
33 ASIO, Cabinet Memorandum 281—Australian Security Intelligence Organisation (ASIO)—National and International Security Committee of Cabinet 25 October 1983—Briefing on the Armenian Terrorist Alert—Decision 2351/Nis, 1983, A13978, 281, p. 2.
34 ASIO, Cabinet Memorandum 281, p. 8.
35 Armenian Terrorist Alert, 1983–85, NAA, A11116, CA1040, Part 1, p. 26.
36 Ibid.
37 Ibid., p. 27.
38 ASIO, Cabinet Memorandum 303—ASIO Submission to the National and International Security Committee of Cabinet—on the Armenian Terrorist Alert—Decision 2053, p. 2.
39 Blaxland and Crawley, *The Secret Cold War*, p. 324.
40 CIA, 'The Armenian Secret Army for the Liberation of Armenian: A Continuing International Threat', CIA Reading Room, <www.cia.gov/readingroom/docs/CIA-RDP 85T00283R000400030009-2.pdf>, accessed 19 February 2021.

41 Armenian Terrorist Alert.
42 Blaxland and Crawley, *The Secret Cold War*, p. 340.
43 Activities of Armenian Terrorists Part 2, pp. 133, 137.
44 Armenian Terrorist Alert, 1983–85, NAA, A11116, CA1040, Part 1, p. 26.
45 Armenian Terrorist Alert.
46 Ibid., p. 3.
47 Armenian Terrorist Alert, pp. 25–24.
48 Armenian Terrorist Alert, p. 1.
49 Activities of Armenian Terrorists Part 3, 1983, NAA, A1209, 1981/1871, pp. 57–56.
50 Activities of Armenian Terrorists Part 2, pp. c.143.
51 Activities of Armenian Terrorists Part 3, p. 58.
52 ASIO Annual Report, Armenian National Committee—General Representations, 1983–91, NAA, A463, 1987/G2015, p. 17.
53 Armenian Revolutionary Army Volume 2, 1985–89, NAA, A6122, 2744, p. 59.
54 Armenian Revolutionary Army Volume 1, 1983–1985, NAA A6122, 2743.
55 'ASIO Goes Public; Report Points to Armenian Danger', *Canberra Times*, 10 May 1984, <http://nla.gov.au/nla.news-article126994389>, accessed 28 April 2021.
56 Armenian Revolutionary Army Volume 1, p. 72.
57 Ibid., p. 39.
58 Ibid., p. 98.
59 Blaxland and Crawley, *The Secret Cold War*, p. 342.
60 Armenian Revolutionary Army Volume 2, p. 105.
61 'Consulate Bomb Case Continues', *Canberra Times*, 18 November 1987, <http://nla.gov.au/nla.news-article122116017>, accessed 19 February 2021.
62 Armenian Revolutionary Army Volume 2, p. 144.
63 Blaxland and Crawley, *The Secret Cold War*, p. 342.
64 Dugan et al., 'Sudden Desistance from Terrorism', pp. 236–37.
65 'Erdogan: Armenia "Genocide" Used to Blackmail Turkey', Al Jazeera News, 5 June 2016, <www.aljazeera.com/news/2016/06/erdogan-armenia-genocide-blackmail-turkey-160604151409300.html>, accessed 19 February 2021.

CHAPTER 7: FIRES IN THE NIGHT
1 Cited in Anthony D. Smith, *National Identity*, Reno: University of Nevada Press, 1991, p. 71.
2 Benedict Anderson, *Imagined Communities: Reflections on the Origin and Spread of Nationalism*, London: Verso, 1983, pp. 48–50.
3 John Perkins, 'Swastikas Down Under: Nazi Activities in Australia, 1933–1939', *Journal of Contemporary History*, vol. 26, 1991, pp. 111–29.
4 ASIO, Nazi Party in Australia Membership Records, 1946–49, NAA, A6122, 161.
5 Department of External Affairs, Nazism, Nazi Activities, 1938–39, NAA, A981, NAZ 1 PART 2.
6 Ibid.
7 Ibid., p. 15.
8 Andrew Moore, 'The Old Guard and "Countrymindedness" During the Great Depression', *Journal of Australian Studies*, vol. 14, no. 27, 1990, p. 52.
9 Richard Evans, 'A Menace to this Realm: The New Guard and the New South Wales Police, 1931–1932', *History Australia*, vol. 5, no. 3, 2008, p. 6.
10 Andrew Moore, 'The New Guard and the Labour Movement, 1931–1935', *Labour History*, vol. 89, 2005, pp. 57–58.

11 Report of Commissioner, 'Inquiry into Matters Relating to the Detention of Certain Members of the "Australia First Movement" Group', 1945, NAA, A374, 1, p. 16.
12 Peter Henderson, 'Frank Browne and the Neo-Nazis', *Labour History*, vol. 89, 2005.
13 Report of Commissioner.
14 'Documenting Numbers of Victims of the Holocaust and Nazi Persecution', United States Holocaust Memorial Museum, <www.ushmm.org/wlc/en/article.php?ModuleId=10008193>, accessed 3 June 2018.
15 Department of Immigration, Nazi Party—National Socialist German Workers Party—NSDAP, 1979–86, NAA, A6980, S251141.
16 Eric Butler, *The International Jew: The Truth About 'the Protocols of Zion'*, Melbourne: New Times Limited, 1946.
17 Andrew Campbell, *The Australian League of Rights: A Study in Political Extremism and Subversion*, Melbourne: Outback Press, 1978, p. 110.
18 John Blaxland and Rhys Crawley, *The Secret Cold War: The Official History of ASIO, 1975–1989*, Sydney: Allen & Unwin, 2017, p. 323.
19 Henderson, p. 74.
20 Henderson, ibid.; 'Secret Report: The impotent Nazis—by ASIO', *The Bulletin*, vol. 96, no. 4932, 16 November 1974, <https://nla.gov.au/nla.obj-1382096721/view?partId=nla.obj-1382979518#page/n17/mode/1up>.
21 The National Socialist Party of Australia, c. 1970s, ASIO, Special Projects Branch Documents 52–67, 1971, NAA, A30, A12389 Part 14, pp. 60–67.
22 Ibid.
23 Department of Prime Minister and Cabinet, Terrorism and Violence in Australia, 1972, NAA, A5882, CO1528, p. 3.
24 The National Socialist Party of Australia, ASIO, Special Projects Branch Documents 52–67, p. 67.
25 Department of Customs and Excise, Importation of Nazi Stickers, 1963, NAA, A425, 1963/13478, p. 16.
26 Department of Customs and Excise, Importation of Nazi Stickers, 1963, NAA, A425, 1963/13478, p. 14.
27 ASIO, Special Projects Branch Documents 52–67, pp. 43–45.
28 Appendix A, Terrorism—Domestic Violence in Australia—General, c. 1978, NAA, A1838, 1652/3/1 Part 1, p. 83.
29 Appendix B, ibid., pp. 81–80.
30 Appendix B, ibid., p. 80.
31 'National Front of Australia', ibid., p. 98.
32 Ibid.
33 Ibid., pp. 97, 98.
34 Ibid., p. 95.
35 David Greason, the author of *I Was a Teenage Fascist*, told the media in 1997 that Tane distributed neo-Nazi literature. '"No Republic" candidate resigns after extremist claims', *The Australian Jewish News* (Sydney, 1990–2008), 31 October 1997, <http://nla.gov.au/nla.news-article261718194>, accessed 4 October 2021.
36 Terrorism—Domestic Violence in Australia—General, c. 1978, NAA, A1838, 1652/3/1, Part 1, p. 95.
37 Ibid., pp. 95–93.
38 Ibid., pp. 91–89.
39 Ibid., p. 88.

40. Charity Register, 'English-Speaking Union Victoria Branch', Australian Charities and Not-for-profits Commission, <https://www.acnc.gov.au/charity/485a3501351da0170579ec7ca6074466#overview>, accessed 24 November 2019.
41. 'National Front of Australia', pp. 86–84.
42. As of 2021, Jim Saleam is the president of the Australia First Party.
43. Matthew Westwood, 'Political Spoilers Who Deal in the Currency of Hatred', *Canberra Times*, 19 July 1989, <http://nla.gov.au/nla.news-article122283735>, accessed 4 January 2019.
44. Kristy Campion, 'Australian Right Wing Extremist Ideology: Narratives of Nemesis and Nostalgia', *Journal of Policing, Intelligence and Counter Terrorism*, vol. 14, no. 3, 2019.
45. Westwood, 'Political Spoilers Who Deal in the Currency of Hatred'.
46. Van Tongeren writes positively about Hitler and Nazi Germany in his self-published book *The ANM Story: The Pre-Revolutionary Years: 1970–1989*, Perth, Western Australia, 2004.
47. 'OPERATION JACKHAMMER', *Canberra Times* (ACT, 1926–95), 30 September 1990, p. 21, <http://nla.gov.au/nla.news-article122314166>, accessed 4 October 2021.
48. 'Court Told of Aryan Army', *Canberra Times*, 11 August 1990, <http://nla.gov.au/nla.news-article122303740>, accessed 4 January 2019.
49. This objective was reiterated by Mr G.F Scott QC later at the trial of the ANM leadership. *Van Tongeren v The Queen*; *Van Blitterswyk v The Queen*, CCA, no. 149 of 1990, Supreme Court of Western Australia, Court of Criminal Appeal, p. 67, <www.austlii.edu.au/au/cases/wa/WASC/1992/229.pdf>.
50. 'Court Told of Aryan Army.'
51. Andrew Fraser, 'Few Marginal Seats to Decide Wa Poll', *Canberra Times*, 4 February 1989, <http://nla.gov.au/nla.news-article120908402>, accessed 4 January 2019.
52. 'Posters Shock a Quiet Community', *Canberra Times*, 7 December 1987, <http://nla.gov.au/nla.news-article122414583>, accessed 4 January 2019.
53. Ibid.
54. 'Members of Racist Group Fined $150 for Bill Posting', *Canberra Times*, 8 August 1989, <http://nla.gov.au/nla.news-article122275082>, accessed 4 January 2019.
55. S.E. Walker, Criminal Code Amendment (Racial Vilification) Bill 2004, Second Reading, Western Australia, *Parliamentary Debates* (Hansard), Legislative Assembly, 15 September 2004, pp. 5973–87.
56. Roy Gibson, 'A Chronicle of Criminal Daring', *Canberra Times*, 30 September 1990, <http://nla.gov.au/nla.news-article122314165>, accessed 4 January 2019.
57. Ibid.
58. 'In Brief: Neo-Nazi on Charges', *Canberra Times*, 27 May 1989, <http://nla.gov.au/nla.news-article122265807>, accessed 16 November 2020; 'Racist Leader Fined for Explosives', *Canberra Times*, 29 July 1989, <http://nla.gov.au/nla.news-article122285644>, accessed 16 November 2020.
59. 'Operation Jackhammer', *Canberra Times*, 30 September 1990, <http://nla.gov.au/nla.news-article122314166>, accessed 4 January 2019.
60. Ibid.
61. 'Supremacist Group "Campaign of Terror" on Asians', *Canberra Times*, 12 June 1990, <http://nla.gov.au/nla.news-article120891774>, accessed 16 November 2020.
62. 'Racist Vows to Fight On', *Canberra Times*, 19 September 1990, <http://nla.gov.au/nla.news-article122311771>, accessed 4 January 2019.
63. 'Savage Beating Brings 12-Month Sentence', *Canberra Times* (ACT, 1926–95), 11 July 1992, p. 6, <http://nla.gov.au/nla.news-article126934683>, accessed 4 October 2021.

64 '"No Plot" to Kill Activist: Accused', *Canberra Times*, 14 June 1990, <http://nla.gov.au/nla.news-article120892319>, accessed 16 November 2020.
65 'Savage Beating Brings 12-Month Sentence'.
66 'Killer Pulls Knife in Court', *Canberra Times*, 21 December 1991, <http://nla.gov.au/nla.news-article122398971>, accessed 16 November 2020.
67 Ibid.
68 Ian McPhedran, 'ASIO Classes 18 Unwanteds in 1994', *Canberra Times*, 25 October 1995, <http://nla.gov.au/nla.news-article130566178>, accessed 7 January 2019.

CHAPTER 8: UNDER SARIN SKIES

1 Daniel A. Metraux, 'Religious Terrorism in Japan: The Fatal Appeal of Aum Shinrikyo', *Asian Survey*, vol. 35, no. 12, 1995, pp. 1140–54.
2 Shoko Asahara, quoted in Susumu Shimazono, 'In the Wake of Aum: The Formation and Transformation of a Universe of Belief', *Japanese Journal of Religious Studies*, vol. 22, nos 3–4, 1995, <http://dx.doi.org/10.18874/jjrs.22.3-4.1995.381-415>, accessed 28 November 2017, p. 385.
3 William Rosenau, 'Aum Shinrikyo's Biological Weapons Program: Why Did It Fail?', *Studies in Conflict and Terrorism*, vol. 24, no. 4, 2001, <http://dx.doi.org/10.1080/10576100120887>, accessed 3 December 2020.
4 Nilay Saiya, 'Confronting Apocalyptic Terrorism: Lessons from France and Japan', *Studies in Conflict and Terrorism*, vol. 43, no. 9, 2020, <http://dx.doi.org/10.1080/1057610X.2018.1499694>, accessed 3 December 2020.
5 A. Nehorayoff Andrea, Ash Benjamin and S. Smith Daniel, 'Aum Shinrikyo's Nuclear and Chemical Weapons Development Efforts', *Journal of Strategic Security*, vol. 9, no. 1, 2016, <https://digitalcommons.usf.edu/jss/vol9/iss1/5>, accessed 27 November 2017, p. 37.
6 Staff Statement, 'A Case Study on the Aum Shinrikyo', United States Senate Government Affairs Permanent Subcommittee on Investigations, 31 October 1995, <https://fas.org/irp/congress/1995_rpt/aum/part05.htm>, accessed 27 November 2017.
7 Andrea, Benjamin and Daniel, 'Aum Shinrikyo's Nuclear and Chemical Weapons Development Efforts', p. 39.
8 Staff Statement, 'A Case Study on the Aum Shinrikyo'.
9 Anthony Tu, 'Aum Shinrikyo's Chemical and Biological Weapons: More Than Sarin', *Forensic Science Review*, vol. 26, no. 2, 2014, p. 119.
10 Andrea, Benjamin and Daniel, 'Aum Shinrikyo's Nuclear and Chemical Weapons Development Efforts', p. 41.
11 Staff Statement, 'A Case Study on the Aum Shinrikyo'.
12 Rosenau, 'Aum Shinrikyo's Biological Weapons Program'.
13 Tu, 'Aum Shinrikyo's Chemical and Biological Weapons', pp. 118–19.
14 Stuart Koschade, 'The Internal Dynamics of Terrorist Cells: A Social Network Analysis of Terrorist Cells in an Australian Context', PhD thesis, Queensland University of Technology, 2017, <https://eprints.qut.edu.au/16591/1/Stuart_Koschade_Thesis.pdf>, accessed 27 November 2017, pp. 215–16.
15 'Lethal Acid Kept in Whisky Bottles on WA Station: Manager', *Canberra Times*, 28 March 1995, <http://nla.gov.au/nla.news-article127520658>, accessed 6 November 2020.
16 'Cult Planned to Use Australian Uranium: Police', *Canberra Times*, 2 July 1995, <http://nla.gov.au/nla.news-article128284841>, accessed 6 November 2020.

17. Koschade, 'The Internal Dynamics of Terrorist Cells', p. 204.
18. Ibid., pp. 206–207.
19. Ibid., p. 207.
20. Tu, 'Aum Shinrikyo's Chemical and Biological Weapons', p. 116.
21. Ibid., p. 117.
22. Ian Bellany, *Terrorism and Weapons of Mass Destruction: Responding to the Challenge*, New York: Routledge, 2007, p. 63.
23. Tomomasa Nakagawa and Anthony T. Tu, 'Murders with VX: Aum Shinrikyo in Japan and the Assassination of Kim Jong-Nam in Malaysia', *Forensic Toxicology*, vol. 36, no. 2, 2018, pp. 542–44.
24. Staff Statement, 'A Case Study on the Aum Shinrikyo'.
25. Ibid.
26. Raymond Zilinskas (ed.), *Biological Warfare: Modern Offense and Defense*, Boulder: Lynne Rienner, 2000, p. 80.
27. Staff Statement, 'A Case Study on the Aum Shinrikyo'.
28. 'Sarin Gas', *Platypus Magazine*, 1995, <http://classic.austlii.edu.au/au/journals/AUFPPlatypus/1995/40.pdf>, accessed 3 December 2020.
29. Staff Statement, 'A Case Study on the Aum Shinrikyo'.
30. Christopher W. Hughes, 'Japan's Aum Shinrikyo, the Changing Nature of Terrorism, and the Post-Cold War Security Agenda', *Pacifica Review*, vol. 10, no. 1, (1998), p. 50.

Battles Cries, 1990 onwards

1. IRA Presence and Support in Australia, Interdepartmental Committee on Counter Terrorism 1974—Part 2, 1974, NAA, A6980, S250143, p. 115.
2. 'Stop Funds for IRA: Opposition', *Canberra Times* (ACT: 1926–95), 30 May 1990, <http://nla.gov.au/nla.news-article122250434>, accessed 20 May 2020.
3. Graeme Dobell, 'Great Australian Foreign Policy Speeches: Howard on 9/11 and the US Alliance', Lowy Institute, 15 August 2014, <www.lowyinstitute.org/the-interpreter/great-australian-foreign-policy-speeches-howard-911-and-us-alliance>, accessed 15 October 2018.

CHAPTER 9: WHITE MEAT
1. 'Operation Alliance', *AFP News*, February 2003.
2. Quinton Temby, 'Imagining an Islamic State in Indonesia: From Darul Islam to Jemaah Islamiyah', *Indonesia*, no. 89, 2010, pp. 1–36.
3. Solahudin, Greg Fealy and Dave Mcrae, *The Roots of Terrorism in Indonesia: From Darul Islam to Jem'ah Islamiyah*, Ithaca, New York: Cornell University Press, 2013, Chapter 2.
4. Interview with Wahid by Department of Foreign Affairs, Indonesia—Islam—Islamic Extremism Part Two, 1975–79, NAA, 1838, 3034/5/1/1, p. 260.
5. Ibid., p. 258.
6. Indonesia: Islam as a Factor in Internal Stability, Indonesia—Islam—Islamic Extremism Part 3, 1979–80, NAA, A1838, 3034/5/1/1 Part 3, paragraph 9.
7. Islamic Revival, Indonesia—Islam—Islamic Extremism Part Two, p. 222.
8. 'A Profile of Islam under the New Order: Muslim/Government Relations', ibid., pp. 253–232.
9. Indonesia: Islam as a Factor in Internal Stability.
10. Solahudin, Fealy and Mcrae, *The Roots of Terrorism in Indonesia*, p. 65.

11 US Department of Defence, 'JTF-GTMO Detainee Assessment: Riduan Isomuddin', 30 October 2008, *Miami Herald*, <https://media.miamiherald.com/static/images/escenic-images/gitmopdfs/us9id-010019dp.pdf>, accessed 30 October 2018.
12 Sally Neighbour, 'The Network—2002', *Four Corners*, ABC TV, 8 August 2011, <www.abc.net.au/4corners/the-network---2002/2841884?site=50y>, accessed 19 April 2021.
13 Natalie O'Brien and Stephen Fitzpatrick, 'Rabiyah and Daughter Married Terror Twins', *The Australian*, 11 December 2006, <www.theaustralian.com.au/news/nation/rabiyah-and-daughter-married-terror-twins/news-story/87ddac9ffbf259f89d6257cb7c577426?sv=9f765ca17e62e60342e9c6f346236d93>, accessed 19 April 2021.
14 Shandon Harris-Hogan and Andrew Zammit, 'Mantiqi IV: Al-Qaeda's Failed Co-optation of a Jemaah Islamiyah Support Network', *Democracy and Security*, vol. 10, no. 4, 2014, pp. 315–34. 'Roche a reluctant, bumbling terrorist', *The Age*, 2 June 2004, <www.theage.com.au/national/roche-a-reluctant-bumbling-terrorist-20040602-gdxym1.html>, accessed 22 July 2021.
15 Sally Neighbour, 'My Life as a Terrorist', *The Australian*, 4 December 2007.
16 Harris-Hogan and Zammit, 'Mantiqi IV'.
17 Mark Baker, Linda Morris and Tom Allard, 'JI Accused of Plot to Bomb 2000 Games', *Sydney Morning Herald*, 4 December 2002, <www.smh.com.au/articles/2002/12/03/1038712936708.html>, accessed 19 April 2021.
18 Neighbour, 'My Life as a Terrorist'.
19 Ibid.
20 Neighbour, 'The Network'.
21 Michael Burleigh, *Blood and Rage: A Cultural History of Terrorism*, New York: Harper Perennial, 2009, p. 462.
22 Ibid.
23 David Royds, Simon W. Lewis and Amelia M. Taylor, 'A Case Study in Forensic Chemistry: The Bali Bombings', *Talanta*, vol. 67, no. 2, 2005, pp. 262–68.
24 'Operation Alliance'.
25 Ibid.
26 Ibid.
27 'Australian Survivors and Relatives of Victims Remember the Bali Bombings 10 Years On', *The Australian*, 7 October 2012.
28 Ibid.
29 Sidney Jones and Solahudin, 'Isis in Indonesia', *Southeast Asian Affairs*, 2015, pp. 154–63.

CHAPTER 10: CALIPHATE DREAMING
1 *R v Thomas* (2006), 14 VR 475, VSCA 165.
2 Ibid.
3 Ian Munro, '"Jihad Jack" Faces 25 Years' Jail', *The Age*, 27 February 2006, <www.theage.com.au/articles/2006/02/26/1140888749187.html>, accessed 12 March 2021.
4 Alyssa Allen, '"Jihad" Jack Thomas Says Australia Is Lucky to Have Not Lost More Lives in Afghanistan', ABC News, 29 October 2013, <www.abc.net.au/local/audio/2013/10/29/3879195.htm>, accessed 12 March 2021.
5 'David Hicks: Former Guantanamo Bay Detainee, Foreign Fighter, Author', ABC News, 23 January 2015, <www.abc.net.au/news/2015-01-23/david-hicks-profile/6032056>, accessed 11 March 2021.
6 *David Hicks v United States of America* (2015), CMCR (US Court of Military Commission Review), 13-004, <https://ccrjustice.org/sites/default/files/attach/2015/05/Hicksv.United%20States_13-004%20Decision_(2015.02.18).pdf>, accessed 11 March 2021.

7. 'David Hicks on His Terrorism Conviction: "I Lost, That's How I Look at It"', *The Guardian*, 19 February 2015, <www.theguardian.com/australia-news/2015/feb/19/david-hicks-on-his-terrorism-conviction-i-lost-thats-how-i-look-at-it>, accessed 11 March 2021.
8. Sam Buckingham-Jones, 'Zaky Mallah Pleads Guilty to Riding a Scooter on a Footpath', *The Australian*, 2 November 2016.
9. Natasha Wallace and Joseph Kerr, 'Not a Terrorist, Just an Angry Loner Starved of Attention', *Sydney Morning Herald*, 7 February 2005, <www.smh.com.au/news/National/Not-a-terrorist-just-an-angry-loner/2005/04/06/1112489565806.html>, accessed 11 March 2021.
10. *R v Lodhi* (2006), NSWSC 691.
11. *R v Ul-Haque* (2007), NSWSC 1251.
12. David Adams, 'CIA Report Unmasks Australian "Terror Boss"', *The Age*, 10 June 2003, <www.theage.com.au/articles/2003/06/09/1055010931902.html>, accessed 14 March 2021.
13. SITE, 'Group Threatens Australia with Ultimatum', SITE Intelligence Group, 1 July 2004, <https://ent.siteintelgroup.com/Jihadist-News/group-threatens-australia-with-ultimatum-07-24-04.html>, accessed 10 March 2021.
14. Tracey Bowden, 'Pre-Dawn Raids Net Terrorism Suspects', *ABC News*, 8 November 2005, <www.abc.net.au/7.30/content/2005/s1500743.htm>, accessed 12 March 2021.
15. Bart Shuurman et al., 'Operation Pendennis: A Case Study of an Australian Terrorist Plot', *Perspectives on Terrorism*, vol. 8, no. 4, 2014, p. 92.
16. SITE, 'A Call for Renewed Attacks on U.S. Allies in Iraq: Italy, Spain, Britain, Japan, and Korea, in a Response to Zarqawi's Recent Message Promoting Support and Unity', SITE Intelligence Group, 30 March 2005, <https://ent.siteintelgroup.com/Jihadist-News/a-call-for-renewed-attacks-on-us-allies-in-iraq-italy-spain-britain-japan-and-korea-in-a-response-to-zarqawis-recent-message-promoting-support-and-unity.html>, accessed on 14 March 2021.
17. *R v Fattal et al.* (2011), VSC 681.
18. Bonnie Malkin, 'Australian Muslims Found Guilty of Terror Plot', *The Telegraph* (London), 23 December 2010, <www.telegraph.co.uk/news/worldnews/australiaandthepacific/australia/8220838/Australian-Muslims-found-guilty-of-terror-plot.html>, accessed 28 April 2021.
19. Stuart Rintoul, 'Two Cleared but Three Convicted over Army Base Terror Attack Plan', *The Australian*, 23 December 2010.
20. Ibid.

CHAPTER 11: CIVILISATION BURNING

1. State Coroner of New South Wales, *Inquest into the Deaths Arising from Lindt Café Siege*, Sydney: Coroner's Court of New South Wales, May 2017, <www.lindtinquest.justice.nsw.gov.au/Documents/findings-and-recommendations.pdf>, accessed 20 March 2021.
2. Michael Ryan, *Decoding Al-Qaeda's Strategy: The Deep Battle against America*, New York: Columbia University Press, 2013.
3. Rachel Olding, 'Tony Abbott's Obsessive Use of the Phrase "Death Cult" Fails to Resonate with Half of Australians', *Sydney Morning Herald*, 12 May 2015, <www.smh.com.au/politics/federal/tony-abbotts-obsessive-use-of-the-phrase-death-cult-fails-to-resonate-with-half-of-australians-20150512-ggzoce.html>, accessed 19 March 2021.
4. Cited in *R v Shoma* (2019), VSC 367.
5. Aaron Y. Zelin, 'Al-Hayat Media Centre Presents New Video Message from the Islamic State: Stories from the Land of the Living: Abu Khalid Al-Kambudi', Jihadology,

<https://jihadology.net/2015/04/21/al-Hayat-Media-Centre-presents-new-video-message-from-The-Islamic-State-Stories-From-the-Land-of-the-Living-Abu-Khalid-al-Kambudi>, accessed 18 November 2018.

6 State Coroner of New South Wales, *Inquest into the Deaths Arising from Lindt Cafe Siege*, p. 5.
7 Abu Musab al-Suri, 'The Military Theory of the Global Islamic Resistance Cell', *The Global Islamic Resistance Call* (c. 2000).
8 *R v Al-Kutobi; R v Kiad* (2016), NSWSC 1760.
9 Michael Safi, 'Revealed: How I Saw Farhad Jabar Change a Week before He Became a Killer', *The Guardian*, 8 October 2015, <www.theguardian.com/australia-news/2015/oct/08/farhad-jabar-troubled-soft-spoken-boy-turned-into-killer>, accessed 19 March 2021.
10 Nick Ralston, 'Farhad Jabar Captured Giving Islamic State Salute before Curtis Cheng Shooting', *Sydney Morning Herald*, 1 May 2017, <www.smh.com.au/national/nsw/farhad-jabar-captured-giving-islamic-state-salute-before-curtis-cheng-shooting-20170501-gvwn36.html>, accessed 11 April 2021.
11 AAP, 'Anzac Day Terror Plot Teen Gets Four More Years Added to His Jail Sentence', news.com, 23 June 2017, <www.news.com.au/national/victoria/courts-law/anzac-day-terror-plot-teen-gets-four-more-years-added-to-his-jail-sentence/news-story/562449fa2c5f0e2a7502926f8fb37009>, accessed 19 March 2021.
12 Sarah Farnsworth, 'Anzac Day Terrorism Plot: Court Documents Reveal Sevdet Besim Wanted to Die a Martyr', ABC News, 12 July 2016, <www.abc.net.au/news/2016-07-12/court-documents-detail-anzac-day-terrorism-plot/7589746>, accessed 19 March 2021.
13 Islamic State, *Rumiyah* magazine, Jihadology, 2016.
14 Tammy Mills et al., '"A Wake-up Call": Police Link Bourke Street Terror Attack to IS', *The Age*, 10 November 2018, <www.theage.com.au/national/victoria/a-wake-up-call-police-link-bourke-street-terror-attack-to-is-20181110-p50f77.html>, accessed 3 July 2019.
15 *R v Shoma*.
16 Ibid.
17 *DPP (Cth) v Ali* (2020), S EAPCR 0118.
18 *R v Khaled Khayat; R v Mahmoud Khayat (No 14)* (2019), NSWSC 1817.
19 Julie Bishop, 'Doorstop—Parliament House, Canberra', Minister for Foreign Affairs (archived website), 29 October 2014, <www.foreignminister.gov.au/minister/julie-bishop/transcript-eoe/doorstop-parliament-house-canberra-0>, accessed 28 April 2021; Rodger Shanahan, 'Typology of Terror—The Backgrounds of Australian Jihadis', Lowy Institute, 21 November 2019, <www.lowyinstitute.org/publications/typology-terror-background-australian-jihadis>, accessed 28 April 2021.
20 James Dowling, 'Jihadi Jake Bilardi Was "Weak" and "Sold His Soul Cheaply", Says Islamic State Online Propaganda', *Herald Sun*, 16 March 2015, <www.heraldsun.com.au/news/victoria/jihadi-jake-bilardi-was-weak-and-sold-his-soul-cheaply-says-islamic-state-online-propaganda/news-story/aeb0881f7b28d5abe5eadce72787b269>, 28 April 2021.
21 Omar Wahid, 'British Runaway Schoolgirl, 16, Marries Australian ISIS Fanatic Dubbed the "Ginger Jihadi" in Syria—as Her New Husband Tells MoS the Terror Group Are "Itching to Attack" the UK and Praises Tunisia Beach Gunman', *Daily Mail*, 2 July 2015, <www.dailymail.co.uk/news/article-3157664/British-runaway-schoolgirl-16-MARRIES-Australian-ISIS-fanatic-dubbed-Ginger-Jihadi-Syria-new-husband-tells-MoS-terror-group-itching-attack-UK-praises-Tunisia-beach-gunman.html>, accessed 28 April 2021.

22 'Australian Teen Abdullah Elmir Warns Tony Abbott in Isis Message—Video', *The Guardian*, 22 October 2014, <www.theguardian.com/world/video/2014/oct/22/australian-teen-abdullah-elmir-isis-video>, accessed 28 April 2021.
23 'Australian Teenager Abdullah Elmir, Who Uses the Alias Abu Khaled', ABC News, 16 June 2015, <www.abc.net.au/news/2015-06-16/australian-teenager-abdullah-elmir-who-calls-himself-abu-khaled/6549256?nw=0>, accessed 28 April 2021.
24 David Wroe, '"Abu Adam" Uses Chilling Video to Urge Terror Attacks against Australia, Philippines', *Sydney Morning Herald*, 8 August 2017, <www.smh.com.au/politics/federal/abu-adam-uses-chilling-video-to-urge-terror-attacks-against-australia-philippines-20170808-gxrqdk.html>, accessed 28 April 2021.
25 David Wroe, 'Australian Foreign Fighters Will Have No Escape from Islamic State Heartland, US Vows', *Sydney Morning Herald*, 5 June 2017, <www.smh.com.au/politics/federal/australian-foreign-fighters-will-have-no-escape-from-islamic-state-heartland-us-vows-20170605-gwkrm5.html>, accessed 3 July 2019.

CHAPTER 12: DARKEST OF HOURS
1 Brenton Tarrant, '*Ahem* No. 12916717', /pol/, 15 March 2019, <http://archive.li/AlIX8>, accessed 3 December 2020.
2 *R v Tarrant: Sentencing Remarks of Mander J*, CRI-2019-009-2468 [2020] NZHC 2192.
3 Matthew M. Sweeney, 'Who's in Charge? How Group Centralization Influences Ideology, Tactics, and Recruitment in American Extremist Groups', PhD thesis, University of Massachusetts Lowell, 2020, pp. 222–34.
4 David Mar, 'One-Way Radio Plays by Its Own Rules', *Sydney Morning Herald*, 13 December 2005, <www.smh.com.au/national/one-way-radio-plays-by-its-own-rules-20051213-gdmmg4.html>, accessed 3 December 2020.
5 Scott Poynting, 'What Caused the Cronulla Riot?', *Race & Class*, vol. 48, no. 1, 2016, pp. 85–92.
6 Geoff Dean, Peter Bell and Zarina Vakhitova, 'Right-Wing Extremism in Australia: The Rise of the New Radical Right', *Journal of Policing, Intelligence and Counter Terrorism*, vol. 11, no. 2, 2016, pp. 121–42.
7 Bianca Hall, 'Restore Australia: The Party That Would Ban Islam', *Sydney Morning Herald*, 1 January 2016, <www.smh.com.au/politics/federal/restore-australia-the-party-that-would-ban-islam-20160101-glxsfh.html>, accessed 3 July 2019.
8 'Reclaiming What?', Reclaim Australia, <www.reclaim-australia.com/reclaim-what-.html>, accessed 18 February 2016.
9 Lella Nouri and Nuria Lorenzo-Dus, 'Investigating Reclaim Australia and Britain First's Use of Social Media: Developing a New Model of Imagined Political Communities Online', *Journal for Deradicalization*, no. 18, Spring 2019, <https://journals.sfu.ca/jd/index.php/jd/article/view/183>, accessed 7 July 2019.
10 Cited by Imogen Richards, 'A Dialectical Approach to Online Propaganda: Australia's United Patriots Front, Right-Wing Politics, and Islamic State', *Studies in Conflict and Terrorism*, vol. 42, nos 1–2, 2019, pp. 43–69.
11 Kristy Campion, 'Australian Right Wing Extremist Ideology: Narratives of Nemesis and Nostalgia', *Journal of Policing, Intelligence and Counter Terrorism*, vol. 14, no. 3, 2019, pp. 208–26.
12 Other groups that contribute and adhere to the same ideological nexus are Identity Australia, the Nationalist Australian Alternative, Australian Traditionalism, the Australian Liberty Alliance, New National Action, and the somewhat amorphous and libertarian freeman/sovereign citizen movement.

13 Alex Mann, 'Haircuts and Hate: Inside Australia's Alt-Right', ABC News, 14 October 2018, <www.abc.net.au/radionational/programs/backgroundbriefing/haircuts-and-hate:-inside-the-rise-of-australias-alt-right/10365948>, accessed 3 July 2019.
14 Kevin Nguyen, 'Christchurch Shooter Brenton Tarrant Sent Death Threat Two Years before Attack', ABC News, 10 April 2019, <www.abc.net.au/news/2019-04-10/brenton-tarrant-alleged-christchurch-shooter-sent-death-threat/10952876>, accessed 3 December 2020.
15 *R v Tarrant: Sentencing Remarks of Mander J.*
16 Ecofascism was developed by prominent Nazis and Italian fascists during World War II, refined by the likes of Savitri Devi in the 1950s, and popularised in recent years on blogs and forums by ecofascists such as Pentti Linkola. Despite it murky and inglorious origins, it has developed significant currency in contemporary society.
17 James Mason, *Siege*, 2nd edn, posted by Ironmarch.org, 2003, p. 199.
18 Brenton Tarrant, 'The Great Replacement', manifesto, 2019.
19 Sam Levin, '"He Came to Kill Hispanics": Peaceful El Paso Left Wounded by Possible Hate Crime', *The Guardian*, 5 August 2019, <www.theguardian.com/us-news/2019/aug/04/el-paso-shooting-reaction-hate-crime-sheriff>, accessed 11 March 2021.
20 Patrick Crusius, 'An Inconvenient Truth', 8chan, 2019.
21 Jacod Aasland Ravndal et al., *Right-Wing Terrorism and Violence in Western Europe, 1990–2019*, Oslo: Centre for Research on Extremism (C-REX), University of Oslo, 2020.
22 'Neo-Nazi Group Praises Norwegian Mosque Shooter among Other Far-Right Terrorist Saints', SITE, 12 August 2019, <https://ent.siteintelgroup.com/Far-Right-/-Far-Left-Threat/neo-nazi-group-praises-norwegian-mosque-shooter-among-other-far-right-terrorist-saints.html>, accessed 11 March 2021.
23 Stephen Balliet, 'A Short Pre-Action Report', manifesto, 2019, accessed 3 June 2020.
24 Sam Levin, 'Police Thwarted at Least Seven Mass Shootings and White Supremacist Attacks since El Paso', *The Guardian*, 23 August 2019, <www.theguardian.com/world/2019/aug/20/el-paso-shooting-plot-white-supremacist-attacks>, accessed 24 October 2019.
25 Ben Strang, 'Muslims on High Alert after Report of Threat against Christchurch Mosque', Stuff, 3 March 2020, <www.stuff.co.nz/national/christchurch-shooting/119957352/muslims-on-high-alert-after-report-of-threat-against-christchurch-mosque?rm=a>, accessed 7 December 2020.
26 Nick McKenzie and Joel Tozer, 'Inside Racism HQ: How home-grown neo-Nazis are plotting white revolution', The Age, 16 August 2021, <https://www.theage.com.au/national/inside-racism-hq-how-home-grown-neo-nazis-are-plotting-a-white-revolution-20210812-p58i3x.html>, accessed 10 September 2021.
27 Daniel McCulloch and Matt Coughlan, 'Dutton Slams "Stupid" Counter-Terror Calls', *Canberra Times*, 4 December 2020, <www.canberratimes.com.au/story/7041125/dutton-slams-stupid-counter-terror-calls>, accessed 7 December 2020.
28 Jacinda Ardern, 'Jacinda Ardern's Speech at Christchurch Memorial—Full Transcript', *The Guardian*, 29 March 2019, <www.theguardian.com/world/2019/mar/29/jacinda-arderns-speech-at-christchurch-memorial-full-transcript>, accessed 6 December 2020.

EPILOGUE

1 'ASIO's Role in the Field of Politically Motivated Violence and Terrorism', ASIO Seminar, February 1976, Politically Motivated Violence and Terrorism, p. 38.

Bibliography

Select books on Australian terrorism and security
Blaxland, John, *The Official History of ASIO: The Protest Years 1963–1975*, Sydney: Allen & Unwin, 2016.
Blaxland, John and Rhys Crawley, *The Official History of ASIO: The Secret Cold War 1975–1989*, Sydney: Allen & Unwin, 2017.
Cain, Frank, *The Australian Security Intelligence Organization: An Unofficial History*, Cass Series: Studies in Intelligence, Ilford, England: F. Cass, 1994.
Cain, Frank, *Terrorism & Intelligence in Australia: A History of ASIO & National Surveillance*, Melbourne: Australian Scholarly Publishing, 2008.
Crown, James, *Australia: The Terrorist Connection*, South Melbourne: Sun Books, 1986.
Department of Foreign Affairs and Trade, *Transnational Terrorism: The Threat to Australia*, Canberra: Australian Government, 2004.
Harris, Steve, *The Prince and the Assassin: Australia's First Royal Tour and Portent of World Terror*, Melbourne: Melbourne Books, 2017.
Healey, Justin, *Terrorism and National Security*, Issues in Society, vol. 321, Thirroul, New South Wales: Spinney Press, 2011.
Hicks, David, *Guantanamo: My Journey*, North Sydney: William Heinemann, 2010.
Landers, Rachel, *Who Bombed the Hilton?*, Sydney: NewSouth Publishing, 2016.
Lynch, Andrew, Nicola McGarrity and George Williams, *Inside Australia's Anti-Terrorism Laws and Trials*, Sydney: NewSouth Publishing, 2015.
Moroney, Peter, *Terrorism in Australia: The Story of Operation Pendennis*, Sydney: New Holland Publishers, 2018.
Neighbour, Sally, *In the Shadow of Swords: On the Trail of Terrorism from Afghanistan to Australia*, Sydney: HarperCollins, 2004.
Peucker, M. and D. Smith (eds), *The Far-Right in Contemporary Australia*, Singapore: Springer Singapore, 2019.

Select scholarly research on terrorism in Australia
Bajc, V., 'National Security, Surveillance and Terror: Canada and Australia in Comparative Perspective', *Canadian Journal of Sociology*, 43(4), 2018, pp. 389–92, doi:10.29173/cjs29522.
Baldino, D. and Lucas, K., 'Anti-government rage: understanding, identifying and responding to the sovereign citizen movement in Australia', *Journal of Policing, Intelligence and Counter Terrorism*, 14(3), 2019, pp. 245–61, doi:10.1080/18335330.2019.1663443.

Brawley, S., '"Days of Rage" Downunder: Considering American Influences on "Home-Grown" Terrorism and ASIO's response in 1970s Australia', *Australian Historical Studies*, 47(2), 2016, pp. 295–310, doi:10.1080/1031461X.2016.1152587.

Campion, K., 'The Ustaša in Australia: A Review of Right-Wing Ustaša Terrorism from 1963–1973, and Factors that Enabled their Endurance', *Salus Journal*, 6(2), 2018, pp. 37–58.

Campion, K., 'Australian Right Wing Extremist Ideology: Narratives of Nemesis and Nostalgia', *Journal of Policing, Intelligence and Counter Terrorism*, 14(3), 2019a, pp. 208–26.

Campion, K., 'A "Lunatic Fringe"? The Persistence of Right Wing Extremism in Australia', *Perspectives on Terrorism*, 13(2), 2019b.

Campion, K., '"Unstructured terrorism"? Assessing left wing extremism in Australia', *Critical Studies on Terrorism*, 13(4), 2020, pp. 545–67, doi:10.1080/17539153.2020.1810992.

Cherney, A. and Murphy, K., 'Police and Community Cooperation in Counterterrorism: Evidence and Insights from Australia', *Studies in Conflict and Terrorism*, 40(12), 2017, pp. 1023–37, doi:10.1080/1057610X.2016.1253987.

Cherney, A. et al., 'Local service provision to counter violent extremism: perspectives, capabilities and challenges arising from an Australian service mapping project', *Behavioral Sciences of Terrorism and Political Aggression*, 10(3), 2018, pp. 187–206, doi:10.1080/19434472.2017.1350735.

Chubb, D., 'Perceptions of terrorism in Australia: 1978–2019', *Australian Journal of International Affairs*, 74(3), 2020, pp. 264–81, doi:10.1080/10357718.2020.1744515.

Evans, R., '"A Menace to This Realm": The New Guard and the New South Wales Police, 1931–32', *History Australia*, 5(3), 2008.

Grossman, M. and Tahiri, H., 'Community perceptions of radicalisation and violent extremism: An Australian perspective', *Journal of Policing, Intelligence and Counter Terrorism*, 10(1), 2015, pp. 14–24, doi:10.1080/18335330.2015.1028773.

Harris-Hogan, S., 'Australian Neo-Jihadist Terrorism: Mapping the Network and Cell Analysis Using Wiretap Evidence', *Studies in Conflict and Terrorism*, 35(4), 2012, pp. 298–314, doi:10.1080/1057610X.2012.656344.

Harris-Hogan, S., 'The importance of family: the key to understanding the evolution of jihadism in Australia', *Security Challenges*, 10(1), 2014, pp. 31–50.

Harris-Hogan, S. and Barrelle, K., 'Young Blood: Understanding the Emergence of a New Cohort of Australian Jihadists', *Terrorism and Political Violence*, 32(7), 2020, pp. 1391–412, doi:10.1080/09546553.2018.1473858.

Harris-Hogan, S., Barrelle, K. and Zammit, A., 'What is countering violent extremism? Exploring CVE policy and practice in Australia', *Behavioral Sciences of Terrorism and Political Aggression*, 8(1), 2016, pp. 6–24, doi:10.1080/19434472.2015.1104710.

Harris-Hogan, S. and Zammit, A., 'Mantiqi IV: Al-Qaeda's Failed Co-Optation of a Jemaah Islamiyah Support Network', *Democracy and Security*, 10(4), 2014a, pp. 315–34, doi:10.1080/17419166.2014.964860.

Harris-Hogan, S. and Zammit, A., 'The Unseen Terrorist Connection: Exploring Jihadist Links Between Lebanon and Australia', *Terrorism and Political Violence*, 26(3), 2014b, pp. 449–69, doi: 10.1080/09546553.2012.729541.

Hutchinson, J., Amarasingam, A., Scrivens, R. and Ballsun-Stanton, B., 'Mobilizing extremism online: comparing Australian and Canadian right-wing extremist groups on Facebook', *Behavioral Sciences of Terrorism and Political Aggression*, 2021, pp. 1–31, doi:10.1080/19434472.2021.1903064.

Lentini, P., 'Demonizing ISIL and Defending Muslims: Australian Muslim Citizenship and Tony Abbott's "Death Cult" Rhetoric', *Islam and Christian Muslim Relations*, 26(2), 2015, pp. 237–52, doi:10.1080/09596410.2015.1007605.

Lentini, P., 'The Neojihadist Cell as a Religious Organization: A Melbourne Jema'ah Case Study', *Journal for the Academic Study of Religion*, 30(1), 2017, pp. 22–51, doi:10.1558/jasr.31615.

Mullins, S., 'Islamist Terrorism and Australia: An Empirical Examination of the "Home-Grown" Threat', *Terrorism and Political Violence*, 23(2), 2011, pp. 254–85, doi:10.1080/09546553.2010.535717.

Mullins, S., 'Counter-terrorism in Australia: practitioner perspectives', *Journal of Policing, Intelligence and Counter Terrorism*, 11(1), 2016, pp. 93–111, doi:10.1080/18335330.2016.1161228.

Peucker, M., Lentini, P., Smith, D. and Iqbal, M., '"Our diggers would turn in their graves": nostalgia and civil religion in Australia's far-right', *Australian Journal of Political Science*, 56(2), 2021, pp. 189–205, doi:10.1080/10361146.2021.1935448.

Shuurman, B., Harris-Hogan, S., Zammit, A. and Lentini, P., 'Operation Pendennis: A Case Study of an Australian Terrorist Plot', *Perspectives on Terrorism*, 8(4), 2014.

Smith, E., 'Keeping the Nazi menace out: George Lincoln Rockwell and the Border Control System in Australia and Britain in the Early 1960s', *Social Sciences*, 9(9), 2020, doi:https://doi.org/10.3390/socsci9090158.

Williams, G. (2011). A decade of Australian anti-terror laws. *Melbourne University law review*, 35(3), 1136–76.

Zammit, A., 'Explaining a Turning Point in Australian Jihadism', *Studies in Conflict and Terrorism*, 36(9), 2013, pp. 739–55, doi:10.1080/1057610X.2013.813264.

Zammit, A., 'Australian Foreign Fighters: Risks and Responses', 2015, retrieved from www.lowyinstitute.org/sites/default/files/australian-foreign-fighters-risks-and-responses.pdf.

Zammit, A., 'The Role of Virtual Planners in the 2015 Anzac Day Terror Plot', *Security Challenges*, 13(1), 2017, pp. 41–58.

Select archival sources

Activities of Armenian Terrorists Part 2, 1981, Series A1209: Control 1981/1871 Part 2, National Archives of Australia, Canberra.

Activities of Armenian Terrorists Part 3, 1983, Series A1209: Control 1981/1871 Part 3, National Archives of Australia, Canberra.

Armenian Revolutionary Army Volume 1, 1983–85, Series A6122: Control 2743, National Archives of Australia, Canberra.

Armenian Revolutionary Army Volume 2, 1985–89, Series A6122: Control 2744, National Archives of Australia, Canberra.

ASIO, Nazi Party in Australia Membership Records, 1946–49, Series A6122/Control 161, National Archives of Australia, Canberra.

ASIO, Special Projects Branch documents 19 to 27: Note on the General Significance of the 'New Left' for the Western World, The 'New (Young) Left' in Australia: Recent Trends in Theory and Strategy, Student Revolutionary Activism: its Implications for the Promotion of Insurrectionary Warfare in Australia, Student Revolutionary Activism in Australia: an Appreciation of Significant Strategical and Tactical Concepts, Trends and Developments in Australia of Counter-Subversion Security Interest and Significance (December 1968), The Role and the Significance of Protest Action in providing 'New Left' Political Trends and Developments in Australia, The Significance of Militant Developments among Secondary School Students in Australia, Report of Anti-War Activists Conference held in Sydney January 27, 28, 29, c. 1968, Series A12389/Control A30, Part 7, National Archives of Australia, Canberra.

ASIO, Special Projects Branch documents 29 to 33: Significant trends and developments in the Australian 'New Left' Movement. Programme for revolution in the High Schools. Violence, political extremism and the revolutionary process in Australia—Basic elements and procedures. The penetration of the Army by the Communist Party of Australia during World War II, 1970, Series 12389: Control A30 Part 8, National Archives of Australia, Canberra.

ASIO, Special Projects Branch Documents 52 to 67: Terrorism, its nature, objectives and revolutionary role, A note on the past, present and future significance of Communism in Australia, Significant demonstrations, including violent incidents claimed by or attributed to terrorist-type groups like the People's Liberation Army, Worker-Student Alliance, the Utashi etc, A note on Terrorist activity, Trotskyism in Australia, The National Socialist Party of Australia (NSPA), Communist Party of Australia (CPA), Socialist Party of Australia (SPA), Comment on a Communist Party of Australia Discussion Document for its 23rd Congress (1971), A note on recent 'New Left' trends in the USA and their significance for the 'Left' in Australia, A note on the 'New Left' in Australia, Urban Guerilla Warfare including Anarchist and radical Violence, The Politically Motivated Act of Violence, Intelligence Report, c. 1971, Series A30/Control A12389, Part 14, National Archives of Australia, Canberra.

ASIO, Special Projects Branch documents 43–45, 1971a, Series 12389/Control A30 Part 12, National Archives of Australia, Canberra.

ASIO, Terrorism and Violence in Australia—Decision 1406 [Cabinet Decision], 1971b, Series A5908: Control 896, National Archives of Australia, Canberra.

ASIO, Seminar February 1976: Politically Motivated Violence and Terrorism, 1976a, Series: 12391/Control R86, National Archives of Australia, Canberra.

ASIO, Special Projects Branch documents 34, 37, 38, 1976b, Series A12389/Control A30 Part 9, National Archives of Australia, Canberra.

ASIO, Cabinet Memorandum 281—Australian Security Intelligence Organisation (ASIO)—National and International Security Committee of Cabinet 25 October 1983—briefing on the Armenian Terrorist Alert—Decision 2351/NIS, 1983a, Series A13978/Control 281, National Archives of Australia, Canberra.

ASIO, Cabinet Memorandum 303—ASIO Submission to the National and International Security Committee of Cabinet—on the Armenian Terrorist Alert—Decision 2053, 1983b, Series A13978/Control 303, National Archives of Australia, Canberra.

Assassination of the Turkish Consul General in Sydney by the Armenian Genocide Justice Commando 17 December 1980 Volume 2, 1980–81, Series A6122/Control 2885, National Archives of Australia, Canberra.

Assassination of the Turkish Consul General in Sydney by the Armenian Genocide Justice Commando 17 December 1980 Volume 3, 1981, Series A6122/Control 2886, National Archives of Australia, Canberra.

Assassination of the Turkish Consul General in Sydney by the Armenian Genocide Justice Commando 17 December 1980 Volume 4, 1981–83, Series A6122/Control 2887, National Archives of Australia, Canberra.

Assassination of the Turkish Consul General in Sydney by the Armenian Genocide Justice Commando 17 December 1980 Volume 5, 1983–91, Series A6122/Control 2888, National Archives of Australia, Canberra.

Branch, C.I., Nazi Activities—Western Australia [with lists of names of Germans], 1935–46, Series A8911/Control 18, National Archives of Australia, Canberra.

Cabinet Submission 2754—Government response to the final reports of the Royal Commission on Australia's Security and Intelligence Agencies (RCASIA)—Decision 5605/SEC, 7 May 1985, Series A14039/Control 2754, National Archives of Australia, Canberra.

Central Intelligence Agency, Yugoslavia—The Ustashi and the Croatian Separatist Problem, 1972, Office of National Assessments, United States of America.

Committee, F.A.a.D., Location of Counter Terrorist Offshore Installations Assault Team (OAT) [Cabinet Minute], 22 July 1981, Decision 16443/Submission 4849, National Archives of Australia, Canberra.

Committee, F.A.a.D., Army Counter Terrorist Facilities—Decision 6783/SEC—Submission 3145, 4 November 1985, Series A14039/Control 3145, National Archives of Australia, Canberra.

Committee, I.a.S., Establishment of a Counter Terrorist Reaction Force [Cabinet Minute], 3 May 1979, Decision 8230/Submission 3098, National Archives of Australia, Canberra.

Croation Extremism—Note from Yugoslavia to Australian Minister—Belgrade, 1972, Series A432/Control 1972/5905, National Archives of Australia, Canberra.

Croation Terrorism: Relations with Yugoslav Government—Part 2, 1975, Series A5034/Control 1973/2136 Part 2, National Archives of Australia, Canberra.

Croation Terrorism: Relations with Yugoslav Government—Part 5, 1977–78, Series A5034/Control 1973/2136 Part 5, National Archives of Australia, Canberra.

Department of Foreign Affairs, C.O., Entry into Australia—Abdul Hamid Abdulla Azzam Al Fatah—Agent, 1973–74, Series A1838/Control 1453/4531 Part 1, National Archives of Australia, Canberra.

Department of Customs and Excise, Importation of Nazi stickers, 1963, Series A425/Control 1963/13478, National Archives of Australia, Canberra.

Immigration, D.o., Nazi Party—National Socialist German Workers Party—NSDAP, 1979–86, Series A6980/Control S251141, National Archives of Australia, Canberra.

Indonesia—Islam—Islamic Extremism Part 2, 1975–79, Series 1838/Control 3034/5/1/1, National Archives of Australia, Canberra.

Indonesia—Islam—Islamic Extremism Part 3, 1979–80, Series A1838/Control 3034/5/1/1 Part 3, National Archives of Australia, Canberra.

Inquiry before Mr Justice Harvey re certain Internees, Irish Republican Brotherhood, c. 1920, Series A5522/Control M770, National Archives of Australia, Canberra.

Investigation into the activities of Ananda Marga in Australia [Submission Nos. 1805, 1848, 1984, 2747 and 3975 refer], 1977–80, Series A10756/Control LC1718 Part 1, National Archives of Australia, Canberra.

Middle East Crisis 1967—Arab Terrorist—Abdul Hamid—Abdullah Azzam, 1967–73, A1838: 181/18/1 Part 1, National Archives of Australia, Canberra.

Middle East Crisis 1967—Arab Terrorist—Abdul Hamid—Abdullah Azzam, 1967–73, A1838: 181/18/1 Part 2, National Archives of Australia, Canberra.

Nazi Activities—Western Australia, 1939–46, Series A8911/Control 18, National Archives of Australia, Canberra.

Police, D.o., Ustashi—Alleged Croatian Terrorist Organisation, 1964–83, Series 39/Item 37399, Queensland State Archives, Brisbane.

Submission No 1805: Interim Report on Commonwealth Recognition or Assistance to the Ananda Marga—Decision 4252(IS), October 1977–November 1977, A12909: 1805, National Archives of Australia, Canberra.

Terrorism—Ananda Marga—Submissions, 1978–80, Series 1838/Control 1652/3/3 Part 2, National Archives of Australia, Canberra.

'Yugoslav denies he aided Nazis', *Canberra Times,* 14 April 1972, p. 3, retrieved from nla.gov.au/nla.news-article102209679.

Yugoslavia—Foreign policy—Extremism—General Part 14, 1977–78, Series A1838/ Control 73/1/3/13 Part 14, National Archives of Australia, Canberra.

Yugoslavia—Foreign policy—Extremism—General Part 25, 1979–1979, Series A1838/Control 73/1/3/13 Part 25, National Archives of Australia, Canberra.

Yugoslavia—Foreign policy—Relations with Australia—Extremism Part 27, 1979–1979, Series A1838/Control 73/1/3/13 Part 27, National Archives of Australia, Canberra.

Yugoslavia—Foreign policy—Relations with Australia—Extremism—Part 31, 1980–81, Series A1838/Control 73/1/3/13 Part 31, National Archives of Australia, Canberra.

Index

1%er (one percenter) 287

A
abadhutas 125
Abase, Amira 308
Abbasid caliphs 233
Abbott, Tony 283–4, 288
Abbullatif, Mahmoud 307
Abby, Hodan 307
Abdulla, Bilal 270
Abdul-Rahman, Taha 267
Abolish Self Government Coalition 206
Abu Ghraib 280
acaryas 125, 127–8
accelerationism 326, 328–9
Adam, Abu *see* Raad, Mounir
Ad Hoc Committee on Palestine 90–1
Adrian IV, Pope 14
Adriatic and Adria Travel agency bombings 61, 76
Advance Australia *see* Restore Australia
Ağca, Mehmet Ali 165
Ahmed, Abdirahman 274–6
Ahmed, Kafeel 270
Ahmed, Sabeel 270
aide-mémoire 76, 83
AK-47 257
Ajmani, Jagdish 134, 146
Alagh, R. 132
Alameddine, Talal 294
Al 'Asifah 88, 95, 101

al-Assad, President Bashar 281
al-Australie, Abu Yousef *see* Kamleh, Tareq
al-Baghdadi, Abu Bakr 277, 281–2
Albury–Wodonga 66, 332–3
Aleph *see* Aum Shinrikyo
Alexander, Jason Holman 127, 138, 143, 145, 148, 150
Alexander I, King of Yugoslavia 62–3
Alexanian, Nina 167, 169, 173
Al Farouk camp 255, 257, 267
al-Faruq, Omar 238, 240–1
Al Fatah
  the Azzam affair 87–9, 100–7
  bombing of consulate and club 110–12
  countering pro-Palestinian extremism 111–14
  domestic connections and support 95–8, 102, 109–10
  historical emergence 36, 88–92
  ideology, factors and fronts 92–6
  international connections 88, 93–7, 99–100, 110
  leadership 87, 95–7
  terrorism activities 99–100, 107–9
Alfred, Duke of Edinburgh 11–14, 16–18
al-Ghozi, Fathur Roman 241–2
Al Hadaf magazine 107
Al-Hayat Media Centre 283
al Iraqi, Abu Nour 308–9
Alister, Paul Shawn 144–5, 146–7, 148

al-Kalaylah, Ahmad Fadhil Nazzal 271, 277, 280–2
al-Kambudi, Abu Khalid *see* Prakash, Neil
Al-Karamah Refugee Camp 95
Al-Kutobi, Omar 292–3
al-Lubnani, Abu Mansour 308
al-Lubnani, Abu Ubaida 307–8
al-Maqdisi, Abu Mohammed 280
Almaouie, Jibryl 291
Almaouie, Mohammed 286, 291
al-Muhajir, Sheikh Abu Sulayman 305
Al Noor Islamic Centre *see* mosques
Al Noor Mosque *see* mosques
Alou, Raban 294
Al-Qaeda
  affiliates and allies 253, 260, 271, 273, 276–7, 280–1
  camps, training and operational 254, 257, 260
  connections with Jemaah Islamiyah 232, 236–44, 247, 250
  counter action 251–2, 255–9, 261–2, 264
  domestic cells inspired by 264–9
  domestic support for 258–63, 265–6, 287, 297–8, 305
  ideology and context 252–4
  statements and claims 244–5, 263–4
  11 September attacks 137, 227–8, 241–2
Alqudsi, Hamdi 309
Al-Shabaab
  emergence and ideology 273
  counter action against 275–6
  Preston cell 273–6
al-Suri, Abu Musab 266, 272, 292
al-wala' wal-bara' 253
al-Zawahiri, Ayman 240, 254, 277, 281, 305
Amundsen, John Howard 269, 271
Ananda Marga (Ánanda Márga Pracáraka Saṁgha)
  counter action against 128–9, 133, 135–8, 142–8, 153
  domestic presence and support 126–7
  Hilton Hotel bombing 121–2, 140–2
  ideology and practices 122–5, 127–8
  other violent extremist activities 129–34, 145–6, 150–2
  sectors and splinters 125–6, 129–30, 138–9
  statements and claims 132, 134, 136

Anandmurti, Shri *see* Sarkar, Prabhat Ranjan
Anarchist Cookbook 152
Anderson, Benedict 183
Anderson, Colin 97
Anderson, John Rex 204
Anderson, Tim 143–6, 148
Andric, Adolf 65, 71, 75–6
Andrić, Ambroz 65, 69–70, 71, 75–6
Anic, Bozenko 82
Antifa (antifascist) 333
anti-government agitators 181, 206
Antipodean Resistance 190, 324
anti-vaxxers 333
anti-war 38, 51, 58
apartheid 55–6, 200
Arab–Israeli War 91
Arab League 92
Arab Liberation Front 96
Arafat, Yasser 87, 94–5, 101
Ardern, Jacinta 312, 334
Arena newsletter 46
Ariyak, Sarik
  assassination of 154, 162–3
  protection of 162, 165, 168
Armenian Revolutionary Army 174–5, 177–9
Armenian Revolutionary Federation 156, 159–61, 164–6, 177, 179
Armenian Revolutionary Federation – Revolutionary Movement 177
Armenian Revolutionary Federation – Youth Federation 159–61, 167
  camps 170, 172–3
  domestic sympathisers 169
  organisational links 174, 176
Armenian Secret Army for the Liberation of Armenia
  domestic ties 165–6
  emergence 160
  terrorism activities 161–2, 171, 177–9
Arnasan 231, 244
Aryan Nations 206, 327
Ashjian, Abraham Ago 160, 174
ash Shami, Abu Yahya *see* Raad, Mounir
assassination plans
  hit lists 72, 108, 187
  kill list 149, 190, 306
asylum 80, 286
Atai, Milad 286, 293–4

INDEX

Atatürk, President Kemal 157
Atef, Mohammed 238, 241–2, 246
Athos, Peter 150, 152
Atik, Izzydeen 266, 269
Atomwaffen Division 328, 332
Attash, Khaled bin 255
Attawaheedi, Abu Mohamed *see* Khazal, Bilal
Attlee, Clement 31
Augustina, Mira 238
Aum Shinrikyo
  activity in Australia 214–17
  counter action 215–16, 219–20
  emergence and ideology 209–12
  violent and terrorism activities 217–20
  weapons programs 212–14, 216–17
Aum Shinsen no Kai 209
AUSI Freedom Scouts 206
Auslandsorganisation (overseas organisation) 185–86
Aussenhandelsamt (Foreign Trade Office) 185
Aussies against Racism 199
Australia–Croatia Society 66
Australia First Movement 187
Australian American Association 50
Australian Arab Association 98
Australian Aryan Army 197
Australian Capital Territory Police 146, 150, 153
Australian Defence Force 142, 257, 261, 287
Australian Defence League 319
Australian Federal Police
  establishment of 153
  protection duties 168, 174
  terrorism investigations 111–12, 178, 216, 219, 245–6, 264, 270, 273, 275–6, 285, 287, 291
Australian Hammerskin Nation 316
Australian Labor Party 53, 58, 153, 191
Australian League of Rights 187–9, 324
Australian Liberation Army 43, 44, 48–52, 54, 58–60
Australian Liberation Front 52
Australian Nationalist Movement
  counter actions against 202–4
  criminal activities of 199–201
  emergence and ideology 195–7
  poster campaign 197–8
  violent extremism 182, 198–201

Australian National Socialist Movement 191
Australian National Socialist Party 189
Australian National Workers Party
  see Australian National Socialist Movement
Australian-Palestinian Solidarity Committee 97
Australian Party 189
Australian Public Service 192
Australian Security Intelligence Organisation
  agent activities 39, 58, 109, 143–4, 147, 173
  prominent assessments and estimates 44, 49, 97, 106, 129, 139, 176, 333
  select surveillance activities 101–2, 136, 167–70, 174, 189, 205, 261
  targeted by extremists/terrorists 51–2, 259, 285
  Venona and establishment of 30–1
Australian Security Service 30, 185
authoritarianism 182–3, 195, 207, 325
Awadhoot, Madhwanand 149
Aweys, Saney 273–6
Ayers, Bill 41
Ayub, Abdul Rahim 238–40, 265
Ayub, Abdul Rahman 239, 265
Azari, Omarjan 285–86
Azmi, Jemal 157
Azzam, Abdullah 236–7, 267
Azzam, Abdulhamid Abdulla *see* Khushia, Ibrahim Ismail Abdullah el Khatib

B

Baader, Andreas 41
Ba'asyir, Abu Bakar 236, 238–40, 248, 250
Baba *see* Sarkar, Prabhat Ranjan
Bachtiar, General Da'i 248
Bain, John 199–200, 202
Bakr, Abu *see* Benbrika, Abdul Nacer
Baladjam, Omar 265, 268
Balian, Dzovig 165–6
Bali bombings 230–2, 243–7
Balkar, Galip 168
Balliet, Stephan 331
Barnett, Harvey 136
Barthou, Louis 63

Bartle, Christopher 197, 199, 202
Baryalei, Mohammad Ali 285, 306, 309
Base 328, 332
Basmadjian, Aram 166
Basmadjian, Esther 166
Bassam, Abu 109
Batra, Ravi 125
Battalion88 322
Bayaat al-Imam (Pledge of Allegiance) 280
Bay'ah 291
Bayda, Sameh 286
Bayston, Martin 205–6
Belmore, Somerset Richard Lowry-Corry, Fourth Earl of 11
Benbrika, Abdul Nacer 265–8, 206
Bennett, John 239
Berg, Nicholas 280
Besim, Sevdet Ramadan 294–5
Bey, Nazim 157
Beydoun, Mohammed Ali 111–12
Bidarp, Christine 122
Bilardi, Jake 306
Billings, Matthew 316
bin Laden, Osama
  death 277, 281
  engagement with Australian context 255, 257, 262, 265–7
  engagement with Indonesian context 236, 238, 240, 241, 244
  engagement with Islamic State 280
Black September Organisation
  counter action against 113–14
  domestic links 95, 106
  Munich Olympics attack 88, 94
  other terrorist attacks 94, 99–100, 105
  trans-organisational links 89, 93–5, 107
Blake, Murray 141
Blood and Honour 206, 315–16, 318–19, 322
Boghossian, Mardik 166–7
border security 5, 36, 97, 114, 120
Boulten, Phillip 259
Bozkurt (Grey Wolves) 165–6
Brahmacaris 125, 127
Breivik, Anders 320, 323, 325
Bremer, Paul 279–80
Brennan, Catherine 321
Breslin, John 19
Bridges, Simon 312

Brighton Siege 297–8
Brigitte, Willie 260
Brook, Gary 245
Brooks, F.H. 52
Browne, Frank 189
Browning, Justine 303
Bund des Deutschtums in Australien und Neuseeland 186
Burmistriw, Paul 122
Burrows, J.B. 105
Butcher of Trebizond *see* Azmi, Jemal
Butković, Ante 65, 81, 83
Butler, David 141
Butler, Eric 188–9

C
Caday, Leonidas 240
Cairns, Jim 53, 68, 71
Cameron, Robert 144–5, 192, 194–5
Camp Bucca 281
Campbell, Eric 186
Canada 64, 79, 83, 125, 171, 175–6, 189, 245
Canbolat, Ismail 155–7
Carlos the Jackal *see* Sánchez, Ilich Ramírez
Carter, Alec 121–2
Catalpa 19–21
Catch the Fire Ministries 318
Cawthorn, Edward 190
Cawthorn, Michael 112
Cerminara, Ralph 319
Chaarani, Abdullah 293
Chand, Ramish 133
Charida, Fuad 96
Cheikho, Khaled 265, 268
Cheikho, Moustafa 268
Chifley, Ben 31
Christchurch terror attack 311–14, 325, 329–32, 334
Citizens Military Forces 54, 66
citizenship 18, 188
  dual 79–80
  excluding from, 63, 136, 184, 193–4
civil aviation authorities 101, 113
Clan na Gael (Clan of the Irish) 18–19, 21, 24
Clayton, Walter Seddon 30
Coco Pops Jihadi 307Cold War 37, 38, 148

INDEX

Collins, Michael 29
colonialism 153
　Indonesian opposition to 232
　Irish opposition to 9–10, 13–18, 24, 29
　Palestinian opposition to 92
Combat 18 315–16, 318–19, 332
committees
　Ad Hoc Committee on Palestine 90–1
　Ananda Marga committees 127
　Australian-Palestinian Solidarity Committee 97
　May 10 Action Committee 56
　National and International Security Committee of Cabinet 169
　Special Interdepartmental Committee on Counter Terrorism 109, 113
　Special Interdepartmental Committee on Domestic Violence 113
　Steering Committee of the National Front 193
Commonwealth Police 30, 72, 77–8, 80, 102–5, 113
　action against Ananda Marga 129, 140, 142–6, 151, 153
communication
　encrypted applications 292, 300, 302, 322, 332
　hand signals 288
　invisible ink 23, 25
　secret code 25, 27, 101, 145–6, 173, 242, 275, 291
Communist International (Comintern) 39
Communist Party of Australia 39, 53, 54, 57–8
Confederate Action Party 206
conscription 44, 47
　opposition to 44, 47–8, 54, 56–8
　policy for 36–8, 40
　slogans 50, 53, 55
Cooks Convicts 323
Counter Espionage Bureau 25–6, 30
Cowan, Sir Zelman 141
Crazy White Boys 318
Creativity Movement 318
Criminal Investigation Bureau 30, 145
Criminal Investigative Service 30–1
Croatian Illegal Revolutionary Organisation 73–4

Croatian Liberation Movement 64–6, 69, 84
Croatian National Resistance 65, 70, 79, 83
Croatian Revolutionary Brotherhood 65–7, 72, 79, 81–3
Cross, William George 13
Crusius, Patrick 329–30
Customs, Australian 36, 101, 114, 169, 215–16

D

Dabiq magazine 282–3, 291, 298
Dabit, Yousef 96
Dahman, Adam 306
Dahman, Maryann 306
Dajani, Thabt 95
Dalton, Maurice 23–4, 27
Darakjian, Hagop 160
Darragh, Thomas 18
Darul Islam Heroes 233, 235–6
Dashnak Party/Dashnaksutyun
　see Armenian Revolutionary Federation
Dashnak Party – Youth Federation
　see Armenian Revolutionary Federation – Youth Federation
Davidson, Nathan 323
Dawson, Katrina 278, 290–1
Dean-Willcocks, James 318
Demirian, Levon 169–70, 172, 177–8
democracy, opposition within
　extreme right ideology 120, 183, 195
　Salafi Jihadist ideology 252, 254
Demolition Man *see* Husin, Dr Azahari
Department of Defence 25, 143, 149, 234
Department of External Affairs 30, 68, 186
Department of Foreign Affairs and Trade 162, 173, 193, 243
Department of Labour and National Service
　see National Service
Desai, Morarji 133–4, 139–40, 142, 148
Desmond, Thomas 19
Deva, Hari 129
Devoy, John 18–19, 21, 24–6
Dharma magazine 132
Dirani, Mustafa 294

DK's Boys 265
Dobson, Kevin Townley 191
Dohrn, Bernardine 41
Dolstra, Derek 45–6
Donaldson, Ian Stuart 315
Donelian, Seta 173
Donelian, Silva 167–70, 173
Doran, John 22–5
Dragoja, Ljubomir 81, 84
Droudis, Amirah 287
Dryer, Albert Thomas 23–4, 26–8
Duff, John William 130–2
Duman, Zehra 307
Dunn, Ross Anthony 144–5, 148
Duong, Minh 318–19
Durack, Peter 136, 164
Dutton, Peter 333
Dylan, Bob 41

E
Ebb, Bill 121–2
ecofascism *see* fascism
Elbaf, Bilal 307
Elbaf, Hamza 307
Elbaf, Omar 307
Elbaf, Taha 307
el Bileisi, Abdel Kadar *see* Meziani, Hamid
elections 48, 190, 192, 197, 212–13, 234
Elkington, L.N. 104
Elmir, Abdullah 308
Elomar, Ahmed 264–5
Elomar Jr, Mohamed Ali 264–5, 267–8, 308
Elomar Sr, Mohamed Ali 264–5, 267–8
Emmet Society 15
Endo, Seiichi 213–15
Engels, Friedrich 22
English Defence League 319
Enright, Thomas Patrick 80–1
Ensslin, Gudrun 41
Erdogan, Recep Tayyip 180
Ergun, Enver 175
ethnostate 182, 184, 229
Eurabia conspiracy 319–20
Eureka Students League 192
Eureka Youth League 192
European Australian Movement 332
Evatt, Herbert Vere 90–1
exclusionary nationalism *see* nationalism
extreme right *see* right-wing extremism

F
Farag, Mostafa *see* al-Muhajir, Sheikh Abu Sulayman
fascism 184–86, 206
  ecofascism 326–8, 330
  fascist organisations 185–6
Fatah, Fouad Abdel *see* Meziani, Hamid
Fattal, Wissam 273–6
Favel, William 121–2
Fenian Brotherhood 14–15, 18, 23
Ferguson, Mark 199, 202–3
Fitzgerald, Thomas A. 24, 27
foreign terrorist fighters
  to Iraq and Syria 282–3, 299, 301, 305–10
  to Ukraine 322
  to Yugoslavia 35–6, 67, 75–6
Fraser, Malcolm 83, 141, 148, 153
Free Aceh Movement 235
Fremantle gaol break 18–21
French, Lord 22
front organisations 68
Frost, Cliff 246
Frost, Jason 200
Fumic, Mika 67
Funde, Eddie 200
Furlan, Robert Valentin 194

G
Gaelic American magazine 24
Galatea 11–13
Galea, Phillip 323–4
Gaza 95, 115–16
Gazette 21
General Post Office *see* Post Office
Georgette 20
Ghazzawy, Ibrahim 291–2
Gietzelt, Arthur 191
Girls Seva Dal 138–9
Girls Volunteers *see* Girls Seva Dal
Gjokmarkovic, Father Marko 69
Greason, David 194
great replacement *see* replacement theory
Greenhalgh, Wayne 296
Greenwood, Ivor 61, 71, 75, 77–8, 113
Griffiths, Terry 122
Guevara, Che 36, 40
Gugenberger, Louis 68–9
Gurey, Joseph *see* Khushia, Ibrahim Ismail Abdullah el Khatib
Gutnick, Joe 239

INDEX

H

Habash, George 96
Haddara, Amer 266–9
Hagopian, Hagop 160
Haider, Abdul Numan 284–5, 294–5, 307
Hakoah Club bombing 110–12
Hamaguchi, Tadahito 217–18
Hambali *see* Isamuddin, Riduan
Hamid, Mustafa 239
Haneef, Dr Mohamed 270–1
Hannan, George 73
Hao, Nick 297
Haq, Huda bin Abdul 243–4
Harders, C.W. 103
Harrington, Michael 18
Harte, Gerald 226
Harvey, John Musgrave 27–8
Hasan, Abdul Rakib 265, 267–8
Hashim, Asman 239
Hassan, Basil 302
Hathaway, Henry 21
Hawke, Bob 108
Hawtin, John 122
Hayakallah, Sheikh 274–5
Hayakawa, Kiyohide 214–15
Heintjes, Antonius 194
Henry II 14
Hicks, David 254, 256–8
Hill, Gordon 198
Hilton hotel bombing 121–2, 140–1
Hitler, Adolf 157, 184, 187, 190, 196, 205, 287, 323
Holt, Mike 320
Hornby, P.A. 48
Hort, Jacob Marshall 319
Horvat, Djuro 75–6
Hougoumont 18
Hovespian, Nubar 114
Hudson, Shannon 318–19
Hurford, Chris 48
Husin, Dr Azahari 243–4, 246, 248–9
Hussein, Irfaan 294, 307
Hussein, Junaid 295
Hussein, Saddam 279
Hutchinson, Rabiyah *see* Hutchinson, Robyn Mary
Hutchinson Robyn Mary 238, 265

I

ideology 2–4
Immigration Control Association 195
imperialism, American 38, 40–1, 45
Imron, Ali 244, 246
Industrial Workers of the World 27
Innes, Ted 153
Inoue, Yoshihiro 214–15
Inspire magazine 272–3
Interpol 77–8, 81
Irish anti-colonialism
 attempted assassination of Prince Alfred 16–18
 domestic groups 15–17, 21–9
 emergence and ideology 12–13
 international groups and networks 18–22, 29–30
Irish National Association 23–4
Irish National Society 28–9
Irish Republican Army 29–30
Irish Republican Brotherhood 15–16, 18, 21–3, 29–30
Irish Republican Brotherhood–Australia 23
 counter action against 26–9
 domestic presence 23–5
 emergence and ideology 14–15, 21–2
Irish Volunteers 21–2
Irving, G.G.H. 28
Isamuddin, Riduan 237–3, 246
Islamic State
 counter action against 283, 285–93, 295–7, 304
 domestic cells 291–3, 301–5
 emergence and ideology 277, 279–84
 foreign terrorist fighters 305–9
 Lindt Café siege 278–9, 286–91
 lone actors, inspired and assisted 284–6, 293–301
 statements and claims 283–4, 298, 308, 310
 trans-organisational links 250, 273, 277, 281, 292
Islamic State of Iraq and Syria *see* Islamic State
Islamic Youth Movement 235
Israeli Consulate bombing 110–12
Italian Red Brigades 160

J

Jabar, Farhad Khalil Mohammad 293–5
Jabar, Shadi 293–4, 307
Jaber, Ibrahim Abou 95
Jabhat al-Nusra 281–2
Jaish-e-Mohammed 267
Jama, Sharky 307
Jama'at al-Tawhid wa'al-Jihad 280
Jamal, Mohammed Omar 265, 268
Jamal, Saleh 265, 268
Japanese Red Army 110, 114, 120, 160
jayhiliyyah 233, 252–3
Jekic, George 135
Jemaah Ansharut Daulah 250
Jemaah Ansharut Tauhid 250
Jemaah Islamiyah
    Bali bombings 230–32, 243
    counter action 243, 245–7, 249–50
    domestic presence in Australia 238–40
    emergence and ideology 232–7
    terrorism activities 240–3, 247–9
    ties to Al Qaeda 232, 236–8, 242–3
Jack Jihad Jack *see* Thomas, Joseph Jack
Johnson, Tori 278–9, 288–91
Jones, Andrew 47–8
Jones, Gerry 77
Jones, Timothy 129
Jordan, Colin 191
Joud, Aimen 266–8
Jurjevic, Marjan 68, 70–1, 73, 75
Justice Commandos of the Armenian Genocide
    assassination of the Turkish consul-general and his bodyguard 154–5, 162–3
    counter action including surveillance activity 163–75, 178
    domestic presence 159–61, 164–5, 169–73
    emergence and ideology 155–61
    statements and claims 155, 163, 175
    terrorism activities 156–7, 161–3, 168–72, 175–9
    trans-organisational links and rivalry 160–1, 175, 177, 179
    Turkish consulate bombing 177–8

K

Kahan, M.J. 191
Kamleh, Tareq 307
Karabegovic, Adnan 272
Karker, Hana 95
Karroum, Amira 307
Kartosuwiryo, Sekarmadji Maridjan 233
Kasic, Reverend Josip 67
Kassab, Dullel 307
Kent, Shane 266–8
Keshishian, Hagob 166
Keshishian, Nerses 165–6
Keskic, Vejsil 75
Keverian, Krikor 169–73
Khaja, Tamim Sahil 296
Khalid, Sulayman 291–2
Khan, Ihsas 296
Khasho, Joseph 109
Khayat, Amer 303–4
Khayat, Dianne 303
Khayat, Khaled 302
Khayat, Mahmoud 302–4
Khayat, Rana 303
Khayat, Tarek 302–5
Khayre, Yacqub 274–6, 297–9
Khazal, Bilal 262–5
Khomeini, Grand Ayatollah Ruhollah 233
Kiad, Mohammad 292–3
Kitchener, Lord 89
Klavins, Daniel Tyrone 316
Kokic, Ivica 64–5
Komando Jihad 235–6
Krull, Walter Heinrich Edward Wilhelm 194
Ku Klux Klan 196, 206, 315, 318, 327
Kumar, Abhiik *see* Alexander, Jason Holman
Kurdistan Workers Party 160, 166, 225, 227
Kushia, Ibrahim Ismail Abdullah el Khatib
    deportation 105–6, 114
    identity 103–6
    interviews 87–8, 102–4
    Melbourne 101–2
    travel record 104, 105

L

Laden, Osama bin *see* bin Laden, Osama
Lads Society 189, 324, 332
Lane, David 315
Lashkar-e-Taiba 253–4, 260–2, 265, 273, 277
Lawrence, Kerry 151
Lazhari *see* Bassam, Abu

left-wing extremism
   cult heroes and leaders 40–1
   emergence and embedment 37–40
   New Left ideology 39–40
Leibler, Isi 108
Lesic, Tomislav 68
Levonian, Hagob 177–8
Liba, Moshe 111
Liberation Tigers of Tamil Eelam 225–7
Lindt Café siege 278–9, 286–91
Lipski, Sam 108
Locke, David 204–5
Lodhi, Faheem Khalid 259–62
Lone Ranger of Leicester see Mark, Sir Robert
Lot's Wife magazine 43
Lovokovic, Fabian 64, 84
Lowry, Clare 110
Loyal Regiment of Australian Guardians 206
Luburić, Vjekoslav 'Maks' 65, 81
Lyons, Judith 197–204

M
Ma, Fiona 289–91
Magarditch, Agop 170–2
Maglicic, Milan 74–5, 79
Makarov, Semen Ivanovich 30
Malaspina, Sisto 299
Mallah, Zaky 258–9
Mallard, Trevor 312
Manshaus, Philip 330–1
Manteghi, Mohammed Hassan 286–91
mantiqis 237, 243–4
   Mantiqi IV 238–40
Marcuse, Herbert 39
Marighella, Carlos 40
Mark, Sir Robert 153
Marsh, Wanda 321
Marvak, Mladenko 74–5
Marx, Karl 39
   Marxism 96, 160
   Marxist–Leninism 47, 225
Mashni 95
Mason, James 328, 332
Matte-Hado, George 297
Mavros, Michael Hayson see Manteghi, Mohammed Hassan
May, Jeremy 192–3
McGing, Michael 24–8

McGuiness, William 24–8
McKeown, Frank 27–8
McMahon, William 77–8
McSweeney, Edmund 24–8
Melke, Edmond 98, 102–3, 106
Melrose, Stephan 226
Meneghini, Michael 134–6
Merhi, Abdul-Karem 303
Merhi, Abdullah 266–9
message boards 312, 330
Meziani, Hamid 95
Mihailović, General Draža 73, 83
Mike the Bomber see al-Ghozi, Fathur Roman
Miles, William J. 187
Miller, Kane 321
Mills, Alexander Rud 187
Minier, David 158
Mir, Sajid 260
Mishra, Lalit Narayan 129
Mohamed, Ahmed 293
Mohamed, Hafsa 307
Mohamed, Walid 274
Mohammad, Sheikh Feiz 264–5
Mohammed, Khalid Sheikh 237–43, 246
Molnar, Ferenc 190
Molomby, Tom 148
Monaghan, William Patrick 204–5
Monis, Man Haron see Manteghi, Mohammed Hassan
Morgan, J.H. 87–8
Morgan, Patrick 45
Moro Islamic Liberation Front 236–7, 241, 243
Morton, Lawrence Ronald 194
Morton-Hoffman, Jarrod 289–91
Mosleh, Sami see Rish, Munif Mohammed Abou
Mosley, Oswald 191
mosques and Islamic centres
   Al-Furqan Islamic Centre (Springvale) 284, 294, 306
   Al Noor Mosque (Christchurch) 311–13, 332, 334
   Al Noor Islamic Centre (Bærum) 331
   Linwood Islamic Centre (Christchurch) 313
   Preston Mosque 273–4
   Shia mosque 293
   Suleymaniye Mosque (Perth) 319

Moukhaiber, Hatim 293
Mucklas *see* Haq, Huda bin Abdul
Mudrinic, Ivan 73–5
Mukhlas *see* Haq, Huda bin Adul
Murphy, Lionel 78–9
Mussolini, Benito 62–3, 184, 187

N
Nagaoka, Hiroyuki 218
Nakagawa, Tomomasa 214–17
Namoa, Alo-Bridget 286
Namrawi, Ibrahim 96–7
Napier, Wayne Robert 204–5
Naruhito, Prince 214
Nasser, Gamal Abdel 92
National Action
  emergence and ideology 195–6
  links to Australian Nationalist Movement 196
  violent extremism 196, 200, 204
National Alliance 195
National Front Australia
  emergence and establishment 192–5
  leaders 144
National Resistance Group 195
national service
  opposition to 37, 40
  targeted premises 47, 49–52, 56
National Socialism *see* Nazism
National Socialist German Workers Party 184–5
National Socialist Network 332–3
National Socialist Party Australia 190–3
nationalism
  Armenian 173
  ethnonationalism 184, 186
  exclusionary 182–4, 187
  Palestinian 92
  white 324, 326
Natsir, Mohammad 234
Nazism
  consequences of WWII 188
  early Nazi outfits in Australia 184–6, 189
  Nazi Party 62–4, 81, 90, 157, 181
  NSW Nazi Party 144
Nazor, Marko 81–2
neo-Nazism
  contemporary groups and individuals 324, 328, 330, 332

  ideological materials and symbols 190–91, 315, 323
  in online forums 312, 322
  internecine violence 203–6
  organisational formations in 1970s 189–95
  shooting of Suleymaniye Mosque 319
  skinhead gang activity 205–7, 318–19
  violent extremism in 1980s *see* Australian Nationalist Movement
Nettleton, Tara 307
New Guard 186–7
New Humanist Society 151–2
New Left 39–40, 42, 44, 58, 60
New South Wales Police
  acquisition of specialist resources 80
  counter actions against Ananda Marga and the Hilton investigation 121–2, 140, 142–3, 147
  counter actions against JCAG 164, 166
  counter actions against pro-Palestine extremists 111–12
  counter actions against right-wing extremists 191, 332
  counter actions against Salafi jihadis 264, 270, 275, 287, 291, 296
Nicholls, Colin 122
Noble, David 205–6
Northern Alliance 254
Northern Territory Police 270
Novakovic, Milan 69
Nurhasyim, Amrozi bin Haji 244–6

O
Obrana magazine 65
O'Brien, Wayne 318–19
O'Callaghan, Paul Maurice 130
Ochida, Otaro 218
O'Connell, Chris 42
Odinism 187, 322
O'Farrell, Henry James 13–17
Official Irish Republican Army 225
Oliver, John 321
Olson, Kyle 218–19
Olympic Games
  Munich Olympic Games 88, 93–4, 98
  Sydney Olympic Games 239–40, 262
O'Mahony, John 15
Omran, Sheikh Mohammed 264–5

INDEX

operations
  Alliance 245–6
  Appleby 285–6
  Castrum 293
  Forbearance 112
  Inherent Resolve 301
  Jackhammer 201–3
  Neath 275–6
  Nemesis 156–7
  Newport 261–2
  Okra 301
  Peace for Galilee 110
  Pendennis 251–2, 264–9
  Peqin 286
  Protective Edge 115
  Rain 270–1
  Rochester 273
  Sparrow 58
  Whip 58
Opperman, Hubert 68
O'Reilly, John Boyle 18–19, 21
Organisation of Monotheism and Jihad *see* Jama'at al-Tawhid wa'al-Jihad
Osman, Maywand 286
O'Sullivan, Paul 234
Ousama, Abu 307

P
Palestinian Arab Club 96–7
Palestinian Liberation Organisation
  alleged claim for Hakoah Club and Israeli Consulate bombings 110–11
  establishment of 92–3
  factions within 93–7
  Oslo Accords 115
Pandey, Pajnath 151
Pangrazio, Peter 178
Pasha, Enver 156
Pasha, Jemal 157
Pasha, Sayid Halim 156
Pasha, Talaat 156
passports
  acquisition of forged or genuine 79, 104, 269, 295, 301
  cancellation of 284–5, 298, 302
  invalid 72
  tampering with 255
  withholding or rejection of 68, 79, 258, 294

Patterson, Rod 299
Pavelić, Ante 62–4, 68
Payne, Marise 309
Pederick, Evan Dunstan 147–8
Peel, Lord William 90
People's Liberation Army 43–4
  emergence 43
  extremist activities 45–9, 50–4
  statements and claims 45
  trans-organisational links 43–4, 58–9
  violent extremism 48, 50–3, 55–7, 59–60
People's Liberation Armed Forces 43
Ping, Kerry Susan 151
Piro (central bureau) 160, 164, 179
Pondok Ngruki 236, 238
Popular Front for the Liberation of Palestine
  counter action against 100, 113–14
  domestic links and support 96–7, 106–7, 109
  emergence of 93, 96
  international attacks 96, 110, 112–13
  Rish affair 107–9
Post Office/Postal Commission 22, 25, 29, 36, 70, 99, 132, 287
Poynting, Scott 317
Prakash, Neil 283, 285, 294, 305–6
Prawiranegara, Lieutenant General Alamsyah 235
Progressive Nationalist Party 195
Progressive Utilisation Theory *see* PROUT
Proud Boys 333
PROUT 125–9, 144, 149
Provisional Irish Republican Army 225–6
purodhas 125

Q
Queensland Police 69, 71, 81, 269–70, 285

R
Raad, Ahmed 266–8
Raad, Ezzit 266–8
Raad, Maryann 306
Raad, Mounir 308–9
Radalj, Gojko 69
Rashed, Mohammed 112
Reclaim Australia 321–3, 325
Red Army Faction 41, 47, 58–9
replacement theory 196, 324, 326–8, 330, 332

Restore Australia 320
Revolutionary Socialist Alliance 43
Revolutionary Socialist Student Alliance 43, 44, 46
Revolutionary Worker Student Alliance 46
right-wing extremism
    Brenton Tarrant *see* Tarrant, Brenton
    definitions and ideology 182–4, 207, 315–16
    nineteenth-century organisations 181, 184–7
    Phillip Galea *see* Galea, Phillip
    20th-century organisations 188–206, 314–16
    21st-century organisations 317–25, 331–3
    Ustaša right-wing extremism *see* Ustaša
Right Wing Resistance 322
Rish, Munif Mohammed Abou 107–9
Ritchie, Leslie 190
Rizal, Jose 241
Robić, Ivo 72
Roche, Jack 239–40, 243, 254, 265
Rockwell, George 191
Rogers, Michael 299
Romita, Salvatore 74
Ross, Brian 48–9
Rover, Srecko 65, 70, 74, 81
Rumiyah magazine 298
Ryan, Thomas J. 28

S
Saadeh, Mahmoud 95
Sadvipras 124, 151
Sakejha, Omar 285
Saleam, James 195–6, 200, 204–5
Samudra, Imam 243–4, 246
Sánchez, Ilich Ramírez 109
Sarkar, Prabhat Ranjan 123–34, 137, 139, 149–52
Sarkissian, Kegham 171
Satnik 65
Sayadi, Fadl 266–8
Sayed, Nayef el 273–6
Seary, Richard 144–5
segregation, racial 182
Sellner, Martin 325
Sever, Engin 154–5, 162–3

Sewell, Thomas 322, 324–5, 332–3
Shakir, Behaeddin 157
Shanahan, Rodger 305
Sharia 233
Sharrouf, Khaled 265–8, 307–8
Sharrouf, Zaynab 307
Shearman, Richard Francis 46, 53
Shia Muslims 277, 280, 286–7, 293, 298, 301, 306
Shilling, Sean 205–6
Shimada, Yasuko 215
Shire Ali, Ali Khalif 301
Shire Ali, Hassan Khalif 298–9
Siege publication 328
Singaravelu, Roger 300
Singh, Darshan 131–2
Singh, Iqbal 130–3
Singh, Steven 163
Sinha, Sovan 151
Sinn Fein 22, 24, 26, 29
Sisson, Rosemary 192–5
Skirmishers 21
Smith, Arthur 189–91
Smith, Wayne David 205
Smurthwaite, Nicholas 199
socialism 41, 43, 58
Society for Democratic Action 42, 44
Soldiers of Odin 321
Solunac, Danica 71
Southern Cross Hammerskins 206, 316
Southern Cross Soldiers 318
Sovereign Citizen Movement 333
Spanos, Nicholas 226
Special Operations Group 297
Spremnost magazine 65
Spry, Charles 66
Stephens, James 15, 21
Stephensen, Percy R. 187
Stephenson, Ron 111
Stewart, John 190
Students for a Democratic Society 40–3, 45, 48, 50, 54
Students Liberation Army Korps 43, 46
Succarieh, Abraham 306
Succarieh, Ahmed 306
Succarieh, Omar 306
Suelkan, Bora 167
Sungkar, Abdullah 236–9
Sunni Islam 234, 277, 280–1, 287, 301–2

Sweetman, Dane 204–6
Syrian Social Nationalist Party 106

T
Taliban 250, 254–8, 277
Tane, Arthur Christian 193
Tarrant, Brenton 313–15, 324–9, 332
 ideology of 326–9
 inspired by 330–2
Tasmania Police 270
tawhid 253–4
The Country 186
The Publicist magazine 187
The Turner Diaries novel 196
Thomas, Joseph Jack 254–6, 258
Thompson, Roger Lindsay 150
Thorne, George 13
Tilling, Ethan 322
Tito, Marshal Josip Broz 36, 66–7, 73, 75, 85
Tokyo subway attack 219
Tomomitsu, Niimi 215, 218
Tone, Wolfe 15, 28
Top, Noordin 243, 246, 249–50
Totenkopf 315, 332
Touma, Mazen 265–8
Trappitt, Bradley Neil 319
True Blue Crew 321, 323
Tsuchiya, Masami 214, 217
Tully, John Andrew 50
Turkish Consulate bombing 177–8
Turner, Sergeant Robert 74–5
Tyndall, John 193

U
ul-Haque, Izhar 260–2
Union of Germans in Australia and New Zealand 186
Union of the United Croatian Youth of the World 73–4
United Croats of West Germany 73, 78
United Development Party 234
United Patriots Front 322–5
Universal PROUTist Revolutionary Federation
 domestic activities and assessments 130–4, 138–9, 143, 149
 international activities 129, 133, 136, 152

Ustaša
 Bugojno incursion and the Croatian Nineteen 75–6, 79
 counter action against 67, 72, 75–84
 domestic groups and support 64–6
 emergence and ideology 62–4, 66–8
 Mudrinic affair 74–5
 terrorism activities 67–73, 76, 81, 83–4
 travel centre bombings 61–2, 76
 Trieste incursion and the Croatian Nine 67
Uzdanica magazine 73

V
van Blitterswyk, John 197–200, 202–3, 316
van Blitterswyk, Wayne 197, 199, 202–3
van Tongeren, Jack 196–204, 316
van Towsey, Julian 145–6
Vial, Mr 13
Victoria Police
 counter actions against potential UPRF/AM 135
 counter actions against right-wing extremists 323–4
 counter actions against Salafi jihadists 264, 267, 275, 285, 297
 protection duties 174
Vietnam Moratorium 53–4, 190
Vietnam War 37–8
 opposition to war 41, 48, 51–2, 57
visas
 bans 120, 139
 cancelling 271
 gaining/issuing 98, 100, 103, 109, 113, 136–7, 286
 overstaying 166, 260, 365
 rejecting/restricting 100, 114, 139, 150–1, 216, 286
Vlasnovic, Mirko 75–6
Voluntary Social Services 138–39, 144, 151
Voters Policy Associations 189

W
Wahid, Abdurrahman 234
Waifus 331
Watt, W.A. 27
Weather Underground Organisation 41, 43–4, 47, 58–9

Wechsler, Maximilian 109
Wenham, Andrew 239
Western Australia Police 170, 219, 319
White, Michael 200
White, Ricky 322
white genocide *see* replacement theory
white supremacy 181, 196, 314–15, 318, 320, 322–3, 329
Whitehouse, Perry John 205
Whitlam, Gough 58, 77–8
Willey, Russell 197–202
Willis, Eric 68
Wilson, James 19
Wilson, Jock 27
Wisudo, Bambang 238
Wisudo, Rahmah 265, 268
Wither, Rodney 122

Women for Aryan Unity 206, 314–16, 318
Women of the Southern Legion 315
Woods, Sir Colin 153

Y
Yanikian, Gourgen 158–9, 161
Yazidi 277, 307–8
Younger Generation of Indonesia Islam 235
Yousef, Ramzi 237

Z
Zahab, Haisem 296
Zarqawi, Abu Musab *see* al-Kalaylah, Ahmad Fadhil Nazzal
Zdrilic, Stanko 67
Zedong, Mao 39
Zic, Nicholas 71